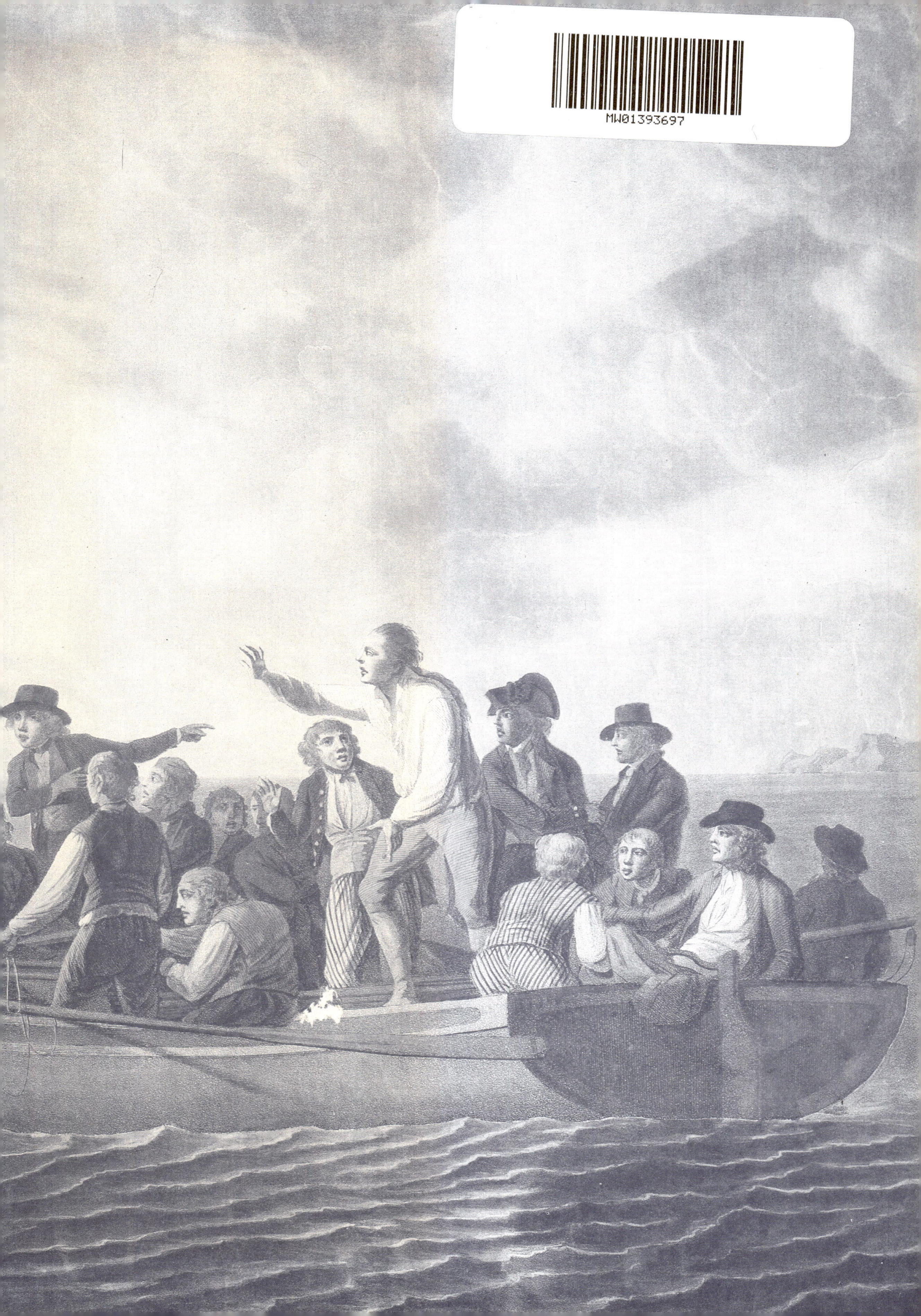

To

Randi, Clarice, Chris & Brian,

I once took an epic journey to the U.S.A.,
A journey I have never forgotten or regretted,
just relished in the fantastic memories.

　　　　　Love.
　　　　　Terry, Jacqui & Dylan Jon.
　　　　　　(July 1992).

AN ILLUSTRATED TREASURY OF
AUSTRALIAN EPIC JOURNEYS

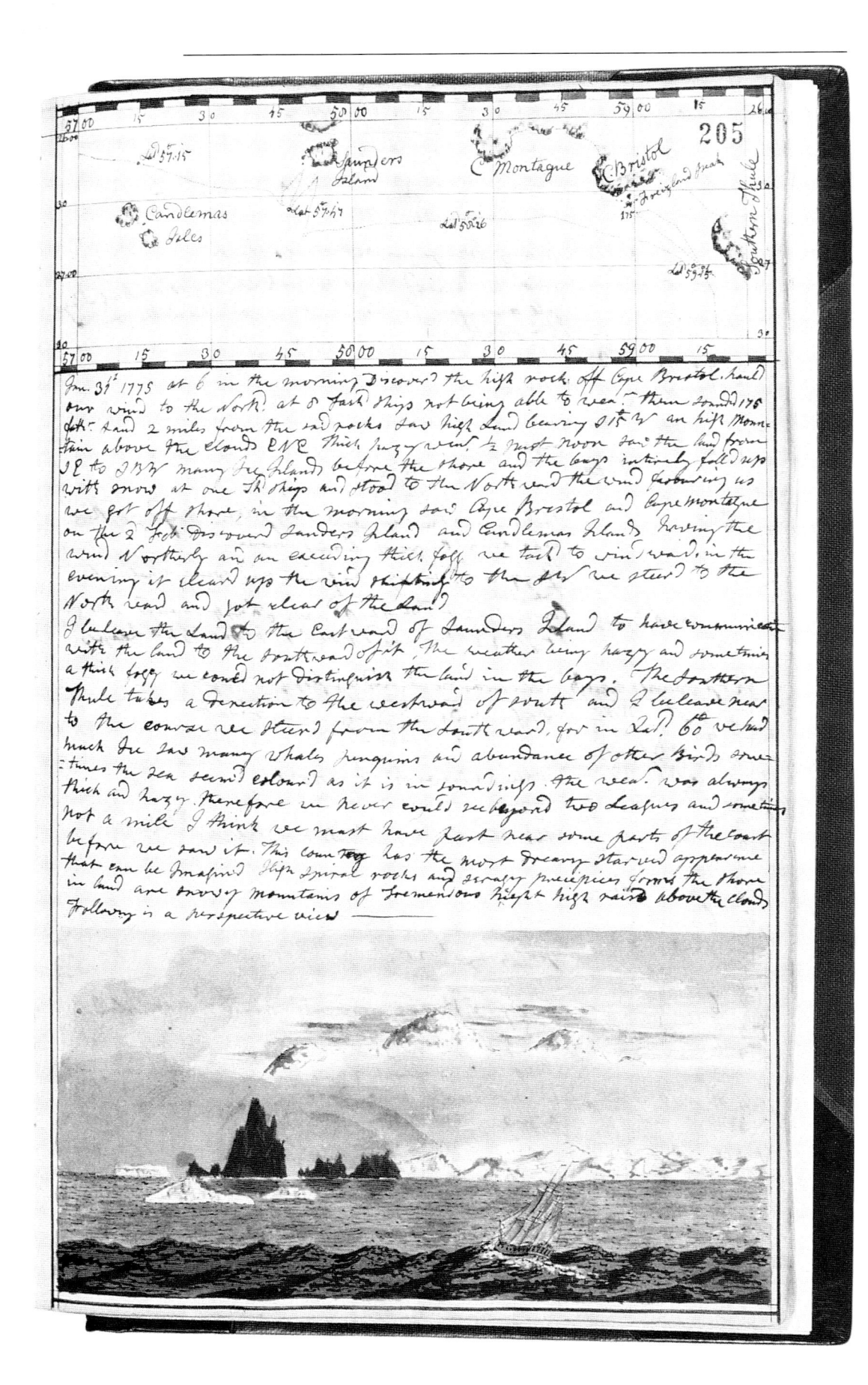

Jan. 31st 1775 at 6 in the morning discover'd the high rocks off Cape Bristol, had our wind to the North at 8 past ship not being able to weather them sound 175 fath. land 2 miles from the said rocks saw high land bearing S 15° W an high Mountain above the clouds ENE thick hazy weath. ½ past Noon saw the land from SE to SBW many Ice Islands before the shore and the bays intirely fill'd up with snow at one Th ships and stood to the North wind favouring us we got off shore, in the morning saw Cape Bristol and Cape Montague on the 2 Feb. Discover'd Saunders Island and Candlemas Islands having the wind Northerly and an exceeding thick fogg we tack'd to windward, in the evening it clear'd up the wind shifting to the SW we steer'd to the Northward and got clear of the land

I believe the land to the Eastward of Saunders Island to have communicat– with the land to the Southward of it, the weather being hazy and sometimes a thick foggy we could not distinguish the land in the bays. The Southern Thule takes a direction to the westward of South and I believe near to the course we steer'd from the Southward, for in Lat.d 60° we had much Ice saw many whales, penguins and abundance of other birds some=times the sea seem'd colour'd as it is in soundings. The weath.r was always thick and hazy therefore we never could see beyond two leagues and sometimes not a mile I think we must have past near some parts of the coast before we saw it. This country has the most dreary starved appearance that can be imagined High spiral rocks and savage precipices forms the shore in land are snowy mountains of tremendous height high raised above the clouds following is a perspective view ————

AN ILLUSTRATED TREASURY OF
AUSTRALIAN EPIC JOURNEYS
SELECTED BY ANTHONY BARKER

M

Page 1. Frederick Garling, Steamship. Garling, a customs official at Port Jackson, was said to have painted every vessel that came to Sydney between 1830 and 1870.

Page 2. Watercolour sketch of the South Sandwich Islands in the logbook of John Gilbert, master of the Resolution.

Created and produced by
Mead & Beckett Publishing
25 Surrey Street Darlinghurst NSW Australia 2010

All rights reserved. No part of this publication may be reproduced or transmitted in any form or by any means without the prior permission of Mead & Beckett.

First published in Australia in 1990 by
The Macmillan Company of Australia Pty Ltd,
107 Moray Street South Melbourne Victoria Australia 3205
6 Clarke Street Crows Nest NSW Australia 2065
Associated companies and representatives throughout the world.

Copyright in this selection © Anthony Barker 1990
Copyright in this edition © Mead & Beckett 1990
Copyright in individual works remains with original copyright holders

National Library of Australia
Cataloguing-in-Publication data:
   1. Adventure and adventurers — Australia — History. 2. Voyages and travels — History. 3. Australia — Description and travel.
   I. Barker A.W. (Anthony Wilhelm), 1930—

919.404

ISBN 0 7329 0328 9

Designed by Barbara Beckett
Picture research by Don Chapman
Maps by Megan Smith
Typeset by Setrite, Hong Kong
Printed by Kyodo-Shing Loong, Singapore

Contents

Introduction 9

ALAN MOOREHEAD
JAMES COOK
James Cook in the Endeavour 12

JOHN WHITE
The Voyage of the First Fleet 25

WILLIAM BLIGH
The Passage of the Bounty's *Launch* 39

JAMES MARTIN
William and Mary Bryant Escape to the North 49

FROM THE *ASIATIC MIRROR*
The Sydney Cove *Survivors* 57

GREGORY BLAXLAND
The Crossing of the Blue Mountains 67

CHARLES STURT
Whaleboat up the Murray 76

EDWARD JOHN EYRE
Round the Great Australian Bight 87

LUDWIG LEICHHARDT
Expedition to Port Essington   103

ANNIE HENNING
Travelling the Great Circle Route   112

IAN MUDIE
JAMES ALLEN
Riverboat Race on the Murray   122

JOHN KING
The Burke and Wills Expedition   131

MARY WATSON
The Heroine of Lizard Island   140

G. E. MORRISON
A Transcontinental Ramble   143

MARY DURACK
The Great Trek of the Duracks   154

DAISY BATES
Three Thousand Miles in a Side-Saddle   161

FRANCIS BIRTLES
Long-Distance Cyclist   168

GEOFFREY DUTTON
The First Crossing of Australia by Motor Car   175

DOUGLAS MAWSON
A Lone Trek in Antarctica   184

FRANK HURLEY
Shackleton's Argonauts   205

ROSS SMITH
The First Flight from England to Australia   216

T. R. NICHOLSON
Francis Birtles Drives from London to Melbourne   225

HECTOR MACQUARRIE
To Cape York by Baby Austin   232

CHARLES KINGSFORD SMITH AND C. T. P. ULM
Pacific Flight of the Southern Cross   238

MICK HEALY
Depression Trackmen   247

NOURMA ABBOTT-SMITH
Ian Fairweather's Raft Voyage   253

DAVID LEWIS
Sailing Alone to Antarctica   261

ROBYN DAVIDSON
Camel Tracks through the Centre   269

DICK SMITH
Round the World in a Helicopter   275

Acknowledgment of Sources   283

Sources of Illustrations   286

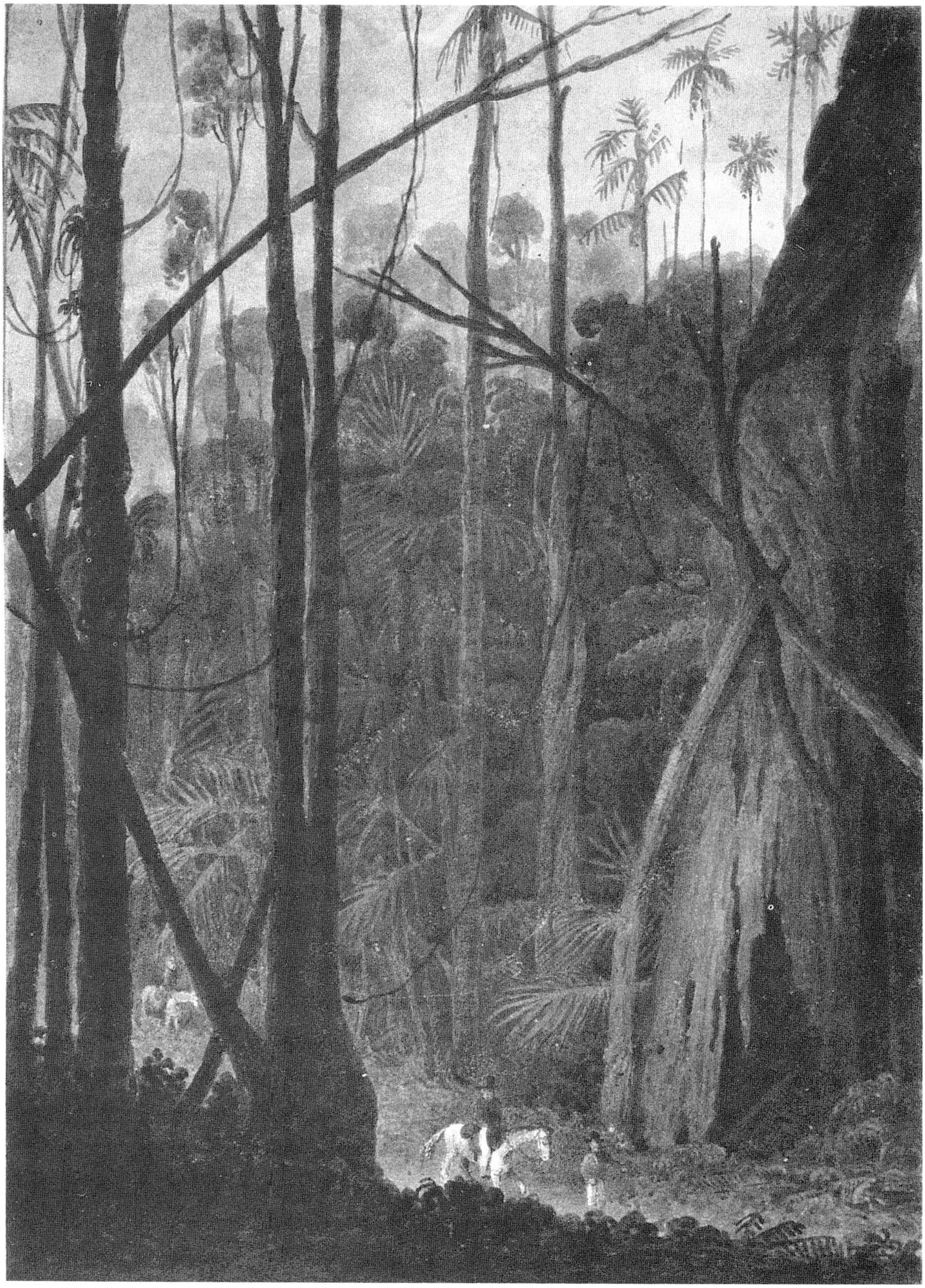

INTRODUCTION

BECAUSE OF its isolation from the rest of the world, its extensive coastline, and its vast, sparsely populated inland, Australia has been the setting for a large number of epic journeys. The explorers' expeditions are perhaps the first to come to mind. Blaxland, Lawson and Wentworth's crossing of the Blue Mountains, Sturt's whaleboat journey up the Murray and Murrumbidgee rivers, Eyre and Wylie's trek round the Great Australian Bight, Leichhardt's expedition to Port Essington, the dash by Burke and Wills to the Gulf of Carpentaria and its tragic outcome at Cooper's Creek are among the better known.

But Australian epic journeys have been undertaken for various reasons. Some were made out of necessity, like William Bligh's remarkable open-boat voyage from Tonga to Timor after the mutiny on the *Bounty*, or the overland journey up the coast to Sydney by the crew of the *Sydney Cove* after its shipwreck in Bass Strait. Others were made in desperation. William and Mary Bryant, with their two children and seven other convicts, made their escape from Port Jackson in Governor Phillip's cutter and sailed it five thousand kilometres to Kupang. Mary Watson, after being attacked by Aborigines on Lizard Island, set out on a tragic voyage with her infant child and a wounded Chinese servant in part of an iron tank.

There were pioneering journeys—the first riverboat trips on the Murray made by William Randell and Francis Cadell; the great overland trek from south-western Queensland to the Kimberleys by the Durack family; Ross and Keith Smith's pioneer flight from England to Australia and Kingsford Smith's crossing of the Pacific in the *Southern Cross*. But many epic journeys were made simply for the hell of it or because of the challenge of the venture. G. E. Morrison rolled his swag in December 1882 and walked across Australia from Normanton to Melbourne. Francis Birtles mounted his bicycle in 1907 and rode thirteen thousand kilometres round Australia. Harry Dutton, on his second attempt in 1908, became the first to drive a motor car across Australia (and met Francis Birtles pedalling furiously in the opposite direction). The artist Ian Fairweather built himself a raft out of scrap, floated out of Port Darwin, and ended up fifteen days later in Indonesia. Robyn Davidson led a team of camels from Alice Springs to the coast of Western Australia. David Lewis sailed a yacht single-handed to Antarctica. Dick Smith flew a helicopter solo round the world.

Augustus Earle, Cabbage Tree Forest, Ilawarra, New South Wales.

INTRODUCTION

My own interest in Australian epic journeys began in 1953 when I travelled from London to Sydney in a 1936 model London taxi. I wondered who was the first to drive a car from England to Australia and found that it was the irrepressible Francis Birtles, who forsook the bicycle for the automobile in 1912 and drove a 25-horsepower Bean from London to Melbourne in 1928. Then, when I was gathering material for my chronology of Australia, *When Was That?*, I realised just how many heroic, pioneering or otherwise remarkable journeys had been made during the past two hundred years.

Only a selection of them have, of course, been included in this book. In the first place, inclusion was governed by the availability of a written account; many epic journeys have no doubt been made and have gone unrecorded and unpublished. I have tried to obtain narratives written by a participant in the journey, and only in a few cases have I used later accounts written by others. I also sought variety in the manner of travelling and the kind of journey. As for eligibility, the term *Australian* has been used loosely to include journeys within, and to and from, Australia. But I have also felt compelled to include two accounts of Australians in Antarctica, as no selection of Australian epic journeys would be complete, it seemed to me, without Douglas Mawson's account of his lone struggle back to winter quarters after the death of his two companions, or Frank Hurley's experiences with the Shackleton expedition trapped for over a year in the pack-ice of the Weddell Sea. But, as in all anthologies, the selection is in the end an individual choice, and inevitably there will be readers who will regret the omission of their own favourite story. That is the lot of the anthologist.

The selection has been arranged chronologically. For consistency and ease of reading, certain editorial changes have been made. Spelling, punctuation, hyphenation, the use of capitals and the treatment of numbers and dates and abbreviations have to some extent been regularised, although unconventional usage has been retained where it gives a distinctive flavour or serves a point. Some obvious typographical errors in the originals have been silently corrected, and later amendments by authors have been incorporated where known. Some re-paragraphing has been done in places. Omission of material of any length has been indicated by the insertion of ellipsis points (three dots) at the end of a sentence or paragraph. As exigencies of space allow the use of only an extract from a lengthy original account, I have supplied an introduction to each piece (and sometimes a conclusion or connecting link) to place the extract in perspective.

ANTHONY BARKER

George Foster, Ice Islands.

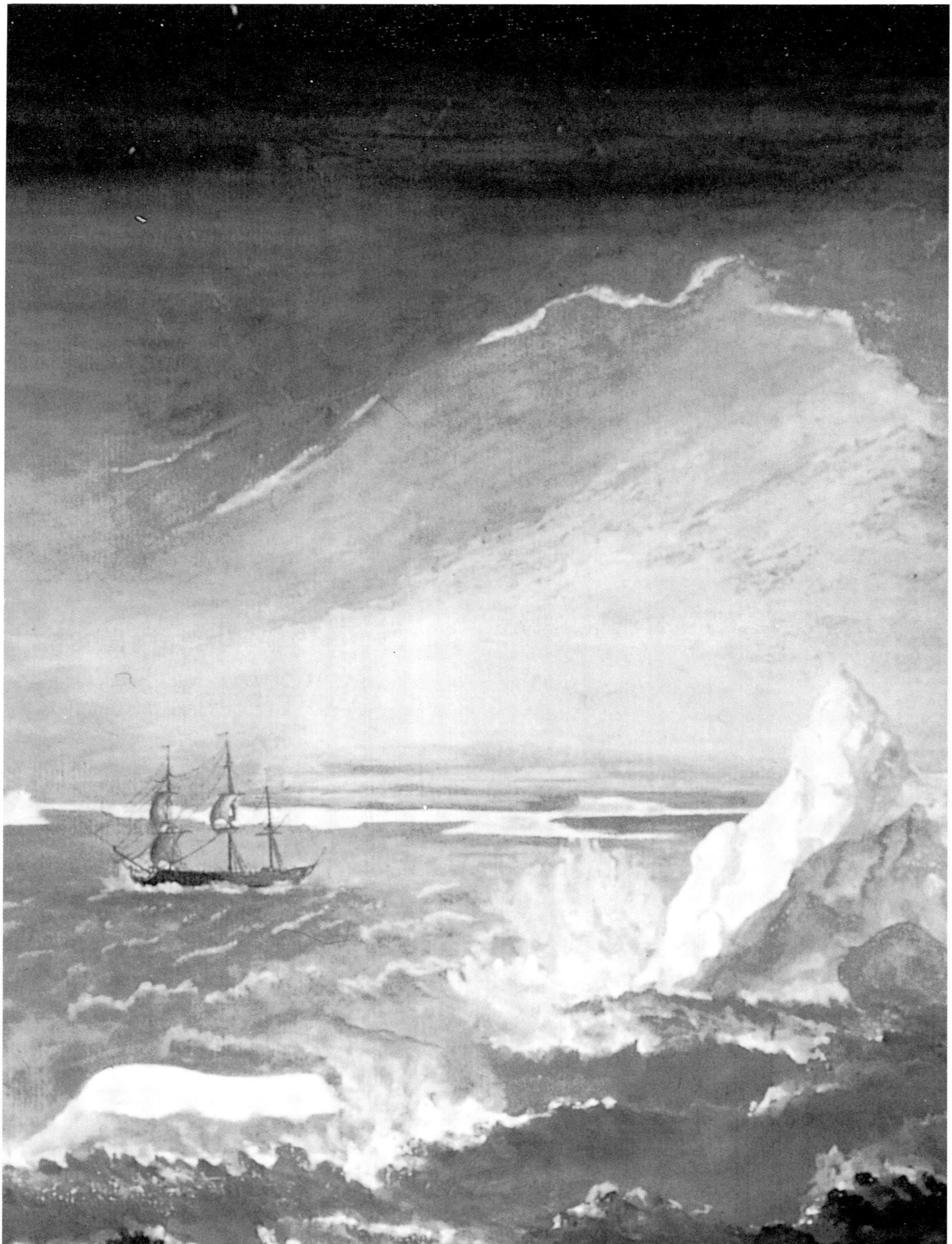

JAMES COOK IN THE ENDEAVOUR

Alan Moorehead
James Cook

IN AUGUST 1768 *the bark* Endeavour, *under the command of Lieutenant James Cook, left England on a voyage to Tahiti to observe the transit of Venus across the sun. The voyage was promoted by the Royal Society, and the scientific party on board included the astronomer Charles Green and a group of naturalists and artists—among them the naturalist D. C. Solander and the natural-history draughtsman Sydney Parkinson—led by a wealthy fellow of the Royal Society, Joseph Banks. But Cook also carried secret instructions from the British Admiralty which he was to open when his work in Tahiti was completed. These instructions ordered him to search for the great south land that was thought to exist in the Southern Hemisphere; he was also to examine the coast of New Zealand, whose western seaboard had been discovered by the Dutch navigator Abel Tasman in 1642, to establish whether or not this was part of the great south land. Cook duly sailed south from Tahiti after the transit to Venus and, finding no great southern continent, turned west and spent six months circumnavigating and mapping the coast of New Zealand. More than a year and a half had now elapsed since he had left England, and it was time to think of returning home. Alan Moorehead in his book* The Fatal Impact *takes up the story:*

THE OBVIOUS ROUTE to take was the one across the south Pacific to Cape Horn, since that would have enabled him to continue his search for a southern continent, but the winter was coming on, barely six months' rations remained, and the *Endeavour*'s sails and rigging, now badly in need of repair, were hardly likely to stand up to the Antarctic gales in that vast stretch of ocean. Consequently another and more promising plan was decided upon: they would strike westward until they reached the eastern seaboard of the country of New Holland and then follow it to the north or wherever it took them until they reached its extremity. Then they would turn west and sail to the Dutch outpost of civilisation at Batavia, where they could refit and revictual the ship.

It was a hazardous proposition. The west coast of New Holland (it was not to be called Australia until half a century later), was known in rough outline, but the east coast was entirely unexplored; no white man had ever been there and the existing maps were merely guesswork. But the *Endeavour*'s crew had been restored to health by their six months' stay in New Zealand, and the officers, on being consulted, were all eager for new discoveries; and so, on 1 April 1770, they set sail for the unknown. It was a fair voyage; the weather

Captain James Cook, an uncharacteristic portrait by William Hodges, a topographical artist who sailed with Cook on his second voyage.

was warm, dolphins leapt about the ship 'like salmons', and *Diomedea exulans*, the wandering albatross, that largest and strongest of all sea birds, came circling trustingly around the rigging, a wonderful target for Banks's gun....

Day after day the dawn disclosed nothing but the empty ocean, and no one knew when he would see land again. Thus it was an event when on the sixteenth day the officer on watch thought—he was not quite certain—that he saw a butterfly, and a little later a small land bird like a sparrow came on board. This was followed by the appearance of a gannet holding a steady course for the west—the *Endeavour*'s course—as though it knew that there was land in that direction. Squally weather set in. Then on 19 April Lieutenant Zachary Hicks cried out at first light that land lay ahead. Cook stood towards it for two hours, and at 8 a.m., when he was fifteen miles from the coast, altered course so that he could run beside it. He had sighted the extreme south-eastern corner of the continent, and he named it Point Hicks—a timely gesture since the lieutenant, like so many other young men in the ship, was to die before the next year was out.

Rain and gales continued through the day—this part of the Tasman Sea is notorious for rough weather—and at one time the grey sky joined the sea between them and the shore in three transparent wavering waterspouts. Next day they had a clear view of the land and Banks thought it looked very promising: 'The country this morn rose in gentle sloping hills which had the appearance of the highest fertility, every hill seemed clothed with trees of no mean size; at noon a smoke was seen a little way inland, and in the evening several more.'

Smoke meant inhabitants, and sure enough on 22 April they saw through their glasses five black men standing on the shore. It was impossible, however, to make a landing; heavy waves were beating on the rocks, and a fresh breeze drove them steadily northwards. Soon they came up with chalky cliffs that reminded them of England, and more natives were seen, two of them carrying a canoe. Cook put out a boat, but heavy surf prevented him from landing and they went on again. At last, on 28 April—nine days after they had first sighted the coast—they saw an opening in the cliffs and the *Endeavour* put in for the shore. There were natives about, some of them spearing fish from canoes, others watching from the rocks and along the cliffs....

Some odd things were happening on the shore as the *Endeavour* approached. One group of natives, about a dozen in all, went up on to a rise to watch, and when the vessel's boat came near they beckoned the sailors to come ashore. On the other hand, no notice at all seemed to be taken of the

Two of the Natives of New Holland, Advancing to Combat, *one of Sydney Parkinson's drawings used to illustrate his* Journal of a Voyage to the South Seas, *which was published posthumously by his brother. Parkinson, the natural-history draughtsman on board the* Endeavour, *was one of several of the ship's company who died from fever contracted in Batavia.*

Endeavour herself. There she was, 100 feet long, with her high masts and her great sails, and when she passed within a quarter of a mile of some fishermen in four canoes they did not even bother to look up. Then when she had anchored close to the shore a naked woman carrying wood appeared with three children. 'She often looked at the ship,' Banks tells us, 'but expressed neither surprise nor concern. Soon after this she lighted a fire and the four canoes came in from the fishing: the people landed, hauled up their boats and began to dress their dinner, to all appearance totally unmoved by us....'

The Englishmen ate their midday meal on board and then in two boats set out for the shore, thinking that these strange quiescent people would allow them to make a peaceful landing. They were wrong. Two natives menaced them from the rocks with long spears, and they were not deterred by the fact that there were at least thirty men in the *Endeavour*'s boats. No amount of pleading with them by signs had any effect, so Cook took a musket and fired it over their heads. Still they held their ground, and Cook fired a second shot at their legs knowing that he could do them little harm, the distance being forty yards. The only result of this was to make one of the natives run off to his hut for a shield and then, as the sailors came ashore, both men threw their spears. Two more shots had to be fired before they were driven off. Cook and Banks went up to the huts, where they found half a dozen children who showed no interest of any kind when they were given presents of beads and ribbons; they left them lying on the ground.

There were some interesting aspects in all this. The sight of the *Endeavour* had apparently meant nothing to these primitives because it was too strange, too monstrous, to be comprehended. It had appeared out of nowhere like some menacing phenomenon of nature, a waterspout or a roll of thunder, and by ignoring it or pretending to ignore it no doubt they had hoped that it would go away. As Sydney Parkinson wrote, the natives 'were so abashed at first they took little notice of us'. But when the small boats had put out from the ship it had been another thing: the English sailors had been instantly recognised as human, a palpable evil, and despite their clothes and pale faces, despite even their roaring incomprehensible shooting-sticks, they had been courageously opposed.

And so it went on for the next few days while the *Endeavour*'s crew came ashore to gather wood and to fill their water casks. Little groups of blacks would appear through the trees and stand for a moment to shout and throw a spear or two. Then they would vanish again into the bush. Every attempt to parley with them or to offer them presents came to nothing. Had they been wild animals they could not have been more difficult to deal with. 'All they seemed to want,' Cook wrote, 'was for us to be gone'....

For the rest it was an excellent landfall. The crew netted enormous quantities of fish in the bay, and there were giant oysters and other shellfish to be found on the rocks as well. The botanists, wandering ashore, came upon trees and plants that had never been described before; the eucalypt, for example, with its long, thin, scented leaves, and a shrub with large, furry nuts which was eventually to become known as the Banksia. The birds were wonderful—great flocks of brightly coloured cockatoos and lorikeets that were entirely strange to European ornithology—and since they had never been shot at before Banks brought down as many as he wished. The skins he preserved, and with the meat the *Endeavour*'s cook made an excellent parrot pie. Sometimes the foraging parties caught glimpses of queer elusive animals: a quadruped about the size of a rabbit, a much larger beast that fed on grass and resembled a stag, another that looked like a wolf, and still another that seemed to be some sort of a polecat or a weasel. But none of these creatures lingered in sight long enough to be described or drawn.

A week went by very pleasantly, and it was marred only by the death of a consumptive seaman named Forby Sutherland, the first white man to be buried on this distant coast.

There was a ceremony on shore before they sailed. The English colours were flown, the ship's name and the date were carved on a tree, and the hospitable harbour which had supplied Banks and Solander with so many new plants was named Botany Bay. It seems ironic that so innocent a name was to become a synonym for all that was heartless and cruel, not only in this new country, but in Georgian civilisation as well.

So now on 6 May 1770 they sailed on to the north, noting from the sea, but not entering, Port Jackson, which was later to be the site of Sydney, one of the largest cities in the Southern Hemisphere; past Cape Byron which was named after Byron's grandfather, the *Dolphin*'s first captain; past the site of Brisbane and so on into the tropics.

Cook was now forcing the pace; his men were growing weary and were eager to reach civilisation again. After so many months on those confined decks, irritations and enmities were beginning to fester; just how much so is revealed by one particularly horrible incident. A clerk named Richard Orton went to bed drunk and someone attacked him and cut off his ears. Life on a British sailing ship in the eighteenth century was tough enough—even brutal by our standards—but this was criminal and Cook was enraged. Yet even the offer of fifteen guineas and fifteen gallons of arrack—a huge reward—could not induce the crew to reveal the name of the culprit. Suspicion fell on Patrick Saunders, one of the midshipmen, but nothing was proved against him. It was significant however that Saunders deserted when the ship eventually reached Batavia.

A month after leaving Botany Bay they were still toiling slowly northward, nearly always in sight of the coast but seldom landing, and on 6 June they arrived at Magnetic Island, so called because it affected the *Endeavour*'s compass. Many tropical islands and coral reefs now began to close round the ship, and Cook sprinkled them liberally with the names of the British aristocracy—Halifax, Sandwich and so on—as he went along. It was a world of water-snakes and turtles, of oysters growing in mangrove swamps, of dolphins and huge sharks, of pandanus palms and pelicans. They shot a wild turkey weighing fifteen pounds and it was the finest meal they had eaten since leaving England nearly two years before.

At times the sea was so full of fish that the nets they let down were torn to pieces. Parkinson, the artist, was kept hard at work drawing the plants they collected while they were still fresh and green; he actually drew ninety-four of them in fourteen days, and still more specimens came in whenever they made a landfall.

Sometimes when they sailed close inshore they saw groups of natives, but the same curious indifference persisted; both men and women would gaze for a moment at the ship and then apparently dismiss it from their minds. If a boat was put ashore they quietly disappeared leaving uneaten shellfish around their camp fires.

With so many reefs about and the tides rising and falling by eighteen to twenty feet, Cook felt his way very gingerly. Everyone dreaded the grounding of the ship on those sharp and beautifully coloured coral antlers, and when this did happen at 11 p.m. on the night of 11 June it was a more fearful thing than any of them could have imagined. They were sailing gently along in the moonlight in a calm sea under double-reefed topsails, and with a man continually sounding the depth. Cook as usual had given his instructions for the night and had just undressed and had gone to sleep. He was awakened by a horrible scraping in the bows and the ship rocked so violently he could scarcely stand upright. Coming on deck in his underclothes he found the vessel stuck fast on the coral and immediately ordered the boats and the anchors to be got out. But no amount of heaving would bring her off, and it became clear that she was badly holed; at midnight the false keel came away and they could see pieces of sheathing boards floating about them in the moonlight. Mercifully it was a calm night, but when the tide began to ebb the ship settled more firmly than ever on the coral and there was every danger of her breaking up. The coast was twenty-four miles away and there was no possible hope of the *Endeavour*'s boats getting them all off. Banks tells us that he packed up his most valuable possessions and prepared to abandon ship.

Meanwhile what could be done to save her was being done; six guns were thrown overboard together with their cannon balls, a quantity of stone ballast, the fresh water and all those casks that contained decayed stores—some forty or fifty tons in all. Dawn found them still afloat and they waited all morning for the rising tide. When it came the ship began to rock again on the coral and to take in water fast. One of their four pumps was out of action, but every man, Cook himself included, now got to work on the other three. There seemed to be only one hope: that they could get the *Endeavour* off before she broke up and then keep her afloat just long enough to beach her on the mainland. With luck, they then might be able to build a smaller vessel out of the wreck and sail her to Batavia or some other civilised port in the East Indies.

At nightfall the water was still gaining on them, and no amount of hauling on the anchors with the capstan could get them off the reef. They could only continue what they were already doing, and since they expected to die the men worked very quietly and efficiently and willingly. There was no panic anywhere on the ship. Then at 10 p.m., twenty-three hours after they had first struck, the hull began to move and within a few minutes they had hauled her into the clear sea. There was nearly four feet of water in the hold, and the carpenter reported that it was gaining so fast that there was little hope of the pumps keeping pace with it. Later he went down to the hold again and discovered he had made a miscalculation—the water was not coming in so rapidly as he had thought; and when this news reached the exhausted men on

'There seemed to be only one hope: that they could get the Endeavour *off before she broke up and then keep her afloat just long enough to beach her on the mainland.'*

The Endeavour *beached at the mouth of the river that now bears its name, where repairs to the ship were carried out. The six weeks' enforced stay enabled Banks and his assistants to collect and study the flora and fauna of the region.*

Sydney Parkinson's sketch of a kangaroo shot at the Endeavour River. The flesh of the young animal was eaten by the ship's company and found good; the skin was dried and, together with the skull, taken back to England, where the kangaroo was reconstructed and given to the animal painter George Stubbs to paint.

the pumps it acted, Cook says, 'like a charm'. When the second dawn broke they were even gaining a little on the leak, and the sails were set for the mainland.

Jonathan Monkhouse, the younger brother of the *Endeavour*'s surgeon, now came forward with a suggestion that they should 'fother' the ship—a thing he had seen done in similar circumstances before—and Cook agreed. A sail was filled with oakum, earth, odd rags and bits of sheep's wool, and then dragged with ropes under the hull until it covered the hole. The pumps instantly began to gain at a faster rate, and by the night of 13 June, the third day after the disaster, they had the ship almost dry. Cook anchored for the night a mile offshore, and in the morning the pinnace was sent off to reconnoitre the coast. It returned at night with the good news that there was a harbour in the estuary of a river a little way to the north.

But now a gale with rain blew up, such a gale as would have destroyed them utterly had they still been on the reef, and they waited all through 15 June and again through 16 June for the wind to drop. Cook himself took the pinnace out and buoyed a channel through the coral into harbour, and at last on 17 June they got in, bumping twice on the passage. They moored within twenty feet of the shore, and the next day they shifted to a steep beach where the ship could be run aground at high water. Immediately they made a ramp to the shore and began taking everything out of her. At least they were all alive; it now remained to see what damage had been done and to estimate what the chances were of repairing her on this primitive coast.

There were natives about—one could see their signal fires—and Cook mounted four of his remaining guns on the quarter-deck in case of attack. Through the next few days a smithy and a sailmaker's workshop were set up on shore, together with tents for the sick and the storage of provisions, and on 22 June they had the vessel empty enough to run up her bows on the beach at high tide, her stern being left afloat. They could now inspect the damage. It was almost as bad as they had imagined. The bottom had been scored by the reef as though someone had attacked it savagely with an axe, but by a miracle of luck a chunk of coral had become wedged in the largest hole and had prevented them from foundering at once. The carpenter believed that within a few weeks he could make provisional repairs, enough at any rate to get them to Batavia. So now, among the mangroves in a tropical river, absolutely isolated from the outside world on an unexplored coast, and with the rain falling upon them, they set about eking out a Robinson Crusoe-like existence until the day they could escape.

The Endeavour *remained at the estuary of the Endeavour River, near present-day Cooktown, for six weeks while repairs were being made. During this time Cook and his companions were able to examine the surrounding countryside. They saw kangaroos for the first time. They were also visited by the Aborigines, who wanted the turtles the crew had caught and attempted to set fire to the ship's tent and equipment when their request was refused. On 4 August the* Endeavour *was ready to resume the homeward voyage. The following extracts from Cook's journal, edited by J. C. Beaglehole, describe the hazardous journey along the coast, in and out of the Great Barrier Reef and into Torres Strait.*

JAMES COOK IN THE ENDEAVOUR

'I had not resolved whether I should beat back to the Southward round all the shoals or seek a passage out to the Eastward or to the northrd, all of which appear'd to be equally difficult and dangerous.'

[*Saturday, 4 August 1770.*] In the PM having pritty Moderate weather I order'd the Coasting anchor and Cable to be laid without the barr to be ready to warp out by, that we might not loose the least oppertunity that might offer, for laying in Port spends time to no purpose, consumes our provisions of which we are very short in many articles, and we have yet a long Passage to make to the East Indies through an unknown and perhaps dangerous Sea; these circumstances considerd makes me very anxious of geting to sea.

[*Sunday, 5 August.*] The wind continued moderate all night and at 5 oClock in the morning when it fell calm, this gave us an oppertunity to warp out. About 7 we got under sail having a light air from the land which soon died away and was succeeded by the Sea breeze from SEbS with which we stood off to Sea EbN, having the Pinnace a head sounding. The Yawl I sent to the Turtle bank to take up the net that was left there but as the wind freshend we got out before her, and a little after noon anchor'd in 15 fathom water Sandy bottom; for I did not think it safe to run in among the Shoals until I had well View'd them at low-water from the Mast head, that I might be better able to judge which way to steer for as yet I had not resolved whether I should beat back to the Southward round all the shoals or seek a passage out to the Eastward or to the northrd, all of which appear'd to be equally difficult and dangerous....

[*Tuesday, 7 August.*] After having well View'd our situation from the mast head I saw that we were surrounded on every side with Shoals and no such thing as a passage to Sea but through the winding channels between them, dangerous to the highest degree in so much that I was quite at a loss which way to steer when the weather would permit us to get under sail; for to beat back to the SE the way we came as the Master would have had me done would be an endless peice of work, as the winds blow now constantly strong from that quarter without hardly any intermission—on the other hand if we do not find a passage to the north^d we shall have to come back at last....

[*Monday, 13 August.*] After well considering both what I had seen my self and the report of the Master, who was of opinion that the Passage to Leeward would prove dangerous; this I was pretty well convince'd of my self that by keeping in with the main land we should be in continual danger besides the risk we should run of being locke'd in within the Main reef at last and have to return back to seek a passage out, an accident of this kind or any other that might happen to the Ship would infallibly loose our passage to the East Indies this season and might prove the ruin of the Voyage, as we have now little more than 3 Months provisions on board and that short allowance in many Articles. These reasons had the same weight with all the officers, I therefore resolved to weigh in the morning and endeavour to quet the coast altogether until we could approach it with less danger.

[*Tuesday, 14 August.*] With this View we got under sail at day light.... By 2 oClock we just fetched to windward of one of the Channels in the outer Reef I had seen from the Island, we now tacked and made a short trip to the SW while the Master in the Pinnace examind the channell, he soon made the Signal for the Ship to follow which we accordingly did and in a short time got safe out, we had no sooner got without the breakers than we had no ground with 150 fathom of line and found a well growen Sea rowling in from the SE, certain signs that neither land nor shoals were in our neighbourhood in that direction, which made us quite easy at being free'd from fears of Shoals &c—after having been intangled among them more or less ever sence the 26th of May, in which time we have saild 360 Leagues without ever having a Man out of the cheans heaving the Lead when the Ship was under way, a circumstance that I dare say never happen'd to any ship before and yet here it was absolutely necessary. It was with great regret I was obliged to quit this coast unexplored to its Northern extremity which I think we were not far off, for I firmly believe that it doth not join to *New Guinea*, however this I hope yet to clear up being resolved to get in with the land again as soon as I can do it with safety and the reasons I have before assigned will I presume be thought sufficient for my haveing left it at this time....

As soon as we were without the reef we brought too and hoisted in the boats, than stood off and on upon a wind all night as I did not care to run to leeward until we had a whole day before us. We now began to find that the Ship had received more damage than we immagined and soon felt the effect the high rowling sea had upon her by increasing her leaks considerably so that it was as much as one Pump could keep her free kept continualy at work; however this was looked upon as trifeling to the danger we had lately made our escape from....

[*Thursday, 16 August.*] By one oClock in the PM or before we saw high land from y*e* Masthead bearing WSW and at 2 oClock saw more land to the NW of the former making in hills like Islands but we judged it to be the continuation of the Main land. An hour after this we saw breakers between us and the land extending to the Southward farther than we could see, but we thought we saw them terminate to the northward abreast of us, this however proved only an opening for soon after we saw the Reef or breakers extend away to the northward as far as we could see, upon this we hauld close upon a wind which was now at ESE. We had hardly trimed our sails before the wind came to EbN which was right upon the Reef and of Course made our clearing of it doubtfull, the northermost of it that we could see at sun set bore from us NbE distant about 2 or 3 Leagues. However this being the best tack to clear it we kept standing to the northward with all the Sail we could set untill 12 oClock at night when fearing to Stand too far up this tack we tacked and stood to the Southward having run 6 Leagues North and NbE sence Sun set.

[*Friday, 17 August.*] We had not stood above 2 Miles SSE before it fell quite Calm, we both sounded now and several times in the night but had no ground with 140 fathoms of line. A little after 4 oClock the roaring of the Surf was plainly heard and at day break the vast foaming breakers were too plainly to be seen not a Mile from us towards which we found the Ship was carried by the waves surprisingly fast. We had at this time not an air of wind and the depth of water was unfathomable so that there was not a possibility of Anchoring, in this distressed situation we had nothing but Providence and the small Assistance our boats could give us to trust to; the Pinnace was under a repair and could not immidiately be hoisted out, the Yawl was put into the water and the Long-boat hoisted out and both sent ahead to tow which together with the help of our sweeps abaft got the Ships head round to the northward which seem'd to be the only way to keep her off the reef or at least to delay time, before this was effected it was 6 oClock and we were not above 80 or 100 Yards from the breakers, the same Sea that washed the sides of the Ship rose in a breaker prodigiously high the very next time it did rise so that between us and distruction was only a dismal Vally the breadth of one wave and even now no ground could be felt with 120 fathoms. The Pinnace by this time was patched up and hoisted out and sent ahead to tow; still we had hardly any hopes of saving the Ship and full as little our lives as we were full 10 Leagues from the nearest land and the boats not sufficient to carry the whole of us, yet in this truly terrible situation not one man ceased to do his utmost and that with as much calmness as if no danger had been near. All the dangers we had escaped were little in comparison of being thrown upon this Reef where the Ship must be dashed to peices in a Moment. A Reef such as is here spoke of is scarcely known in Europe, it is a wall of Coral Rock rising all most perpendicular out of the unfathomable Ocean, always overflown at high-water generally 7 or 8 feet and dry in places at low-water; the large waves of the vast Ocean meeting with so sudden a resistance make a most terrible surf breaking mountains high especially as in our case when the general trade wind blowes directly upon it. At this critical juncture when all our endeavours seem'd too little a small air of wind sprung up, but so small that at any other time in a Calm we should not have observed it, with this and the assistance of our boats we could observe the Ship to move off from the Reef in a slanting direction, but in less than 10 Minutes we had as flat a Calm as ever when our fears were again renewed for as yet we were not above 200 Yards from the breakers. Soon after our friendly breeze Viseted us again and lasted about as long as before. A small opening was now seen in the Reef about a quarter of a Mile from us which I sent one of the Mates to examine, its breadth was not more than the length of the Ship but within was smooth water, into this place it was resolve'd to push her if possible haveing no other probable Views to save her, for we were still in the very jaws of distruction and it was a doubt whether or no we could reach this opening, however we soon got off it when to our surprise we found the Tide of Ebb gushing out like a Mill stream so that it was impossible to get in; we however took all the advantage possible of it and it carried us out about a $\frac{1}{4}$ of a Mile from the breakers, but it was too narrow for us to keep in long; how ever what with the help of Ebb and our boats we by noon had got an offing of one and a half or two Miles, yet we could hardly flater our selves with hopes of getting clear even if a breeze should spring up as we were by this time imbayed by the Reef, and the Ship in spite of our endeavours driving before the Sea into the bight, the Ebb had been in our favour and we had reason to suppose that the flood which was now making would be against us, the only hopes we had was another opening we saw about a Mile to the Westward of us which I sent Lieutenant Hicks in the Small boat to examine.

While Mr Hicks was examining the opening we strugled hard with the flood some times gaining a little and at other times looseing. At 2 oClock Mr Hicks returned with a favourable account of the opening, it was immidiately resolved to try to secure the Ship in it, narrow and dangerous as it was it seem'd to be the only means we had of saving her as well as our selves. A

'...we had got quite within the Reef where we anchor'd in 19 fathom a Corally & Shelly bottom happy once more to incounter those shoals which but two days ago our utmost wishes were crowned by getting clear of, such are the Vicissitudes attending this kind of service and must always attend an unknown Navigation.'

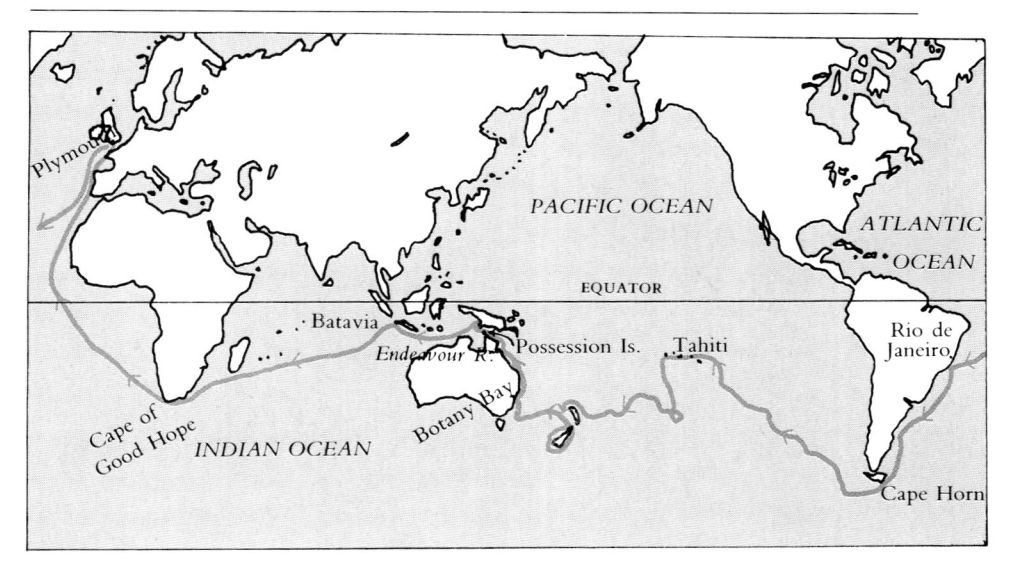

light breeze soon after sprung up at ENE which with the help of our boats and a flood tide we soon enter'd the opening and was hurried through in a short time by a rappid tide like a Mill race which kept us from driving againest either side, tho the channell was not more than a quarter of a Mile broad, we had however two boats a head to direct us through, our depth of water in the Channell was from 30 to 7 fathom very erregular soundings and foul ground until we had got quite within the Reef where we anchor'd in 19 fathom a Corally & Shelly bottom happy once more to incounter those shoals which but two days ago our utmost wishes were crowned by geting clear of, such are the Vicissitudes attending this kind of service and must always attend an unknown Navigation....

I now came to a fix'd resolution to keep the Main land on board in our rout to the norward let the concequence be what it will, indeed now it was not adviseable to go without the reef, for by it we might be carried so far from the Coast as not to be able to determine whether or no New Guinea joins to or makes a part of this land. This doubtfull point I had from my first coming upon the Coast determined if possible to clear up....

[*Tuesday, 21 August.*] By one oClock we had run nearly the length of the southermost of the two Islands before mentioned, and finding that we could not well go to windward of them without carrying us too far from the Main land, we bore up and run to Leeward where we found a fair open passage. This done we steer'd NbW in a Parallel direction with the Main land leaving a small Island between us and it, and some low sandy Isles and shoals without us, all of which we lost sight off by 4 oClock; neither did we see any more before the sun went down at which time the farthest part of the Main in sight bore NNW¼W. Soon after this we Anchord in 13 fathom soft ground about 5 Leagues from the land where we lay until day light....

[*Wednesday, 22 August.*] We got again under sail, having first sent the Yawl ahead to sound. We steerd NNW by Compass from the norther-most land in sight. Variation 3°6' East. Seeing no danger in our way we took the Yawl in tow and made all the Sail we could until 8 oClock, at which time we discovered Shoals ahead and on our Larboard bow and saw that the norther-

The route of the Endeavour *on Cook's first voyage to the South Seas. The ship left Plymouth on 25 August 1768, coasted eastern Australia between April and August 1770, and arrived back in England on 13 July 1771.*

most land, which we had taken to be a part of the Main, was an Island or Islands between which and the Main their appear'd to be a good passage, thro' which we might pass.... The Point of the Main which forms one side of the Passage before mentioned and which is the northern Promontary of this country I have named *York Cape* in honour of His late Royal Highness the Duke of York....

At 4 oClock we anchor'd about a Mile and a half or 2 Miles within the entrance in 6½ fathom clear ground, distant from the Islands on each side of us one mile, the Main land extending away to the SW, the farthest point of which that we could see bore from us S 48° West and the South-wester-most point of the Islands on the NW side of the Passage bore S 76° West. Between these two points we could see no land so that we were in great hopes that we had at last found a Passage into the Indian Seas, but in order to be better informd I landed with a party of Men accompan'd by Mr Banks and Dr Solander upon the Island which lies at the SE point of the Passage. Before and after we Anchor'd we saw a number of People upon this Island arm'd in the same manner as all the others we have seen, except one man who had a bow and a bundle of Arrows, the first we have seen on this coast. From the appearance of these People we expected that they would have opposed our landing but as we approached the Shore they all made off and left us in peaceable posession of as much of the Island as served our purpose. After landing I went upon the highest hill which however was of no great height, yet not less than twice or thrice the height of the Ships Mast heads, but I could see from it no land between SW and WSW so that I did not doubt but what there was a passage. I could see plainly that the Lands laying to the NW of this passage were composed of a number of Islands of various extent both for height and circuit, rainged one behind another as far to the Northward and Westward as I could see, which could not be less than 12 or 14 Leagues. Having satisfied my self of the great Probability of a Passage, thro' which I intend going with the Ship, and therefore may land no more upon this Eastern coast of *New Holland*, and on the Western side I can make no new discovery the honour of which belongs to the Dutch Navigators; but the Eastern Coast from the Latitude of 38° South down to this place I am confident was never seen or viseted by any European before us, and Notwithstanding I had in the Name of His Majesty taken posession of several places upon this coast, I now once more hoisted English Coulers and in the Name of His Majesty King George the Third took posession of the whole Eastern Coast from the above Latitude down to this place by the name of *New South Wales*.

From the Endeavour Strait, as this passage within Torres Strait was named, Cook sailed to the southern coast of New Guinea and on to the Dutch colonial port of Batavia, where the Endeavour *was repaired and reprovisioned. By the time they were ready to leave, on 27 December, several of the crew had died from dysentery and malaria, and others were to die on the voyage back to England via the Cape of Good Hope, among them the astronomer Charles Green, the artist Sydney Parkinson, and Midshipman Monkhouse, who had suggested fothering the ship. The* Endeavour *arrived back in England on 13 July 1771, after a voyage of nearly three years.*

THE VOYAGE OF THE FIRST FLEET

John White

SINCE *early in the eighteenth century the British government had been sentencing criminals to transportation—in effect, banishment—mainly to the colonies of Virginia and Maryland. With the outbreak of the American War of Independence in 1775, those destinations were closed to Britain and transportation was discontinued. A project of building model prisons, or penitentiaries, along the lines proposed by prison reformers John Howard and Jeremy Bentham, was slow to be put into effect; meanwhile, the gaols in Britain filled with convicts and the overflow were held in prison hulks moored in the River Thames or at Portsmouth and Plymouth. In 1784 the idea of transportation was revived, and after rejecting destinations in the West Indies and Africa, the British government selected Captain Cook's discovery, Botany Bay, as the site of a new convict settlement. Accordingly, a fleet of eleven ships—HMS* Sirius *and the armed tender* Supply; *the convict transports* Alexander, Charlotte, Friendship, Lady Penrhyn, Prince of Wales *and* Scarborough; *and the storeships* Borrowdale, Fishburn *and* Golden Grove—*carrying about 750 convicts, 211 marines and some 70 officials, wives and children, under the command of Captain Arthur Phillip, was assembled off Portsmouth. On 13 May 1787, escorted by HMS* Hyaena, *under Captain Michael de Courcy, the fleet set out on its long voyage to New South Wales. The following extracts are from the journal of John White, Surgeon-General of New South Wales, who travelled on the* Charlotte.

THIS MORNING the *Sirius* and her convoy weighed again, with an intention of going through St Helen's; but the wind being fair for the Needles, we ran through them, with a pleasant breeze. The *Charlotte*, Captain Gilbert, on board of which I was, sailing very heavy, the *Hyaena* took us in tow, until she brought us ahead of the *Sirius*, and then cast us off.

15 May. An accident of a singular nature happened today. Corporal Baker of the marines, on laying a loaded musquet down, which he had just taken out of the arms chest, was wounded by it in the inner ankle of the right foot. The bones, after being a good deal shattered, turned the ball, which, taking another direction, had still force enough left to go through a harness-cask full of beef, at some distance, and after that to kill two geese that were on the other side of it. Extraordinary as this incident may appear, it is no less true. The corporal being a young man, and in a good habit of body, I had the pleasure, contrary to the general expectation, of seeing him return to his duty in three months, with the perfect use of the wounded joint.

Surgeon-General John White and colleagues, with a party of soldiers, visiting Aborigines at Botany Bay, by an anonymous artist. White is presumed to be the tall central figure.

20 May. A discovery of a futile scheme, formed by the convicts on board the *Scarborough*, was made by one of that body, who had been recommended to Captain Hunter previous to our sailing. They had laid a plan for making themselves masters of the ship; but being prevented by this discovery, two to the ringleaders were carried on board the *Sirius*, where they were punished, and afterwards put on board the *Prince of Wales* transport, from which time they behaved very well. Being now near one hundred leagues to the westward of Scilly, and all well, Captain Phillip found it no longer necessary to keep the *Hyaena* with him; therefore, having committed his letters to the care of the Hon. Captain De Courcey, he in the course of this day sent her back.

28 May. Departed this life, Ismael Coleman, a convict, who, worn out by lowness of spirits and debility, brought on by long and close confinement, resigned his breath without a pang.

30 May. In the forenoon passed to the southward of Madeira, and saw some turtle of the hawks-bill kind.

2 June. Saw and passed the Salvages. These islands are not laid down in any of the charts we had on board, except a small one, by Hamilton Moore, in the possession of the second mate. They lie, by our observation, in lat. 30°10′N, long. 15°9′W.

3 June. This evening, after seeing many small fish in our way from the Salvages, we arrived at Teneriffe, and anchored in Santa Cruz road, about a mile to the north-east of the town of that name, in sixteen fathom water; some of the ships came to in twenty fathom. We were visited the same night, as is the custom of the port, by the harbour master, and gained permission to water and procure such refreshments as the island afforded. The marines were now served with wine in lieu of spirits; a pound of fresh beef was likewise daily distributed to them as well as to the convicts, together with a pound of rice instead of bread, and such vegetables as could be procured. Of the latter indeed the portion was rather scanty, little besides onions being to be got; and still less of fruit, it being too early in the season....

8 June. During the night, while the people were busily employed in taking in water on board the *Alexander,* a service in which some of the convicts assisted, one of them, of the name of Powel, found means to drop himself unperceived into a small boat that lay along-side and under cover of the night to cast her off without discovery. He then drifted to a Dutch East Indiaman that had just come to an anchor, to the crew of which he told a plausible story and entreated to be taken on board; but, though they much wanted men, they would have nothing to do with him. Having committed himself again to the waves, he was driven by the wind and the current, in the course of the night, to a small island lying to leeward of the ships, where he was the next morning taken. The boat and oars, which he could not conceal, led to a discovery; otherwise he would probably have effected his escape. When brought back by the party sent after him, Captain Phillip ordered him into irons, in which state he remained for some time; but at length, by an artful petition he got written for him, he so wrought on the governor's humanity as to procure a release from his confinement....

10 June. This morning the fleet got under way with a light breeze, which carried us out of Santa Cruz, but left us two days becalmed between Teneriffe and the Grand Canary. After this a fine breeze sprang up from the north-east; and no occurrence worthy of notice happened for some days. We crossed the tropical line in 18°20′ west longitude, and was nearly pressed on board the *Lady Penrhyn* transport, whose people did not attend to her steerage, being deeply engaged in sluicing and ducking all those on board who had never crossed it....

18 June. Early this morning the *Sirius* threw out the *Supply's* signal to make sail, and look out ahead. She immediately obeyed, and at eight o'clock made the signal for seeing land, which was repeated by the *Sirius* to the convoy. At eleven we passed the Isle of Sal, in lat. 16°38′N. long. 22°5W., and in the evening Bonavista; two of the Cape de Verd islands, a cluster of islands so called from a cape of that name situated opposite to them on the continent of Africa....

23 June. The weather became exceedingly dark, warm, and close, with heavy rain, a temperature of the atmosphere very common on approaching the Equator, and very much to be dreaded, as the health is greatly endangered thereby. Every attention was therefore paid to the people on board the *Charlotte,* and every exertion used to keep her clean and wholesome between decks. My first care was to keep the men, as far as was consistent with the regular discharge of their duty, out of the rain; and I never suffered the convicts to come upon deck when it rained, as they had neither linen nor clothing sufficient to make themselves dry and comfortable after getting wet: a line of conduct which cannot be too strictly observed, and enforced, in those latitudes.

To this, and to the frequent use of oil of tar, which was used three times a week, and oftener if found necessary, I attribute, in a great degree, the uncommon good health we enjoyed. I most sincerely wish oil of tar was in more general use throughout His Majesty's navy than it is. If it were, I am certain that the advantage accruing from it to the health of seamen, that truly useful and valuable class of the community, and for whose preservation too much cannot be done, would soon manifest itself. This efficacious remedy wonderfully resists putrefaction, destroys vermin and insects of every kind; wherever it is applied overcomes all disagreeable smells; and is in itself both agreeable and wholesome.

In the evening it became calm, with distant peals of thunder, and the most vivid flashes of lightning I ever remember. The weather was now so immoderately hot that the female convicts, perfectly overcome by it, frequently fainted away; and these faintings generally terminated in fits. And yet, notwithstanding the enervating effects of the atmospheric heat, and the inconveniences they suffered from it, so predominant was the warmth of their constitutions, or the depravity of their hearts, that the hatches over the place where they were confined could not be suffered to lay off, during the night, without a promiscuous intercourse immediately taking place between them and the seamen and marines.

> '*At night the sea, all around the ship, exhibited a most delightful sight. This appearance was occasioned by the gambols of an incredible number of various kinds of fish, who sported about us, and whose sudden turnings caused an emanation which resembled flashes of lightning darting in quick succession.*'

What little wind there was, which was only at intervals, continuing adverse, and the health of these wretches being still endangered by the heat, Captain Phillip, though anxious to prevent as much as possible this intercourse, gave an order, on my representing the necessity of it, that a grating should be cut, so as to admit a small wind sail being let down among them. In some of the other ships, the desire of the women to be with the men was so uncontrollable, that neither shame (but indeed of this they had long lost sight), nor the fear of punishment, could deter them from making their way through the bulk heads to the apartments assigned the seamen....

5 July. The wind south-west by south, the fleet tacked by signal and stood to the eastward. In the evening, a more numerous shoal of porpoises than ever remembered to be seen by the oldest seaman on board, presented themselves to our view. They were, as we conjectured, in pursuit of some wounded fish; and so very intent were they on the object of their chase that they passed through the fleet, and close to some of the ships, without showing any disposition to avoid them. The sailors and mariners compared them to a numerous pack of hounds, scouring through watery ground; and, indeed, when the rays of the sun beamed upon them I know not what they resembled more.

The weather being moderate, I went round the ships, and was really surprised, considering the damp and unfavourable weather we had had, to find the people look so well, and to be in so good a state of health....

6 July. The wind continuing adverse and the fleet making little progress in their voyage, Captain Phillip put the officers, seamen, marines, and convicts to an allowance of three pints of water per day (not including a quart allowed each man a day for boiling pease and oatmeal); a quantity scarcely sufficient to supply that waste of animal spirits the body must necessarily undergo, in the torrid zone, from a constant and violent perspiration, and a diet consisting of salt provisions. Necessity, however, has no law in this instance as well as in every other; and I am fully persuaded the commander acted upon this occasion from the best of motives, and for the good of the whole....

7 July. Dark, cloudy, unpleasant, sultry weather; the wind south by east. We saw many fish, and caught two bonitoes. The boat swain struck, with a pair of grains, out of the cabin window, a most beautiful fish, about ten pounds weight. In shape it a good deal resembled a salmon, with this difference, that its tail was more forked. It was in colour of a lovely yellow; and when first taken out of the water, it had two beautiful stripes of green on each side, which, some minutes after, changed to a delightful blue, and so continued. In the internal formation of this fish I observed nothing particular, except that its heart was larger, and its respirations contracted and dilated longer than I had ever seen before in any aquatic animal, a tortoise not excepted. As we were at a loss what appellation to give it, having never met with a fish of this species, and it being a non-descript, the sailors gave it the name of the Yellow Tail....

14 July. About five in the evening we crossed the Equator, without any wish or inclination being shewn by the seamen to observe the ceremony usually practised in passing under it. The longitude was 26°37′W, the wind at east the weather moderate and clear. In lat. 1°24′S, long. 26°22′W, the boatswain caught sixteen fine bonitoes, which proved a very seasonable and acceptable supply.

At night the sea, all around the ship, exhibited a most delightful sight. This appearance was occasioned by the gambols of an incredible number of various kinds of fish, who sported about us, and whose sudden turnings caused an emanation which resembled flashes of lightning darting in quick succession. What I before spoke of as the spawn, I am now fully convinced were rather the fish themselves, turning up their white bellies at some little distance below the surface of the water, and these sudden evolutions were what gave the sea the luminous appearance observed on it before....

18 July. Being informed that several of the mariners and convicts on board the *Alexander* were suddenly taken ill, I immediately visited that ship, and found that the illness complained of was wholly occasioned by the bilge water, which had by some means or other risen to so great a height that the pannels of the cabin, and the buttons on the clothes of the officers, were turned nearly black by the noxious effluvia. When the hatches were taken off, the stench was so powerful that it was scarcely possible to stand over them.

How it could have got to this height is very strange; for I well know that Captain Phillip gave strict orders (which orders I myself delivered) to the masters of the transports to pump the ships out daily, in order to keep them

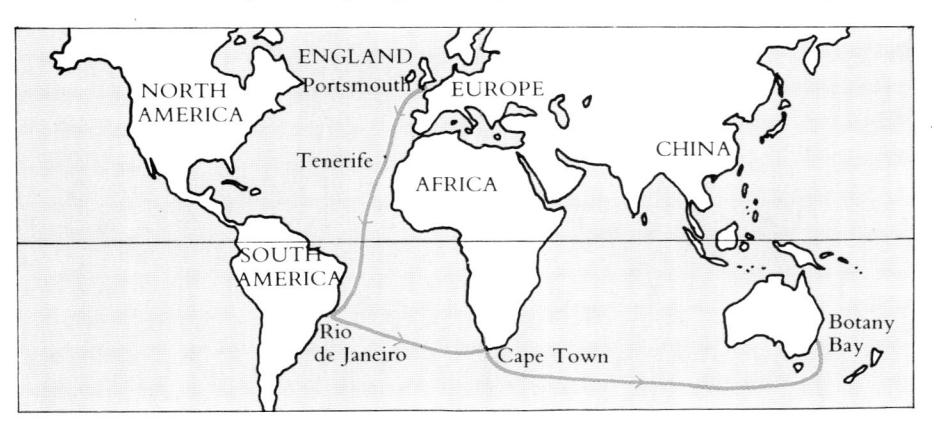

The route taken by the First Fleet, a voyage of eight months duration, from May 1787 to January 1788.

sweet and wholesome; and it was added that if the ships did not make water enough for that purpose they were to employ the convicts in throwing water into the well, and pumping it out again, until it become clear and untinged. The people's health, however, being endangered by the circumstance, I found a representation upon the subject to Captain Phillip needful, and accordingly went on board the *Sirius* for that purpose.

Captain Phillip, who upon every occasion showed great humanity and attention to the people, with the most obliging readiness sent Mr King, one of his lieutenants, on board the *Alexander* with me, in order to examine into the state of the ship, charging him, at the same time, with the most positive and pointed instructions to the master of the ship instantly to set about sweetening and purifying her. This commission Mr King executed with great propriety and expedition; and, by the directions he gave, such effectual means were made use of that the evil was soon corrected: and not long after all the people, who, suffering from the effects of it, were under Mr Balmain, my assistant's care, got quite rid of the complaint.

I now returned to the *Sirius* and solicited an increase of water, which Captain Phillip with equal readiness complied with; and as we had by this time got into a regular south-east trade wind our allowance served tolerably well, every man having three quarts a day....

2 August. Being now in expectation of soon seeing land, the commodore made the *Supply*'s signal to look out ahead, and the *Alexander*'s and *Prince of Wales*'s to take their station in the order of sailing, being too far ahead. At three in the afternoon the *Supply* made the signal for seeing land, which was repeated by the commodore to the convoy. At nine at night, being well in with Cape Frio, we shortened sail, running at an easy rate until morning, when the wind was little and variable.

3 August. This evening, finding it impossible to get hold of anchorage, the commodore dispatched Lieutenant King in the *Supply*, which sailed well in light winds, to the viceroy, with information that he was, with his convoy, arrived near the mouth of the harbour. He then made the signal for the ships to bring to, with their heads to the southward, about six miles from the shore, Rio de Janeiro Sugar Loaf bearing west half north, distant about six leagues. In the course of the day we saw many whales playing about.

4 August. This morning, standing in for the harbour, the wind headed us, which obliged us to tack, and stand out to sea a little, in order to prevent our falling to leeward of the port, which it would have been no easy matter to have regained.

5 August. Still calm. This morning a boat came alongside, in which were three Portugueze and six slaves, from whom we purchased some oranges, plantains, and bread. In trafficking with these people, we discovered that one Thomas Barret, a convict, had, with great ingenuity and address, passed some quarter dollars which he, assisted by two others, had coined out of old buckles, buttons belonging to the marines, and pewter spoons, during their passage from Teneriffe. The impression, milling, character, in a word, the whole was so inimitably executed that had their metal been a little better the fraud, I am convinced, would have passed undetected. A strict and careful search was made for the apparatus wherewith this was done, but in vain; not

The Sirius *and convoy at anchor in the harbour of Rio de Janeiro, a drawing by Lieutenant William Bradley of the* Sirius. *The fleet remained at Rio for a month while reprovisioning. Phillip and his officers were treated well, for Phillip had previously served with distinction in the Portuguese navy.*

the smallest trace or vestige of any thing of the kind was to be found among them. How they managed this business without discovery, or how they could effect it at all, is a matter of inexpressible surprise to me, as they never were suffered to come near a fire and a centinel was constantly placed over their hatchway, which, one would imagine, rendered it impossible for either fire or fused metal to be conveyed into their apartments. Besides, hardly ten minutes ever elapsed without an officer of some degree or other going down among them. The adroitness, therefore, with which they must have managed, in order to complete a business that required so complicated a process, gave me a high opinion of their ingenuity, cunning, caution, and address; and I could not help wishing that these qualities had been employed to more laudable purposes.

The officers of marines, the master of the ship, and myself fully explained to the injured Portugueze what villains they were who had imposed upon them. We were not without apprehensions that they might entertain an unfavourable opinion of Englishmen in general from the conduct of these rascals; we therefore thought it necessary to acquaint them that the perpetrators of the fraud were felons doomed to transportation, by the laws of their country, for having committed similar offences there.

About one o'clock a gentle breeze from the east carried us within about a mile of the bar, where, at nine o'clock, we anchored in sixteen-fathom water. The calms had baffled the *Supply* so much that she had only dropped her anchor a little while before us.

6 August. Early this morning, it being quite calm, the commodore dispatched an officer to the viceroy, who met with a courteous reception, and about eleven o'clock returned with the boat nearly full of fruit and vegetables, sent as presents to the commodore from some of his old friends and acquaintances.

Some years ago Captain Phillip was on this coast, commander of a Portugueze man-of-war. During that time he performed several gallant acts, which, aided by his other amiable qualities, rendered him extremely popular here, and recommended him to the notice of the court of Lisbon. Shortly after, his

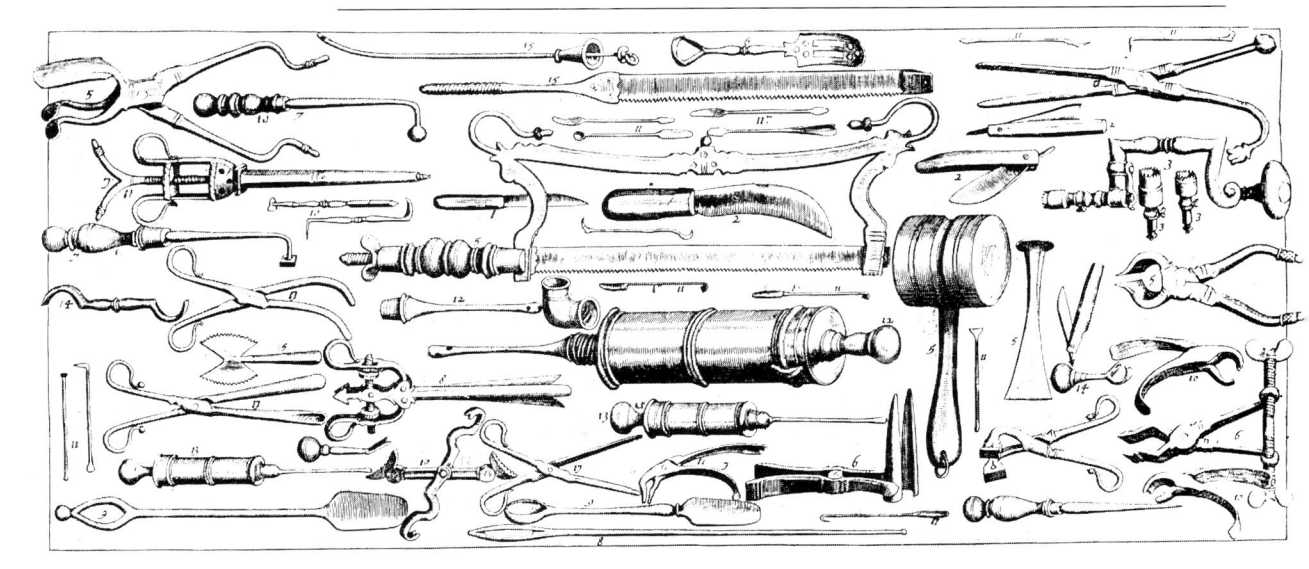

A sea surgeon's instruments at the time of the First Fleet. The illustration is from Viaticum, or Pathway to the Surgeon's Chest, *by John Woodall, Surgeon-General to the East India Company, published in 1639; however, the pattern of instruments changed little until the end of the eighteenth century.*

own country having a claim to his services, on the breaking out of a war, he declined a command offered him by the Portugueze, and returned to the English navy, where he served some time as lieutenant (a rank he had held before he had engaged in the service of Portugal) on board the *Alexander*, under the command of that brave and exemplary character, Lord Longford.

About two o'clock we got under way, with a gentle sea-breeze, which ran us into the harbour. In passing Santa Cruz fort, the commodore saluted it with thirteen guns, which was returned with an equal number. This day a Portugueze ship sailed for Lisbon, which gave us an opportunity of writing short letters to our friends in England....

11 August. The commodore ordered six female convicts, who had behaved well, to be removed from the *Friendship* into the *Charlotte*; and at the same time an equal number, whose conduct was more exceptionable, to be returned to the *Friendship* in their stead. The commodore's view was (a matter not easily accomplished) to separate those whose decent behaviour entitled them to some favour from those who were totally abandoned and obdurate.

13 August. Cornelius Connell, a private in the marines, was, according to the sentence of a court martial, punished with a hundred lashes for having an improper intercourse with some of the female convicts, contrary to orders. Thomas Jones was also sentenced to receive three hundred lashes, for attempting to make a centinel betray his trust in suffering him to go among the women; but in consideration of the good character he bore previous to this circumstance the court recommended him to the clemency of the commanding officer and, in consequence thereof, he was forgiven. John Jones and James Reiley, privates, accused of similar offences to that of Connell's, were acquitted for want of evidence, there being no witnesses to support the charge except convicts, whose testimony could not be admitted....

4 September. At six the fleet weighed with a light land breeze. On the commodore's approaching Santa Cruz Fort, he was saluted from the batteries with twenty-one guns; which he returned from the *Sirius* with an equal number. About ten o'clock we got clear of the land, steering to the eastward with a gentle breeze.

Thomas Brown, a convict, was punished with a dozen lashes for behaving insolently to one of the officers of the ship. This was the first that had received any punishment since their embarkation on board the *Charlotte*....

7, 8 September. The weather continued dark and cloudy, with some heavy showers of rain. On the evening of the 8th, between the hours of three and four, Mary Broad, a convict, was delivered of a fine girl....

19 September. William Brown, a very well-behaved convict, in bringing some clothing from the bowsprit end, where he had hung them to dry, fell overboard. As soon as the alarm was given of a man being overboard, the ship was instantly hove to, and a boat hoisted out, but to no purpose. Lieutenant Ball of the *Supply*, a most active officer, knowing from our proceedings (as we were at the time steering with a fair wind, and going near six knots an hour) that some accident must have happened, bore down; but, notwithstanding every exertion, the poor fellow sank before either the *Supply* or our boat could reach him. The people on the forecastle, who saw him fall, say that the ship went directly over him, which, as she had quick way through the water, must make it impossible for him to keep on the surface long enough to be taken up, after having received the stroke from so heavy a body....

13 October. The *Sirius* made the signal for seeing land; and at seven in the evening we came to, in Table Bay, at the Cape of Good Hope, in seventeen-fathom water, abreast of Cape Town, distant about a mile or a mile and half. As soon as the *Sirius* anchored, the commodore and commissary went on shore and took up their residence in lodgings at the house of Mrs De Witt. They were soon followed by such officers as could be spared from the duty of the fleet, all wishing to prepare themselves, by the comforts and refreshments to be enjoyed on shore, for the last and longest stage of their voyage.

14 October. The contract for provisions being settled with Messrs De Witts and Caston, the troops, men, women, and children, were served with a pound and half of soft bread, and an equal quantity of beef or mutton daily, and with wine in lieu of spirits. The convicts, men, women, and children, had the same allowance as the troops, except wine.

16 October. Commodore Phillip, attended by most of the officers of the fleet, paid a complimentary visit to his excellency Mynheer Van Graaf, the Dutch governor, by whom we were received with extreme civility and politeness. A few hours after we had taken leave, he called on the commodore at his lodgings, to return his visit, and the next day returned the visit of such officers, residing on shore, as had paid their respects to him.

Notwithstanding this studied politeness, several days elapsed before the commodore could obtain a categorical answer to the requisition he had made for the supplies he stood in need of for the expedition: and had it not been for the judicious perseverance Commodore Phillip observed, in urging his particular situation, and the uncommon exigency of the service he was engaged in, it was believed the governor fiscal and council would have sheltered their refusal under the pretence that a great scarcity had prevailed in the Cape colony the preceding season, particularly of wheat and corn, which were the articles we stood most in want of.

This idea they wished to impress us with; but, as just observed, the commodore's sagacity and industrious zeal for the service subdued and got over the supineness shown by the governor etc., and procured permission for the contractor to supply us with as much stock, corn, and other necessaries as we could stow. It is, however, much to be lamented that the quantity we could find room for fell very short of what we ought to have taken in, as the only spare room we had was what had been occasioned by the consumption of provisions etc., since we left Rio de Janeiro, and the removal of twenty female convicts from the *Friendship* into the *Charlotte*, the *Lady Penrhyn*, and the *Prince of Wales*....

11 November. Having got on board such animals, provisions &c. as we could stow, the commodore, with all the officers that had lodgings on shore, embarked. Previous to the commodore's embarkation he gave a public dinner to some of the gentlemen of the town and the officers of his fleet. The Dutch governor was to have been of the party but by some unforeseen event was detained in the country, where he had been for some days before. Commodore Phillip had his band of music on shore upon the occasion, and the day was spent with great cheerfulness and conviviality.

13 November. About half past one o'clock we sailed from the Cape of Good Hope....

17 November. The wind variable, inclining to the southward and eastward, with hazy weather, an epidemic dysentry appeared among the convicts, which very soon made its way among the marines, and prevailed with violence and obstinacy until about Christmas, when it was got under by an unremitting attention to cleanliness, and every other method proper and essential for the removal and prevention of contagion. It gives me pleasure to be able to add that we only lost one person by this disease, violent and dangerous as it was, and that was Daniel Cresswell, one of the troops intended for the garrison, who was seized on 19 November and died the 30th of the same month, the eleventh day of his illness. From the commencement of his disorder, he was in the most acute agonising pain I ever was witness to; nor was it in the power of medicine to procure him the shortest interval of ease. His case being a very singular one, I have transmitted it, with some others, to a medical friend in London, with permission to make what use of them he may think proper....

25 November. The commodore removed into the *Supply* armed tender, and took with him Lieutenant King of the *Sirius*, and Mr Dawes of the marines, whom I had before occasion to mention as having undertaken the astronomical observations during the voyage. Having likewise selected some artificers from among the convicts, he went on, taking the *Alexander, Scarborough,* and *Friendship* with him, being fast sailing vessels; leaving the heavy sailers, both transports and victuallers, under the direction of Captain Hunter of the *Sirius*. Major Ross, commanding officer of the troops, removed into the *Scarborough*, as did the adjutant....

20 December. Wind variable, inclining to the south. I visited the *Prince of Wales*, where I found some of the female convicts with evident symptoms of the scurvy, brought on by the damp and cold weather we had lately experienced. The two succeeding days the wind to the westward, though at times variable, with dark, wet, gloomy weather; in lat. 41°18′ south, long. 90°7′

east. We saw and passed some seaweed. On those days the scurvy began to show itself in the *Charlotte*, mostly among those who had the dysentery to a violent degree; but I was pretty well able to keep it under by a liberal use of the essence of malt and some good wine, which ought not to be classed among the most indifferent antiscorbutics. For the latter we were indebted to the humanity of Lord Sydney and Mr Nepean, principal and undersecretaries of state.

24 December. The weather still dark and gloomy. Had several birds round the ship of the albatross and petrel kind; with what appeared to me to be something of the sea-hawk species....

4 January 1788. Cloudy weather, in latitude 44°2′S. The *Sirius* made the signal for the longitude by lunar observation, which was found to be 135°30′ east. In the evening some birds, called Mother Carey's Chickens, were round the ship.

5 January. The weather cold and clear, the wind NW. Passed some seaweed. In the morning the third mate thought he saw some divers; but, as they were not seen by any other person, not much attention was paid to the report. At night we had some squalls, with light showers of rain.

7 January. Early in the morning the *Lady Penrhyn* made the signal for seeing land; but it only proved to be a fogbank; a circumstance that often deceives the anxious mariner. About two o'clock in the afternoon the *Prince of Wales*, being the headmost ship, made the same signal. The *Charlotte* being next in succession, the signal was scarcely displayed before we also discovered it very plainly through the haze, and repeated the signal, which was answered by the *Sirius*.

Bradley's view of the First Fleet at the Cape of Good Hope, in Table Bay, with Table Mountain in the background. Livestock and more provisions were obtained at Cape Town, though at high prices, for the colony was short of food and the governor was unhelpful.

By our last lunar observation this land appears to be well laid down in Maskelyne's Tables, and in the journals of the celebrated Cook: but to the surprise of every one on board, we found a small chart, published by Steele, and which was held in little estimation, to be not only accurate as to the situation, but also to give a tolerable appearance and description of Van Diemen's Land: indeed such as may prove extremely useful to ships coming this way, and fully sufficient to enable them to avoid all danger if the weather be clear. For my own part, I see no hazard that attends making this land by day (such an attempt by night would be very incautious and absurd), as nature has been very particular in pointing out where it lies, by rocks which jutt out of the sea like so many beacons.

I believe a convoy was never conducted with more care, or made the land with greater accuracy and certainty, than this. Indeed, ability and experienced nautical knowledge were never more fully evinced on all occasions than by Captain Hunter; who is, I may venture to pronounce, without much risk of having my veracity called in question, one of the most assiduous and accurate observers, and able navigators, the present day furnishes. His appointment to this expedition by Lord Howe is strongly marked with that prudence and wisdom which are known to govern His Lordship's conduct. Captain Hunter has a pretty turn for drawing, which will enable him, no doubt, to give such a description of this coast as will do credit to himself, and be of singular advantage, as well to those whose lot it may be to visit, hereafter, this extensive coast, as to navigation at large.

The assistance of Lieutenant Bradley, first [lieutenant] of the *Sirius* (who likewise is an officer of more than common abilities), as a navigator in conducting a convoy in a track so little known, must have been pleasing to Captain Hunter.

As we ran in with the land, which is pretty high, we were surprised to see, at this season of the year, some small patches of snow. The haze being dispersed by a gentle breeze at NNW, we could observe, and hear, as we were not more than six or seven miles from the shore, the surf beating high and loudly against some uneven rocks which jutted out, in strange projections, into the sea. This part of the coast, as far as we could see, is bold, irregular, and craggy; and very few trees, or appearance of verdure, to be seen.

At four in the afternoon, being about six or eight miles to the eastward of the eastward-most rock, called the Mewstone (there being several others which we distinctly saw), bearing NNW, we discovered to the westward of them some eminences which probably might be islands; or, if not, some land running a considerable way into the sea. For my own part I am inclined to believe the latter to be the case; though the distance was too great to hazard a conclusive opinion upon it, as a large smoke was seen close to the innermost height.

About seven, steering to the eastward, along shore, nearly at the distance of four miles, being well in with the westward-most point of a very large bay, called Storm Bay, laid down in lat. 44°3′S and long. 146°E, we discovered Swilly bearing SE½S and a little to the eastward of it a small rock rising out of the sea, distinguished by the name of the Eddystone, from its resemblance to the Eddystone lighthouse off Plymouth, which was very perceptible at the

> '*I believe a convoy was never conducted with more care, or made the land with greater accuracy and certainty, than this. Indeed, ability and experienced nautical knowledge were never more fully evinced on all occasions than by Captain Hunter;*'

distance we were then from it. Our being close in with the land prevented us from seeing either of these before, as they lie at least six or seven leagues out to sea. From the SW cape, which lies in lat. 43°39′S and long. 145°50′E to the SE cape, which is admitted to be Tasman's South Cape, is about the distance of fifteen or sixteen leagues. As we got to the eastward, we saw many trees, mostly of a dwarf or stunted kind, with a whitish bark, and perfectly leafless.

This part of the country still continued to be a rough, rugged, uneven tract, with very little appearance of fertility. Some small patches of verdure were discovered about Storm Bay, and the trees seemed to increase in number and size. Between eight and nine at night we saw a large fire on the east point of land which forms this bay, made by the natives, none of whom could we see during the day, though close in with the shore: nor did we perceive any other indication of its being inhabited but this fire, and the smoke mentioned to be seen on our first falling in with the land. The distance between the smoke and the fire was eight leagues, a space that would surely have exhibited some other proofs of populosity had it been thickly peopled....

8 January. The wind and weather variable; could perceive nothing of the land. I went on board the *Fishburn*, to see the boatswain, who, on the first night of the new year, having probably drunk more grog than he ought, and the ship labouring much, had fallen from the topsail yard, by which he bruised himself in a dreadful manner. The man being highly scorbutic, the parts soon mortified, and he died about half an hour after I got on board.

The master of the ship showed evident marks of great concern for this *invaluable* man, as he termed him. He declared to me that, sooner than venture again on so long a voyage without a surgeon, he would put to sea with less than half his complement of men; for he was strongly of opinion that if the poor fellow had received immediate assistance he would have recovered. I should have seen him sooner, but was prevented by my own indifferent state of health. How owners of ships can think of sending them through such a variety of climates, and a voyage of so great a length, without a surgeon, is to me a matter of surprise. The *Lady Penrhyn*, owned by Alderman Curtis, was the only merchant ship in our fleet that had a surgeon. What the others will do on their return, Heaven only knows; but this I well know, that they would never have reached thus far but for the succour given them by myself and my assistants.

9 January. Wind variable, and weather hazy, damp and dark; with some vivid flashes of lightning, succeeded by distant peals of loud thunder. On the morning of this day died Edward Thomson, a convict, worn out with a melancholy and long confinement. Had he lived, I think he would have proved a deserving member of society, as he seemed sensible of the impropriety and imprudence of his former life, and studious to atone for it....

11–12 January. The wind variable, inclining to the southward and westward, and still an unpleasant cross troublesome sea. We saw a whale, several seals, and many large oceanous birds, which we frequently fired at, without their betraying the smallest symptom of fear either at the report, or at the balls, which frequently dropped close to them. A conclusion may be drawn from hence, that they had never been harassed with firearms before; if they had, they would undoubtedly have shown some fear, a sensation they seemed

The Sirius *and the remainder of the First Fleet transports entering Botany Bay on 20 January 1788. Captain Phillip had transferred from the* Sirius *to the* Supply *and had gone ahead with three of the faster-sailing vessels to make preparations for the landing.*

to be totally unacquainted with. In all our firings we did not kill one of them.

19 January. In the evening we saw the land over Red Point, bearing W by N the extremes of the land from SSW to N. We were then about three leagues from the shore, and, finding it unlikely to get in that night, Captain Hunter made the signal for the convoy to come within hail, when he acquainted them that the entrance into Botany Bay bore NNW: adding that for the night be intended to stand off and on, and early in the morning make sail for the bay.

20 January. At four in the morning the *Sirius* and convoy made sail, and at eight o'clock anchored in eight fathom water; Cape Banks ESE, Point Solander SSE, and the entrance of the bay, between these two lands, WSW.

We found here the *Supply* tender, which had arrived the 18th, and the *Alexander, Scarborough,* and *Friendship* transports, who had only arrived the day before. To see all the ships safe in their destined port, without ever having, by any accident, been one hour separated, and all the people in as good health as could be expected or hoped for, after so long a voyage, was a sight truly pleasing, and at which every heart must rejoice.

THE PASSAGE OF THE BOUNTY'S LAUNCH

William Bligh

JUST BEFORE SUNRISE *on 29 April 1789 the commander of HMS* Bounty, *William Bligh, was seized by his acting lieutenant, Fletcher Christian, and other mutinous crewmen and cast adrift with eighteen others in the ship's launch. The open boat was seven metres long with a beam measurement of just over two metres. The mutineers gave Bligh 68 kilograms of bread, or ship's biscuit, sixteen pieces ($14\frac{1}{2}$ kilograms) of salt pork, about seven litres of rum and six bottles of wine, 127 litres of water and four empty water casks, as well as his sextant and nautical tables and four cutlasses.*

At the time, they were in the vicinity of Tonga, and Bligh first made for the island of Tofua, where he landed and stayed until 4 May, obtaining breadfruit and coconuts and filling their water casks before being attacked and driven off by the natives, who killed one of the seamen. Although the Bounty *had left England seven months after the First Fleet, Bligh had no way of knowing if the penal colony had in fact been established at Botany Bay, so he resolved to sail to the north coast of New Holland and follow Cook's route along the Barrier Reef and through Torres Strait with the hope of reaching a settlement in what is now Indonesia. The six-week voyage was a triumph of seamanship. Bligh kept a log during the voyage and wrote up a detailed account of the mutiny and its aftermath on his return to England. The following extracts are taken from his book* Narrative of the Mutiny on Board His Majesty's Ship 'Bounty', *beginning at the time he and his party made their escape from Tofua.*

IT WAS about eight o'clock at night when we bore away under a reefed lug-foresail, and having divided the people into watches and got the boat in a little order, we returned God thanks for our miraculous preservation, and, fully confident of His gracious support, I found my mind more at ease than it had been for some time past.

At daybreak the gale increased, the sun rose very fiery and red—a sure indication of a severe gale of wind. At eight it blew a violent storm and the sea ran very high, so that between the seas the sail was becalmed, and when on the top of the sea it was too much to have set; but we could not venture to take in the sail, for we were in very imminent danger and distress, the sea curling over the stern of the boat, which obliged us to bale with all our might. A situation more distressing has perhaps seldom been experienced.

Our bread was in bags and in danger of being spoiled by the wet: to be starved to death was inevitable if this could not be prevented. I therefore began to examine what clothes there were in the boat, and what other things could be spared; and having determined that only two suits should be kept for each person, the rest was thrown overboard, with some rope and spare sails, which lightened the boat considerably, and we had more room to bale the water out. Fortunately the carpenter had a good chest in the boat, in which we secured the bread the first favourable moment. His tool-chest also was cleared and the tools stowed in the bottom of the boat, so that this became a second convenience.

I served a teaspoonful of rum to each person (for we were very wet and cold), with a quarter of a bread-fruit, which was scarce eatable, for dinner. Our engagement was now strictly to be carried into execution, and I was fully determined to make our provisions last eight weeks, let the daily proportion be ever so small.

At noon I considered our course and distance from Tofoa to be WNW¾W eighty-six miles, latitude 19°27′S. I directed the course to the WNW, that we might get a sight of the islands called Fiji, if they lay in the direction the natives had pointed out to me.

The weather continued very severe, the wind veering from NE to ESE. The sea ran higher than in the forenoon, and the fatigue of baling, to keep the boat from filling, was exceedingly great. We could do nothing more than keep before the sea, in the course of which the boat performed so well that I no longer dreaded any danger in that respect. But among the hardships we were to undergo, that of being constantly wet was not the least. The night was very cold, and at daylight our limbs were so benumbed that we could scarce find the use of them. At this time I served a teaspoonful of rum to each person, from which we all found great benefit....

Friday, 8 May. As our lodgings were very miserable and confined for want of room, I endeavoured to remedy the latter defect by putting ourselves at watch and watch; so that one-half always sat up while the other lay down on the boat's bottom, or upon a chest, with nothing to cover us but the heavens. Our limbs were dreadfully cramped, for we could not stretch them out; and

A plan of the Bounty's *launch in which Bligh and the seventeen other crew members made their heroic voyage.*

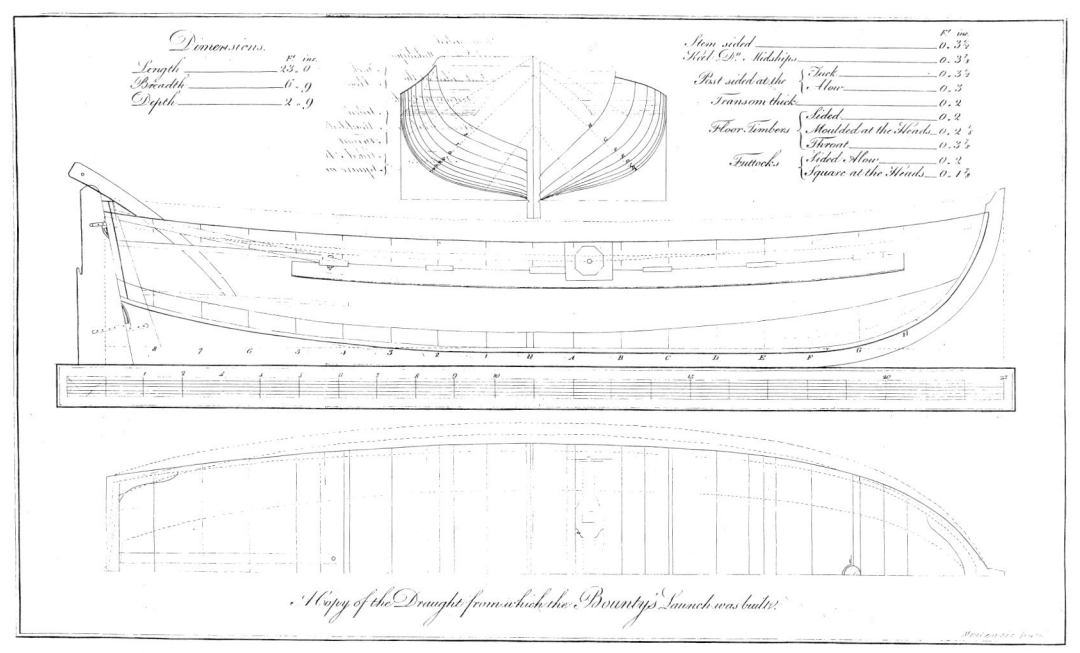

THE PASSAGE OF THE BOUNTY'S LAUNCH

the nights were so cold, and we so constantly wet, that after a few hours' sleep we could scarce move.

At dawn of day we again discovered land from WSW to WNW, and another island NNW, the latter a high round lump of but little extent; the southern land that we had passed in the night was still in sight. Being very wet and cold, I served a spoonful of rum and a morsel of bread for breakfast....

I imagine these to be the islands called Fiji, as their extent, direction, and distance from the Friendly Islands answers to the description given of them by those islanders. Heavy rain came on at four o'clock, when every person did their utmost to catch some water, and we increased our stock to thirty-four gallons, besides quenching our thirst for the first time since we had been at sea; but an attendant consequence made us pass the night very miserably, for being extremely wet, and having no dry things to shift or cover us, we experienced cold and shiverings scarce to be conceived. Most fortunately for us the forenoon turned out fair, and we stripped and dried our clothes. The allowance I issued today was an ounce and a half of pork, a teaspoonful of rum, half a pint of coconut milk, and an ounce of bread. The rum, though so small in quantity, was of the greatest service. A fishing-line was generally

An engraving by Robert Dodd, published in 1790, depicting the Bounty *mutineers casting Bligh and some of the other officers and crew adrift in the ship's launch.*

towing from the stern of the boat, but though we saw great numbers of fish, we could never catch one....

In the afternoon we cleaned out the boat, and it employed us till sunset to get everyting dry and in order. Hitherto I had issued the allowance by guess, but I now made a pair of scales with two coconut shells; and having accidentally some pistol-balls in the boat, twenty-five of which weighed one pound, or sixteen ounces, I adopted one as the proportion of weight that each person should receive of bread at the times I served it. I also amused all hands with describing the situation of New Guinea and New Holland, and gave them every information in my power, that in case any accident happened to me those who survived might have some idea of what they were about, and be able to find their way to Timor, which at present they knew nothing of more than the name, and some not even that. At night I served a quarter of a pint of water and half an ounce of bread for supper.

Saturday, 9 May. In the morning, a quarter of a pint of coconut milk and some of the decayed bread was served for breakfast; and for dinner I divided the meat of four coconuts with the remainder of the rotten bread, which was only eatable by such distressed people.

At noon I observed the latitude to be 15°47′S; course since yesterday N75°W, distance sixty-four miles; longitude made, by account, 8°45′W.

In the afternoon I fitted a pair of shrouds for each mast, and contrived a canvas weather-cloth round the boat, and raised the quarters about nine inches by nailing on the seats of the stern-sheets, which proved of great benefit to us.

The wind had been moderate all day, in the SE quarter, with fine weather, but about nine o'clock in the evening the clouds began to gather, and we had a prodigious fall of rain, with severe thunder and lightning. By midnight we caught about twenty gallons of water. Being miserably wet and cold, I served to the people a teaspoonful of rum each, to enable them to bear with their distressed situation. The weather continued extremely bad, and the wind increased; we spent a very miserable night, without sleep, except such as could be got in the midst of rain. The day brought no relief but its light. The sea broke over us so much that two men were constantly baling, and we had no choice how to steer, being obliged to keep before the waves for fear of the boat filling.

The allowance now regularly served to each person was one twenty-fifth of a pound of bread, and a quarter of a pint of water, at eight in the morning, at noon, and at sunset. Today I gave about half an ounce of pork for dinner, which, though any moderate person would have considered only as a mouthful, was divided into three or four....

Monday, 11 May. In the morning at daybreak I served to every person a teaspoonful of rum, our limbs being so cramped that we could scarce move them. Our situation was now extremely dangerous, the sea frequently running over our stern, which kept us baling with all our strength....

In the evening it rained hard, and we again experienced a dreadful night. At length the day came, and showed to me a miserable set of beings, full of wants, without anything to relieve them. Some complained of great pain in their bowels, and every one of having almost lost the use of his limbs. The

---

'The day brought no relief but its light. The sea broke over us so much that two men were constantly baling, and we had no choice how to steer, being obliged to keep before the waves for fear of the boat filling.'

little sleep we got was no ways refreshing, as we were covered with sea and rain. I served a spoonful of rum at day-dawn, and the usual allowance of bread and water for breakfast, dinner, and supper....

Friday, 15 May. At one in the morning another island was discovered, bearing WNW, five leagues distance.... The sight of these islands served only to increase the misery of our situation. We were very little better than starving, with plenty in view; yet to attempt procuring any relief was attended with so much danger that prolonging of life, even in the midst of misery, was thought preferable while there remained hopes of being able to surmount our hardships. For my own part, I consider the general run of cloudy and wet weather to be a blessing of Providence. Hot weather would have caused us to have died with thirst, and probably being so constantly covered with rain or sea protected us from that dreadful calamity.

As I had nothing to assist my memory, I could not then determine whether these islands were a part of the New Hebrides or not. I believed them to be a new discovery, which I have since found true; but though they were not seen either by Monsieur Bougainville or Captain Cook, they are so nearly in the neighbourhood of the New Hebrides that they must be considered as part of the same group. They are fertile, and inhabited, as I saw smoke in several places....

Saturday, 16 May. In addition to our miserable allowance of one twenty-fifth of a pound of bread and a quarter of a pint of water, I issued for dinner about an ounce of salt pork to each person. I was often solicited for this pork, but I considered it more proper to issue it in small quantities than to suffer it to be all used at once or twice, which would have been done if I had allowed it....

Sunday, 17 May. At dawn of day I found every person complaining, and some of them solicited extra allowance; which I positively refused. Our situation was miserable; always wet, and suffering extreme cold in the night, without the least shelter from the weather. Being constantly obliged to bale, to keep the boat from filling, was perhaps not to be reckoned an evil, as it gave us exercise.

The little rum we had was of great service. When our nights were particularly distressing I generally served a teaspoonful or two to each person, and it was always joyful tidings when they heard of my intentions....

Wednesday, 20 May. Fresh breezes ENE, with constant rain; at times a deluge. Always baling.

At dawn of day some of my people seemed half dead; our appearances were horrible, and I could look no way but I caught the eye of someone in distress. Extreme hunger was now too evident, but no one suffered from thirst, nor had we much inclination to drink, that desire perhaps being satisfied through the skin. The little sleep we got was in the midst of water, and we constantly awoke with severe cramps and pains in our bones. This morning I served about two teaspoonfuls of rum to each person, and the allowance of bread and water as usual. At noon the sun broke out and revived every one. I found we were in latitude 14°49′S; longitude made 25°46′W; course S88°W distance seventy-five miles.

All the afternoon we were so covered with rain and salt water that we could scarcely see. We suffered extreme cold, and every one dreaded the approach of night. Sleep, though we longed for it, afforded no comfort: for my own part I almost lived without it. About two o'clock in the morning we were overwhelmed with a deluge of rain. It fell so heavy that we were afraid it would fill the boat, and were obliged to bale with all our might. At dawn of day I served a larger allowance of rum. Towards noon the rain abated and the sun shone, but we were miserably cold and wet, the sea breaking constantly over us; so that notwithstanding the heavy rain, we had not been able to add to our stock of fresh water. Latitude, by observation, 14°29'S, and longitude made, by account, from Tofoa, 27°25'W; course, since yesterday noon, N78°W, ninety-nine miles. I now considered myself nearly on a meridian with the east part of New Guinea.

Friday, 22 May. Strong gales from ESE to SSE, a high sea, and dark dismal night.

Our situation this day was extremely calamitous. We were obliged to take the course of the sea, running right before it, and watching with the utmost care, as the least error in the helm would in a moment have been our destruction.

At noon it blew very hard, and the foam of the sea kept running over our stern and quarters. I, however, got propped up, and made an observation of the latitude, in 14°17'S; course N85°W, distance one hundred and thirty miles; longitude made 29°38'W.

The misery we suffered this night exceeded the preceding. The sea flew over us with great force, and kept us baling with horror and anxiety. At

The Bounty's *launch at sea, as portrayed in the Dutch edition of Bligh's* Narrative.

dawn of day I found every one in a most distressed condition, and I began to fear that another such night would put an end to the lives of several, who seemed no longer able to support their sufferings. I served an allowance of two teaspoonfuls of rum; after drinking which, having wrung our clothes and taken our breakfast of bread and water, we became a little refreshed.

Towards noon the weather became fair, but with very little abatement of the gale, and the sea remained equally high. With some difficulty I observed the latitude to be 13°44′S; course since yesterday noon N74°W, distance one hundred and sixteen miles; longitude made 31°32′W from Tofoa.

The wind moderated in the evening and the weather looked much better, which rejoiced all hands, so that they ate their scanty allowance with more satisfaction than for some time past. The night also was fair; but being always wet with the sea, we suffered much from the cold. A fine morning, I had the pleasure to see, produced some cheerful countenances, and the first time for fifteen days past we experienced comfort from the warmth of the sun. We stripped and hung our clothes up to dry, which were by this time become so threadbare that they would not keep out either wet or cold....

As the sea began to run fair and we shipped but little water, I took the opportunity to examine into the state of our bread, and found that according to the present mode of issuing there was a sufficient quantity remaining for twenty-nine days' allowance; by which time I hoped we should be able to reach Timor. But as this was very uncertain, and it was possible that after all we might be obliged to go to Java, I determined to proportion the allowance so as to make our stock hold out six weeks. I was apprehensive that this would be ill received, and that it would require my utmost resolution to enforce it; for small as the quantity was which I intended to take away for our future good, yet it might appear to my people like robbing them of life; and some, who were less patient than their companions, I expected would very ill brook it. However, on my representing the necessity of guarding against delays that might be occasioned in our voyage by contrary winds or other causes, and promising to enlarge upon the allowance as we got on, they cheerfully agreed to my proposal. It was accordingly settled that every person should receive one twenty-fifth of a pound of bread for breakfast, and the same quantity for dinner; so that by omitting the proportion for supper, we had forty-three days' allowance.

Monday, 25 May. At noon some noddies came so near to us that one of them was caught by hand. This bird was about the size of a small pigeon. I divided it, with its entrails, into eighteen portions, and by a well-known method at sea, of 'Who shall have this?'[1] it was distributed, with the allowance of bread and water for dinner, and ate up bones and all, with salt water for sauce. I observed the latitude 13°32′S; longitude made 35°19′W; course N89°W, distance one hundred and eight miles.

In the evening several boobies flying very near to us, we had the good fortune to catch one of them. This bird is as large as a duck. Like the noddy, it has received its name from seamen, for suffering itself to be caught on the

> *'A fine morning, I had the pleasure to see, produced some cheerful countenances, and the first time for fifteen days past we experienced comfort from the warmth of the sun.'*

---

1. One person turns his back on the object that is to be divided; another then points separately to the portions, at each of them asking aloud, 'Who shall have this?' to which the first answers by naming somebody. This impartial method of division gives every man an equal chance of the best share.

masts and yards of ships. They are the most presumptive proofs of being in the neighbourhood of land of any sea-fowl we are acquainted with. I directed the bird to be killed for supper, and the blood to be given to three of the people who were the most distressed for want of food. The body, with the entrails, beak, and feet, I divided into eighteen shares, and with an allowance of bread, which I made a merit of granting, we made a good supper compared with our usual fare....

To make the bread a little savoury, most of the people frequently dipped it in salt water; but I generally broke mine into small pieces and ate it in my allowance of water, out of a coconut shell, with a spoon, economically avoiding to take too large a piece at a time, so that I was as long at dinner as if it had been a much more plentiful meal.

The weather was now serene, which nevertheless was not without its inconveniences, for we began to feel distress of a different kind from that which we had lately been accustomed to suffer. The heat of the sun was so powerful that several of the people were seized with a languor and faintness which made life indifferent. We were so fortunate as to catch two boobies in the evening. Their stomachs contained several flying fish and small cuttlefish, all of which I saved to be divided for dinner the next day.

Wednesday, 27 May. A fresh breeze at ESE, with fair weather. We passed much driftwood this forenoon and saw many birds; I therefore did not hesitate to pronounce that we were near the reefs of New Holland....

Thursday, 28 May. At one in the morning the person at the helm heard the sound of breakers, and I no sooner lifted up my head than I saw them close under our lee, not more than a quarter of a mile distant from us. I immediately hauled on a wind to the NNE, and in ten minutes' time we could neither see nor hear them....

In the morning, at daylight, we could see nothing of the land or of the reefs. We bore away again, and at nine o'clock saw the reefs. The sea broke furiously over every part, and we had no sooner got near to them than the wind came at E, so that we could only lie along the line of the breakers; within which we saw the water so smooth that every person already anticipated the heart-felt satisfaction he should receive as soon as we could get within them. I now found we were embayed, for we could not lie clear with the sails, the wind having backed against us, and the sea set in so heavy towards the reef that our situation was become unsafe. We could effect but little with the oars, having scarce strength to pull them, and I began to apprehend that we should be obliged to attempt pushing over the reef. Even this I did not despair of effecting with success, when happily we discovered a break in the reef about one mile from us, and at the same time an island of a moderate height within it, nearly in the same direction, bearing W$\frac{1}{2}$N. I entered the passage with a strong stream running to the westward, and found it about a quarter of a mile broad, with every appearance of deep water....

Being now happily within the reefs, and in smooth water, I endeavoured to keep near them to try for fish, but the tide set us to the NW. I therefore bore away in that direction, and having promised to land on the first convenient spot we could find, all our past hardships seemed already to be forgotten....

We now returned God thanks for His gracious protection, and with much content took our miserable allowance of a twenty-fifth of a pound of bread and a quarter of a pint of water for dinner.

As we advanced within the reefs the coast began to show itself very distinctly, in a variety of high and low land, some parts of which were covered with wood. In our way towards the shore we fell in with a point of a reef which is connected with that towards the sea, and here we came to a grapnel and tried to catch fish, but had no success.... Two islands lay about four miles to the W by N, and appeared eligible for a resting-place, if for nothing more; but on our approach to the nearest island, it proved to be only a heap of stones, and its size too inconsiderable to shelter the boat. We therefore proceeded to the next, which was close to it and towards the main. On the NW side of this I found a bay and a fine sandy point to land at.... We landed to examine if there were any signs of the natives being near us. We saw some old fireplaces, but nothing to make me apprehend that this would be an unsafe situation for the night. Every one was anxious to find something to eat, and it was soon discovered that there were oysters on the rocks, for the tide was out; but it was nearly dark, and only a few could be gathered. I determined therefore to wait till the morning, when I should better know how to proceed, and I directed that one-half of our company should sleep on shore and the other half in the boat. We would gladly have made a fire, but as we could not accomplish it we took our rest for the night, which happily was calm and undisturbed.

Friday, 29 May. The dawn of day brought greater strength and spirits to us than I expected, for notwithstanding every one was very weak, there appeared

A page from the small leather-bound notebook in which Bligh, under almost impossible conditions, kept a daily record of events and made navigational calculations. Whenever conditions were more favourable, he wrote up his notes in the ship's logbook.

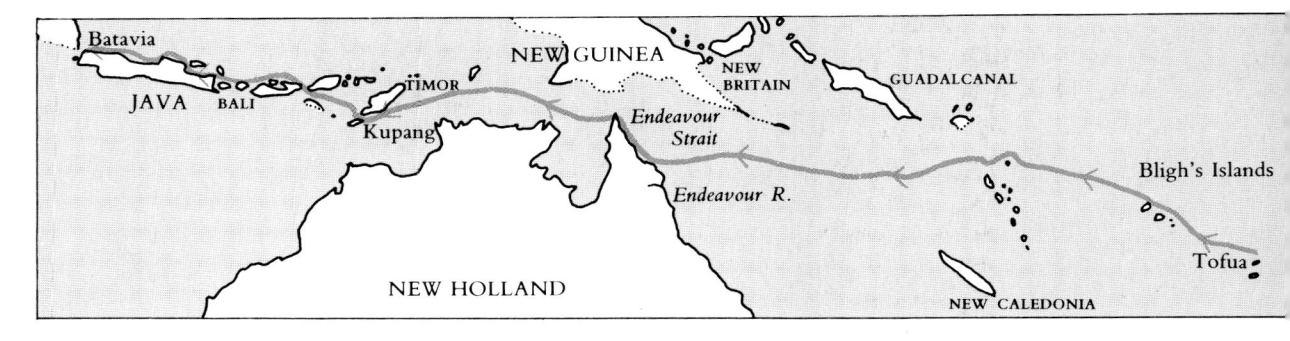

The track of the Bounty's launch from Tofua, in the Tongan islands, to Kupang in Timor, and the subsequent voyage to Batavia. The map is copied from Bligh's own chart of the route published in his Narrative.

strength sufficient remaining to make me conceive the most favourable hopes of our being able to surmount the difficulties we might yet have to encounter.

As there were no appearances to make me imagine that any of the natives were near us, I sent out parties in search of supplies, while others of the people were putting the boat in order, that we might be ready to go to sea in case any unforeseen cause should make it necessary....

The parties returned, highly rejoiced at having found plenty of oysters and fresh water. I had also made a fire, by the help of a small magnifying glass; and what was still more fortunate, we found among the few things which had been thrown into the boat and saved, a piece of brimstone and a tinder-box, so that I secured fire for the future.

One of the people had been so provident as to bring away with him from the ship a copper pot. By being in possession of this article we were enabled to make a proper use of the supply we now obtained, for with a mixture of bread and a little pork we made a stew that might have been relished by people of far more delicate appetites, and of which each person received a full pint.

The general complaints of disease among us were a dizziness in the head, great weakness of the joints, and violent tenesmus; most of us having had no evacuation by stool since we left the ship. I had constantly a severe pain at my stomach, but none of our complaints were alarming. On the contrary, every one retained marks of strength that, with a mind possessed of a tolerable share of fortitude, seemed able to bear more fatigue than I imagined we should have to undergo in our voyage to Timor....

This day being the anniversary of the restoration of King Charles the Second, and the name not being inapplicable to our present situation (for we were restored to fresh life and strength), I named this Restoration Island.

After a brief stay at Restoration Island, Bligh and his party sailed north between the mainland of Cape York Peninsula and the Great Barrier Reef. On 3 June, they rounded Cape York and passed through Torres Strait into the Arafura Sea. A week later they came in sight of Timor, and on 15 June they arrived at Kupang, having travelled 3,700 nautical miles in forty-two days without loss of life and with provisions for eleven days remaining. At Kupang Bligh bought a small schooner, which he sailed to Batavia towing the launch behind. He and his clerk and servant took the first available ship to England, leaving the others to follow as soon as they could. One had died in Kupang, and only nine of the fourteen left in Batavia reached England.

WILLIAM AND MARY BRYANT ESCAPE TO THE NORTH

James Martin

THE STORY of Mary Bryant is the stuff of historical romance. In March 1786, at the Exeter assizes, Mary Broad of Fowey in Cornwall was convicted of assault and robbery and sentenced to be hanged. The sentence was commuted to transportation for seven years, and after a few months in a prison hulk off Plymouth she was sent to Botany Bay in the Charlotte, one of the transports of the First Fleet. During the voyage she gave birth to a child, which she named Charlotte, and four days after landing at Sydney Cove married a fellow convict, William Bryant, in the first marriage ceremony conducted in the colony. An experienced fisherman, William Bryant was put in charge of the boats engaged in catching fish for the settlement. He was thus in a favourable position to put into operation a plan he devised with seven other convicts to escape from the colony.

The plan was well prepared and carried out. Food and equipment were secretly acquired and stockpiled over a period of months, and Bryant bought from the master of the Dutch vessel Waaksamheyd, which had arrived at Port Jackson in December 1790 with supplies for the colony, a quadrant and compass, a chart (probably a copy of Cook's chart of the Australian coast), two muskets and ammunition, and foodstuffs. On 28 March 1791, under cover of darkness, he and his wife and two children (a son, Emanuel, had been born twelve months before), with the seven other convicts, stole the governor's six-oared cutter, slipped quietly out of Port Jackson, and headed north.

Sixty-nine days later, after a hazardous voyage of more than five thousand kilometres, they arrived safely at Kupang, Timor, where they posed as survivors of a wrecked whaler. Their real identity was, however, eventually revealed, and they were placed in custody. By a remarkable coincidence, some genuine British shipwreck survivors—of HMS Pandora, which had been sent to search for the Bounty mutineers—arrived in Kupang at that time, and the Pandora's Captain Edwards took the Bryants and their party in charge and conveyed them in a chartered ship to Batavia to await transhipment to England. There William Bryant and the boy Emanuel sickened and died. On the subsequent voyage to England, Mary Bryant's remaining child, Charlotte, also died, as did two of her companions; another jumped or fell overboard.

Back in England, Mary and her four remaining companions were committed to Newgate prison for an indefinite sentence. Their exploits were given much publicity, and public sympathy was aroused. One of those influenced by their plight was James Boswell, the author of the Life of Samuel Johnson. Boswell, a lawyer noted for his defence of well-nigh hopeless cases and for his spirited espousal of causes that aroused his sympathy, appealed to the Home Secretary on behalf of Mary Bryant over a period of several months and was eventually successful in obtaining an unconditional pardon for her. She subsequently returned to her home town in Cornwall.

The following account of the Bryants' remarkable journey was written by James Martin (or Martyn), one of the survivors, while he was in Newgate prison. It was discovered nearly 150 years later by a research student, Charles Blount, among papers of the prison reformer Jeremy Bentham. The manuscript was written in four different hands, apparently begun by the almost illiterate Martin and then, when the effort became too great for him, dictated to three fellow prisoners—perhaps the other three survivors. The following account is presented as it was originally written and published by Charles Blount in 1937. For the sake of easier reading, an occasional full stop has been inserted and a new paragraph made.

ON THE 28 Day of March Made My Escape in Comp^y with 7 men more and me with one woman and two Child^n—in an open six oar Boat—having of provision on B^d one hundred w^t of flower and one hund^d w^t of Rice 14 lb of pork and aBout Eight galons of water—having a Copass Quardrant and Chart. After two Days sail reach a little Creek about 2 Degrees to they Northward of port Jackson[1] there found a quantity of fine

1. [Probably in the vicinity of Nobby's, Hunter River.]

Convicts of New Holland, *by Juan Ravenet of the Spanish scientific expedition led by Alessandro Malaspina which visited Sydney in March 1793. The convicts William and Mary Bryant had both been sentenced to transportation for seven years, he for 'resisting revenue officers who attempted to seize some smuggled property he had', she for assaulting a spinster and robbing her of a silk bonnet and other goods.*

Sydney Cove, Port Jackson, in 1791, the year the Bryants and their companions made their escape. The view, by Lieutenant Bradley of the Sirius, shows the original Government House.

Burn^g Coal there Remained 2 nights and one Day and found a Varse Quantty of Cabage tree which we Cut Down and procured they Cabage. Then they Natives Came Down to which we gave some Cloathes and other articles and they went away very much satisfied. They apperanance of they land appears more better here than at Sidney Cove here we got avarse Quantity of fish which of a great Refresment to us.

After our stay of 2 nights and one Day we proceeded our Voyage to they Northward after 2 Days sail we made a very fine harbour Seeming to run up they Country for Many miles and Quite Comodious for they Anchorage of Shipping[2]—here we found aplenty of fresh water—hawld our Boat ashore to repair her Bottom being very leaky they Better to pay her Bottom with some Beeswax and Rosin which we had a small Quantity Thereof—But on they Same night was Drove of By they natives—which meant to Destroy us—we Launchd our Boat and Road off in they strame Quite out of Reach of them—that being Sunday Monday we were of in ye stream we rowed Lower Down thinging To Land Some Miles Below—on Monday Morn^g we Attempted to land when we found a place Convenient for to Repair our Boat we accord^g we put Some of our things—part being ashore there Came they natives in Vase Numbers With Speers and Sheilds etc we formed in parts one party of us Made towards them they Better By signes to pasify them But they not taking they least notice accordingly we fired a musket thinking to afright them But they took not they least notice Thereof—on perceving them Rush more forward we were forsed to take to our Boat and to get out of their reach as fast as we Could—and what to Do we Could not tell But on Consulting with each other it was Detirmined for to row up they harbour which accordingly we rowed up they harbour 9 or 10 miles till we made a little white Sandy Isl^d in they Middle of they harbour—which land^d upon

2. [Probably Port Stephens.]

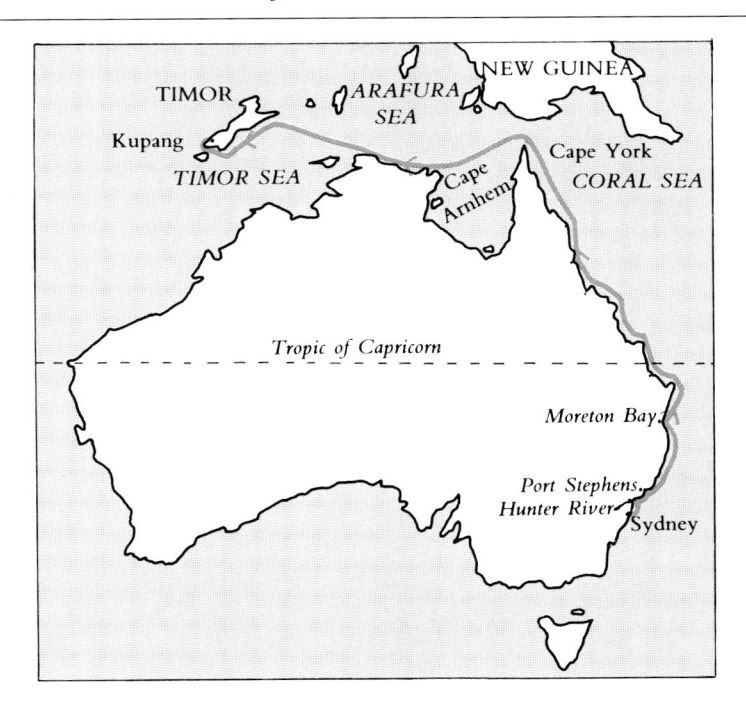

The route taken by the Bryants on their voyage from Sydney to Kupang. The epic boat journey has been compared to that of Bligh in the Bounty's *launch, and Bligh himself, a man not given to praising others, remarked that William Bryant 'must have been a determined and enterprising man'.*

and hawld up our Boat and repair her Bottom with what Little materials we had. Whilst our Stay of 2 Days we had no Interupon from they Natives.

Then we rowed of to they main where we took in fresh water and a few cabage trees—and then put out to sea—they natives here is quiet naked of a Copper Colour—shock hair—they have Cannoos made of bark then we proceed^d they Northard, having a lead^g Breez from they S:W—But that night they wind Changed and Drove us Quite out of sight of Land—which we hawld our wind having a set of Sails in they Boat accordingly they next Day we Made Close into they land But they Surf run^g so very hard we C^d not attempt to land but kept along shore but Making no harbour or Creek for nere three weeks we were much Distress^d for water and wood—accordingly perceving they Surf to abate Two of our men swam on shore thinking to get some water But being afraid of they natives which they see in numbers they return^d without any, But a little wood which threw into they water which we took up We put over on the other side of the Bay expecting to meet with a Convenient Harbour we found a little River which with great difficulty we got up our Boat being very leaky at that Time that it was with great difficulty we Could keep her above Water—were we Landed and hawled her up putting some soap in the Seams which Answered very well—at this Place we Cou'd get no Shell Fish or Fish of any kind in this Bay here we stopped two days and two Nights.

Then we left this Place and went down the Bay about 20 Miles expecting to meet with a Harbor to get some refreshment—but cou'd see none nor the End of the Bay the Wind being favourable we Tack'd about and put to sea the Land here seem'd to be much the same as at Botany Bay—accordingly we up grapling so stood to they Northward but our Boat being very Deep we were Obliged to trow all our Cloathing over Board they Better to lighten our Boat as they Sea Breaking over us Quite rapid—that Night we ran into an Open Bay and Could see no Place to land at the Surf running that we were Afraid of Staving our Boat to Pieces—We Came to a Grapling in that Bay the same Night about 2 oClock in the Morn^g our Grapling Broke and we were drove in the Middle of the Surf Expecting every Moment that our Boat wou'd be Staved to Pieces and every Soul Perish but as God wou'd have we Got our Boat save on Shore without any Loss or damage excepting one Oar we Hauld our Boat up and there remaind two days and 2 Nights there we kindled a Fire with great difficulty every thing that we had being very Wet—we Got Plenty of Shell Fish there and Fresh Water the Natives Came down in great Numbers we discharged a Musquet over their Heads and they dispersed immediately and we saw no more of them we put our things in the Boat and with great difficulty we Got out to Sea.

For 2 or 3 days we had very Bad Weather our Boat Shipping many heavy Seas, so that One Man was always Employed in Bailing out the Water to keep her up—the next Place we made was White Bay[3] being in Latt^d 27^d oo we ran down that Bay 2 or 3 Leagues before we cou'd see a convenient Place to Land the Surf running very High we saw two Women and 2 Children with a Fire Brand in their Hands at this Place we Landed the two Women being Frightened ran away but we made Signs that we wanted a Light which they Gave us Crying at the same Time in their Way we took our things out of the Boat and put them in two Huts which was there—the next Morn^g about 11 o Clock a great Number of the Natives Came towards us—as soon as we saw we went to meet them and Fired a Musquet over their Heads as

Boats were a valuable and scarce commodity at Port Jackson in the early days of settlement, so it was a serious loss to the colony when the Bryants stole the governor's cutter to make their escape. William Bradley's picture shows two of the settlement's boats and their crews conducting the 'First Interview with the Native Women at Port Jackson'.

3. [Moreton Bay.]

soon as they Heard the report they ran into the Woods and we saw no more of them the Natives there is Quite Naked—there we Stopped two days and two Nights.

The Surf running so very High that we were in great danger of Staving y^e Boat that Night we were drove out to Sea by a heavy Gale of Wind and Current, expecting every Moment to go to the Bottom next Morn^g saw no Land the Sea running Mountains high we were Under a Close reeft Mainsail and kept so until Night and then came too under a droge all the Night with her Head to the Sea thinking every Moment to be the last the sea Coming in so heavy upon us every now and then that two Hands was Obliged to keep Bailing out and it rained very hard all that Night the next Morn^g we took our droge in but Could see no Land but Hawling towards the Land to make it as soon as possible the Gale of Wind still Continuing we kept on under a Close reeft Mainsail but cou'd make no Land all that day—I will Leave you to Consider what distress we must be in the Woman and the two little Babies was in a bad Condition everything being so Wet that we Cou'd by no Means light a Fire we had nothing to Eat except a little raw rice.

At Night we Came too under a droge as we did the Night before the next Morn^g we took in our droge and kept to the North^{wd} on purpose to make the Land about 8 o Clock we made Land which proved to be a little Island about 30 Leagues from the Main the Surf running so very High we were rather fearful of going in for fear of Staving our Boat but we Concluded amongst Ourselves that we might as well Venture in there as to keep out to Sea seeing no Probability that if we kept out to Sea that we shou'd every Soul Perish—All round this Island there was nothing but reefs but a little sandy Beach which we got in safe without much damage and haul'd our Boat up out of the way of the Surf we got all our things out of the Boat then we Went to get a Fire which with great difficulty we got a Fire which being almost Starving we put on a little rice for to Cook when we went to this Island we had but one Gallon of fresh Water for there was not a drop of fresh Water to be had on this Island the Island was about one Mile in Circumference.

After the Tide fell we went to Look for some Shell Fish but found a great Quantity of very fine Large Turtles which was left upon the reef which we turned five of them and hawled them upon the Beach this reef runs about a Mile and half out in the Sea and Intirely dry when low Water we took and killed One of the Turtles and had a Noble Meal this Night it rain'd very Hard when we spread our Mainsail and filled our two Breakers full of Water—We staid on this Island six days during that Time we Killed twelve Turtles and some of it we Took and dry'd over the Fire to take to sea with us. It seemed to us that there had never been any Natives on this Island there is a kind of Fruit grows like unto a Bellpepper which seemed to Taste very well there was a great Quantity of Fowls which stayed at Night in Holes in the ground we Could not think of taking any live Turtles with us because our Boat wou'd not admit of it.

We Paid the Seams of our Boat all over with Soap before we put to sea at 8 o Clock in the Morn^g and Steered to the Northward: this Island was in Lat. 26^d 27^m we made the main Land in the Evening we passed a great Number of Small Islands which we put into a great many of them expecting to find

'The Surf running so very High that we were in great danger of Staving y^e Boat that Night we were drove out to Sea by a heavy Gale of Wind and Current, expecting every Moment to go to the Bottom'

Leaves of the false sarsaparilla vine (Smilax glycyphylla), a native plant used by the settlers at Port Jackson to make 'sweet tea'. The packet was found among the papers of James Boswell, with the inscription in Boswell's handwriting, and it is presumed he obtained the leaves from Mary Bryant, whom he had befriended.

some Turtle but never found any in any of the Islands we put into Afterwards we found a great Quantity of Shell Fish but none of them very fit to Eat but being very Hungred we were Glad to Eat them and Thank God for it if it had not been for the Shell Fish and the little Turtle that we had we must have Starved very seldom put into any Place but found plenty of Fresh Water but nothing We could find fit to Eat.

When we Came to the Gulf of Carpentara which is in Latt. 10^d 11^m we ran down the Gulf Nine or Ten Miles we saw several small Islands on which we saw several of the Natives in two Canoes landing on One of the small Islands we steered down towards them as soon as they saw us they sent their two Canoes round to the Back of the Island with one Man in each of them when we Came down to them they seemed to stand in a posture of defence against us we fired a Musquet over them and immediately they began Firing their Bows and Arrows at us we immediately hoisted up our Sails and rowed away from them but as God wou'd have it none of their Arrows Came into the Boat but dropped along side we Could not get Hold of any of them but they seemed to be about Eighteen Inches long the Natives seemed to be very Stout and fat and Blacker they were in other Parts we seen before there was One which we took to be the Chief with some Shells Around his Shoulders.

We rowed down a little farther down the Gulf and landed upon the Main for to get some Water we found plenty of fresh Water we saw a small Town of Huts about 20 of them just by were the fresh Water was there was none of the Inhabitants in their Huts or about them that we Could see their Huts was large enough for six or seven of them to Stand upright in they were made of Bark and Covered Over with Grass we filled our 2 Breakers with fresh Water and Came on Board of our Boat again for we were Afraid of Staying on Shore for fear of the Natives we went three or four Miles from the Shore and dropt our Killock and there Stopped all Night the next Morn^g we was detirmined to Go to the same Place to recruit our Water but as we were making to the Shore we saw two very large Canoes coming towards us we did not know what to do for we were Afraid to meet them there seemed to us to be 30 or 40 Men in each Canoe they had Sails in their Canoes seemed to made of Matting one of their Canoes was a Head of the others a little Way Stopt untill the other Came up and then she Hoisted her Sails and made after us as soon as we saw that we Tack'd about with what Water we had— Detirmined to Cross the Gulf which was about five Hundred Miles Across which as God wou'd have it we Out run them they followed us untill we Lost sight of them we having but little fresh Water and no Wood to make a Fire with but in four days and a half we made the other side of the Gulf we put on Shore to look for some fresh Water but Cou'd find none at that Place but we kept along Shore untill the Even^g we saw a small river which we made to and Got plenty of Fresh Water.

We put of to Sea the same Night we saw no more Land untill we Came into the Lattitude of North End of the Island we hawled up to make the land to get some fresh Water but saw no Land but a heavy Swell running which had liked to have swallowed us up then we Concluded as the best Way to shape our Course for the Island of Timor with what little Water we had which we made it in 36 Hours after Which we run along the Island of Timor till we came to the Dutch Settlements where we went on Shore to the Governors house where he behaved extremely well to us filled our Bellies and Cloathed Double with every that was wore on the Island.

We rem^d very happy at our work for two Months till Wm Bryant had words With his wife went and informed against himself Wife and Children and all of us which we was immediately taken Prisoners and was put into the Castle we were strictly Examined after been Examined we were allowed to Go out of the Castle 2 at a time for one Day and the next Day 2 more and so we continued till Captain Edwards who had been on search of the Bounty Pirates which had taken some of the Pirates at Otaheite which he lost the Pandora frigate betwixt New Guinea and New Holland which he made Island of Timor in the Pinnace Two yawls and his Long boat and 120 hands which was saved which Captain Edwards came to us to know what we were which we told him we was Convicts and had made our Escape from Botany Bay which he told us we was his prisoners and put us on board the Rambang Dutch Companys Ship and put us Both Legs in Irons Called the bilboes which we was Conveyed to bretava which we was taken out of the Rambang and put on board a Dutch Guardship in Irons again there we Lost the Child 6 Days after the father of the Child was taken Bad and Died which was both buried at Bretava 6 weeks after we was put on 3 different Ships bound to the Cape of Good hope which we was 3 months before we reached the Cape.

When we came there the Gorgon man of war which had brought the marines from Botany Bay which we was Put on board of Gorgon which we was known well by all the marine officers which was all Glad that we had not perished at sea was brought home to England in the Gorgon we was Brought ashore at Purfleet and from there Conveyed by the Constables to Bow st office London and was taken before Justice Bond and was fully committed to Newgate/Wm Moatton Navigatoter of the Boat Died James Cox Died Saml Burd Died Wm Bryant Died A Boy of 12 months old Died A Little Girl 3 Yrs and a Quarter old Died the mother of the 2 Children Mary Bryant alive James Martin alive Wm Allen alive John Brown alive Nathl Lilly alive.

'...we run along the Island of Timor till we came to the Dutch Settlements where we went on Shore to the Governors house where he behaved extremely well to us filled our Bellies and Cloathed Double with every that was wore on the Island.'

THE SYDNEY COVE SURVIVORS

From the Asiatic Mirror

THE FIRST *lengthy overland journey by non-Aborigines in Australia was made by the survivors of the ship* Sydney Cove, *which was wrecked on Preservation Island in Bass Strait in February 1797 while en route from Calcutta to Port Jackson. Seventeen of the crew set out in the ship's longboat to sail to Sydney for help. Their boat was wrecked on the mainland, probably near the northern end of Ninety-Mile Beach, and the men were forced to continue on foot. Only three completed the gruelling, eleven-week journey, a distance of some six hundred kilometres in a direct line but considerably farther travelling along the coast as they did. The three survivors were found by fishermen near Wattamolla, south of Port Hacking. The following account was published in the* Asiatic Mirror, *Calcutta, in December 1797 and January 1798. It is taken from a journal kept by one of the survivors, probably the* Sydney Cove's *supercargo, W. Clarke.*

THE LONGBOAT, being equipped and ready for sea, was dispatched on 28 February, as already stated, in order to proceed to Port Jackson with intelligence of the shipwreck. Mr Thomson, late chief mate of the *Sydney Cove*, Mr Clark, supercargo, three European seamen, and twelve lascars, in all seventeen persons, embarked. They pursued a [northerly] course till March, lat. 38°S by account, having had no observation for several days. On the evening of this day it began to blow, and soon increased to a stormy gale, with a heavy sea, by which the boat was in great danger of foundering. They were at an inconsiderable distance from the shore; but the surf broke with such violence as to prevent the possibility of approaching with safety. Being unable to land, the only chance of preservation was to come to with both anchors, which was accordingly done. The boat lay in the most imminent danger from being often almost entirely filled with water by the heavy sea, which during the night continued to break over her. In this perilous situation they remained till daylight, when they cut both cables and set the foresail; but the boat at this time suddenly filling, it was not without the utmost difficulty that they got her through the surf, when she went to pieces a few minutes after the people had gained the beach.

Imagination cannot picture a situation more melancholy than that to which the unfortunate crew was reduced—wrecked a second time on the inhospitable shore of New South Wales; cut off from all hopes of rejoining their companions; without provisions, without arms, or any probable means either of

Although the Sydney Cove *was wrecked on an island in Bass Strait, the existence of the Strait was not yet determined, and sailing ships making the voyage from such places as Calcutta to Sydney took the long and sometimes tempestuous route around the bottom of Tasmania. Here George Raper, an officer of the First Fleet, portrays the* Sirius *weathering Tasman's Head, the southern tip of Bruny Island off Tasmania's south coast.*

subsistence or defence, they seemed doomed to all the horrors of a lingering death, with all their misfortunes unknown and unpitied. In this trying situation they did not abandon themselves to despair; they determined to proceed to the northward in the hopes of reaching Port Jackson, although the distance of the settlement, the unfrequented deserts they were to traverse, and the barbarous hordes among whom they had to gain their way, presented difficulties that required no ordinary share of fortitude to encounter and perseverance to overcome; but danger and difficulty lessen as they approach—the mind, as if its ultimate strength were reserved for arduous occasions, reconciles itself with calm resignation to sufferings from which, on a more distant view, it would recoil with horror.

It was thus with our little party: the dangers that surrounded them served but to excite them to exertion; they resolved to brave every difficulty, and to commence their journey without delay. The three days following the loss of their boat were spent in collecting such articles as had been thrown on shore from the wreck. On the 15th they began their march. The principal occurrences in the course of the journey are related in the following abstract of a journal, compiled partly from recollection and partly from the assistance of memoranda written with a pencil.

15 March. We began our journey for Port Jackson.

16 March. Walked sixteen or eighteen miles along a sandy beach.

17 March. Passed several small rivers, and one so large that we were obliged to construct a raft to cross it. From the detention this occasioned walked only eight miles.

18 March. Forded several branches of rivers. We this day fell in with a party of natives, about fourteen, all of them entirely naked. They were struck with astonishment at our appearance, and were very anxious to examine every part of our clothes and body, in which we readily indulged them. They viewed us most attentively. They opened our clothes, examined our feet, hands, nails, &c., frequently expressing their surprise by laughing and loud shoutings. From their gestures during this awkward review it was easy to perceive that they considered our clothes and bodies as inseparably joined. Having made them a present of a few stripes of cloth, which they appeared highly delighted with, we pursued our journey, and halted in the evening, after a march of thirty miles.

The natives on this part of the coast appear strong and muscular, with heads rather large in proportion to their bodies. The flat nose, the broad thick lips which distinguish the African, also prevail amongst the people on this coast. Their hair is long and straight, but they are wholly inattentive to it, either as to cleanliness or in any other respect. It serves them in lieu of a towel to wipe their hands as often as they are daubed with blubber or shark oil, which is their principal article of food. This frequent application of rancid grease to their heads and bodies renders their approach exceedingly offensive. Their ornaments consist chiefly of fish-bones or kangaroo-teeth, fastened with gum or glue to the hair of the temples and on the forehead. A piece of reed or bone is also worn through the septum, or cartilage, of the nose, which is pierced for the admission of this ornament. Upon the whole, they present the most hideous and disgusting figures that savage life can possibly afford.

19 March. Met with a pretty large river, which we were unable to cross till low water, there being no wood from which we could construct a raft. A few natives on the opposite bank of the river ran off at our approach.

20 March. This day we procured a few shellfish on the rocks. We walked about sixteen miles along the seaside, part of the way over very high bluffs and sharp rocks.

21 March. This morning went inland about three or four miles. Made a raft and crossed a large river. Its banks were delightful; the trees, tall and majestic, added dignity to the stream, and gave the surrounding country a beautiful and picturesque appearance. Saw a few of the natives, who, at first sight, advanced, but on a nearer approach they fled and concealed themselves in the woods. Among the different groups of natives it is remarkable we have not yet seen a woman. Walked sixteen miles this day.

22 March. This day's walk was rendered very disagreeable by constant heavy rain.

23 March. The weather today was delightful; the agreeable temperance, together with the beautiful scenery that opened to our view through a most delightful country, compensated in a great measure for the inclemency of yesterday's journey. We had a distant prospect inland of some very high hills, covered to their summit with lofty trees. In the evening we halted, after a march of eighteen miles.

24 March. We had travelled about seven miles when our progress was stopped by an immense river, which emptied itself in the ocean by several branches. We began to prepare a raft, in order to cross the river before us.

25, 26 and 27 March. These three days were employed in completing the raft and crossing the different branches of the river.

28 March. In the course of this day's journey we reached an island, about five miles distant from the seashore. This place appears well suited to afford shelter to shipping, being completely landlocked and covered from the wind.

In the latter part of the day's march we had to traverse hills of sands, which made it exceedingly fatiguing; nevertheless we travelled about twelve miles.

29 March. On crossing a narrow but deep river one of the natives threatened to dispute our landing, but approaching with a determined appearance no actual resistance was attempted, and a reconciliation was effected by the distribution of a few stripes of cloth. A good understanding being thus established, the men called to their wives and children, who were concealed behind the rocks, and who now ventured to show themselves. These were the first women we had seen; from their cries and laughing it is evident they were greatly astonished at our appearance. The men did not think proper to admit of our coming sufficiently near to have a full or perfect view of their ladies, but we were near enough to discern that they were the most wretched objects we had ever seen—equally filthy as the men, coarse and ill-featured, and so devoid of delicacy or any appearance of it that they seem to have nothing even human about them but the form. We pursued our way and walked about ten miles.

30 March. Crossed a small river this morning, and walked about eight miles through a country interspersed with hills and covered with heath. We came to a pretty large river, which, being too deep to ford, we began to prepare a raft, which we could not have completed till next day had not three of our native friends, from whom we parted yesterday, rejoined us and assisted us over. We were much pleased with their attention, for the act was really kind, as they knew we had this river to cross and appear to have followed us purposely to lend their assistance. In the evening we travelled about four miles farther, and rested for the night.

31 March. Walked about eighteen miles round a very deep bay and many small rivers opening into it.

1 April. Passed through a very pleasant country, whose delightful verdure, strewed over with a variety of flowers, rendered a walk of twenty miles this day extremely agreeable.

2 April. Travelled eight miles this forenoon. Between nine and ten o'clock we were most agreeably surprised by meeting five of the natives, our old friends, who received us in a very amicable manner, and kindly treated us with some shellfish, which formed a very acceptable meal, as our small pittance of rice was nearly expended. After this little repast we proceeded six miles further and halted.

3 April. Had a fatiguing march over very high bluffs, sharp rocks, and afterwards through very thick brushwood, interspersed with stumps of trees and other sharp substances, by which our feet were so much bruised and wounded that some of the party remained lame for some time afterwards; and to aggravate our sufferings we were now living upon a quarter of a pint of dry rice per diem. As we got out of this harassing thicket we missed two of our unhappy fellow-travellers. At 4 p.m. we provided ourselves a lodging for the night, having walked, or rather crawled, ten miles, over the ground above described.

4 April. Waited for our missing companions until twelve o'clock, when, to our great joy, they made their appearance; we then proceeded on our journey, and in the evening came to a very broad river. It being low water, some

> '*1 April. Passed through a very pleasant country, whose delightful verdure, strewed over with a variety of flowers, rendered a walk of twenty miles this day extremely agreeable.*'

places were very shallow, which enabled us to catch a few small skate, which were, indeed, very acceptable. Walked this day eight miles.

5 April. Reached the opposite bank of the river, where we remained a few hours to catch some more fish, in which we happily succeeded; among them was a very fine shark about four feet long; this was a refreshment for which we offered our thanks to Providence, the rice, our only certain resource, being now nearly at an end.

6 April. Having got a tolerable supply of fish, pursued our journey for about eighteen miles through a delightful plain, interspersed here and there with a few scattered trees.

7 April. Went some way into the country, over hills and valleys. After a walk of sixteen miles we halted at twilight, and as we reclined our heads to rest on a bank we could just hear the roaring of the surf on the seashore.

8 April. Bent our way towards the beach this morning, and travelled along about nine miles, when we were stopped by our old impediment, a river, at which we were obliged to wait until low water before we could cross. We had scarcely surmounted this difficulty when a greater danger stared us in the face, for here we were met by about fifty armed natives. Having never before seen so large a body collected, it is natural to conclude that we were much alarmed. However, we resolved to put the best appearance on the matter, and to betray no symptoms of fear. In consequence of the steps we took, and after some preliminary signs and gestures on both sides, we came to some understanding, and the natives were apparently amicable in their designs. We presented them with a few yards of calico, for they would not be satisfied with small stripes, and, indeed, we were glad to get rid of them at any

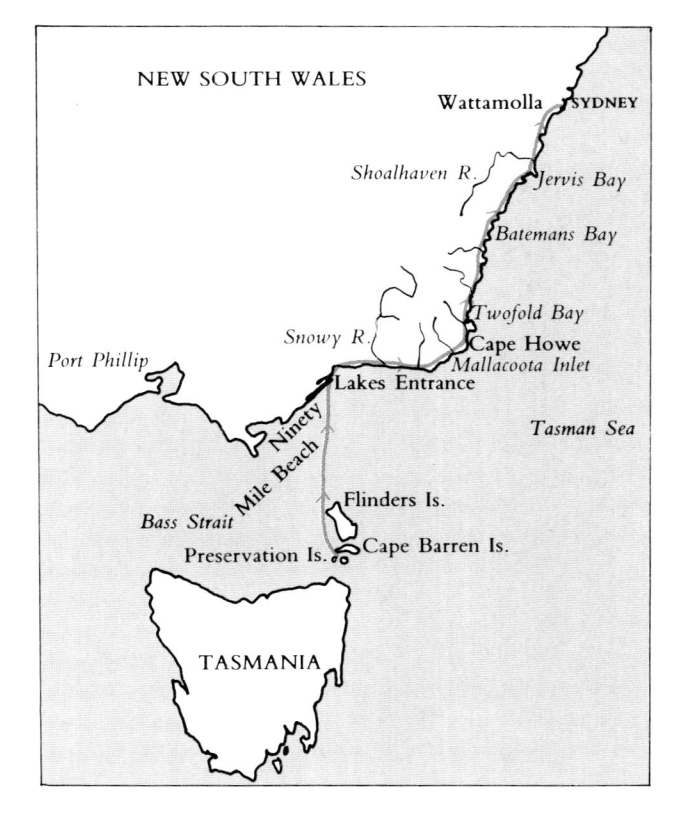

The route taken by the Sydney Cove *survivors on their boat journey and forced march from Preservation Island, in the Furneaux Group, Bass Strait, to Wattamolla, about twenty-five kilometres south of Botany Bay.*

expense, for their looks and demeanour were not such as to invite greater intimacy.

9 April. Proceeding this morning on our journey, we were again alarmed at the approach of the party who detained us yesterday, and whom we so justly suspected of treacherous intentions. They came on with dreadful shoutings which gave us warning to prepare for defence, and to give them a warm reception in case violence should be offered. Fortunately, however, from the particular attention we paid to their old men, whom we supposed to be their chiefs, and making them some small presents, they soon left us. This dispersion gave our little party general satisfaction, as we were doubtful how the affair might have terminated. During our conference, and at their departure, several of them had placed their spears in the throwing-sticks, ready to discharge at us. We now pursued our route, and walked about ten miles.

> '13 April. *Came to a large river, where we met with a few natives, who appeared very timorous at seeing us; but in a short time we came to a better understanding, and they kindly carried us over in their canoes.*'

10 April. We were overtaken by a few of the natives with whom we parted yesterday, but seeing us on our guard, with our one gun, two pistols, and two small swords, while others were armed with clubs, and perceiving our resolution not to be imposed upon, they acted with more prudence than heretofore. We did not at this meeting indulge them with any presents, but to one gave a piece of cloth, in exchange for a large kangaroo's tail, with which we endeavoured to make some soup, by adding a little of the rice we had remaining, from which we received great nourishment, being much weakened by the fatigue and want which we had suffered in these inhospitable regions. Our walk of fourteen miles this day was performed over a number of rugged and disagreeable heights, until we came to a river, which we crossed, and then betook ourselves to the cheerless turf until the morning.

11 April. Walked eight miles and came to a river, where we met fourteen natives, who conducted us to their miserable abodes in the wood adjoining to a large lagoon, and kindly treated us with mussels, for which unexpected civility we made them some presents. These people seemed better acquainted with the laws of hospitality than any of their countrymen whom we had yet seen, for to their benevolent treat was added an invitation to remain with them for the night. They did not, however, lodge us in their nominal huts, but after we were seated around our resting-place they brought their women and children to see us, and certainly, to judge from the attention with which they surveyed us, we afforded them no small share of entertainment. As far as we could understand, these natives were of a different tribe from those we had seen, and were then at war with them. They possessed a liberality to which the others were strangers, and freely gave us a part of the little they had, which the others were so far from doing that they would have deprived us of the last article in our possession had they not been overawed by the sight of arms, against which they knew not how to defend themselves. We endeavoured to make our entertainers sensible by signs how rudely their neighbours had behaved to us; to compensate for which both the old and the young were anxious to give us part of their shellfish.

12 April. Met with another party of the natives who did not attempt to molest us. Walked sixteen miles over rising ground and along the seaside, where we found a dead skate, which, though a little tainted, would not have

Australian Aborigines in bark canoes, by 'the Artist of the Chief Mourner'. The Aborigines were of great help to the Sydney Cove *crewmen in conveying them across many of the rivers and inlets along the coast.*

been unacceptable to an epicure with our appetite.

13 April. Came to a large river, where we met with a few natives, who appeared very timorous at seeing us; but in a short time we came to a better understanding, and they kindly carried us over in their canoes. This was not accomplished without several duckings, for their rude little vehicles formed of bark, tied at both ends with twigs, and not exceeding eight feet in length, by two in breadth, are precarious vessels for one unacquainted with them to embark in, though the natives, of whom they will carry three or four, paddle about in them with the greatest facility and security. After crossing the river, and receiving a few small fish at parting, we walked ten miles.

14 April. Met with no obstruction during a walk of eighteen miles.

15 April. We were joined by our last friends, who ferried us over a very large river in their canoes. Whether this meeting was the effect of chance or one of their fishing excursions, or that perceiving we should find it difficult they had come to our assistance, we could not determine; but had it not been for their aid we must have been detained here for some time in making a raft. The greatest part of the wood of the country being very heavy will not swim, unless it has been felled for some time and exposed to the sun, a fact which we had already been taught by miserable experience. Having walked nine miles after crossing the river, we rested for the night, and boiled a few shellfish we had picked up by the way like good œconomists, making them serve for both dinner and supper, for our little evening's cookery formed the only meal we could daily afford ourselves, unless we ventured to eat a few wild plants which we sometimes picked up.

16 April. Having walked about twelve miles we once more met with our friends, who, a third time, conveyed us over a large river at a shallow part, which they pointed out. On the banks of this river we remained for the

Aborigines Spearing Fish, by the convict artist Joseph Lycett. The coastal Aborigines encountered by the Sydney Cove *crewmen provided them with a plentiful supply of fish.*

night. Our poor unfortunate companions, worn out by want and excessive fatigue, now began to drop behind very fast. At this place we were under the painful necessity of leaving nine of our fellow-sufferers behind, they being totally unable to proceed further; but we flattered ourselves they would be able to come up with us in a day or two, as we now often stopped some time with the natives when we found them kind to us, or loitered about the rocks to pick up shellfish or collect herbs.

17 April. Had a pleasant walk about five miles along the seacoast until we came to a narrow but deep river, in endeavouring to cross which an unlucky accident happened to Mr Thomson, and which nearly proved fatal. We found an old canoe on the bank, in which three or four of our party got to the opposite side, and proceeded on their journey. Mr Thomson, who could not swim, in making an effort to cross, was left struggling in the water by the canoe sinking under him. This was witnessed by four Bengal blacks, who, though they were adepts at swimming, stood unmoved spectators. I instantly jumped in and flew to his relief, although very much fatigued and very cold. I seized him by the hair and drew him to the shore motionless. My first care was to place him over a rock with his head downwards, pressing him at the same time on the back, by which means he discharged much sea water by the mouth, and in a little time recovered.

18 April. The illness of Mr Thomson, occasioned by the accident, prevented our walking more than eight miles this day.

19 April. Came up with those who went before us the 17th. Were again stopped by a very large river, which the violence of the wind prevented us from crossing. We therefore employed ourselves in collecting mussels, which, in our present situation, was a great relief, having been without a more generous nourishment for two days before.

20 April. Got over the river and had a long walk, about eighteen miles, through an immense wood, the plain of which was covered with long grass. We had the good fortune this day to have a friendly native in company, who undertook to be our guide, by whose good-natured assistance we were enabled to avoid several high points and cut off a great deal of ground.

21 April. Had a pleasant walk for about fourteen miles, during which we met a party of natives who gave us plenty of fishes. It seems they had met the Moor whose friendship we experienced yesterday, and were by him informed of our distress, so that we were indebted to that kind-hearted fellow for his guidance and this day's protection.

22 April. The natives accompanied us a few miles and returned, leaving with us a plentiful supply of fish. This day we walked twelve miles.

23, 24 and 25 April. Walked ten or twelve miles each day, without meeting with any natives, and being wholly without nourishment almost perished for want.

26 April. At 9 a.m. observed several natives on the top of a high bluff, who came down to us as we approached, and remained with us for some time. When we had made signs to them that we were hungry and much exhausted, they brought us plenty of fish and treated us very kindly. After we had refreshed ourselves and put up some fish to carry with us, we were preparing to proceed, when about fifty strong natives made their appearance, of whom we soon took leave, giving them such little presents as we could afford, and with which they were apparently well satisfied. We had not parted more than twenty or thirty minutes when a hundred more approached us, shouting and hallowing in a most hideous manner, at which we were all exceedingly alarmed. In a short time a few of them began throwing their spears, upon which we made signs to them to desist, giving them some presents, and appearing no ways dismayed at their conduct—any other demeanour on our part would have been quite superfluous, having only one musket unloaded and two pistols out of repair, and at best were only six opposed to such a multitude, for our little company were daily dropping off. No sooner had we turned our backs on this savage mob than they renewed hostilities and wounded three of us, viz., Mr Hugh Thomson, myself, and my servant. Notwithstanding this disaster, we, in our painful situation, proceeded eight miles, to get clear, if possible, of these savages; but just as we came up to a very deep bay they overtook us again. This pursuit induced us all to suppose they intended to murder us—as we were, however, to make a virtue of necessity, and to remain among them all that night, though it may be well supposed that the anguish of our minds and the pain of our wounds prevented the possibility of sleep.

27 April. Our disagreeable and treacherous companions continued with us on our journey until about 9 a.m., when they betook themselves to the woods, leaving us extremely happy at their departure. We continued our route along this extensive bay ten miles.

29 April. Met with some brackish water, which we eagerly swallowed; indeed, all the rivers we examined were impregnated with salt water from their connection with the sea. Walked fourteen miles.

30 April. We this morning reached the largest river we had met with since we came to this large bay. Its width put us entirely to a stand and prevented our crossing over until the evening. As we were devising means to accomplish our design six natives very fortunately came to our assistance. They seemed, however, suspicious of us, for when we reached the opposite bank we made signs that we wanted water, and, under pretence of going for some, they set off, but never returned. We were not able to proceed any more than three miles this day.

The fifteen following days of our journey were much the same as the preceding, until we very fortunately met with a fishing-boat about fourteen miles to the southward of Botany Bay.

Two days before they were rescued, Clarke and his companions had discovered a large quantity of coal, and Clarke later accompanied George Bass on an expedition to examine the area, near present-day Coalcliff. They also found the remains of the chief mate, Thomson, and the ship's carpenter, who had been left behind between the vicinity of Coalcliff and Wollongong. Two vessels, the Francis *and the* Eliza, *were sent from Sydney to rescue the remaining crew members of the* Sydney Cove *on Preservation Island and to salvage the cargo. The* Francis *subsequently returned to Sydney, but the* Eliza *was never seen again after leaving Preservation Island.*

THE CROSSING OF THE BLUE MOUNTAINS

Gregory Blaxland

BY THE YEAR 1813 the infant colony of New South Wales had outgrown its territory on the Cumberland Plain. More land was needed by the increasing number of settlers to graze their flocks and herds. A way had to be found over the Blue Mountains, which for twenty-five years had formed an impenetrable barrier to the west. Several attempts had been made over the years to cross the mountains, but all had been thwarted by the precipitous cliffs at the end of every valley. On 11 May 1813 three explorers—the wealthy free settler Gregory Blaxland; the soldier-farmer William Lawson, an experienced surveyor; and the youthful William Charles Wentworth, later to become the leading force in the movement for self-government in New South Wales—set out with four convicts to find a way across the mountains by keeping to the ridge tops. By 28 May they had reached Mount York, a spur off the central ridge on the western side of the mountains, and on the 31st reached their furthest point, Mount Blaxland, just over the Cox River beyond its junction with the River Lett. Although they turned back before crossing the main section of the Great Dividing Range, they had conquered the toughest barrier, the Blue Mountains, and had sighted the plains on the other side. The following is Blaxland's account of the journey, an unembroidered record written in the third person.

ON TUESDAY, 11 May 1813, Mr Gregory Blaxland Mr William Wentworth, and Lieutenant Lawson, attended by four servants, with five dogs, and four horses laden with provisions, ammunition, and other necessaries, left Mr Blaxland's farm at the South Creek for the purpose of endeavouring to effect a passage over the Blue Mountains, between the Western River[1] and the River Grose. They crossed the Nepean, or Hawkesbury River, at the ford, on to Emu Island, at four o'clock, p.m., and having proceeded, according to their calculation, two miles in a south-west direction, through forest land and good pasture, encamped at five o'clock at the foot of the first ridge. The distance travelled on this and on the subsequent days was computed by time; the rate being estimated at about two miles per hour. Thus far they were accompanied by two other gentlemen.

On the following morning, 12 May, as soon as the heavy dew was off, which was about 9 a.m., they proceeded to ascend the ridge at the foot of which they had encamped the preceding evening. Here they found a large

---

1. [Warragamba River.]

lagoon of good water, full of very coarse rushes. The high land of Grose Head appeared before them at about seven miles distance, bearing north by east. They proceeded this day about three miles and a quarter, in a direction varying from south-west to west-north-west; but, for a third of the way, due west. The land was covered with scrubby brushwood, very thick in places, with some trees of ordinary timber, which much incommoded the horses. The greater part of the way, they had deep rocky gullies on each side of their track, and the ridge they followed was very crooked and intricate. In the evening they encamped at the head of a deep gully,[2] which they had to descend for water; they found but just enough for the night, contained in a hole in the rock, near which they met with a kangaroo, who had just been killed by an eagle. A small patch of grass supplied the horses for the night.

They found it impossible to travel through the brush before the dew was off, and could not, therefore, proceed at an earlier hour in the morning than nine. After travelling about a mile on the third day, in a west and north-west direction, they arrived at a large tract of forest land, rather hilly, the grass and timber tolerably good, extending, as they imagine, nearly to Grose Head, in the same direction nearly as the river. They computed it at two thousand acres. Here they found a track marked by a European, by cutting the bark of the trees. Several native huts presented themselves at different places. They had not proceeded above two miles when they found themselves stopped by a brushwood much thicker than they had hitherto met with. This induced them to alter their course and to endeavour to find another passage to the westward; but every ridge which they explored proved to terminate in a deep rocky precipice; and they had no alternative but to return to the thick brushwood, which appeared to be the main ridge, with the determination to cut a way through for the horses on the next day. This day, some of the horses, while standing, fell several times under their

2. [Between present-day Warrimoo and Valley Heights.]

The track pioneered by Blaxland, Lawson and Wentworth across the Blue Mountains in 1813.

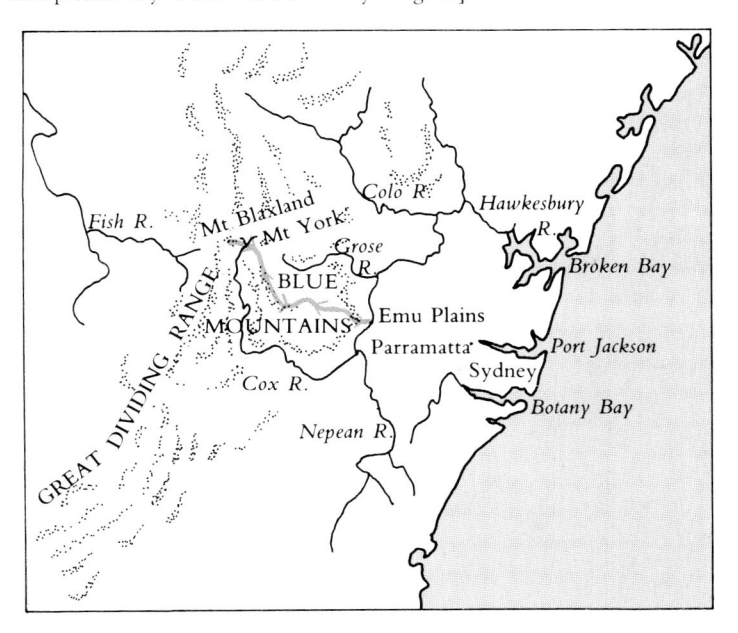

Gregory Blaxland, generally regarded as the initiator and leader of the expedition that first found a way over the Blue Mountains, although his journal and that of Lawson make no mention of anyone being the leader.

loads. The dogs killed a large kangaroo. The party encamped in the forest tract, with plenty of good grass and water.[3]

On the next morning, leaving two men to take care of the horses and provisions, they proceeded to cut a path through the thick brushwood, on what they considered as the main ridge of the mountain, between the Western River and the River Grose; keeping the head of the gullies which were supposed to empty themselves into the Western River, on their left hand, and into the River Grose on their right. As they ascended the mountain, these gullies became much deeper and more rocky on each side. They now began to mark their track by cutting the bark of the trees on two sides. Having cut their way for about five miles, they returned in the evening to the spot on which they had encamped the night before. The fifth day was spent in prosecuting the same tedious operation; but, as much time was necessarily lost in walking twice over the tract cleared the day before, they were unable to cut away more than two miles further. They found no food for the horses the whole way. An emu was heard on the other side of the gulley, calling continually in the night.

On Sunday they rested, and arranged their future plan. They had reason, however, to regret this suspension of their proceedings, as it gave the men leisure to ruminate on their danger; and it was for some time doubtful whether, on the next day, they could be persuaded to venture farther. The dogs this day killed two small kangaroos. They barked and ran off continually during the whole night; and at daylight a most tremendous howling of native dogs was heard, who appeared to have been watching them during the night.

On Monday, the 17th, having laden the horses with as much grass as could be put on them, in addition to their other burdens, they moved forward along the path which they had cleared and marked, about six miles and a

3. [Near Springwood railway station.]

half. The bearing of the route they had been obliged to keep along the ridge varied exceedingly; it ran sometimes in a north-north-west direction, sometimes south-east, or due south, but generally south-west, or south-south-west. They encamped in the afternoon between two very deep gullies,[4] on a narrow ridge, Grose Head bearing north-east by north; and Mount Banks north-west by west. They had to fetch water up the side of the precipice, about six hundred feet high, and could get scarcely enough for the party. The horses had none this night: they performed the journey well, not having to stand under their loads.

The following day was spent in cutting a passage through the brushwood, for a mile and a half farther. They returned to their camp at five o'clock, very much tired and dispirited. The ridge, which was not more than fifteen or twenty yards over, with deep precipices on each side, was rendered almost impassable by a perpendicular mass of rock, nearly thirty feet high, extending across the whole breadth, with the exception of a small broken rugged tract in the centre. By removing a few large stones, they were enabled to pass.

On Wednesday, the 19th, the party moved forward along this path; bearing chiefly west and west-south-west. They now began to ascend the second ridge of the mountains, and from this elevation they obtained for the first time an extensive view of the settlements below. Mount Banks bore north-west: Grose Head, north-east; Prospect Hill, east by south; the Seven Hills, east-north-east; Windsor, north-east by east. At a little distance from the spot at which they began the ascent, they found a pyramidical heap of stones, the work, evidently, of some Eruopean, one side of which the natives had opened, probably in the expectation of finding some treasure deposited in it. This pile they concluded to be the one erected by Mr Bass, to mark the end of his journey. That gentleman attempted, some time ago, to pass the mountains and to penetrate into the interior; but having got thus far, he gave up the undertaking as impracticable, reporting, on his return, that it was impossible to find a passage even for a person on foot. Here, therefore, the party had the satisfaction of believing that they had penetrated as far as any European had been before them.

They encamped this day to refresh their horses, at the head of a swamp covered with a coarse rushy grass, with a small run of good water through the middle of it. In the afternoon they left their camp to mark and cut a road for the next day.

They proceeded with the horses on the 20th nearly five miles, and encamped at noon at the head of a swamp about three acres in extent, covered with the same coarse rushy grass as the last station, with a stream of water running through it.[5] The horses were obliged to feed on the swamp grass, as nothing better could be found for them. The travellers left the camp as before, in the afternoon, to cut a road for the morrow's journey. The ridge along which their course lay now became wider and more rocky, but was still covered with brush and small crooked timber, except at the heads of the different streams of water which ran down the side of the mountain, where the land was swampy and clear of trees. The track of scarcely any animal was to be

4. [Near Linden railway station.]
5. [Probably just beyond Hazelbook station.]

seen, and very few birds. One man was here taken dangerously ill with a cold. Bearing of the route at first, south-westerly; afterwards north north-west, and west-north-west.

Their progress, the next day, was nearly four miles, in a direction still varying from north-west by north to south-west. They encamped in the middle of the day, at the head of a well-watered swamp, about five acres in extent;[6] pursuing, as before, their operations in the afternoon. In the beginning of the night, the dogs ran off, and barked violently. At the same time, something was distinctly heard to run through the brushwood, which they supposed to be one of the horses got loose; but they had reason to believe afterwards that they had been in great danger; that the natives had followed their track and advanced on them in the night, intending to have speared them by the light of their fire, but that the dogs drove them off.

On Saturday, the 22nd instant, they proceeded in the track marked the preceding day, rather more than three miles in a south-westerly direction, when they reached the summit of the third and highest ridge of the mountains southward of Mount Banks. From the bearing of Prospect Hill, and Grose Head, they computed this spot to be eighteen miles in a straight line from the River Nepean, at the point at which they crossed it. On the top of this ridge they found about two thousand acres of land clear of trees, covered with loose stones, and short coarse grass such as grows on some of the commons in England. Over this heath they proceeded for about a mile and a half, in a south-westerly direction, and encamped by the side of a fine stream of water, with just wood enough on the banks to serve for firewood.[7] From the summit, they had a fine view of all the settlements and country eastward, and of a great extent of country to the westward and south-west. But their progress in both the latter directions was stopped by an impassable barrier of rock, which appeared to divide the interior from the coast as with a stone wall, rising perpendicularly out of the side of the mountain.

'But their progress in both the latter directions was stopped by an impassable barrier of rock, which appeared to divide the interior from the coast as with a stone wall, rising perpendicularly out of the side of the mountain.'

In the afternoon, they left their little camp in the charge of three of the men, and made an attempt to descend the precipice, by following some of the streams of water, or by getting down at some of the projecting points where the rocks had fallen in; but they were baffled in every instance. In some places, the perpendicular height of the rocks above the earth below could not be less than four hundred feet. Could they have accomplished a descent, they hoped to procure mineral specimens which might throw light on the geological character of the country, as the strata appeared to be exposed for many hundred feet, from the top of the rock to the beds of the several rivers beneath. The broken rocky country on the western side of the cow pasture has the appearance of having acquired its present form from an earthquake, or some other dreadful convulsion of nature, at a much later period than the mountains northward, of which Mount Banks forms the southern extremity. The aspect of the country, which lay beneath them, much disappointed the travellers: it appeared to consist of sand and small scrubby brushwood, intersected with broken rocky mountains, with streams of water running between them to the eastward, towards one point, where

6. [Near Bullaburra station.]
7. [Near the Wentworth Falls sanatorium.]

they probably form the Western River, and enter the mountains.

They now flattered themselves that they had surmounted half the difficulties of their undertaking, expecting to find a passage down the mountain more to the northward.

On the next day, they proceeded about three miles and a half; but the trouble occasioned by the horses when they got off the open land induced them to recur to their former plan of devoting the afternoon to marking and clearing a track for the ensuring day, as the most expeditious method of proceeding, notwithstanding that they had to go twice over the same ground. The bearing of their course this day was, at first, north-east and north; and then changed to north-west, and north-north-west. They encamped on the side of a swamp, with a beautiful stream of water running through it.[8]

Their progress on the next day was four miles and a half, in a direction varying from north-north-west to south-south-west: they encamped, as before, at the head of a swamp.[9] This day, between 10 and 11 a.m., they obtained a sight of the country below, when the clouds ascended. As they were marking a road for the morrow, they heard a native chopping wood very near them, who fled at the approach of the dogs.

On Tuesday, the 25th, they could proceed only three miles and a half in a varying direction, encamping at two o'clock at the side of a swamp.[10] The underwood, being very prickly and full of small thorns, annoyed them very much. This day they saw the track of the Woombat for the first time. On the 26th, they proceeded two miles and three quarters. The brush still continued to be very thorny. The land to the westward appeared sandy and barren. This day they saw the fires of some natives below: the number they computed at about thirty, men, women, and children. They noticed also more tracks of the Woombat. On the 27th they proceeded five miles and a quarter; part of the way over another piece of clear land, without trees; they saw more native fires, and about the same number as before, but more in their direct course. From the top of the rocks, they saw a large piece of land below, clear of trees, but apparently a poor reedy swamp. They met with some good timber in this day's route. The bearing of the route for the last three days had been chiefly north and north-west.

On the 28th they proceeded about five miles and three-quarters. Not being able to find water, they did not halt till five o'clock, when they took up their station on the edge of the precipice.[11] To their great satisfaction, they discovered that what they had supposed to be sandy barren land below the mountain was forest land, covered with good grass, and with timber of an inferior quality. In the evening, they contrived to get their horses down the mountain, by cutting a small trench with a hoe, which kept them from slipping, where they again tasted fresh grass for the first time since they left the forest land on the other side of the mountain. They were getting into miserable condition. Water was found about two miles below the foot of the mountain. The second camp of natives moved before them about three

'Part of the descent was so steep that the horses could but just keep their footing without a load, so that, for some way, the party were obliged to carry the packages themselves.'

---

8. [North of Wentworth Falls railway station.]
9. [Near Leura railway station.]
10. [Not far from the historic Explorers' Tree, Katoomba.]
11. [Mount York.]

miles. In this day's route, little timber was observed fit for building.

On the 29th, having got up the horses, and laden them, they began to descend the mountain at seven o'clock, through a pass in the rock, about thirty feet wide, which they had discovered the day before, when the want of water put them on the alert. Part of the descent was so steep that the horses could but just keep their footing without a load, so that, for some way, the party were obliged to carry the packages themselves. A cart road might, however, easily be made by cutting a slanting trench along the side of the mountain, which is here covered with earth. This pass is, according to their computation, about twenty miles north-west in a straight line from the point at which they ascended the summit of the mountain. They reached the foot at nine o'clock a.m., and proceeded two miles, north-north-west, mostly through open meadow land, clear of trees, the grass from two to three feet high. They encamped on the bank of a fine stream of water.[12] The natives, as observed by the smoke of their fires, moved before them as yesterday. The dogs killed a kangaroo, which was very acceptable, as the party had lived on

12. [River Lett.]

Augustus Earle's painting of the Wentworth Falls gives a contemporary portrayal of the rugged terrain of the Blue Mountains through which Blaxland, Lawson and Wentworth had to find a route.

salt meat since they caught the last. The timber seen this day appeared rotten and unfit for building.

Sunday the 30th they rested in their encampment. One of the party shot a kangaroo with his rifle, at a great distance across a wide valley. The climate here was found very much colder than that of the mountain, or of the settlements on the east side, where no signs of frost had made its appearance when the party set out. During the night, the ground was covered with a thick frost, and a leg of the kangaroo was quite frozen. From the dead and brown appearance of the grass, it was evident that the weather had been severe for some time past. They were all much surprised at this degree of cold and frost, in the latitude of about 34. The track of the emu was noticed at several places near the camp.

On the Monday they proceeded about six miles, south-west and west, through forest land, remarkably well watered, and several open meadows, clear of trees, and covered with high good grass. They crossed two fine streams of water. Traces of the natives presented themselves in the fires they had left the day before, and in the flowers of the honeysuckle tree scattered around, which had supplied them with food. These flowers, which are shaped like a bottlebrush, are very full of honey. The natives on this side of the mountains appear to have no huts like those on the eastern side, nor do they strip the bark, or climb the trees. From the shavings and pieces of sharp stones which they had left, it was evident that they had been busily employed in sharpening their spears.

The party encamped by the side of a fine stream of water,[13] at a short distance from a high hill, in the shape of a sugar loaf. In the afternoon, they ascended its summit, from whence they descried all around, forest or grass land, sufficient in extent, in their opinion, to support the stock of the

An artist's impression of Blaxland, Lawson and Wentworth gazing over the fertile land to the west from their vantage point on Mount York.

13. [Cox River beyond its junction with the River Lett.]

Colony for the next thirty years. This was the extreme point of their journey. The distance they had travelled, they computed, at about fifty-eight miles nearly north-west; that is, fifty miles through the mountain (the greater part of which they had walked over three times) and eight miles through the forest land beyond it, reckoning the descent of the mountain to be half a mile to the foot.

The timber observed this day still appeared unfit for building. The stones at the bottom of the rivers appeared very fine large-grained dark-coloured granite, of a kind quite different from the mountain rocks, or from any stones which they had ever seen in the Colony. Mr Blaxland and one of the men nearly lost the party today, by going too far in the pursuit of a kangaroo.

They now conceived that they had sufficiently accomplished the design of their undertaking, having surmounted all the difficulties which had hitherto prevented the interior of the country from being explored, and the Colony from being extended. They had partly cleared, or, at least marked out, a road by which the passage of the mountain might easily be effected. Their provisions were nearly expended, their clothes and shoes were in very bad condition, and the whole party were ill with bowel complaints. These considerations determined them, therefore, to return home by the track they came. On Tuesday 1 June they arrived at the foot of the mountain which they had descended, where they encamped for the night. The following day, they began to ascend the mountain at seven o'clock, and reached the summit at ten; they were obliged to carry the packages themselves part of the ascent. They encamped in the evening at one of their old stations. One of the men had left his greatcoat on the top of the rock, where they re-loaded the horses, which was found by the next party who traversed the mountain. On the 3rd they reached another of their old stations. Here, during the night, they heard a confused noise arising from the eastern settlements below, which, after having been so long accustomed to the death-like stillness of the interior, had a very striking effect. On the 4th, they arrived at the end of the marked track, and encamped in the forest land where they had cut the grass for their horses. One of the horses this day fell with his load, quite exhausted, and was with difficulty got on, after having his load put on the other horses. The next day, the 5th, was the most unpleasant and fatiguing they had experienced. The track not being marked, they had great difficulty in finding their way back to the river, which they did not reach till four o'clock, p.m. They then once more encamped for the night, to refresh themselves and their horses. They had no provisions now left, except a little flour, but procured some from the settlement on the other side of the river. On Sunday, 6 June, they crossed the river after breakfast, and reached their homes, all in good health. The winter had not set in on this side of the mountain, nor had there been any frost.

'Traces of the natives presented themselves in the fires they had left the day before, and in the flowers of the honeysuckle tree scattered around, which had supplied them with food. These flowers, which are shaped like a toothbrush, are very full of honey.'

WHALEBOAT UP THE MURRAY

Charles Sturt

THE SOLDIER-EXPLORER Charles Sturt, having traced the course of the Macquarie River and discovered the Darling, set out from Sydney on 3 November 1829 to determine the course of the Murrumbidgee. His river party comprised George Macleay, the young son of the Colonial Secretary of New South Wales; Sturt's regimental servant, John Harris; two soldiers named Hopkinson and Fraser; a carpenter named Clayton; and two convicts, Macnamee and Mulholland. Sturt also took several dogs. As well, there was a small supporting land party under a man named Robert Harris. A whaleboat 7.6 metres long with a 1.5-metre beam was carried in sections and assembled at a point on the Murrumbidgee near the present township of Maude, where Sturt took to the river waters.

On 14 January, having travelled down the Murrumbidgee for a week, they entered 'a broad and noble river' which Sturt named the Murray. They continued their voyage downstream, having several dangerous encounters with Aborigines, to the Murray's termination in Lake Alexandrina. Here Sturt tried to reach the sea, with the intention of rowing round to Gulf St Vincent, where a ship was to pick them up, but he was unable to do so. Since their food was running low, they had to start back without delay, the way they had come—but now against the current.

Charles Sturt in later years. A soldier who had been sent to New South Wales in charge of convicts, Sturt became military secretary to Governor Darling before being appointed to lead exploratory expeditions. Later he was to hold important appointments in South Australia, a colony founded as a result of his discoveries on the Murrumbidgee-Murray expedition.

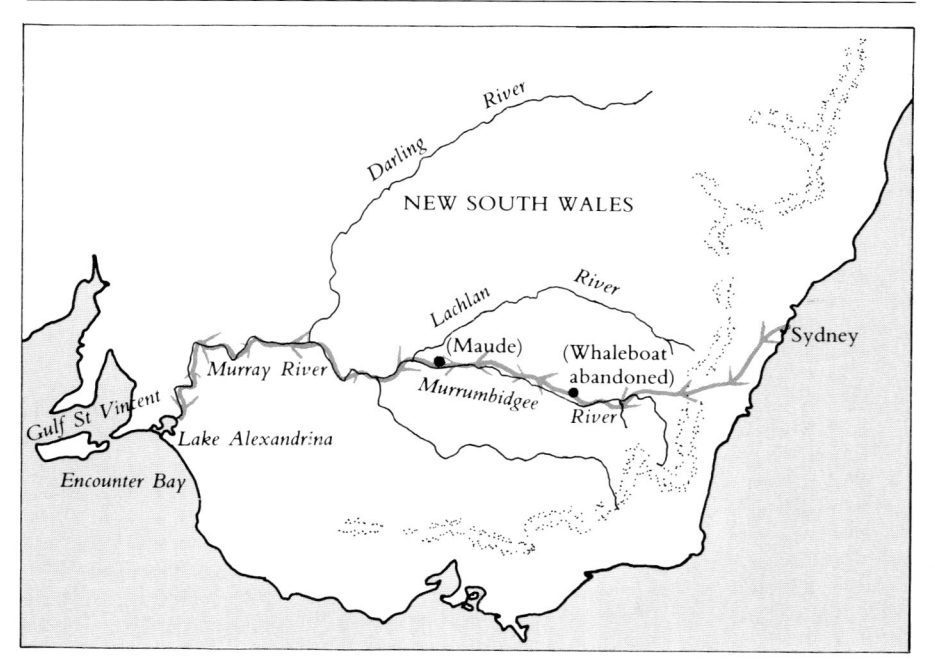

The route of Sturt's expedition on the Murrumbidgee-Murray rivers. The party set out from Sydney, reached the Murrumbidgee near the site of Jugiong, and took to the river in their prefabricated whaleboat near the site of Maude. Their return journey up-river from Lake Alexandrina to a point near the site of Narrandera was a rowing feat of heroic proportions.

WE HAD now only to make the best of our journey, rising at dawn and pulling to seven and often to nine o'clock. I allowed the men an hour from half past eleven to half past twelve to take their bread and water. This was our only fare, if I except an occasional wild duck; but these birds were extremely difficult to kill, and it cost us so much time that we seldom endeavoured to procure any. Our dogs had been of no great use, and were now too weak to have run after anything if they had seen either kangaroos or emus; and for the fish, the men loathed them, and were either too indifferent or too much fatigued to set the nightlines. Shoals frequently impeded us as we proceeded up the river, and we passed some rapids that called for our whole strength to stem. A light wind assisted us on two or three of these occasions, and I never failed hoisting the sail at every fitting opportunity. In some parts the river was extremely shallow, and the sandbanks of amazing size; and the annoyance of dragging the boat over these occasional bars was very great....

When we came down the river, I thought it advisable to lay its course down as precisely as circumstances would permit: for this purpose I had a large compass always before me, and a sheet of foolscap paper. As soon as we passed an angle of the river, I took the bearings of the reach before us, and as we proceeded down it, marked off the description of country, and any remarkable feature. The consequence was that I laid down every bend of the Murray River, from the Morumbidgee downwards. Its creeks, its tributaries, its flats, its valleys, and its cliffs, and, as far as I possibly could do, the nature of the distant interior. This chart was, of course, erroneous in many particulars, since I had to judge the length of the reaches of the river, and the extent of its angles, but I corrected it on the scale of the miles of latitude we made during the day, which brought out an approximate truth at all events. The hurried nature of our journey would not allow me to do more; and it will be remembered that my observations were all siderial, by reason that the sextant would not embrace the sun in its almost vertical position at noon. Admitting, however, the imperfection of this chart, it was of inconceivable value and comfort to us on our return, for, by a reference to it, we discovered our place upon the river, and our distance from our several encampments. And we should often have stopped short of them had not the chart shewn us that a few reaches more would bring us to the desired spots. It cheered the men to know where they were, and gave them conversation. To myself it was very satisfactory, as it enabled me to prepare for our meetings with the larger tribes, and to steer clear of obstacles in the more difficult navigation of some parts of the stream.

On the 21st, by dint of great labour, we reached our camp of 2 February, from which it will be remembered the Murray took up a southerly course, and from which we likewise obtained a first view of the coast ranges. The journey to the sea and back again had consequently occupied us twenty days. From this point we turned our boat's head homewards; we made it, therefore, a fixed position among the stages into which we divided our journey. Our attention was now directed to the junction of the principal tributary, which we hoped to reach in twelve days, and anticipated a close to our labours on the Murray in eight days more from that stage to the Morumbidgee....

On the 23rd, we stove the boat in for the first time. I had all along anticipated such an accident, from the difficulty of avoiding obstacles, in consequence of the turbid state of the river. Fortunately the boat struck a rotten log. The piece remained in her side and prevented her filling, which she must, otherwise, inevitably have done, ere we could have reached the shore. As it was, however, we escaped with a little damage to the lower bags of flour only. She was hauled up on a sandbank, and Clayton repaired her in less than two hours, when we reloaded her and pursued our journey. It was impossible to have been more cautious than we were, for I was satisfied as to the fate that would have overtaken the whole of us in the event of our losing the boat, and was proportionably vigilant.

At half past five we came to an island, which looked so inviting, and so quiet, that I determined to land and sleep upon it. We consequently ran the boat into a little recess, or bay, and pitched the tents; and I anticipated a respite from the presence of any natives, as did the men, who were rejoiced at my having taken up so snug a berth. It happened, however, that a little after sunset, a flight of the new parroquets perched in the lofty trees that grew on the island, to roost: when we immediately commenced the work of death, and succeeded in killing eight or ten. The reports of our guns were heard by some natives up the river, and several came over to us. Although I was annoyed at their having discovered our retreat, they were too few to be troublesome. During the night, however, they were joined by fresh numbers, amounting in all to about eighty, and they were so clamorous that it was impossible to sleep.

As the morning broke, Hopkinson came to inform me that it was in vain that the guard endeavoured to prevent them from handling every thing, and from closing in round our camp. I went out, and from what I saw I thought it advisable to double the sentries. M'Leay, who was really tired, being unable to close his eyes amid such a din, got up in ill-humour and went to see into the cause, and to check it if he could. This, however, was impossible. One man was particularly forward and insolent, at whom M'Leay, rather imprudently, threw a piece of dirt. The savage returned the compliment with as much good will as it had been given, and appeared quite prepared to act on the offensive. At this critical moment my servant came to the tent in which I was washing myself, and stated his fears that we should soon come to blows, as the natives shewed every disposition to resist us. On learning what had passed between M'Leay and the savage, I pretended to be equally angry with both, and with some difficulty forced the greater part of the blacks away from the tents. I then directed the men to gather together all the minor articles in the first instance, and then to strike the tents; and, in order to check the natives, I drew a line round the camp, over which I intimated to them they should not pass. Observing, I suppose, that we were on our guard, and that I whom they well knew to be the chief, was really angry, they crept away one by one, until the island was almost deserted by them. Why they did not attack us, I know not, for they had certainly every disposition to do so, and had their shorter weapons with them, which, in so confined a space as that on which we were, would have been more fatal than their spears.

They left us, however; and a flight of red-crested cockatoos happening to settle on a plain near the river, I crossed in the boat in order to shoot one. The plain was upon the proper left bank of the Murray. The natives had passed over to the right. As the one channel was too shallow for the boat, when we again pursued our journey we were obliged to pull round to the left side of the island. A little above it the river makes a bend to the left, and the angle at this bend was occupied by a large shoal, one point of which rested on the upper part of the island, and the other touched the proper right bank of the river. Thus a narrow channel (not broader indeed than was necessary for the play of our oars) alone remained for us to pass up against a strong current. On turning round the lower part of the island, we observed that the natives occupied the whole extent of the shoal, and speckled it over like skirmishers. Many of them had their spears, and their attention was evidently directed to us. As we neared the shoal, the most forward of them pressed close to the edge of the deep water, so much so that our oars struck their legs. Still this did not induce them to retire. I kept my eye on an elderly man who stood one of the most forward, and who motioned to us several times to stop, and at length threw the weapon he carried at the boat. I immediately jumped up and pointed my gun at him to his great apparent alarm. Whether the natives hoped to intimidate us by a show of numbers, or what immediate object they had in view, it is difficult to say; though it was most probably to seize a fitting opportunity to attack us. Seeing, I suppose, that we were not to be checked, they crossed from the shoal to the proper right bank of the river, and disappeared among the reeds that lined it.

Shortly after this, eight of the women, whom we had not before noticed, came down to the waterside and gave us the most pressing invitation to land. Indeed they played their part uncommonly well, and tried for some time to allure us by the most unequivocal manifestations of love. Hopkinson, however,

'On turning round the lower part of the island, we observed that the natives occupied the whole extent of the shoal, and speckled it over like skirmishers. Many of them had their spears, and their attention was evidently directed to us.'

'Junction of the Supposed Darling with the Murray', an illustration from Sturt's Two Expeditions into the Interior, *from a sketch by the author. He correctly assumed the river to be the Darling, whose upper part he had discovered the previous year.*

who always had his eyes about him, observed the spears of the men among the reeds. They kept abreast of us as we pulled up the stream, and, no doubt, were anticipating our inability to resist the temptations they had thrown in our way. I was really provoked at their barefaced treachery and should most undoubtedly have attacked them had they not precipitately retreated on being warned by the women that I was arming my men, which I had only now done upon seeing such strong manifestations of danger. M'Leay set the example of coolness on this occasion; and I had some doubts whether I was justified in allowing the natives to escape with impunity, considering that if they had wounded any one of us the most melancholy and fatal results would have ensued.

We did not see anything more of the blacks during the rest of the day, but the repeated indications of hostility we perceived as we approached the Darling made me apprehensive as to the reception we should meet from its numerous population; and I was sorry to observe that the men anticipated danger in passing that promising junction.

Having left the sea breezes behind us, the weather had become oppressive; and as the current was stronger, and rapids more numerous, our labour was proportionably increased. We perspired to an astonishing degree, and gave up our oars after our turn at them with shirts and clothes as wet as if we had been in the water. Indeed Mulholland and Hopkinson, who worked hard, poured a considerable quantity of perspiration from their shoes after their task. The evil of this was that we were always chilled after rowing, and, of course, suffered more than we should otherwise have done....

A little below the Lindesay, a rapid occurs. It was with the utmost difficulty that we stemmed it with the four oars upon the boat, and the exertion of our whole strength. We remained, at one time, perfectly stationary, the force we employed and that of the current being equal. We at length ran up the stream obliquely; but it was evident the men were not adequate to such exertion for any length of time. We pulled that day for eleven successive hours, in order to avoid a tribe of natives who followed us. Hopkinson and Fraser fell asleep at their oars, and even the heavy Clayton appeared to labour....

The least circumstance, in our critical situation, naturally raised my apprehensions, and I feared the river would be swollen in the event of any heavy rains in the hilly country; I hoped, however, we should gain the Morumbidgee before such a calamity should happen to us, and it became my object to press for that river without delay.

Although we had met with frequent rapids in our progress upwards, they had not been of a serious kind, nor such as would affect the navigation of the river. The first direct obstacle of this kind occurs a little above a small tributary that falls into the Murray from the north, between the Rufus and the cliffs we have alluded to. At this place a reef of coarse grit contracts the channel of the river. No force we could have exerted with the oars would have taken us up this rapid; but we accomplished the task easily by means of a rope which we hauled upon, on the same principle that barges are dragged by horses along the canals.

As we neared the junction of the two main streams, the country on both sides of the river became low, and its general appearance confirmed the opinion I have already given as to its flooded origin. The clouds that obscured the sky, and had threatened to burst for some time, at length gave way, and we experienced two or three days of heavy rain. In the midst of it we passed the second stage of our journey, and found the spot lately so crowded with inhabitants totally deserted. A little above it we surprised a small tribe in a temporary shelter; but neither our offers nor presents could prevail on any of them to expose themselves to the torrent that was falling. They sat shivering in their bark huts in evident astonishment at our indifference. We threw them some trifling presents and were glad to proceed unattended by any of them.

It will be remembered that in passing down the river the boat was placed in some danger in descending a rapid before we reached the junction of the Murray with the stream supposed by me to be the Darling. We were now gradually approaching the rapid, nor did I well know how we should surmount such an obstacle. Strength to pull up it we had not, and I feared our ropes would not be long enough to reach to the shore over some of the rocks, since it descended in minor declivities to a considerable distance below the principal rapid, in the centre of which the boat had struck. We reached the commencement of these rapids on the 6th, and ascended the first by means of ropes, which were hauled upon by three of the men from the bank; and, as the day was pretty far advanced, we stopped a little above it, that we might attempt the principal rapid before we should be exhausted by previous exertion. It was fortunate that we took such a precaution. The morning of the 7th proved extremely dark, and much rain fell. We commenced our journey in the midst of it, and soon gained the tail of the rapid. Our attempt to pull up it completely failed. The boat, as soon as she entered the ripple, spun round like a top, and away we went with the stream. As I had anticipated, our ropes were too short; and it only remained for us to get into the water and haul the boat up by main force. We managed pretty well at first and drew her alongside a rock to rest a little. We then recommenced our efforts and had got into the middle of the channel. We were up to our armpits in the water and only kept our position by means of rocks beside us. The rain was falling, as if we were in a tropical shower, and the force of the current was such that if we had relaxed for an instant we should have lost all the ground we had gained. Just at this moment, however, without our being aware of their approach, a large tribe of natives, with their spears, lined the bank, and took us most completely by surprise. At no time during this anxious journey were we ever so completely in their power, or in so defenceless a situation. It rained so hard that our firelocks would have been of no use, and had they attacked us, we must necessarily have been slaughtered without committing the least execution upon them. Nothing, therefore, remained for us but to continue our exertions. It required only one strong effort to get the boat into still water for a time, but that effort was beyond our strength, and we stood in the stream, powerless and exhausted.

The natives, in the meanwhile, resting on their spears, watched us with earnest attention. One of them, who was sitting close to the water, at length called to us, and we immediately recognised the deep voice of him to whose singular interference we were indebted for our escape on 23 January. I desired Hopkinson to swim over to him, and to explain that we wanted assistance. This was given without hesitation; and we at length got under the lee of the rock, which I have already described as being in the centre of the river. The natives launched their bark canoes, the only frail means they possess of crossing the rivers with their children. These canoes are of the simplest construction and rudest materials, being formed of an oblong piece of bark, the ends of which are stuffed with clay, so as to render them impervious to the water. With several of these they now paddled round us with the greatest care, making their spears, about ten feet in length (which they use at once as poles and paddles) bend nearly double in the water. We had still the most difficult part of the rapid to ascend, where the rush of water was the strongest, and where the decline of the bed almost amounted to a fall. Here the blacks could be of no use to us. No man could stem the current, supposing it to have been shallow at the place, but it was on the contrary extremely deep. Remaining myself in the boat, I directed all the men to land, after we had crossed the stream, upon a large rock that formed the left buttress as it were to this sluice, and, fastening the rope to the mast instead of her head, they pulled upon it. The unexpected rapidity with which the boat shot up the passage astonished me, and filled the natives with wonder, who testified their admiration of so dexterous a manoeuvre by a loud shout.

It will, no doubt, have struck the reader as something very remarkable that the same influential savage to whom we had already been indebted should have been present on this occasion, and at a moment when we so much needed his assistance. Having surmounted our difficulties, we took leave of this remarkable man and pursued our journey up the river.

It may be imagined we did not proceed very far; the fact was, we only

'View on the Morumbidge River', from a sketch by Sturt. On their return upriver, Sturt's party had to row against the Murrumbidgee in flood after heavy rain.

pushed forward to get rid of the natives, for, however pacific, they were always troublesome, and we were seldom fitted for a trial of temper after the labours of the day were concluded. The men had various occupations in which, when the natives were present, they were constantly interrupted, and whenever the larger tribes slept near us, the utmost vigilance was necessary on the part of the night guard, which was regularly mounted as soon as the tents were pitched. We had had little else than our flour to subsist on. Hopkinson and Harris endeavoured to supply M'Leay and myself with a wildfowl occasionally, but for themselves, and the other men, nothing could be procured to render their meal more palatable....

Sturt's party continued slowly up the Murray, rowing from daylight to dark. After another difficult encounter with the Aborigines, they re-entered the Murrumbidgee on 16 March, having rowed back up the Murray, against the current, in a heroic twenty-three days, three days less than they had taken to travel downstream. Their provisions were now extremely low, and they were anxious to reach the depot where they hoped to find Robert Harris and the others with fresh supplies.

At noon, I stopped about a mile short of the depôt to take sights. After dinner we pulled on, the men looking earnestly out for their comrades whom they had left there, but none appeared. My little arbour, in which I had written my letters, was destroyed, and the bank on which our tents had stood was wholly deserted. We landed, however, and it was a satisfaction to me to see the homeward track of the drays. The men were sadly disappointed, and poor Clayton, who had anticipated a plentiful meal, was completely chop-fallen. M'Leay and I comforted them daily with the hopes of meeting the drays, which I did not think improbable.

Thus, it will appear, that we regained the place from which we started in seventy-seven days, during which we could not have pulled less than two thousand miles. It is not for me, however, to make any comment, either on the dangers to which we were occasionally exposed, or the toil and privations we continually experienced in the course of this expedition. My duty is simply to give a plain narrative of facts, which I have done with fidelity, and with as much accuracy as circumstances would permit. Had we found Robert Harris at the depôt, I should have considered it unnecessary to trespass longer on the patient reader, but as our return to that post did not relieve us from our difficulties, it remains for me to carry on the narrative of our proceedings to the time when we reached the upper branches of the Morumbidgee.

The hopes that had buoyed up the spirits of the men, ceased to operate as soon as they were discovered to have been ill founded. The most gloomy ideas took possession of their minds, and they fancied that we had been neglected, and that Harris had remained in Sydney. It was to no purpose that I explained to them that my instructions did not bind Harris to come beyond Pontebadgery, and that I was confident he was then encamped upon that plain.

'The river had fallen below its former level, and rocks and logs were now exposed above the water, over many of which the boat's keel must have grazed, as we passed down with the current. I really shuddered frequently, at seeing these complicated dangers...'

We had found the intricate navigation of the Morumbidgee infinitely more distressing than the hard pulling up the open reaches of the Murray, for we were obliged to haul the boat up between numberless trunks of trees, an operation that exhausted the men much more than rowing. The river had fallen below its former level, and rocks and logs were now exposed above the water, over many of which the boat's keel must have grazed, as we passed down with the current. I really shuddered frequently, at seeing these complicated dangers, and I was at a loss to conceive how we could have escaped them. The planks of our boat were so thin that if she had struck forcibly against any one branch of the hundreds she must have grazed, she would inevitably have been rent asunder from stem to stern.

The day after we passed the depôt, on our return, we began to experience the effects of the rains that had fallen in the mountains. The Morumbidgee rose upon us six feet in one night, and poured along its turbid waters with proportionate violence. For seventeen days we pulled against them with determined perseverance, but human efforts, under privations such as ours, tend to weaken themselves, and thus it was that the men began to exhibit the effects of severe and unremitting toil. Our daily journeys were short, and the head we made against the stream but trifling. The men lost the proper and muscular jerk with which they once made the waters foam and the oars bend. Their whole bodies swung with an awkward and laboured motion. Their arms appeared to be nerveless; their faces became haggard, their persons emaciated, their spirits wholly sunk; nature was so completely overcome that from mere exhaustion they frequently fell asleep during their painful and almost ceaseless exertions. It grieved me to the heart to see them in such a state at the close of so perilous a service, and I began to reproach Robert Harris that he did not move down the river to meet us; but, in fact, he was not to blame. I became captious, and found fault where there was no occasion, and lost the equilibrium of my temper in contemplating the condition of my companions. No murmur, however, escaped them, nor did a complaint reach me that was intended to indicate that they had done all they could do. I frequently heard them in their tent, when they thought I had dropped asleep, complaining of severe pains and of great exhaustion. 'I must tell the captain, tomorrow,' some of them would say, 'that I can pull no more.' Tomorrow came, and they pulled on, as if reluctant to yield to circumstances. Macnamee at length lost his senses. We first observed this from his incoherent conversation, but eventually from his manner. He related the most extraordinary tales, and fidgeted about eternally while in the boat. I felt it necessary, therefore, to relieve him from the oars.

Amidst these distresses, M'Leay preserved his good humour and endeavoured to lighten the task and to cheer the men as much as possible. His presence at this time was a source of great comfort to me. The uniform kindness with which he had treated his companions gave him an influence over them now, and it was exerted with the happiest effect.

On 8 and 9 April we had heavy rain, but there was no respite for us. Our provisions were nearly consumed, and would have been wholly exhausted if we had not been so fortunate as to kill several swans. On the 11th, we gained our camp opposite to Hamilton's Plains, after a day of severe exertion. Our tents were pitched upon the old ground, and the marks of our cattle were around us. In the evening, the men went out with their guns, and M'Leay and I walked to the rear of the camp, to consult undisturbed as to the most prudent measures to be adopted under our embarrassing circumstances. The men were completely sunk. We were still between eighty and ninety miles from Pontebadgery, in a direct line, and nearly treble that distance by water. The task was greater than we could perform, and our provisions were insufficient. In this extremity I thought it best to save the men the mortification of yielding, by abandoning the boat; and on further consideration I determined on sending Hopkinson and Mulholland, whose devotion, intelligence, and indefatigable spirits I well knew, forward to the plain.

The joy this intimation spread was universal. Both Hopkinson and Mulholland readily undertook the journey, and I, accordingly, prepared orders for them to start by the earliest dawn. It was not without a feeling of sorrow that I witnessed the departure of these two men, to encounter a fatiguing march. I had no fears as to their gaining the plain if their reduced state would permit them. On the other hand, I hoped they would fall in with our old friend the black, or that they would meet the drays; and I could not but admire the spirit and energy they both displayed upon the occasion. Their behaviour throughout had been such as to awaken in my breast a feeling of the highest approbation. Their conduct, indeed, exceeded all praise, nor did they hesitate one moment when I called upon them to undertake this last trying duty, after such continued exertion. I am sure the reader will forgive me for bringing under his notice the generous efforts of these two men; by me it can never be forgotten.

Six days had passed since their departure; we remaining encamped. M'Leay and myself had made some short excursions but without any result worthy of notice. A group of sandhills rose in the midst of the alluvial deposits, about a quarter of a mile from the tents, that were covered with coarse grasses and banksias. We shot several intertropical birds feeding in the latter and sucking the honey from their flowers. I had, in the meantime, directed Clayton to make some plant cases of the upper planks of the boat, and then to set fire to her, for she was wholly unserviceable, and I felt a reluctance to leave her like a neglected log on the water. The last ounce of flour had been served out to the men, and the whole of it was consumed on the sixth day from that on which we had abandoned the boat. I had calculated on seeing Hopkinson again in eight days, but as the morrow would see us without food, I thought, as the men had had a little rest, it would be better to advance towards relief than to await its arrival.

On the evening of the 18th, therefore, we buried our specimens and other stores, intending to break up the camp in the morning. A singular bird, which invariably passed it at an hour after sunset, and which, from its heavy flight, appeared to be of unusual size, had so attracted my notice that in the evening M'Leay and I crossed the river, in hope to get a shot at it. We had, however, hardly landed on the other side when a loud shout called us back to witness the return of our comrades.

They were both of them in a state that beggars description. Their knees and ankles were dreadfully swollen, and their limbs so painful, that as soon as they arrived in the camp they sank under their efforts, but they met us with smiling countenances, and expressed their satisfaction at having arrived so seasonably to our relief. They had, as I had foreseen, found Robert Harris on the plain, which they reached on the evening of the third day. They had started early the next morning on their return with such supplies as they thought we might immediately want. Poor Macnamee had in a great measure recovered, but for some days he was sullen and silent: the sight of the drays gave him uncommon satisfaction. Clayton gorged himself; but M'Leay, myself, and Fraser could not at first relish the meat that was placed before us.

It was determined to give the bullocks a day of rest, and I availed myself of the serviceable state of the horses to visit some hills about eighteen miles to the northward. I was anxious to gain a view of the distant country to the NW, and to ascertain the geological character of the hills themselves. M'Leay, Fraser, and myself left the camp early in the morning of the 19th, on our way to them.... We returned to the camp at midnight.

On the following morning we left our station before Hamilton's Plains. We reached Pondebadgery on the 28th, and found Robert Harris, with a plentiful supply of provisions. He had everything extremely regular, and had been anxiously expecting our return, of which he at length wholly despaired. He had been at the plain two months, and intended to have moved down the river immediately, had we not made our appearance when we did.

'Their knees and ankles were dreadfully swollen, and their limbs so painful, that as soon as they arrived in the camp they sunk under their efforts, but they met us with smiling countenances, and expressed their satisfaction at having arrived so seasonably to our relief.'

ROUND THE GREAT AUSTRALIAN BIGHT

Edward John Eyre

EDWARD JOHN EYRE *was born in England and came to Australia in 1833 for health reasons. After taking up land in New South Wales, he made a series of droving trips to the Port Phillip District and then overlanded sheep and cattle to South Australia, where he eventually settled. In 1839 he made two exploratory expeditions, one from Adelaide to the north, on which he discovered Lake Torrens, the other from Port Lincoln to Streaky Bay and across to the head of Spencer Gulf. Early in 1840 he took a shipment of sheep and cattle to Albany and overlanded them from there to Perth. In June that year he set off once again from Adelaide to explore the country to the north, sighting Lake Eyre (which he thought was Lake Torrens) and reaching Mount Hopeless before turning back towards the coast, where he set up base at Fowlers Bay on the Great Australian Bight. After further unsuccessful attempts to penetrate to the north, he decided to try to travel overland to King George Sound and on 25 February 1841, together with his overseer, John Baxter, three Aborigines, nine horses, a pony and a foal, and six sheep (which were eaten on the way), set out from Fowlers Bay for Albany, fifteen hundred kilometres across difficult and partly desert country.*

They had been travelling for two months when tragedy struck. While Eyre was watching the horses one night some distance from their camp on the cliffs above the Bight, two of the Aborigines killed Baxter and ran off with much of the food and equipment. Eyre was left to continue the journey with the remaining Aboriginal, Wylie, whom he had brought back from Albany the previous year. Eyre's journal records his feelings at the time.

'The horrors of my situation glared upon me in such startling reality as for an instant almost to paralyse the mind.'

THE HORRORS of my situation glared upon me in such startling reality as for an instant almost to paralyse the mind. At the dead hour of night, in the wildest and most inhospitable wastes of Australia, with the fierce wind raging in unison with the scene of violence before me, I was left, with a single native, whose fidelity I could not rely upon, and who for aught I knew might be in league with the other two, who perhaps were even now lurking about with the view of taking away my life as they had done that of the overseer. Three days had passed away since we left the last water, and it was very doubtful when we might find any more. Six hundred miles of country had to be traversed before I could hope to obtain the slightest aid or assistance of any kind, whilst I knew not that a single drop of water or an ounce of flour had been left by these murderers, from a stock that had previously been so small.

With such thoughts rapidly passing through my mind, I turned to search for my double-barrelled gun, which I had left covered with an oilskin at the head of my own breakwind. It was gone, as was also the double-barrelled gun that had belonged to the overseer. These were the only weapons at the time that were in serviceable condition, for though there were a brace of pistols they had been packed away, as there were no cartridges for them, and my rifle was useless, from having a ball sticking fast in the breech, and which we had in vain endeavoured to extract. A few days' previous to our leaving the last water, the overseer had attempted to wash out the rifle not knowing it was loaded, and the consequence was that the powder became wetted and partly washed away, so that we could neither fire it off nor get out the ball; I was, therefore, temporarily defenceless and quite at the mercy of the natives had they at this time come upon me. Having hastily ripped open the bag in which the pistols had been sewn up, I got them out, together with my powder flask and a bag containing a little shot and some large balls. The rifle I found where it had been left, but the ramrod had been taken out by the boys to load my double-barrelled gun with, its own ramrod being too short for that purpose; I found it, however, together with several loose cartridges, lying about near the place where the boys had slept, so that it was evident they had deliberately loaded the firearms before they tried to move away with the things they had stolen; one barrel only of my gun had been previously loaded, and I believe neither barrels in that of the overseer.

After obtaining possession of all the remaining arms, useless as they were at the moment, with some ammunition, I made no further examination then,

Below: Wylie, the Aboriginal from King George Sound who accompanied Eyre round the Great Australian Bight to Albany, from an illustration in Eyre's Journal of Expeditions in Central and Southern Australia in 1840.

Right: Edward John Eyre in 1845. From 1841 to 1845 Eyre was resident magistrate and protector of Aborigines at Moorundie, South Australia. The following year he was appointed Lieutenant-Governor of New Zealand and later was Governor-in-Chief of Jamaica.

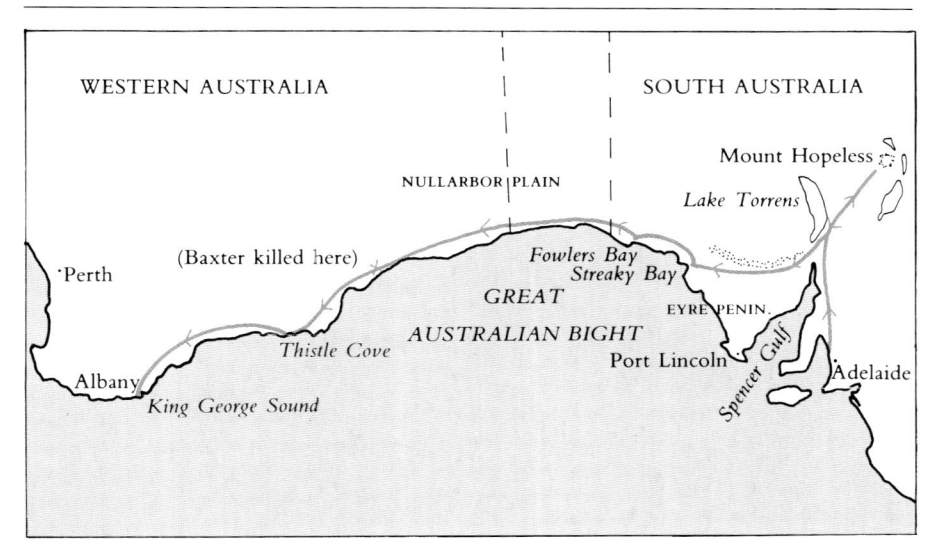

The route of Eyre's journey in 1840–41.

but hurried away from the fearful scene, accompanied by the King George's Sound native, to search for the horses, knowing that if they got away now, no chance whatever would remain of saving our lives. Already the wretched animals had wandered to a considerable distance; and although the night was moonlight, yet the belts of scrub, intersecting the plains, were so numerous and dense that for a long time we could not find them; having succeeded in doing so at last, Wylie and I remained with them, watching them during the remainder of the night; but they were very restless and gave us a great deal of trouble. With an aching heart, and in most painful reflections, I passed this dreadful night. Every moment appeared to be protracted to an hour, and it seemed as if the daylight would never appear. About midnight the wind ceased, and the weather became bitterly cold and frosty. I had nothing on but a shirt and a pair of trousers, and suffered most acutely from the cold; to mental anguish was now added intense bodily pain. Suffering and distress had well nigh overwhelmed me, and life seemed hardly worth the effort necessary to prolong it. Ages can never efface the horrors of this single night, nor would the wealth of the world ever tempt me to go through similar ones again.

30 April. At last, by God's blessing, daylight dawned once more, but sad and heart-rending was the scene it presented to my view, upon driving the horses to what had been our last night's camp. The corpse of my poor companion lay extended on the ground, with the eyes open, but cold and glazed in death. The same stern resolution, and fearless open look, which had characterised him when living, stamped the expression of his countenance even now. He had fallen upon his breast four or five yards from where he had been sleeping, and was dressed only in his shirt. In all probability, the noise made by the natives, in plundering the camp, had awoke him; and upon his jumping up, with a view of stopping them, they had fired upon and killed him.

Around the camp lay scattered the harness of the horses and the remains of the stores that had been the temptation to this fatal deed.

As soon as the horses were caught, and secured, I left Wylie to make a fire, whilst I proceeded to examine into the state of our baggage, that I might decide upon our future proceedings. Among the principal things carried off by the natives were the whole of our baked bread, amounting to twenty pounds weight, some mutton, tea and sugar, the overseer's tobacco and pipes, a one-gallon keg full of water, some clothes, two double-barrelled guns, some ammunition, and a few other small articles.

There were still left forty pounds of flour, a little tea and sugar, and four gallons of water, besides the arms and ammunition I had secured last night.

From the state of our horses, and the dreadful circumstances we were placed in, I was now obliged to abandon everything but the bare necessaries of life. The few books and instruments I had still left, with many of the specimens I had collected, a saddle, and some other things, were thrown aside to lighten somewhat more the trifling loads our animals had to carry. A little bread was then baked, and I endeavoured once more to put the rifle in serviceable condition, as it was the only weapon we should have to depend upon in any dangers that might beset us. Unable in any way to take out the breech, or to extract the ball, I determined to melt it out, and for that purpose took the barrel off the stock, and put the breech in the fire, holding the muzzle in my hand. Whilst thus engaged, the rifle went off, the ball whizzing close past my head; the fire, it seems, had dried the powder, which had been wetted, not washed out; and when the barrel was sufficiently heated, the piece had gone off, to the imminent danger of my life, from the incautious way in which I held it. The gun, however, was again serviceable; and after carefully loading it, I felt a degree of confidence and security I had before been a stranger to.

At eight o'clock we were ready to proceed; there remained but to perform the last sad offices of humanity towards him whose career had been cut short in so untimely a manner. This duty was rendered even more than ordinarily painful by the nature of the country where we happened to have been encamped. One vast unbroken surface of sheet rock extended for miles in every direction and rendered it impossible to make a grave. We were some miles away from the seashore, and even had we been nearer, could not have got down the cliffs to bury the corpse in the sand. I could only, therefore, wrap a blanket around the body of the overseer and, leaving it enshrouded where he fell, escape from the melancholy scene, accompanied by Wylie, under the influence of feelings which neither time nor circumstances will ever obliterate. Though years have now passed away since the enactment of this tragedy, the dreadful horrors of that time and scene are recalled before me with frightful vividness and make me shudder even now when I think of them. A lifetime was crowded into those few short hours, and death alone may blot out the impressions they produced.

For some time we travelled slowly and silently onwards, Wylie preceding, leading one of the horses, myself following behind and driving the others after him, through a country consisting still of the same alternations of scrub and open intervals as before. The day became very warm, and at eleven, after travelling ten miles to the west, I determined to halt until the cool of the evening. After baking some bread and getting our dinners, I questioned Wylie as to what he knew of the sad occurrence of yesterday. He positively

> '*Though years have now passed away since the enactment of this tragedy, the dreadful horrors of that time and scene are recalled before me with frightful vividness and make me shudder even now when I think of them.*'

denied all knowledge of it—said he had been asleep, and was awoke by the report of the gun, and that upon seeing the overseer lying on the ground he ran off to meet me. He admitted, however, that after the unsuccessful attempt to leave us and proceed alone to King George's Sound, the elder of the other two natives had proposed to him again to quit the party and try to go back to Fowler's Bay to the provisions buried there. But he had heard or knew nothing, he said, of either robbery or murder being first contemplated.

My own impression was that Wylie had agreed with the other two to rob the camp and leave us—that he had been cognisant of all their proceedings and preparations, but that when, upon the eve of their departure, the overseer had unexpectedly awoke and been murdered, he was shocked and frightened at the deed and, instead of accompanying them, had run down to meet me. My opinion upon this point received additional confirmation from the subsequent events of this day; but I never could get Wylie to admit even the slightest knowledge of the fatal occurrence, or that he had even intended to have united with them in plundering the camp and deserting. He had now become truly alarmed; and independently of the fear of the consequences which would attach to the crime, should we ever reach a civilised community again, he had become very apprehensive that the other natives, who belonged to quite a different part of Australia to himself, ... would murder him as unhesitatingly as they had done the white man.

We remained in camp until four o'clock and were again preparing to advance when my attention was called by Wylie to two white objects among the scrub at no great distance from us, and I at once recognised the native boys, covered with their blankets only and advancing towards us. From Wylie's account of their proposal to go back towards Fowler's Bay, I fully hoped that they had taken that direction and left us to pursue our way to the Sound unmolested. I was therefore surprised, and somewhat alarmed, at finding them so near us. With my rifle and pistols I felt myself sufficiently a match for them in an open country, or by daylight. Yet I knew that as long as they followed like bloodhounds on our tracks our lives would be in their power at any moment that they chose to take them whilst we were passing through a scrubby country, or by night. Whatever their intention might be, I knew that if we travelled in the same direction with them, our lives could only be safe by their destruction. Although they had taken fully one-third of the whole stock of our provisions, their appetites were so ravenous, and their habits so improvident, that this would soon be consumed, and then they must either starve or plunder us; for they had already tried to subsist themselves in the bush, and had failed.

As these impressions rapidly passed through my mind, there appeared to me but one resource left, to save my own life and that of the native with me: that was, to shoot the elder of the two. Painful as this would be, I saw no other alternative, if they still persisted in following us. After packing up our few things, and putting them upon the horses, I gave the bridles to Wylie to hold, whilst I advanced alone with my rifle towards the two natives. They were now tolerably near, each carrying a double-barrelled gun, which was pointed towards me, elevated across the left arm and held by the right hand. As I attempted to approach nearer they gradually retreated.

Finding that I was not likely to gain ground upon them in this way, I threw down my weapons and advanced unarmed, hoping that if they let me near them I might suddenly close with the eldest and wrest his gun from him. After advancing about sixty or seventy yards towards them, I found that they again began to retreat, evidently determined not to let me approach any nearer, either armed or unarmed. Upon this I halted and endeavoured to enter into parley with them, with a view to persuading them to return towards Fowler's Bay and thus obviate the painful necessity I should have been under of endeavouring, for my own security, to take away the life of the eldest whenever I met with him, should they still persist in going the same road as myself. The distance we were apart was almost too great for parley, and I know not whether they heard me or not; though they halted, and appeared to listen, they did not reply to what I said, and plainly wished to avoid all closer contact. They now began to call incessantly to Wylie, and in answer to my repeated efforts to get them to speak to me, only would say, 'Oh massa, we don't want you, we want Wylie.' Thus fully confirming me in the opinion I had formed, that Wylie had agreed to go with them before the deed of violence was committed. It was now apparent to me that their only present object in following us had been to look for Wylie, and get him to join them. In this they were unsuccessful; for he still remained quietly where I left him holding the horses, and evidently afraid to go near them. There was no use wasting further time, as I could not get them to listen to me. The sun, too, was fast sinking in the horizon, we had been four days without finding water, and the probability was we had very far still to go before we could hope to procure any; every moment, therefore, was precious.

Having returned to Wylie, I made him lead one of the horses in advance, and I followed behind, driving the rest after him, according to the system of march I had adopted in the morning. As soon as the two natives saw us moving on, and found Wylie did not join them, they set up a wild and plaintive cry, still following along the brush parallel to our line of route, and never ceasing in their importunities to Wylie, until the denseness of the scrub, and the closing in of night, concealed us from each other.

I was now resolved to make the most of the opportunity afforded me and, by travelling steadily onwards, to gain so much distance in advance of the two natives as to preclude the possibility of their again overtaking us until we had reached the water, if indeed we were ever destined to reach water again. I knew that they would never travel more than a few miles before lying down, especially if carrying all the bread they had taken, the keg of water, guns, and other articles. We had, however, seen none of these things with them. except the firearms.

Our road was over scrubby and stony undulations, with patches of dry grass here and there; in other parts, we passed over a very sandy soil of a red colour, and overrun by immense tufts of prickly grass (spinifex), many of which were three and four yards in diameter. After pushing on for eighteen miles, I felt satisfied we had left the natives far behind and finding a patch of grass for the horses, halted for the remainder of the night. It was quite impossible, after all we had gone through, to think of watching the horses, and my only means of preventing them from straying was to close the chains of their hobbles so tight that they could not go far; having thus secured them, we lay down, and for a few hours enjoyed uninterrupted and refreshing sleep.

Moving on again on 1 May, as the sun was above the horizon, we passed through a continuation of the same kind of country for sixteen miles, and then halted for a few hours during the heat of the day. We had passed many recent traces of natives, both yesterday and today, who appeared to be travelling to the westward. After dividing a pot of tea between us, we again pushed on for twelve miles, completing a stage of twenty-eight miles, and halting, with a little dry grass for the horses.

It was impossible they could endure this much longer, they had already been five days without water, and I did not expect to meet with any for two days more, a period which I did not think they could survive. As yet no very great change had taken place in the country; it was still scrubby and rocky, but the surface stone now consisted of a cream-coloured limestone of a fine compact character, and full of shells. The cliffs, parallel with which we were travelling, were still of about the same height, appearance, and formation as before, whilst the inland country increased in elevation, forming scrubby ridges to the back, with a few open grassy patches here and there. One circumstance in our route today cheered me greatly, and led me shortly to expect some important and decisive change in the character and formation of the country. It was the appearance for the first time of the Banksia, a shrub which I had never before found to the westward of Spencer's Gulf, but which I knew to abound in the vicinity of King George's Sound, and that description of country generally. Those only who have looked out with the eagerness and anxiety of a person in my situation, to note any change in the vegetation or physical appearance of a country, can appreciate the degree of satisfaction with which I recognised and welcomed the first appearance of the Banksia. Isolated as it was amidst the scrub, and insignificant as the stunted specimens were that I first met with, they led to an inference that I could not be mistaken in, and added, in a tenfold degree, to the interest and expectation with which every mile of our route had now become invested. During the day the weather had been again cloudy, with the appearance of rain; but the night turned out cold and frosty, and both I and the native suffered extremely. We had little to protect us from the severity of the season, never being able to procure firewood of a description that would keep burning long at once, so that between cold and fatigue, we were rarely able to get more than a few moments rest at a time and were always glad when daylight dawned to cheer us, although it only aroused us to the renewal of our unceasing toil.

2 May. We again moved away at dawn, through a country which gradually became more scrubby, hilly, and sandy. The horses crawled on for twenty-one miles, when I halted for an hour to rest and to have a little tea from our now scanty stock of water. The change which I had noticed yesterday in the vegetation of the country was greater and more cheering every mile we went, although as yet the country itself was as desolate and inhospitable as ever. The smaller banksias now abounded, whilst the *Banksia grandis*, and many other shrubs common at King George's Sound, were frequently met with. The natives whose tracks we had so frequently met with, taking the

> 'Those only who have looked out with the eagerness and anxiety of a person in my situation, to note any change in the vegetation or physical appearance of a country, can appreciate the degree of satisfaction with which I recognised and welcomed the first appearance of the Banksia.'

same course as ourselves to the westward, seemed now to be behind us; during the morning we had passed many freshly lit fires, but the people themselves remained concealed; we had now lost all traces of them, and the country seemed untrodden and untenanted. In the course of our journey this morning, we met with many holes in the sheets of limestone which occasionally coated the surface of the ground; in these holes the natives appeared to procure an abundance of water after rains, but it was so long since any had fallen that all were dry and empty now. In one deep hole only did we find the least trace of moisture; this had at the bottom of it perhaps a couple of wineglasses full of mud and water, and was most carefully blocked up from the birds with huge stones: it had evidently been visited by natives not an hour before we arrived at it, but I suspect they were as much disappointed as we were upon rolling away all the stones to find nothing in it.

'After travelling two and a half miles, however, we were cheered and encouraged by the sight of sandy hills, and a low coast stretching beyond the cliffs to the south-west, though they were still some distance from us.'

After our scanty meal, we again moved onwards, but the road became so scrubby and rocky, or so sandy and hilly, that we could make no progress at all by night, and at eight miles from where we dined we were compelled to halt, after a day's journey of twenty-nine miles; but without a blade even of withered grass for our horses, which was the more grievous, because for the first time since we left the last water, a very heavy dew fell and would have enabled them to feed a little had there been grass. We had now traversed 138 miles of country from the last water and, according to my estimate of the distance we had to go, ought to be within a few miles of the termination of the cliffs of the Great Bight.

3 May. The seventh day's dawn found us early commencing our journey. The poor horses still crawled on, though slowly. I was surprised that they were still alive, after the continued sufferings and privations they had been subject to. As for ourselves, we were both getting very weak and worn out, as well as lame, and it was with the greatest difficulty I could get Wylie to move if he once sat down. I had myself the same kind of apathetic feeling and would gladly have lain down and slept for ever. Nothing but a strong sense of duty prevented me from giving way to this pleasing but fatal indulgence.

The road today became worse than ever, being one continued succession of sandy, scrubby and rocky ridges, and hollows formed on the top of the cliffs along which our course lay. After travelling two and a half miles, however, we were cheered and encouraged by the sight of sandy hills, and a low coast stretching beyond the cliffs to the south-west, though they were still some distance from us. At ten miles from where we had slept, a native road led us down a very steep part of the cliffs, and we descended to the beach. The wretched horses could scarcely move; it was with the greatest difficulty we got them down the hill, and now, although within sight of our goal, I feared two of them would never reach it. By perseverance we still got them slowly along, for two miles from the base of the cliffs, and then turning in among the sand-drifts, to our great joy and relief, found a place where the natives had dug for water; thus at twelve o'clock on the seventh day since leaving the last depot, we were again encamped at water, after having crossed 150 miles of a rocky, barren, and scrubby tableland....

8 May. About two hours before daylight, rain began to fall and continued steadily though lightly for three hours, so that enough had fallen to deposit water in the ledges or holes of the rocks. The day was wild and stormy, and we did not start until late. Even then we could only get the tired horse along for three miles, and were again compelled to halt. Water was still procured, by digging under the sandhills, but we had to sink much deeper than we had lately found occasion to do. It was now plain that the tired horse would never be able to keep pace with the others and that we must either abandon him or proceed at a rate too slow for the present state of our commissariat. Taking all things into consideration, it appeared to me that it would be better to kill him at once for food, and then remain here in camp for a time, living upon the flesh, whilst the other horses were recruiting, after which I hoped we might again be able to advance more expeditiously. Upon making this proposal to Wylie, he was quite delighted at the idea, and told me emphatically that he would sit up and eat the whole night. Our decision arrived at, the sentence was soon executed. The poor animal was shot, and Wylie and myself were soon busily employed in skinning him. Leaving me to continue this operation, Wylie made a fire close to the carcass, and as soon as he could get at a piece of the flesh he commenced roasting some, and continued alternately eating, working and cooking. After cutting off about a hundred pounds of the best of the meat, and hanging it in strips upon the trees until our departure, I handed over to Wylie the residue of the carcass, feet, entrails, flesh, skeleton, and all, to cook and consume as he pleased, whilst we were in the neighbourhood. Before dark he had made an oven and roasted about twenty pounds, to feast upon during the night. The evening set in stormy, and threatened heavy rain, but a few drops only fell. The wind then rose very high and raged fiercely from the south-west. At midnight it lulled, and the night became intensely cold and frosty, and both Wylie and myself suffered severely; we could only get small sticks for our fire, which burned out in a few minutes, and required so frequently renewing that we were obliged to give it up in despair and bear the cold in the best way we could. Wylie, during the night, made a sad and dismal groaning, and complained of being very ill, from pain in his throat, the effect he said of having to work too hard. I did not find that his indisposition interfered very greatly with his appetite, for nearly every time I awoke during the night I found him up and gnawing away at his meat; he was literally fulfilling the promise he had made me in the evening, 'By and bye, you see, Massa, me "pta" (eat) all night.'

9 May. The day was cold and cloudy, and we remained in camp to rest the horses and diminish the weight of meat, which was greater than our horses could well carry in their present state. On getting up the horses to water them at noon, I was grieved to find the foal of my favourite mare (which died on 28 March) missing; how we had lost it I could not make out, but as its tracks were not anywhere visible near the camp, it was evident that it had never come there at all. In leaving our last halting place my time and attention had been so taken up with getting the weak horse along that I had left it entirely to Wylie to bring up the others and had neglected my usual precaution of counting to see if all were there before we moved away. The little creature must have been lying down behind the sandhills asleep, when we left, or otherwise it would never have remained behind the others. Being very desirous not to lose this foal, which had now accompanied me so far and got through all the worst difficulties, I saddled the strongest of the horses, and mounting Wylie, I set off myself on foot with him to search for it. We had not gone far from the camp when Wylie wished me to go back, offering to go on by himself; and as I was loth to leave our provisions and ammunition to the mercy of any native that might chance to go that way, I acceded to his request, and delivering to him the rifle, returned to the encampment. Wylie had pledged himself to the due execution of this errand, and I had some confidence that he would not deceive me. Hour after hour passed away without his return, and I began to be uneasy at his long delay and half repented that I had been so foolish as to trust the rifle in his hands. At last, a little after dark, I was delighted to see him return, followed by the foal, which he had found six miles away and still travelling backwards in search of the horses. Having given him an extra allowance of bread as a reward for his good conduct, we took our tea and lay down for the night.

During the day, whilst Wylie was absent, I had employed my time in collecting firewood from the back of the sandhills. In this occupation I was pleased to meet with the silver-bark teatree, another change in the vegetation, which still further convinced me that we were rapidly advancing into a more practicable country.

10 May. The morning was spent in washing my clothes, cooking meat, and preparing to move on in the afternoon. Wylie, who knew that this was his last opportunity, was busy with the skeleton of the horse and never ceased eating until we moved on in the afternoon. As we took away with us nearly a hundred pounds of the flesh, the poor horses were heavily laden for the condition they were in. The scrubby and swampy nature of the country behind the shore compelled us too to keep to the beach, where the sands were loose and heavy. Our progress was slow, and at eight miles I halted. Here we found a little dry grass not far from the sea, and as the horses did not require water, they fared tolerably well. This was the first grass we had met with since we descended the cliffs on the 3rd instant, the horses having entirely subsisted since then on the wiry vegetation which binds the sand-drifts together. Although we had water in the canteens for ourselves, and the horses did not require any, I was curious to know whether fresh water could be procured where we were encamped—a long, low and narrow tongue of sandy land, lying between the sea on one side and extensive salt swamps on the other, and in no part elevated more than a few feet above the level of the sea itself. After tea I took the spade and commenced digging, and to my great surprise at six feet I obtained water, which though brackish was very palatable. This was very extraordinary, considering the nature of the position we were in, and that there were not any hills from which the fresh water could drain.

The night was again bitterly cold and frosty, and we suffered severely. Now the winter had set in, and we were sadly unprepared to meet its inclemency; the cold at nights became so intense as to occasion me agonies of pain; and the poor native was in the same predicament. . . .

12 May. I intended this morning to have walked down to the beach but

> '*I was pleased to meet with the silver-bark teatree, another change in the vegetation, which still further convinced me that we were rapidly advancing into a more practicable country.*'

was suddenly taken ill with similar symptoms to those I had experienced on 19 and 21 April; and, as formerly, I attributed the illness entirely to the unwholesome nature of the meat diet. Wylie was ill too, but not to so great a degree; nor was I surprised at his complaining; indeed, it would have been wonderful if he had not, considering the enormous quantity of horse flesh that he daily devoured. After his feasts, he would lie down and roll and groan and say he was 'mendyt' (ill), and nothing would induce him to get up or to do anything. There were now plenty of stingray fish along the beach again, and I was desirous, if possible, to get one for a change of diet; my friend, however, had so much to eat that though he said he should like fish too I could not get him to go about a mile to the back of the sandhills, to cut a stick from the scrub, to make a spear for catching them.

13 May. After breakfast, Wylie said he thought he could catch some bandicoots, by firing the scrub near the sandhills, and went out for an hour or two to try, but came back as he went. During his absence, I was employed in repairing my only two pair of socks now left, which were sadly dilapidated, but of which I was obliged to be very careful, as they were the only security I had against getting lame. In the afternoon I walked down to the beach, to try to spear stingray, but the sea was rough, and I saw none. In my ramble, I found plenty of the beautiful white clematis, so common both to the north and south of Sydney.

14 May. I was again seized with illness, though I had been particularly careful in the quantity of flesh which I had used. For many hours I suffered most excruciating pains; and after the violence of the attack was over, I was left very weak and incapable of exertion. Wylie was also affected. It was evident that the food we were now living upon was not wholesome or nutritious. Day after day we felt ourselves getting weaker and more relaxed, whilst the least change of weather, or the slightest degree of cold, was most painfully felt by both of us. What we were to do in the wet weather, which might daily be expected, I knew not, suffering as we did from the frosts and dews only. In the state we now were in, I do not think that we could have survived many days' exposure to wet....

17 May. This morning I felt rather better, but very weak, and wishing to give the horses an opportunity of drinking, which they would not do very early on a cold morning, I did not break up the camp until late. Upon lying down last night Wylie had left the meat on the ground at some distance from our fire, instead of putting it up on a bush as I had directed him; the consequence was that a wild dog had stolen about fourteen pounds of it whilst we slept, and we were now again reduced to a very limited allowance.

After travelling about five miles we found a great and important change in the basis rock of the country; it was now a coarse imperfect kind of grey granite, and in many places the low-water line was occupied by immense sheets of it. Other symptoms of improvement also gradually developed themselves. Mountain ducks were now, for the first time, seen upon the shore, and the trunk of a very large tree was found washed up on the beach: it was the only one we had met with during the whole course of our journey to the westward, and I hailed it with a pleasure which was only equalled by finding, not far beyond, a few drops of water trickling down a huge granite

'*Mountain ducks were now, for the first time, seen upon the shore, and the trunk of a very large tree was found washed up on the beach: it was the only one we had met with during the whole course of our journey to the westward, and I hailed it with a pleasure which was only equalled by finding, not far beyond, a few drops of water trickling down a huge granite rock abutting on the sea shore.*'

rock abutting on the sea shore. This was the only approximation to *running* water which we had found since leaving Streaky Bay, and though it hardly deserved that name, yet it imparted to me as much hope, and almost as much satisfaction, as if I had found a river. Continuing our course around a small sand-drifts behind a rocky point of the coast, from which the islands we had seen yesterday bore E47°S, Cape Pasley, SW, Point Malcolm, S33°W, and Mount Ragged W32°N. Several reefs and breakers were also seen at no great distance from the shore.

Our stage today was only twelve miles, yet some of our horses were nearly knocked up, and we ourselves in but little better condition. The incessant walking we were subject to, the low and unwholesome diet we had lived upon, the severe and weakening attacks of illness caused by that diet, having daily, and sometimes twice a day, to dig for water, to carry all our firewood from a distance upon our backs, to harness, unharness, water, and attend to the horses, besides other trifling occupations, making up our daily routine, usually so completely exhausted us that we had neither spirit nor energy left. Added to all other evils, the nature of the country behind the seacoast was as yet so sandy and scrubby that we were still compelled to follow the beach, frequently travelling on loose heavy sands that rendered our stages doubly fatiguing: whilst at nights, after the labours of the day were over, and we stood so much in need of repose, the intense cold, and the little protection we had against it, more frequently made it a season of most painful suffering than of rest, and we were glad when the daylight relieved us once more. On our march we felt generally weak and languid—it was an effort to put one foot before the other, and there was an indisposition to exertion that it was often very difficult to overcome. After sitting for a few moments to rest—and we often had to do this—it was always with the greatest unwillingness we ever moved on again. I felt, on such occasions, that I could have sat quietly and contentedly and let the glass of life glide away to its last sand. There was a dreamy kind of pleasure, which made me forgetful or careless of the circumstances and difficulties by which I was surrounded, and which I was always indisposed to break in upon. Wylie was even worse than myself; I had often much difficulty in getting him to move at all, and not infrequently was compelled almost forcibly to get him up. Fortunately he was very good tempered and on the whole had behaved extremely well under all our troubles since we had been travelling together alone.

18 May. This morning we had to travel upon a soft heavy beach, and moved slowly and with difficulty along, and three of the horses were continually attempting to lie down on the road. At twelve miles, we found some nice green grass, and although we could not procure water here, I determined to halt for the sake of the horses. The weather was cool and pleasant. From our camp Mount Ragged bore N35°W, and the island we had seen for the last two days, E18°C. Having seen some large kangaroos near our camp, I sent Wylie with the rifle to try and get one. At dark he returned bringing home a young one large enough for two good meals; upon this we feasted at night, and for once Wylie admitted that his belly was full. He commenced by eating a pound and a half of horseflesh, and a little bread, he then ate the entrails, paunch, liver, lights, tail, and two hind legs of the young kangaroo, next followed a penguin that he had found dead upon the beach, upon this he forced down the whole of the hide of the kangaroo after singeing the hair off, and wound up this meal by swallowing the tough skin of the penguin; he then made a little fire and lay down to sleep and dream of the pleasures of eating, nor do I think he was ever happier in his life than at that moment.

The two travellers continued their gruelling journey round the coast, supplementing their meagre food supplies with kangaroos shot by Wylie and fish and crabs caught by Eyre. On 2 June they arrived at Thistle Cove, near present-day Esperance, where Eyre planned to kill the foal for food and rest for a while beside the freshwater lake that Matthew Flinders had discovered there during his voyage in the Investigator. *Instead, to their delight, they found a French whaler, the* Mississippi, *at anchor in the bay. For the next twelve days they lived aboard the* Mississippi, *enjoying the hospitality of Captain Rossiter, an Englishman, and when they left to continue their journey they were well supplied with food and clothing. Another two weeks of travelling and they were in Wylie's home territory. Eyre's journal records the last few days:*

5 *July.* Another rainy day, and so excessively cold that we were obliged to walk to keep ourselves at all warm; we spent a miserable time, splashing through the wet underwood, and at fifteen miles we passed a freshwater lake, in a valley between some hills. This Wylie recognised as a place he had once been at before, and told me that he now knew the road well, and would act as guide, upon which I resigned the post of honour to him, on his promising always to take us to grass and water at night. Two miles and a half beyond the lake, we came to a freshwater swamp, and a mile beyond that to another, at which we halted for the night, with plenty of water, but very little grass. During the day, we had been travelling generally through a very heavily timbered country.

At night the rain set in again, and continued to fall in torrents at intervals; we got dreadfully drenched, and suffered greatly from cold and want of rest, being obliged to stand or walk before the fire, nearly the whole night.

6 *July.* The morning still very wet and miserably cold. With Wylie acting as guide, we reached in eight miles the Candiup River, a large chain of ponds, connected by a running stream, and emptying into a wide and deep arm of the sea, with much rich and fertile land upon its banks. The whole district was heavily timbered and had good grass growing amongst the trees. From the very heavy rains that had fallen, we had great trouble in crossing many of the streams, which were swollen by the floods into perfect torrents. In the Candiup River I had to wade, cold and chill as I was, seven times through, with the water breast high, and a current that I with difficulty could keep my feet against, in order to get the horses over in safety; the only fordable place was at a narrow ledge of rocks, and with so strong a stream, and such deep water below the ledge, I dared not trust Wylie to lead any of them, but went back and took each horse across myself. The day was bitterly cold and rainy, and I began to suffer severely from the incessant wettings I had been subject to for many days past.

Panoramic View of King George Sound, the first two sections of a lithograph, dated 1834, taken from a painting by the surveyor-explorer Lieutenant Robert Dale. A settlement had been established on King George Sound at Albany in 1826 to forestall a possible French settlement.

Four miles beyond the Candiup River, we came to King's River, a large salt arm of Oyster Harbour; here my friend Wylie, who insisted upon it that he knew the proper crossing place, took me into a large swampy morass, and in endeavouring to take the horses through, three of them got bogged and were nearly lost, and both myself and Wylie were detained in the water and mud for a couple of hours, endeavouring to extricate them. At last we succeeded, but the poor animals were sadly weakened and strained, and we were compelled to return back to the same side of the river, and encamp for the night, instead of going on to King George's Sound as I had intended!

Fortunately there was tolerable grass, and fresh water lay everywhere about in great abundance, so that the horses would fare well, but for ourselves there was a cheerless prospect. For three days and nights we had never had our clothes dry, and for the greater part of this time we had been enduring in full violence the pitiless storm—whilst wading so constantly through the cold torrents in the depth of the winter season, and latterly being detained in the water so long a time at the King's River, had rendered us rheumatic and painfully sensitive to either cold or wet. I hoped to have reached Albany this evening, and should have done so, as it was only six miles distant, if it had not been for the unlucky attempt to cross King's River. Now we had another night's misery before us, for we had hardly lain down before the rain began to fall again in torrents. Wearied and worn-out as we were with the sufferings and fatigues of the last few days, we could neither sit nor lie down to rest; our only consolation under the circumstances being that, however bad or inclement the weather might be, it was the last night we should be exposed to its fury.

7 July. Getting up the horses early, we proceeded up the King's River, with a view of attempting to cross, but upon sounding the depths in one or two places, I found the tide, which was rising, was too high; I had only the alternative, therefore, of waiting for several hours until the water ebbed, or else of leaving the horses and proceeding on without them. Under all the circumstances, I decided upon the latter; the rain was still falling very heavily, and the river before us was so wide and so dangerous for horses, from its very boggy character, that I did not think it prudent to attempt to force a passage, or worth while to delay to search for a proper crossing place. There was good feed for the horses where they were, and plenty of water, so that I knew they would fare better by remaining than if they were taken on to the Sound; whilst it appeared to me more than probable that I should have no difficulty, whenever I wished to get them, to procure a guide to go for and conduct them safely across, at the proper crossing place.

Having turned our horses loose, and piled up our baggage, now again greatly reduced, I took my journals and charts, and with Wylie forded the river about breast high. We were soon on the other side and rapidly advancing towards the termination of our journey; the rain was falling in torrents, and we had not a dry shred about us, whilst the whole country through which we passed had, from the long-continued and excessive rains, become almost an uninterrupted chain of puddles. For a great part of the way we walked up to our ankles in water. This made our progress slow and rendered our last day's march a very cold and disagreeable one. Before reaching the Sound, we met a native, who at once recognised Wylie and greeted him most cordially. From him we learnt that we had been expected at the Sound some months ago but had long been given up for lost, whilst Wylie had been mourned for and lamented as dead by his friends and his tribe. The rain still continued falling heavily as we ascended to the brow of the hill immediately overlooking the town of Albany—not a soul was to be seen—not an animal of any

Eyre and Wylie arriving at Albany, from an illustration in Eyre's Journal.

kind—the place looked uninhabited, so completely had the inclemency of the weather driven both man and beast to seek shelter from the storm.

For a moment I stood gazing at the town below me—that goal I had so long looked forward to, had so laboriously toiled to attain, was at last before me. A thousand confused images and reflections crowded through my mind, and the events of the past year were recalled in rapid succession. The contrast between the circumstances under which I had commenced and terminated my labours stood in strong relief before me. The gay and gallant cavalcade that accompanied me on my way at starting—the small but enterprising band that I then commanded, the goodly array of horses and drays, with all their well-ordered appointments and equipment were conjured up in all their circumstances of pride and pleasure; and I could not restrain a tear as I called to mind the embarrassing difficulties and sad disasters that had broken up my party and left myself and Wylie the two sole wanderers remaining at the close of an undertaking entered upon under such hopeful auspices.

Whilst standing thus upon the brow overlooking the town, and buried in reflection, I was startled by the loud shrill cry of the native we had met on the road, and who still kept with us: clearly and powerfully that voice rang through the recesses of the settlement beneath, whilst the blended name of Wylie told me of the information it conveyed. For an instant there was a silence still almost as death—then a single repetition of that wild joyous cry, a confused hum of many voices, a hurrying to and fro of human feet, and the streets which had appeared so shortly before gloomy and untenanted, were now alive with natives—men, women and children, old and young, rushing rapidly up the hill, to welcome the wanderer on his return, and to receive their lost one almost from the grave.

EXPEDITION TO PORT ESSINGTON

Ludwig Leichhardt

THE PRUSSIAN-BORN *scientific traveller Ludwig Leichhardt arrived in Sydney in February 1842. After spending two years examining the geology and botany of the Sydney and Hunter River regions and making lone overland journeys to Moreton Bay, he obtained support from a number of pastoralists and businessmen for an expedition from Brisbane to the settlement at Port Essington in what is now the Northern Territory. At the time there was much speculation about the nature of the country in the northern part of the continent. The party of ten men that left the last outpost on the Darling Downs on 1 October 1844 comprised the leader, Leichhardt, two acquaintances he had met on board ship, nineteen-year-old James Calvert and John Murphy, a hunchbacked youth of fifteen; John Gilbert, a naturalist employed by John Gould; William Phillips, a ticket-of-leave convict; two Aborigines, Harry Brown and Charlie Fisher; and a young squatter named Pemberton Hodgson and an American Negro named Caleb—the last two returned to the Darling Downs only six weeks after setting out. Stores and equipment were carried by a number of packhorses and draft bullocks.*

The great trek of more than four thousand kilometres took fourteen months and seventeen days, during which Leichhardt made important discoveries of major rivers and streams and much valuable pastoral country. It was an exhausted and haggard party that arrived at Port Essington on 17 December 1845, having long been given up for dead. The following extracts from Leichhardt's published account describe a typical day's routine halfway through their travels and the tragic encounter with Aborigines near the Mitchell River in which the naturalist Gilbert was speared and killed.

OUR TWO black companions, who until now had been like brothers—entertaining each other by the relation of their adventures to a late hour of the night; singing, chatting, laughing, and almost crying together; making common cause against me; Brown even following Charley into his banishment—quarrelled yesterday, about a mere trifle, so violently that it will be some time before they become friends again. When Mr Calvert and Brown returned yesterday to the camp, they remarked that they had not seen the waterfall of which Charley had spoken whilst at our last camp; upon which Charley insinuated that they had not seen it because they had galloped their horses past it. This accusation of galloping their horses irritated Brown, who was very fond and proud of his horse, and a serious quarrel of a rather ridiculous character ensued. Keeping myself entirely neutral, I soon found that I derived the greatest advantage from their animosity to each other, as each tried to outdo the other in readiness to serve me. Today, Charley, who was usually the last to rise in the morning, roused even me and brought the horses before our breakfast was ready. Brown's fondness for spinning a yarn will soon, however, induce him to put an end to this feud with his companion and countryman.

In the early part of our journey, one or other of our party kept a regular night watch, as well to guard us from any night attack of the natives as to look after our bullocks; but, latterly, this prudential measure, or rather its regularity, has been much neglected. Mr Roper's watch was handed from one to another in alphabetical rotation at given intervals, but no one thought of actually watching; it was, in fact, considered to be a mere matter of form. I did not check this, because there was nothing apparently to apprehend from the natives, who always evinced terror in meeting us; and all our communications with them have been accidental and never sought by them. On that point, therefore, I was not apprehensive; and, as to the bullocks, they were now accustomed to feed at large, and we seldom had any difficulty in recovering them in the morning.

I shall here particularise the routine of one of our days, which will serve as an example of all the rest. I usually rise when I hear the merry laugh of the

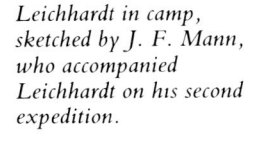

Leichhardt in camp, sketched by J. F. Mann, who accompanied Leichhardt on his second expedition.

Leichhardt's Aboriginal guides, Charlie Fisher and Harry Brown, drawn by Charles Rodius, a convict artist noted for his lithographs of Aborigines.

laughing-jackass (Dacelo gigantea), which, from its regularity, has not been unaptly named the settlers' clock; a loud cooee then rouses my companions—Brown to make tea, Mr Calvert to season the stew with salt and marjoram, and myself and the others to wash and to prepare our breakfast, which, for the party, consists of two pounds and a half of meat, stewed overnight; and to each a quart pot of tea. Mr Calvert then gives to each his portion, and, by the time this important duty is performed, Charley generally arrives with the horses, which are then prepared for their day's duty. After breakfast, Charley goes with John Murphy to fetch the bullocks, which are generally brought in a little after seven o'clock a.m. The work of loading follows, but this requires very little time now, our stock being much reduced; and at about a quarter to eight o'clock we move on, and continue travelling four hours, and, if possible, select a spot for our camp.

The Burdekin, which has befriended us so much by its direct course and constant stream, already for more than two degrees of latitude and two of longitude, has not always furnished us with the most convenient camps for procuring water. The banks generally formed steep slopes descending into a line of hollows parallel to the river, and thickly covered with a high, stiff grass; and then another steep bank covered with a thicket of drooping teatrees rose at the water's edge; and, if the descent into the bed of the river was more easy, the stream frequently was at the opposite side, and we had to walk several hundred yards over a broad sheet of loose sand, which filled our moccasins when going to wash. At present, the river is narrower, and I have chosen my camp twice on its dry sandy bed, under the shade of casuarinas and melaleucas, the stream being there comparatively easy of access, and not ten yards off. Many unpleasant remarks had been made by my companions at my choice of camping places; but, although I suffered as much inconvenience as they did, I bore it cheerfully, feeling thankful to Providence for the pure stream of water with which we were supplied every night. I had naturally a great antipathy against comfort-hunting and gourmandising, particularly on an expedition like ours, on which we started with the full expectation of suffering much privation, but which an Almighty Protector had not only allowed us to escape hitherto but had even supplied us frequently with an abundance—in proof of which we all got stronger and improved in health, although the continued riding had rather weakened our legs. This antipathy I expressed, often perhaps too harshly, which caused discontent; but on these occasions my patience was sorely tried.

I may, however, complete the picture of the day: as soon as the camp is pitched, and the horses and bullocks unloaded, we have all our alloted duties; to make the fire falls to my share; Brown's duty is to fetch water for tea; and Mr Calvert weighs out a pound and a half of flour for a fat cake, which is enjoyed more than any other meal; the large teapot being empty, Mr Calvert weighs out two and a half pounds of dry meat to be stewed for our late dinner; and during the afternoon everyone follows his own pursuits, such as washing and mending clothes, repairing saddles, pack-saddles, and packs; my occupation is to write my log and lay down my route, or make an excursion in the vicinity of the camp to botanise, etc., or ride out reconnoitring. My companions also write down their remarks, and wander about gathering seeds or looking for curious pebbles. Mr Gilbert takes his gun to shoot birds. A loud cooee again unites us towards sunset round our tablecloth; and, whilst enjoying our meals, the subject of the day's journey, the past, the present, and the future, by turns engage our attention or furnish matter for conversation and remark, according to the respective humour of the parties. Many circumstances have conspired to make me strangely taciturn, and I am now scarcely pleased even with the chatting humour of my youngest companion, whose spirits, instead of flagging, have become more buoyant and lively than ever. I consider it, however, my invariable duty to give every information I can, whenever my companions inquire or shew a desire to learn, and I am happy to find that they are desirous of making themselves familiar with the objects of nature by which they are surrounded, and of understanding their mutual relations. Mr Roper is of a more silent disposition; Mr Calvert likes to speak, and has a good stock of 'small talk' with which he

Leichhardt's route on his successful journey from the Darling Downs to Port Essington between October 1844 and December 1845.

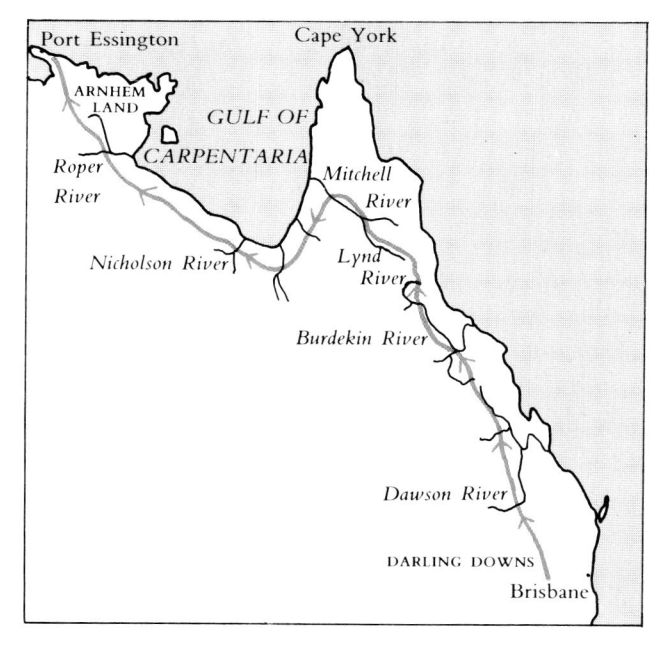

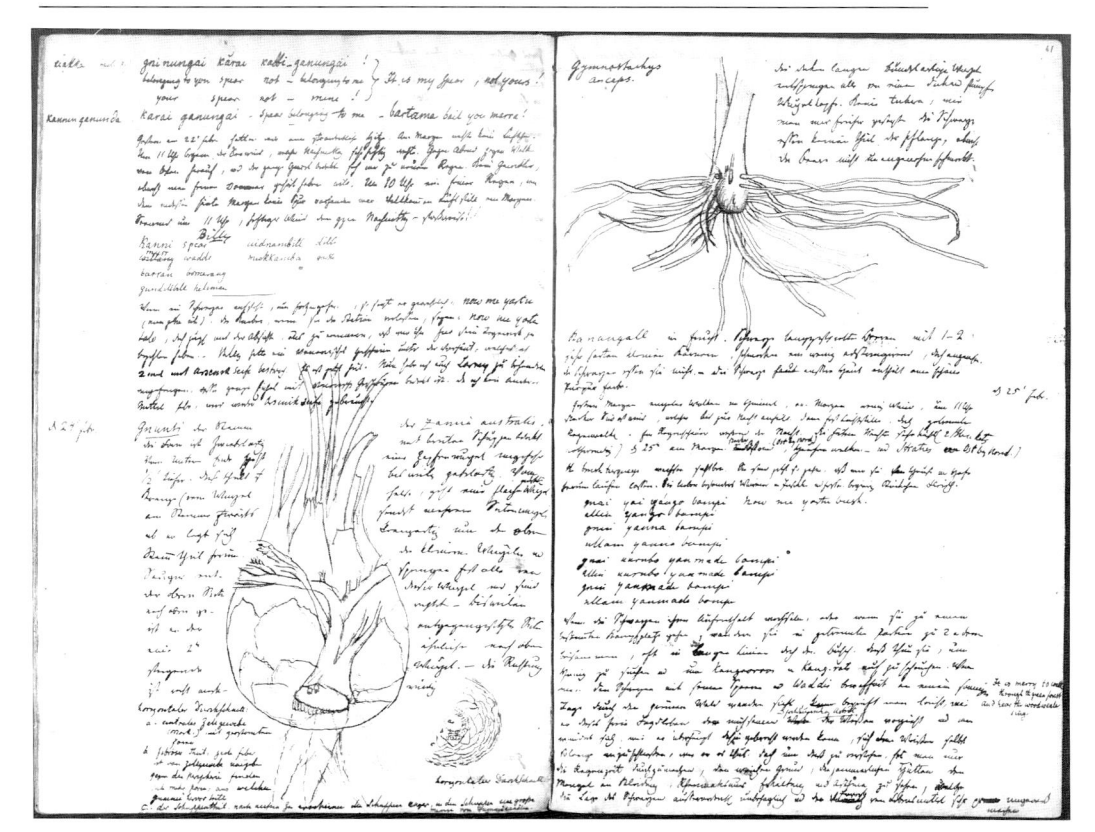

Pages from Leichhardt's notebook and diary, written in old-style Gothic German script, which show his consuming interest in botany.

often enlivens our dinners; he is in that respect an excellent companion, being full of jokes and stories, which, though old and sometimes quaint, are always pure, and serve the more to exhilarate the party. Mr Gilbert has travelled much, and consequently has a rich store of *impressions de voyage*: his conversation is generally very pleasing and instructive in describing the character of countries he has seen and the manners and customs of the people he has known. He is well informed in Australian ornithology.

As night approaches, we retire to our beds. The two blackfellows and myself spread out each our own under the canopy of heaven, whilst Messrs Roper, Calvert, Gilbert, Murphy, and Phillips have their tents. Mr Calvert entertains Roper with his conversation; John amuses Gilbert; Brown tunes up his corroborri songs, in which Charley, until their late quarrel, generally joined. Brown sings well, and his melodious plaintive voice lulls me to sleep when otherwise I am not disposed. Mr Phillips is rather singular in his habits; he erects his tent generally at a distance from the rest, under a shady tree, or in a green bower of shrubs, where he makes himself as comfortable as the place will allow by spreading branches and grass under his couch and covering his tent with them, to keep it shady and cool, and even planting lilies in blossom (*Crinum*) before his tent, to enjoy their sight during the short time of our stay. As the night advances, the blackfellows' songs die away; the chatting tongue of Murphy ceases, after having lulled Mr Gilbert to sleep; and at last even Mr Calvert is silent, as Roper's short answers became few and far between. The neighing of the tethered horse, the distant tinkling of the bell, or the occasional cry of night-birds, alone interrupt the silence of our camp. The fire, which was bright as long as the corroborri songster kept it stirred, gradually gets dull, and smoulders slowly under the large pot in which our meat is simmering; and the bright constellations of heaven pass unheeded over the heads of the dreaming wanderers of the wilderness, until the summons of the laughing jackass recalls them to the business of the coming day.

A circumstance occurred today which gave me much concern, as it showed that the natives of this part were not so amicably disposed towards us as those we had hitherto met: whilst Charley and Brown were in search of game in the vicinity of our camp, they observed a native sneaking up to our bullocks, evidently with the intention of driving them towards a party of his black companions, who with poised spears were waiting to receive them. Upon detecting this manœuvre, Charley and his companion hurried forward to prevent their being driven away, then the native gave the alarm, and all took to their heels, with the exception of a lame fellow, who endeavoured to persuade his friends to stand and fight. Charley, however, fired his gun, which had the intended effect of frightening them; for they deserted their camp, which was three hundred yards from ours, in a great hurry, leaving, among other articles, a small net full of potatoes, which Charley afterwards picked up. The gins had previously retired; a proof that mischief was intended.

28 June. We crossed the creek, near which we had encamped, and travelled about nine miles west, over a most beautifully varied country of plains, of forest land, and chains of lagoons. We crossed a large creek or river, which I believed to be the main branch of the Nassau. It was well supplied with waterholes, but there was no stream. Loose clayey sandstone cropped out in its bed, and also in the gullies which joined it. A small myrtle tree with smooth bark, and a leafless tree resembling the casuarina, grew plentifully on its banks. We saw smoke rising in every direction, which showed how thickly the country was inhabited. Near the lagoons we frequently noticed bare spots of a circular form, about twelve or fifteen feet in diameter, round each of which was a belt of ten, twelve, or more fireplaces, separated from each other by only a few feet. It seems that the natives usually sit within the circle of fires; but it is difficult to know whether it belonged to a family, or whether each fire had an independent proprietor. Along the Lynd and Mitchell, the natives made their fires generally in heaps of stones, which served as ovens for cooking their victuals. Bones of kangaroos and wallabies, and heaps of mussel shells, were commonly seen in their camps; but fish bones were very rarely observed. It was very different, however, when we travelled round the head, and along the western side, of the gulf; for fish seemed there to form the principal food of the natives.

At the end of our stage, we came to a chain of shallow lagoons, which were slightly connected by a hollow. Many of them were dry; and fearing that, if we proceeded much farther, we should not find water, I encamped on one of them, containing a shallow pool; it was surrounded by a narrow belt of small teatrees, with stiff broad lanceolate leaves. As the water occupied only the lower part of this basin, I deposited our luggage in the upper part. Mr Roper and Mr Calvert made their tent within the belt of trees, with its

'We crossed the creek, near which we had encamped, and travelled about nine miles west, over a most beautifully varied country of plains, of forest land, and chains of lagoons.'

opening towards the packs; whilst Mr Gilbert and Murphy constructed theirs amongst the little trees, with its entrance from the camp. Mr Phillips's was, as usual, far from the others, and at the opposite side of the water. Our fireplace was made outside of the trees, on the banks. Brown had shot six *Leptotarsis eytoni* (whistling ducks) and four teals, which gave us a good dinner, during which the principal topic of conversation was our probable distance from the sea coast, as it was here that we first found broken seashells, of the genus *Cytherea*. After dinner, Messrs Roper and Calvert retired to their tent, and Mr Gilbert, John, and Brown were plaiting palm leaves to make a hat, and I stood musing near their fireplace, looking at their work, and occasionally joining in their conversation. Mr Gilbert was congratulating himself upon having succeeded in learning to plait; and, when he had nearly completed a yard, he retired with John to their tent. This was about seven o'clock; and I stretched myself upon the ground as usual, at a little distance from the fire, and fell into a doze, from which I was suddenly roused by a loud noise and a call for help from Calvert and Roper. Natives had suddenly attacked us. They had doubtless watched our movements during the afternoon and marked the position of the different tents and, as soon as it was dark, sneaked upon us and threw a shower of spears at the tents of Calvert, Roper, and Gilbert, and a few at that of Phillips, and also one or two towards the fire. Charley and Brown called for caps, which I hastened to find, and, as soon as they were provided, they discharged their guns into the crowd of the natives, who instantly fled, leaving Roper and Calvert pierced with several spears, and severely beaten by their waddies. Several of these spears were barbed and could not be extracted without difficulty. I had to force one through the arm of Roper to break off the barb; and to cut another out of the groin of Mr Calvert. John Murphy had succeeded in getting out of the tent and concealing himself behind a tree, whence he fired at the natives, and severely wounded one of them, before

'Peak Range from the north-west', an illustration from Leichhardt's *Journal of an Overland Expedition in Australia from Moreton Bay to Port Essington.*

Brown had discharged his gun. Not seeing Mr Gilbert, I asked for him, when Charley told me that our unfortunate companion was no more! He had come out of his tent with his gun, shot, and powder, and handed them to him, when he instantly dropped down dead. Upon receiving this afflicting intelligence, I hastened to the spot, and found Charley's account too true. He was lying on the ground at a little distance from our fire, and, upon examining him, I soon found, to my sorrow, that every sign of life had disappeared. The body was, however, still warm, and I opened the veins of both arms, as well as the temporal artery, but in vain; the stream of life had stopped, and he was numbered with the dead. As soon as we recovered from the panic into which we were thrown by this fatal event, every precaution was taken to prevent another surprise; we watched through the night, and extinguished our fires to conceal our individual position from the natives.

A strong wind blew from the southward, which made the night air distressingly cold; it seemed as if the wind blew through our bodies. Under all the circumstances that had happened, we passed an anxious night, in a state of most painful suspense as to the fate of our still surviving companions. Mr Roper had received two or three spear wounds in the scalp of his head;

Before setting out on his expedition to Port Essington, Leichhardt spent some time at Durandur station in the upper Brisbane Valley, where he pursued his botanical investigations (becoming the first scientist to describe the macadamia tree) and studied the local Aborigines. In his diary he sketched and noted the physical measurements of 'Paddy, a Badda man on Durandur station'.

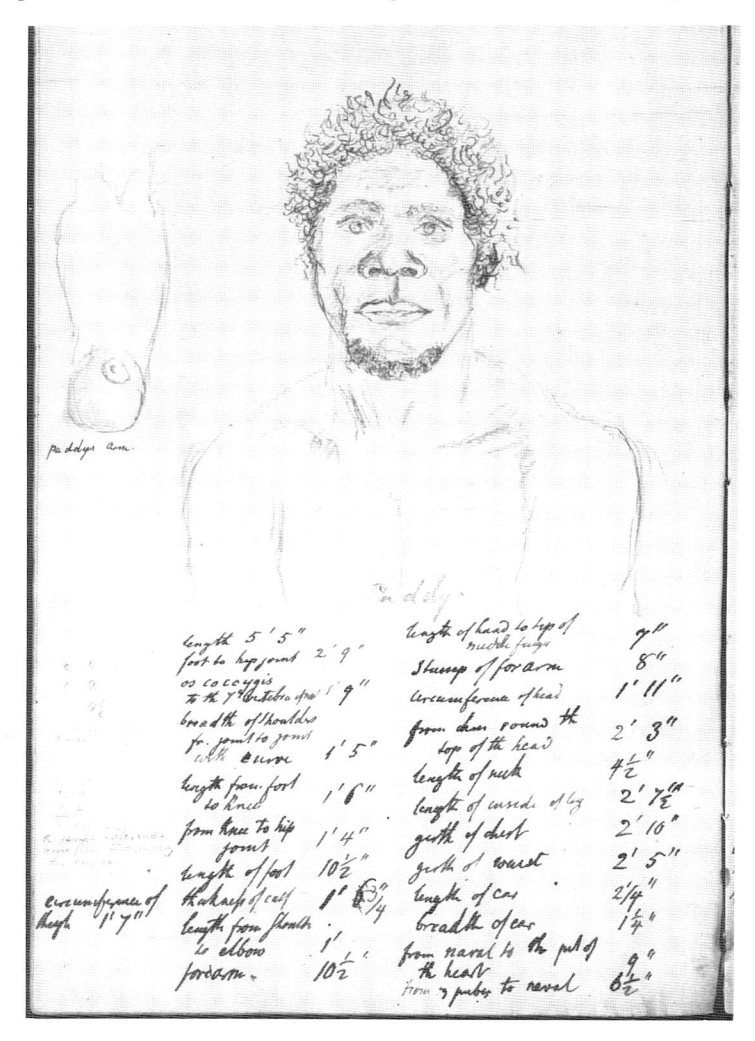

one spear had passed through his left arm, another into his cheek below the jugal bone, and penetrated the orbit, and injured the optic nerve, and another in his loins, besides a heavy blow on the shoulder. Mr Calvert had received several severe blows from a waddy; one on the nose which had crushed the nasal bones; one on the elbow, and another on the back of his hand; besides which, a barbed spear had entered his groin; and another into his knee. As may be readily imagined, both suffered great pain and were scarcely able to move. The spear that terminated poor Gilbert's existence had entered the chest, between the clavicle and the neck, but made so small a wound that for some time I was unable to detect it. From the direction of the wound, he had probably received the spear when stooping to leave his tent.

The dawning of the next morning, the 29th, was gladly welcomed, and I proceeded to examine and dress the wounds of my companions, more carefully than I had been able to do in the darkness of the night.

Very early in the morning we heard the cooees of the natives, who seemed wailing, as if one of their number was either killed or severely wounded: for we found stains of blood on their tracks. They disappeared, however, very soon, for, on reconnoitring about the place, I saw nothing of them. I interred the body of our ill-fated companion in the afternoon, and read the funeral service of the English Church over him. A large fire was afterwards made over the grave, to prevent the natives from detecting and disinterring the body. Our cattle and horses fortunately had not been molested.

The cold wind from the southward continued the whole day; at night it fell calm, and continued so until the morning of 30 June, when a strong easterly wind set in, which afterwards veered round to the north-west.

Calvert and Roper recovered wonderfully, considering the severe injuries they had received; and the wound which I feared as being the most dangerous promised with care and patience to do well. As it was hazardous to remain long at the place, for the natives might return in greater numbers, and repeat their attack, as well on ourselves as the cattle, I determined to proceed, or at least to try if my wounded companions could endure to be removed on horseback. In a case like this, where the lives of the whole party were concerned, it was out of the question to attend only to the individual feelings and wishes of the patients; I felt for their position to the fullest extent that it was possible for one to feel towards his fellow creatures so situated; but I had equal claims on my attention. I had to look exclusively to the state of their wounds, and to the consequences of the daily journey on their constitutions; to judge if we could proceed or ought to stop; and I had reason to expect, or at least was sanguine enough to hope, that although the temporary feelings of acute pain might make them discontented with my arrangements, sober reflection at the end of our journey would induce them to do me justice.

The constant attention which they required, and the increased work which fell to the share of our reduced number, had scarcely allowed me time to reflect upon the melancholy accident which had befallen us, and the ill-timed death of our unfortunate companion. All our energies were roused, we found ourselves in danger, and, as was absolutely necessary, we strained every nerve to extricate ourselves from it: but I was well aware that the more coolly we went to work, the better we should succeed.

> *'All our energies were roused, we found ourselves in danger, and, as was absolutely necessary, we strained every nerve to extricate ourselves from it: but I was well aware that the more coolly we went to work, the better we should succeed.'*

TRAVELLING THE GREAT CIRCLE ROUTE

Annie Henning

'We lunched again in Mr Gray's room; we get a better lunch, ham and tongue, intead of cheese, and it makes a change being there and it helps to fill up the morning which passes rather wearily sometimes.'

AFTER GOLD *was discovered in Victoria in the 1850s, tens of thousands of people in Britain and Europe were anxious to get to Australia as quickly as possible, before the gold was worked out. Shipping companies vied with one another to cut travelling time. Fast clipper ships were put into service, and a new route was devised—a route that followed as closely as practicable a 'great circle' on the earth's surface. While this cut travelling time by many days, it meant sailing much farther south than usual, beyond the roaring forties into the fifties as far as icebergs would allow. It meant also that no land would be seen from the time the ship left the Cape Verde Islands in the North Atlantic until it entered Bass Strait. Comfort was sacrificed for speed, and emigrants of all classes suffered the discomfort caused by the severe weather and cramped conditions and the boredom caused by a lack of things to do on the long, unbroken journey. Among the emigrants of the 1850s were members of the Henning family. Rachel Henning was to become posthumously famous for her sensitive and revealing letters to her family, which were published in 1952. She made the voyage to Australia in the* Calcutta *with her sister Amy in 1854. But the year before, another sister, Annie, and her brother, Biddulph, made the trip in the* Great Britain, *a pioneer propeller-driven steamship which also carried sail. The following extract from Annie's journal of the voyage begins when the ship is deep in the South Atlantic, about midway between the Cape of Good Hope and Cape Horn.*

THURSDAY, 15 SEPTEMBER, *lat. 33°44′S, long. 29°22′W.* We had a walk after breakfast and it was fortunate, for the rain commenced at eleven and did not cease the whole day. We lunched again in Mr Gray's room; we get a better lunch, ham and tongue, instead of cheese, and it makes a change being there and it helps to fill up the morning which passes rather wearily sometimes. All the afternoon I was busily engaged in mending my afternoon dress which I tore to pieces yesterday evening.

Friday, 16 September, lat. 37°26′S, long. 27°20′W. It rained incessantly all day so that we were not able to get out. There are numbers of birds that follow the ship now. They come from the Cape (three thousand miles off) and are often five months at a time on the water without seeing land. They look exceedingly pretty. There are Cape hens, Cape pigeons and a few albatrosses—the Ancient Mariner's birds—I have seen but one yet, and that a small one.

Saturday, 17 September, lat. 41°16′S, long. 24°40′W. Still too wet to go out and the wind very high, but against us; indeed the wind has not been really favourable since we have been out, and we have gone considerably out of our course in consequence.

I read the fortune-telling cards to two different audiences yesterday, and this evening, between dinner and tea. They afforded great amusement and were wonderfully appreciated. Chiefly, I fear however, from the utter lack of anything to do.

After tea Mr Stevens gave us some songs. It was exceptionally rough, everything rolling about in the saloon, so that it was almost impossible to keep one's seat, much more to walk. About ten one of the rudder chains broke but they set it to rights again without any ill consequences. It was a tremendous night, the wind being very high and dead against us so that the ship rolled and lurched awfully. No one could sleep; it was as much as we could do to keep in our berths. Many of the passengers were terribly frightened and when a worse sea than usual struck the ship it made it quiver all through. There were such lamentations to be heard.

Sunday, 18 September, lat. 44°36′S, long. 21°34′W. The sea was not come down and it was a difficult matter to keep the breakfast things on the table. It was expected there would be no service but the Captain was determined to have it and as Mr Savigny was ill (of course), he read it himself. We were very glad. The Captain reads very nicely and his printed sermons are as good or better than Mr S.'s manuscript ones.

After morning service some of the ladies went on deck. It was difficult to walk but well worth bearing the wind and cold for the sake of the magnificent sea we saw. The waves sometimes as high as the quarterdeck. After tea a wave struck the ship, burst in two of the porthole windows and flooded the cabins. Luckily none of ours were among the number.

The 3,500-ton auxiliary steamer Great Britain. *For the ship's first two voyages to Australia (Annie Henning was on the second), Captain B. R. Matthews was in command and Lieutenant John Gray, RNR, was first officer. Gray became the ship's commander in 1854 and remained so until 1868.*

The great circle route. The earth being a sphere, the shortest distance between two points on its surface is the arc of the 'great circle' (which divides the earth into two halves) connecting them. As the great circle from Liverpool to Melbourne crosses the Antarctic continent, it was impossible for ships to follow it exactly, but they went as far south as their masters dared.

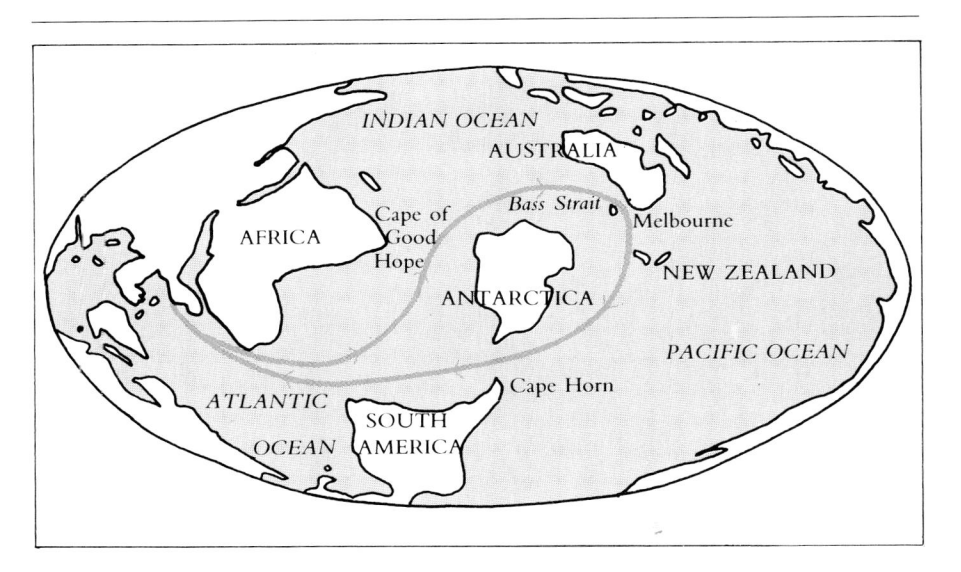

Monday, 19 September, lat. 47°33′S, long. 17°30′W. The last was a wretched night and scarcely anyone slept a wink, we were rolling about so. I believe there was no damage, however, unless of losing part of the masts from rolling. It is extremely cold now and everyone has put on winter dresses.

After breakfast it was calmer and we walked on the deck until lunch. Took another walk after dinner in the dusk with Mr Gray and Captain Matthews. A storm of snow came on and drove us down.

There was an engagement today between two of the passengers, a Mr Hutchinson and Miss Mary Fitzgerald, the youngest and prettiest of the two sisters. Mr Hutchinson is a young man from the fore saloon, good looking and about twenty. He sings well and began his acquaintance with his intended by singing duets together. Miss Fitzgerald went twenty-one yesterday. She is going out with her sister to find situations as governesses in Sydney. They are Irish and their father lost, or squandered away, a fortune: there are fourteen of them at home and these are the two eldest. They both play and sing well. The marriage is not to take place yet as Mr Hutchinson has no fortune. They seem very fond of each others and the circumstance is an advantage in every way as it gives the whole ship's company something to talk about.

Tuesday, 20 September, lat. 48°19′S, long. 13°29′W. Several of the passengers are ill. Mrs McDermot, Miss Smythe's sister for one, and a Dutchman, Mr Pit, with rheumatic fever. It was rather a quieter night and we all slept better, though not all first rate even now.

Walked on deck after breakfast, took a navigation lesson with Mr Gray after lunch, then had another walk, and again from dinner to tea without stopping, a space of two hours. The whole of our table, almost, took a walk then, two and two, round and round the deck and we had great fun. The weather is so cold that walking is the only way to keep oneself warm. It is very draughty everywhere but in the saloon, which they warm with pipes filled with steam, running along under the tables. They are very comfortable to put your feet on when not too hot, but make a bad smell of sulphur.

One of the gentlemen, Mr Bowdon, kept a birthday in the smoking room this evening and gave punch to all the gentlemen. He sent in mulled port to the ladies, which was very acceptable this cold weather.

I will just give the names and places of our table as we sit, now that it has come into my head.

Mr Laing

Miss Henning	Miss Smythe
Mr Forbes	Mr Morley
Captain McDonald	Mr Hoole
Mr Sibbald	Mr Henning
Mr Higginbotham	Miss White
(Mr Smith)	Mr Woodrup
(Mr Bowdon)	Mr Foster

The last two are only occasional visitors.

Mr Laing is a young Scotchman, very handsome and Supercargo of the vessel. Mr Sibbald is likewise a Scotchman, young and pleasant, he is going out to his mother in Melbourne. Mr Forbes is Scotch also, going into the Army in two years and travelling now for his pleasure. He is nineteen and a wonderful talker, been in Germany and France all his life, very amusing but quite a boy in many things and gets very much teased.

Mr Higginbotham is come out by the *Great Britain* for a change and

An advertisement for the Great Britain's voyage of 15 February 1861. Annie Henning and her brother, as first-class passengers, in the after saloon, paid seventy guineas each for their passages in 1852.

returns by her. He used to get very tipsy but has been better lately, having taken to cards instead. Mr Morley is from Yorkshire, going out I believe principally for pleasure. Mr Hoole is going to set up some mills near Sydney; he is very handsome—and agreeable when not seasick, as generally is the case.

Miss White is Captain Matthews's niece. Mr Woodrup is nephew to Mr Foster who has come out merely to establish him in business. They are both from Stockport and consequently what are called 'Manchester Men', although very pleasant and all that. With this exception all at our table are really *gentlemen*, as far as I can judge at least.

Wednesday, 21 September, lat. 49°35′S, long. 7°6′W. Were fortunate enough to have a quiet and consequently good night which was a great refreshment. Pouring with rain in the morning so no one could go out on deck. There is a great deal of wind but it is all in our favour so we are going at a rate of fifteen knots, the most we have made yet.

Commenced rolling a good deal after breakfast and one of the blocks belonging to the rudder gave way. They managed to put it right again before long—had it been in the night it might have been very dangerous with so much wind as we have now, as for a time they could not guide the ship. It was excessively cold and rained all day. Some of us played consequences in the afternoon before dinner. After dinner the gentlemen went on deck. It was so slippery from the damp that several fell down and one (Mr Booth) injured himself considerably.

The day before yesterday, Mr Laing, our Supercargo, saw someone throw a sandwich overboard. He was angry since the ship's provisions were limited, so said there should be no more cut for supper. There was a regular insurrection among the ladies and, as might be expected, Mr Laing was so beset that he was obliged to give in and we had them again tonight, but under limitations: no one being allowed more than three, which I consider an ample supply but some want five or six. The children are not allowed any.

Thursday, 22 September, lat. 50°41′S, long. 1°29′W. A sunny frosty day, reminding one of a bright December day in England. Very pleasant for walking and we were on deck until eleven, then to Mr Gray's room for a lesson, after which we had lunch there with him, Mr Laing and the Doctor.

I mended my dress after dinner, an occupation one or other of the ladies are continually engaged in. The nails in the hen coops on deck catch them so. Mr Forbes declared that one of the *ducks* caught hold of mine and tore it, but I did not believe that or indeed anything else that he says.

We walked on deck again after dinner to tea; the stars came out very brightly and it was pleasant though cold. We found Dr Sicler on deck and made him promise to play for us after tea, so he came to tea and gave us some beautiful music.

There are great complaints that the music room is always occupied by the lovers, Mr Hutchinson and Miss Fitzgerald, to the exclusion of anyone else, as even if they have not the door shut, no one likes to intrude upon them. Except Mr Forbes who insisted on going in yesterday and was forcibly withdrawn by the coat-tails.

Friday, 23 September, lat. 50°47′S, long. 4°29′E. We were all awakened at a quarter to six by a noise on deck, occasioned by the rudder getting out of order for the *fourth* time. This time it was one of the bolts that gave way. All the sails were taken in directly but not before one of the studding sails had taken *itself* in without assistance.

On coming down to breakfast found the Captain very angry about it—he says there must have been great neglect somewhere, that the vessel was not properly looked to before leaving Liverpool. It seems the rudder is not strong enough, unless the steam is on, to break the force of the waves, as each time that an accident has happened to it the steam has been stopped. They are not going to stop it again, which will be but wise.

It snowed a great part of the morning and we had icicles brought down from the deck. It was so cold we did not walk and I spent the morning in the music room listening to Miss Middleton, who plays very nicely.

Saturday, 24 September, lat. 50°36′S, long. 11°59′E. Went on deck in the morning, very cold and frosty. After lunch went for my lesson into Mr Gray's room. Mrs McDermot is ill and Miss Smythe is obliged to be with her, so she could not come. We went on deck after dinner, but after nearly breaking our legs thrice or four times, to say nothing of being almost blown over the side, were obliged to retreat again. It was a rough evening and a great deal of crockery was broken.

Sunday, 25 September, lat. 50°36′S, long. 18°59′E. Almost all the passengers have had colds from going out of the heated saloon into the draughty passages below. The attendance both at service and table was consequently very small this morning but Mr Savigny preached us a beautiful sermon.

Everyone went on deck, after lunch and again between dinner and tea, and walked as usual round the deck in The Grand Circle as we call it—two by two—this way of walking is great fun and prevents any stoppages from people running foul of each other. The noise is very great in the saloon, however, for those who are foolish enough to stay there. It sounds like a regiment of soldiers marching overhead.

At dinner today one of the Sunday visitors—an officer—took too much wine and was slightly excited in consequence. He was on the point of giving the table an impromptu song when we retreated. The other gentlemen were very much scandalised and say he is not to come again.

Miss White 'went out to dinner' at another table. Miss Smythe 'went out' to tea yesterday, and I was invited out tonight but I declined. It is rather amusing though to change sometimes.

Monday, 26 September, lat. 51...S, long. 25°5′E. Snowing as usual in the morning. Some of the gentlemen put up a notice to the effect that they had ascertained by astronomical calculations that Friday next, 30 September, answers in these latitudes to 14 February in England and that they have consequently appointed that day to be Saint Valentine's. The letters are all to be delivered at breakfast on that day and I suppose we shall have some fun.

After lunch we went in to help Mr Gray prick off our course from the day we left England, on a new chart.

'The late severe gales' have so damaged our crockery lately that at dinner we had to drink our water out of champagne glasses and we expect to have tea cups introduced in a day or two.

> 'Everyone went on deck, after lunch and again between dinner and tea, and walked as usual round the deck in The Grand Circle as we call it—two by two—this way of walking is great fun and prevents any stoppages from people running foul of each other.'

In the evening Miss Smythe and I played whist with Mr Gray and Mr Morley. Biddulph was playing with others. We had some music afterwards, not for the love of it, but for the sake of driving Miss Fitzgerald and Mr Hutchinson out of the room which they had occupied the whole day to the great indignation of everyone.

The sea was most beautiful this evening, rising in great mountains and looking as if it would break over the stern every moment. There were a great many porpoise to be seen this morning.

Tuesday, 27 September, lat. 51°58'S, long. 32°30'E. It was snowing all the morning so much that we could not go on deck. We went in to the Purser's room and to the bar to see all that was to be seen, for lack of other amusement. It is just above the engine room and is very dirty and cold there.

After lunch we, that is Miss Smythe and I, went to Mr Gray's room. I had just finished my lesson and we were talking, when we heard a great noise overhead. Mr Gray jumped up and ran on deck. We waited in quiet anxiety to know what it was. There was not a voice to be heard, only a great trampling of feet above us at the stern of the vessel. Mr Gray came down again in less than a quarter of an hour and said they had lost a man overboard.

He was on the main topgallant yard arm with another man when he was struck by one end of the sail; his companion held on but he lost his balance and fell straight into the sea. They cut down a lifebuoy and threw it over to him, but he had not reached it when last they saw him and perhaps it was best not, for it could only have kept him alive for an hour or two longer and there was no chance of his being saved or picked up by another vessel as few or none come into these latitudes. There was most unfortunately a strong breeze and the ship was going very quickly at the time (twelve knots) so that they could not lower a boat without stopping her, and by the time this could be done we should have been at least six miles off.

I suppose the Captain was right in at all events he was more likely to know than the passengers. But most of *them* thought that something ought at least to have been *tried* to save the man. It seemed so dreadful to sail on leaving him to perish. He was out of sight in little more than five minutes, and they said he must have been insensible before reaching the water, from the height the fell from.

Mr Gray was terribly grieved about it. The poor man was a countryman of his and indeed came from the same place (one of the Shetland Isles) but he felt it most on account of its being at his persuasion that Ramsay came on board the *Great Britain* this voyage instead of sailing with a small vessel as he first intended. He was but twenty-five and has a father and sister living whom he supported almost entirely.

I had a narrow escape the same afternoon. It was snowing very hard and, on leaving Mr Gray's room Miss Smythe and I went down the smoking room stairs which are close. The stairs were very slippery and the ship gave a lurch just as I put my foot on the first of them. As I had my hands full I could not save myself and fell straight from the top to the bottom where, by some marvellous means, I lighted on my feet with no other injury than a strained back, and not much of that. I fully expected to break my leg at least.

The dinner today was a very silent and gloomy one on account of what

A group of Henning family and friends photographed in later years in Australia. Annie (Mrs George Hedgeland) is in the middle, sitting, third from left.

had just happened; most people felt it very much. There were some gentlemen, however, who were playing cards at the time the man fell overboard; they ran on deck to see what was the matter and then came down again, took off their hats, and quietly went on with their game.

Wednesday, 28 September, lat. 54°8′S, long. 37°12′E. On coming into the saloon this morning we found there was an iceberg in sight. It was a small one and a good way off, so we could see little beyond a white mass (more like a small cloud than anything else) shining in the sun. There had been a great deal of snow during the night so the gentlemen amused themselves by throwing snowballs.

There was a subscription got up after breakfast for the father of poor Ramsay and they collected altogether upwards of fifty pounds. We hear that for the last few days before the accident he had been very nervous about going up to the masthead or on the rigging; he told some of the other sailors so but, very foolishly, not any of the officers or he would not have been sent aloft again. Mr Gray showed me a hymn that was found in his pocket this morning.

We went on deck a little between dinner and tea. It was a rough night and very dark.

Thursday, 29 September, lat. 52°7′S, long. 44°12′E. Two whirlwinds passed the ship this morning at a little distance, throwing up water like a water spout. If they had come right in our course it would have been very dangerous as we might in that case have lost both sails and masts, or part of the latter at least.

Everyone was writing valentines all the morning and evening. After lunch we went to Mr Gray's room.

'Sketches on board an emigrant ship', an illustration from the Illustrated Australian News *of 24 March 1875.*

Friday, 30 September, lat. 53°43′S, long. 47°58′E. It was so dark when we got up at half past eight that I could not believe it was more than six. The sea was rolling very much, the wind making a great noise in the sails, and a thick snow storm so that they could not see the length of the ship forward on deck. In short it was a regular gale, the first we have had and I hope the last. The deadlights were drawn over all the windows and everyone rather out of spirits; indeed for a wonder the card playing was stopped. The wind was dead against us so that instead of keeping on our course we were running due south right among the icebergs and with such thick weather that we might run into one before it was seen almost, and a very poor chance we should have then.

However, the weather cleared and the wind shifted a little by the middle of the day so that they were able to turn the ship towards the east again. Everyone on board is very dissatisfied with coming so far south for the sake of saving four days and they all note this 'circular sailing' a failure, saying (and I think very truly) that for the little advantage in point of time gained it is hardly worth while to risk the lives of all the passengers, besides bringing us down into these cold latitudes, giving nearly everyone colds and influenza if nothing worse. The Captain himself is sorry for it, I believe, and will change her course as soon as the wind allows.

The valentines were delivered after lunch; almost everyone had one and most of the ladies four or five. The weather was much calmer by dinner time so that we were able to enjoy them and they made great fun. After dinner Miss Smythe, I, Biddulph and Mr Morley had a game of whist.

Saturday, 1 October, lat. 52°3'S, long. 52°4'E. We had an exceedingly rough night, scarcely anyone slept an hour. I am so accustomed to it, however, that I do not think that I should have been awake but for a gathering on my finger which gives me too much pain to sleep. I ran a splinter of wood into it the other day and in consequence of the cold weather it has gathered. We had a very small muster at breakfast today; half the people are ill.

Monday, 3 October. Dr Sicler came in to play after tea and Mr A. kept his birthday by giving an extra punch night in the smoking room for gentlemen, sending in negus to the ladies.

The Jews had a grand assembly, both tonight and yesterday evening, in one of the boudoirs, to celebrate the commencement of their year—this day being, according to them, the anniversary of the Creation.

One of the card players won seventy pounds tonight in less than two hours. There are only half a dozen who play high, and I am sure I do not know how they can afford it. Many of the gentlemen do not play at all and scarcely any for any amount of money.

Tuesday, 4 October, lat. 51°20'S, long. 70°11'E. Snowing again all day. We had been in hopes of seeing Kerguelen Island but have gone too far south for it. I believe the *Great Britain* is the first steamer that has been in these latitudes and I should hope for the comfort and health of the passengers, she will be the last. Half the sailors are laid up for cold or fatigue consequent on the bad weather we have had down here. They say that if they had had an idea we were coming so far south, they would never have engaged.

After lunch today a court martial was held on a sailor who has been misconducting himself for a long time and brought his crimes to a climax yesterday by insulting a lady and kicking one of the officers. The court was held in the smoking room and the Captain and all the officers and midshipmen attended, in their uniforms with swords on, which report says they did not very well know what to do with, but got them continually hitched between their legs and among the benches, thereby creating much confusion. The prisoner was sentenced to receive twelve lashes at six o'clock tomorrow morning.

The officers all dined in the saloon after the trial. We had music after dinner for it was too wet to go on deck and after tea Captain Matthews sang for the amusement of the ladies.

Wednesday, 5 October, lat. 51°8'S, long. 76°21'E. Many of the gentlemen got up at six o'clock this morning to see the man flogged, but I am glad to say they were disappointed, for after he had been tied up to the mast and sufficiently frightened, he was let off at the intercession of Captain Snell. Of course this was all arranged with Captain Matthews beforehand and he was only brought up at all to save appearances with the sailors. Snowing again all the morning.

RIVERBOAT RACE ON THE MURRAY

Ian Mudie
James Allen

FOR EIGHTY YEARS *from the 1850s, the riverboat trade on the Murray-Darling-Murrumbidgee system played an important and colourful part in Australian life. The first steamboat to take to the waters of the Murray was William and Thomas Randell's* Mary Ann, *a wooden vessel 16.8 metres long that the Randells built themselves. They made an unsuccessful voyage in it during the low-water season in March 1853, navigating from Goolwa, near the Murray mouth, to an uncrossable sand bar some three hundred kilometres upriver. The following August, after the annual rise of the Murray, they set off again from Noa-No, near present-day Mannum, taking a small cargo of stores to sell to settlers on the banks of the river. Their destination was Swan Hill, or as far as they could get.*

Meanwhile, another man with ideas of navigating the Murray, Francis Cadell, had had a steamboat built in Sydney. His vessel, the Lady Augusta, *was bigger and faster than the* Mary Ann; *thirty-two metres long, it was built to accommodate sixteen first-class and eight second-class passengers. It was brought round the coast from Sydney and arrived at Goolwa on 16 August, the day after the* Mary Ann *left Noa-No. Nine days later, with the barge* Eureka *lashed alongside, the* Lady Augusta *set out in pursuit of the* Mary Ann. *The South Australian government had offered a bonus of two thousand pounds each for the first two vessels of certain specifications to navigate the Murray to the junction of the Darling. However, neither the* Mary Ann *nor the* Lady Augusta *met these specifications. In his book* Riverboats, *Ian Mudie describes what developed into a race between the two steamers and a degree of enmity between their owners, William and Thomas Randell and Francis Cadell.*

WILLIAM AND TOM took with them an engine-driver, two 'knockabout hands', and a passenger William referred to as a 'knockabout parson'.

William's recollections of the voyage were still vivid fifty years later:

> Of course we did not know our way a bit—we were like blind men in the dark. Every evening we ran alongside the bank and made fast to a tree for the night. There was plenty of game to be had up the river, and the settlers at every station greeted us with open-handed hospitality. They used to send fresh meat down to the boat, half a bullock, or a few sheep. Of course they were pleased to see us, because the fact that we proved the river navigable increased the

The Lady Augusta *with the barge* Eureka *lashed alongside.*

value of their stations considerably. There was little incident on that trip. The blacks we met were not hostile, and became quite friendly when we gave them some flour, sugar, or tobacco. At that time there were plenty of snags in the river, and we had to keep a constant look-out for them. They were sticking out in ridges in some places like a regiment of soldiers.

The Randells travelled slowly, feeling their way carefully along the river, even though there was far more water than there had been on their previous voyage. When they came to the sand bar that had turned them back before, they found there was now between twenty and thirty feet where there had earlier been only three.

On 3 September the *Mary Ann* arrived at the Darling Junction—and so reached the point where, had she been eligible, she would have qualified for the first of the two government bonuses of two thousand pounds. Eleven days later, 770 miles from the sea, Randell passed the Murrumbidgee Junction, and went on a few miles before tying up for the night. As he says:

> We were now within three days' journey of Swan Hill, and after having moored the boat at the bank of the river, and gone to rest, we were awakened by an unusual noise upon the water, and when we turned out to ascertain the cause of the commotion we beheld the *Lady Augusta*, steaming up the river at the rate of three or four knots.

He did not let Francis Cadell's *Lady Augusta* steam on unchallenged. Although they had up till then steamed only by day, he and his crew immediately lit the furnace and got up steam. On his return to South Australia he was to tell the story of the next twenty-four hours or so.

> It was then near eleven o'clock at night, and although our sleep had been disturbed, we followed in a few hours, and passed her again next morning. During the day, however, as we were stopping at a station, the *Lady Augusta* came up, and for the rest of the afternoon and night we were not far from each other; in fact, we had a race, which lasted till long after sunset, and during which we passed and

repassed each other four or five times. At last we resolved on a temporary cessation of the struggle, and, putting off the steam, allowed the *Lady Augusta* to pass, and came to for the night.

One place the steamers called at that day was Windomal, an out-station of Canally. Many years later, Nehemiah Bartley, in talking of the arrival there of the *Lady Augusta*, described the effect the coming of the steamers had on life in the river districts. He stressed the social revolution they brought about:

> No teams had been up, or down, for two years. There were two seasons' wool stored in the sheds; the remaining flour was awfully musty; boots, saddlery, tinware, 'slops', and the like had, long since, given out in the store.
>
> I remember we used to boil 'fat hen' (a weed which resembles dandelion) for vegetables, and we bore the musty flour as best we could, when, presto! all the muddle came to an end.... The two years' siege was raised. Fifty-pound bags of pure white flour, fresh from the mills of Adelaide, spick and span boxes of loaf sugar, and equally spick and span cases of Van Martell's brandy, and sperm candles also clean; and other goods too numerous to mention. *Not covered with the mud and dust of 800 miles of bush travel; not doled out in occasional dray-loads of 30 cwt. at a time, but fresh and clean only a week ago from the Adelaide stores....* Here was a metamorphosis with a vengeance, and the congested wool stores soon afforded ample return loading for the steamer and her barge. And station property round those parts known as 'Riverina' at once rose 100 per cent. in the market.

Almost ten miles past Windomal, Cadell turned up the Wakool. Randell, thinking the *Lady Augusta* was following the Murray, took the *Mary Ann* in behind her. As he was not expecting the river to narrow suddenly, the *Mary Ann* struck an overhanging tree, and one of her masts was carried away.

Below: Captain Francis Cadell of the Lady Augusta.

Right: Captain William Randell of the Mary Ann.

The *Lady Augusta* went only a few miles up the Wakool, then turned back to the Murray. Some time after midnight she reached Coghill's station, Piangil, fifty miles below Swan Hill, after a run that had aroused the admiration of the passengers:

> For all those hours Captain Cadell had been on deck, scarcely leaving it even for his meals. His powers of endurance are really as remarkable as his energy and courage; it must require no small share of each to direct two vessels by night along an almost unknown river, amidst dangers seen and unseen.

Next day Cadell left the *Eureka* barge behind to take on wool. In the evening he overhauled the *Mary Ann* again, and soon afterwards the *Lady Augusta* struck a form of trouble that was to affect many riverboats—shallow-draught vessels as they were, operating in the comparatively limited space of the rivers. She 'got into a regular fix', through being blown into a patch of overhanging trees, and was not freed until two in the morning.

At about midday next day, several hours ahead of the *Mary Ann*, the *Lady Augusta* arrived at Swan Hill, almost nine hundred miles from Goolwa. The entire population turned out to welcome Cadell—ten white men, two white women, and fifteen Aborigines. There's a story that the *Mary Ann* arrived at Swan Hill in need of repairs. This really applies to a voyage Randell made twelve months later, when his streamer was snagged a number of times on the way to Swan Hill.

Soon after Randell arrived he visited Cadell on the *Lady Augusta*, and arranged that Mr Davis, the knock-about parson of the *Mary Ann*, should hold a service aboard the *Lady Augusta* next day. On Sunday morning, however, so many settlers from the surrounding districts turned up that in the end Davis read the service on the veranda of the inn.

The Lady Augusta *and the* Mary Ann *at Swan Hill, a drawing by James Allen illustrating his* Journal of an Experimental Trip by the 'Lady Augusta'.

The *Lady Augusta* left Swan Hill on Monday morning. Randell stayed till the afternoon and sold most of his cargo. 'We obtained,' he said, 'good prices for the goods we sold, and on the whole it was a profitable trip, considering the small quantity the boat was able to carry.' Early next morning the *Mary Ann* overtook Cadell's steamer while the crew and passengers of the *Lady Augusta* were ashore cutting wood for the boilers, and went on to be the first past the post of what was to be the *Lady Augusta*'s highest point, Gannawarra—and so won the race up-river.

There is a story that the reason why Randell went on past Swan Hill was that Cadell had employed him to pick up a cargo of wool. Several pieces of evidence make this story appear incorrect; the Randells were merely following their original intention when they went on, leaving Cadell to turn back from a point 924 miles above Goolwa, and nearly 450 miles short of 'the village of Albury' for which he had set out.

On Saturday, 24 September, the *Mary Ann* passed Hopwood's Ferry (Echuca) and went on the couple of miles to Maiden's Punt (Moama), 1,068 river-miles from the sea, three hundred miles downstream from Albury. Maiden made Randell and the crew his guests for the two days of their stay, and offered to pilot them—apparently up the Goulburn—to within a few miles of the diggings and 'get us a lot of passengers'. It is said that several settlers offered Randell a cargo of wool, but that he declined to take it as he knew nothing of insurance and the business side of carriage by water.

> '*Randell's voyage above Swan Hill was appreciated by the settlers. "On both sides of the Murray, up and down, as he passed, shouts rent the air, from all the inhabitants, both white and black."*'

Randell's voyage above Swan Hill was appreciated by the settlers. 'On both sides of the Murray, up and down, as he passed, shouts rent the air, from all the inhabitants, both white and black.'

On 3 October the *Mary Ann* again caught up with the *Lady Augusta*, a little above Euston. Randell arrived just after the *Eureka* had, for some unexplained reason, lurched and swung backwards and forwards two or three times before she could be caught and lashed down—thirty-five bales of wool being shot into the river. He offered to carry this wool to Goolwa for three pounds a bale, 'but Captain Cadell offered, at our last moment of starting, £100 for doing so, and promised to make a cargo at the Darling'. That night the steamers lay at Euston, where they 'had some dancing and singing in Mr Commissioner Cole's drawing room'.

Up till this time there had been no sign of enmity between Randell and Cadell. Next day, however, it seems, Randell had some unpleasant things to say of his rival. Of the descriptions of that pioneering voyage by the two steamers, only one, that of a schoolboy passenger on the *Lady Augusta*, B.T.N. Finniss, refers to the matter. Finniss, who hero-worshipped Cadell, writes that when the *Lady Augusta* reached Keane and Orr's station, Kulkyne, some time after the *Mary Ann*,

> We were told by Mr Orr that Mr Randell of the *Mary Ann* had been spreading reports that we lost half our wool in the river, and that we had only got on as well as we had by trickery—and many other shabby falsehoods.

From Kulkyne down, Randell kept ahead of the *Lady Augusta*. It is hard to say whether he continued to nurse a resentment against Cadell, although those who were his friends say it is unlikely. He carried dispatches from the

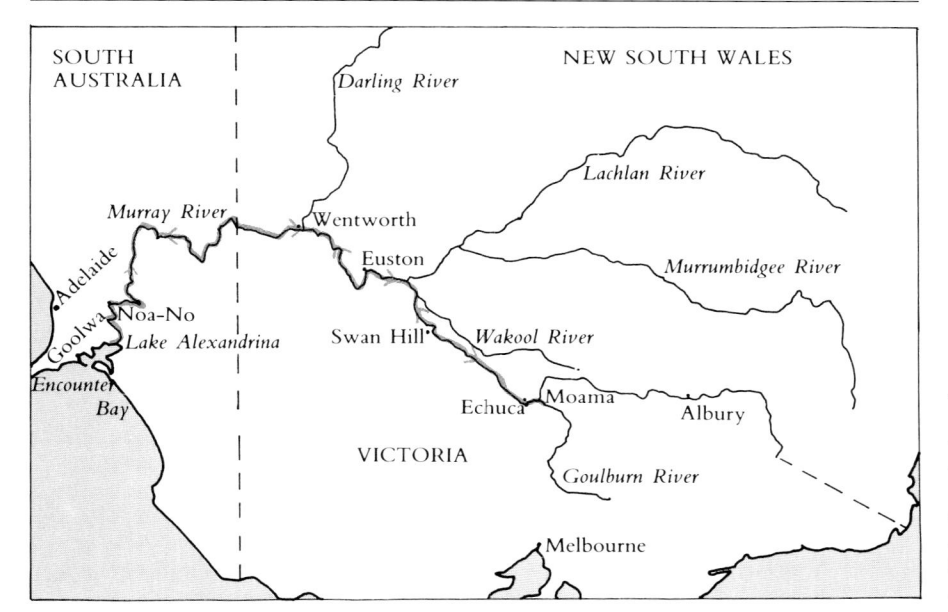

The Murray River system, showing the extent of the pioneer riverboat voyages of William Randell and Francis Cadell. The Lady Augusta *navigated from Goolwa to Gannawarra, above Swan Hill; the* Mary Ann *from Noa-No to Moama, just beyond Echuca.*

Governor, and reports for the press from the two journalists who were aboard the *Lady Augusta*. He arrived at Noa-No on October 11, and then went on down to Goolwa to deliver Cadell's wool.

Among the passengers aboard the Lady Augusta *was James Allen, who later published his* Journal of an Experimental Trip by the 'Lady Augusta'. *Here are some extracts from the journal.*

Thursday, 1 September. Shortly after starting this morning before daylight we met two branches of the river proceeding to the right and left, and it being dark at the time, we unfortunately took the wrong passage. This we found out shortly afterwards, however, by the narrowness of the passage and the shallowing of the stream. Without much difficulty we backed out, and proceeded on our right course.

If we proceed at our present speed, which is about six miles an hour, we shall make one hundred miles today. At present it is not determined, I believe, whether we shall proceed further than Swan Hill.

The *Mary Ann* steamer, I have just heard, passed the Warru station on Wednesday, 24 August, and Chambers's station on Saturday the 27th....

Shortly after nightfall, and just as we were expecting to reach Chapman's, a native canoe came paddling out to us from the bank of the river, containing two or three natives, anxious to inspect the 'big one mongoe' (the native name for canoe), which had arrived in their waters. One of the natives remained on board, and piloted us up to Chapman's station, which was a few miles further on, and opposite to which we anchored for the night at about eight o'clock p.m. On our arrival there, the right-hand bank of the river was lined with natives, who, as a means of welcoming us, I suppose, had lit large bonfires along the edge of the river, which, with their dark figures flitting here and there before the flames, gave the scene a singularly wild appearance....

Wednesday, 7 September.... One of the lady passengers met with a narrow escape from being drowned this morning while bathing in the river, having slipped her foot into a hole where the water was beyond her depth. She sank below the water, but eventually recovered her footing, and with the assistance of a lady who accompanied her, regained the shore. Her health for a day or two subsequently was seriously affected by it.

After shipping some firewood, which was finished by three o'clock, and taking on board some cargo for Messrs Jamieson's station, as well as half a score of natives to assist them as shepherds, we started at three o'clock, and proceeded about half a mile down the Darling, where the junction of the Murray with it takes place, and then proceeded up the main stream.

The country improves very much in appearance, particularly on the New South Wales side, being thickly timbered, principally with gum trees. We find the wood we shipped at the Darling (peppermint wood) very inferior, and, from the small power of steam it generates, we are making but little way. Anchored tonight at ten o'clock, having made only twenty miles since our departure this afternoon from the Darling. Having moonlight now in our favour, we shall, if necessary, be able to travel during the night....

Wednesday, 14 September.... While wooding this morning, the men belonging to the vessel were subjected to much interference from some of the shepherds on the station, who were intoxicated, and who became so abusive, from Captain Cadell refusing them the sale of any spirits, as to lead to a quarrel. They became so violent in their conduct to Mr Copeland, the first mate of the *Eureka*, as to result in an open battle between them, who, though attacked by three of them at once, succeeded in giving them a sound thrashing, and sent them away with broken heads to repent over their conduct. They slunk away in the most abject manner, although they had bragged before the encounter, in the most absurd language, of what they would do. Mr Ross, the owner of the station, expressed his satisfaction at their thus receiving their deserts.

It will be a matter of great regret if steamers trading on the river make a practice of supplying spirituous liquors to men employed at the different stations, who are too ready to take advantage of such a course. It will prove a counteraction to the advantages to be gained by th trade of the steamers, from the men engaged by the settlers being unfitted for the duties which they agree to perform. One influential settler on the Murray declared that, sooner than such a course should be pursued, he would relinquish the anticipated advantages to be gained on the other hand. I am glad to say that the impolicy of this course Captain Cadell is fully alive to, who has refused most scrupulously in every case, in the passage of the *Lady Augusta* up the river, any supply of intoxicating liquors, which he sees would have such an injurious effect.

After accomplishing the shipment of our wood at Ross's station, we left our moorings about half past eight o'clock a.m., and proceeded on our course up the river. Passed McCallum's station about midday, at which there are thirteen thousand sheep, and reached the junction of the Murrumbidgee by ten o'clock. At half past ten o'clock we sighted the *Mary Ann* steamer, which was moored by the bank of the river, and continued steaming until midnight, when we anchored. From the force of the current where we were stationed, the *Lady Augusta* lay over on her side to such a degree as to cause great inconvenience to the passengers, the declivity being so great as to affect the safety of the occupants of the sleeping berths in the saloon, many of whom, as a preventative against tumbling out on the floor, were necessitated to rise. This discomfort, however, was soon rectified by the vessel being trimmed to her natural level.

Wednesday, 20 September.... Arrived at Poonboon, or Westmeath—our destination—at half past ten o'clock, where we remained for the purpose of shipping 220 bales of wool lying on the banks of the river.

Here the ceremony of shipping the first bale of wool was performed shortly after our arrival. The first woolpack was accordingly rolled down the bank of the river to the plank communicating with the vessel, and then passed on board jointly by Mrs Younghusband, Mrs Finniss, and Miss Younghusband. The bale of wool was then hoisted up to the masthead of the *Eureka* with a sailor seated upon it, and on his giving the signal a gun was fired, which was succeeded by three cheers for the first shipment of wool on the Murray, and again by three more for the success of the present expedition. The scene altogether had a very pleasing effect, and the appearance of the ladies, who were collected on the top of the wool bales, which were piled up along the bank, was highly picturesque. After this ceremony was gone through, the crew retired to drink success to the commerce of the Murray, the passengers at the same time repeating the toast: one gentleman facetiously wishing Captain Cadell 'Success to his wool-gathering'. The rest of the day was occupied in loading the wool, which, with the exception of a few bales, was finished by nightfall....

Friday, 30 September. On our way at half past five o'clock, and at nine o'clock landed the carpenters, who are about to build two cargo boats for Captain Cadell. The timber here is extremely fine.

Entered the Murray at half past nine o'clock a.m., and reached Phelps's cattle station at eleven. Here we shipped fifty bales more wool on board the *Eureka*. On this station there are about nine hundred head of cattle. Mr Phelps has several sheep stations, one on the Lachlan, and in all musters a flock of about four thousand. The wool shipped was the remainder of his last year's clip, and he was about to commence shearing this year's in a few days.

Left Phelps's station at four o'clock.

Shortly after our departure from there a most melancholy occurrence took place, viz., the loss of one of the crew overboard, who, not being able to swim, perished before assistance could be rendered. The unfortunate man was a stoker on board the *Lady Augusta*, named William Teague, and arrived in this colony as a government emigrant by the *Osceola* in the early part of 1851; and from his address discovered amongst his papers, appears to have come originally from Devonport. He formerly followed the trade of blacksmith at the Goolwa, but shipped himself on board the steamer as a stoker. It appears that while leaning over the side rail of the vessel to draw a bucket of water, the rail, which was a shifting one opposite to the gangway, gave way, and precipitated him into the water. The cry of 'a man overboard' immediately

'From the force of the current where we were stationed, the Lady Augusta *lay over on her side to such a degree as to cause great inconvenience to the passengers, the declivity being so great as to affect the safety of the occupants of the sleeping berths in the saloon.'*

resounded through the ship. The engines were stopped and reversed, and the boat dragging at the stern was immediately manned and shaped towards the spot where the drowning man was seen struggling, with his head below the water, and his hands beating about above, in his vain endeavours to support himself, and which, instead of doing so, more speedily hastened his end. When the boat reached within two oars' lengths of him he was seen sinking, with both his hands raised, and about three or four feet below the surface of the water. Another moment and he would have been saved; but, alas! he sank to rise no more. For half an hour the steamer remained near the spot, it being hoped that his body might rise, but without the wished-for result. It was satisfactory, however, to feel under this heart-rending occurrence that everything was done, and that in the most expeditious manner, to rescue him from a watery grave. We continued our course with heavy hearts, and a gloom has spread over our proceedings which will not be dispelled for some time.

A familiar scene on the Murray, Darling and Murrumbidgee rivers from the 1850s till after the First World War. Riverboat traffic was at its peak in the 1870s but declined with the development of the railway system.

THE BURKE AND WILLS EXPEDITION

John King

THE GREAT NORTHERN EXPLORATION EXPEDITION, *led by Robert O'Hara Burke with William Wills as second in command, was the most elaborate and best-equipped expedition ever mounted in Australia. No expense was spared in fitting out the party of seventeen men with more than twenty tonnes of stores and equipment, twenty-three horses, and twenty-five camels specially imported (with three Indian camel drivers) for the expedition. A huge crowd assembled in Melbourne to watch the explorers' procession leave there on 20 August 1860 after an official farewell by the mayor and the Exploration Committee of the Royal Society of Victoria.*

The object of the expedition was to cross the continent from south to north through the centre. Burke made first for Menindee, on the Darling, where he set up a depot, leaving most of his staff and equipment there while he moved on with six men and fifteen camels to Cooper's Creek. After setting up another depot there, Burke sent William Wright, the manager of a cattle station who had shown them the route to Cooper's Creek, back to Menindee to bring up the remainder of the party, but when they had not arrived after six weeks an impatient Burke decided to make a dash for the Gulf of Carpentaria. He set out with three others—Wills, Charles Gray and John King—taking six camels, four horses and three months' provisions. The rest of the party and equipment were to remain at Cooper's Creek to await their return.

On 11 February 1861 they reached the tidal waters of the Flinders River at the Gulf and two days later started back for Cooper's Creek. Their supplies were running low, the weather was bad, and they were suffering from sickness and exhaustion. On 17 April Gray died. The remaining three struggled back to Cooper's Creek, only to find the depot deserted. A message in a bottle left buried with a month's supply of rations revealed that the depot party had left that very morning to return to Menindee, as some of them were sick with scurvy, Wright had not come back with the others, and Burke's party were long overdue.

The story of the three explorers' desperate struggle for survival is one of the great tragedies of Australian exploration. The sole survivor, John King, was found on 15 September by a search party led by Alfred Howitt. King had been living with the Aborigines since Burke and Wills died. At a subsequent royal commission of inquiry into the conduct of the expedition, King gave the following narrative of events that followed their arrival back at Cooper's Creek.

'*All the provisions we then had consisted of one and a half pound of dried meat.*'

MR BURKE, MR WILLS, and I reached the depot at Cooper's Creek on 21 April, about half past seven in the evening, with two camels, all that remained of the six Mr Burke took with him. All the provisions we then had consisted of one and a half pound of dried meat. We found the party had gone the same day; and, looking about for any mark they might have left, found the tree with 'DIG, Ap. 21'. Mr Wills said the party had left for the Darling. We dug and found the plant of stores. Mr Burke took the papers out of the bottle and then asked each of us whether we were able to proceed up the creek in pursuit of the party; we said not, and he then said that he thought it was his duty to ask us, but that he himself was unable to do so, but that he had decided upon trying to make Mount Hopeless, as he had been assured by the Committee in Melbourne that there was a cattle station within 150 miles of Cooper's Creek. Mr Wills was not inclined to follow this plan, and wished to go down our old track, but at last gave in to Mr Burke's wishes. I also wished to go down by our old track.

We remained four or five days to recruit, making preparations to go down the creek by stages of four or five miles a day, and Mr Burke placed a paper in the plant stating what were our plans. Travelling down the creek, we got some fish from the natives; and some distance down, one of the camels, Landa, got bogged, and although we remained there that day and part of the next, trying to dig him out, we found our strength insufficient to do so. The evening of the second day we shot him as he lay, and having cut off as much meat as we could, we lived on it while we stayed to dry the remainder. Throwing all the least necessary things away, we made one load for the remaining camel, Rajah, and each of us carried a swag of about twenty-five pounds. We were then tracing down the branches of the creek running south, and found that they ran out into earthy plains. We had understood that the creek along Gregory's track was continuous; and finding that all these creeks ran out into plains, Mr Burke returned, our camel being completely knocked up. We then intended to give the camel a spell for a few days and to make a new attempt to push on forty or fifty miles to the south in the hope of striking the creek.

During the time that the camel was being rested, Mr Burke and Mr Wills

Robert O'Hara Burke (left), William Wills (seated) and John King—an unsigned and undated painting.

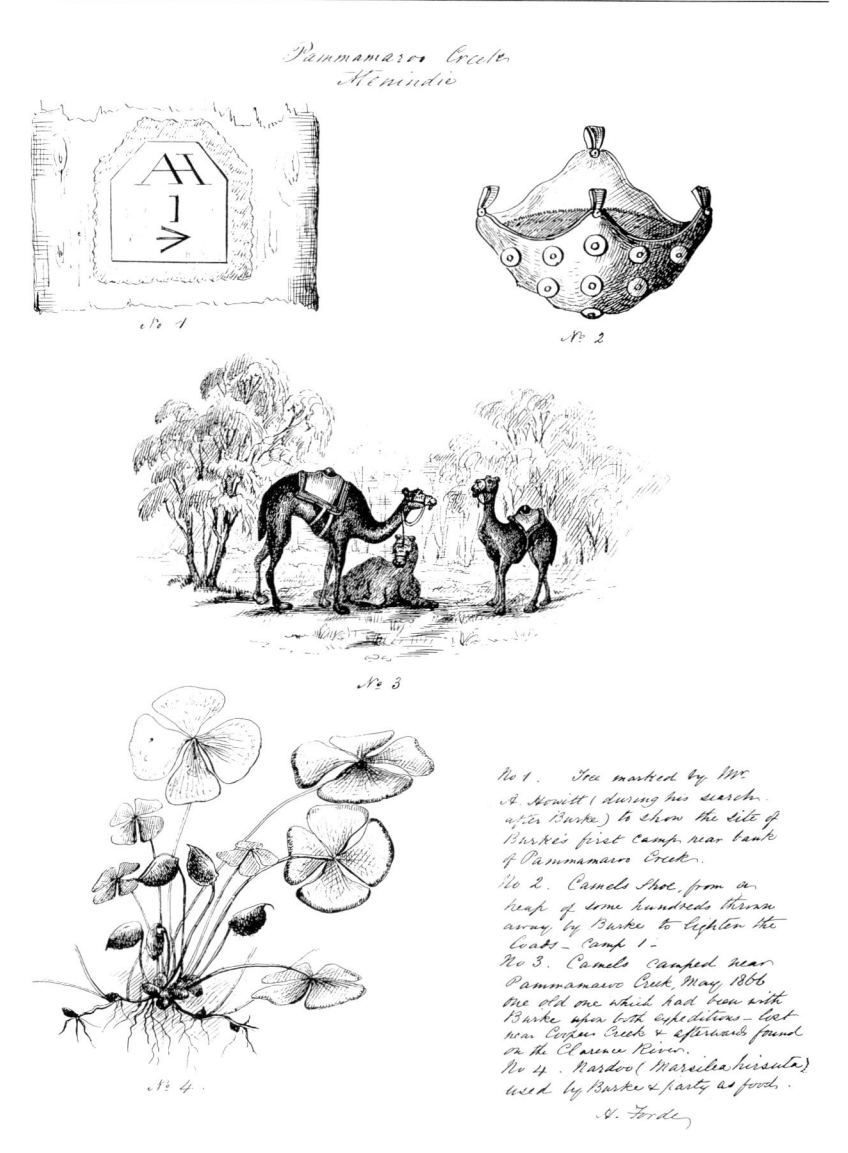

Pen sketches made by Helena Forde, who visited Menindee a few years after the Burke and Wills expedition. They show: a tree marked by Alfred Howitt, who found King, indicating the site of Burke's first camp; one of the many camel shoes discarded by Burke to lighten the load carried; camels camped near Pammamaroo Creek, Menindee; and the nardoo plant, used by Burke, Wills and King as food.

went in search of the natives, to endeavour to find out how the nardoo grew. Having found their camp, they obtained as much nardoo cake and fish as they could eat but could not explain that they wished to be shown how to find the seed themselves. They returned on the third day, bringing some fish and nardoo cake with them. On the following day the camel Rajah seemed very ill, and I told Mr Burke I thought he could not linger out more than four days, and as on the same evening the poor brute was on the point of dying, Mr Burke ordered him to be shot. I did so, and we cut him up with two broken knives and a lancet. We cured the meat and planted it, and Mr Burke then made another attempt to find the nardoo, taking me with him. We went down the creek expecting to find the natives at the camp where they had been last seen, but found that they had left, and not knowing whether they had gone up or down the creek, we slept in their gunyahs that night, and on the following morning returned to Mr Wills.

The next day, Mr Burke and I started up the creek but could see nothing of them and were three days away, when we returned and remained three days in our camp with Mr Wills. We then made a plant of all the articles we could not carry with us, leaving five pounds of rice and a quantity of meat, and then followed up the creek to where there were some good native huts. We remained at that place a few days, and finding that our provisions were beginning to run short, Mr Burke said that we ought to do something and that if we did not find the nardoo we should starve, and that he intended to save a little dried meat and rice to carry us to Mount Hopeless. The three of us then came to the conclusion that it would be better to make a second attempt to reach Mount Hopeless, as we were then as strong as we were likely to be, our daily allowance being then reduced. Mr Burke asked each of us whether we were willing to make another attempt to reach South Australian settlements, and we decided on going. We took with us what remained of the provisions we had planted—two and a half pounds of oatmeal, a small quantity of flour, and the dried meat; this, with powder and shot, and other small articles, made up our swags to thirty pounds each, and Mr Burke carried one billy of water, and I another.

We had not gone far before we came on a flat, where I saw a plant growing which I took to be clover, and on looking closer saw the seed, and called out that I had found the nardoo. They were very glad when I found it. We travelled three days and struck a watercourse coming south from Cooper's Creek. We traced this as it branched out and re-formed in the plains, until we at last lost it in flat country. Sandhills were in front of us, for which we made, and travelled all day but found no water. We were all greatly fatigued as our rations now consisted of only one small johnnycake and three sticks of dried meat daily.

We camped that evening about four o'clock, intending to push on next day until two o'clock p.m., and then, should we find no water, to return. We travelled and found no water, and the three of us sat down and rested for one hour and then turned back. We all felt satisfied that had there been a few days rain we could have got through; we were then, according to Mr Wills's calculation, forty-five miles from the creek. We travelled, on the day we turned back, very late, and the following evening reached the nearest water at the creek. We gathered some nardoo and boiled the seeds, as we were unable to pound them.

The following day we reached the main creek, and knowing where there was a fine waterhole and native gunyahs, we went there intending to save what remained of our flour and dried meat for the purpose of making another attempt to reach Mount Hopeless. On the following day Mr Wills and I went out to gather nardoo, of which we obtained a supply sufficient for three days, and finding a pounding stone at the gunyahs, Mr Burke and I pounded the seed, which was such slow work that we were compelled to use half flour and half nardoo. Mr Burke and Mr Wills then went down the creek for the remainder of the dried meat which we had planted; and we had now all our things with us, gathering nardoo and living the best way we could.

Mr Burke requested Mr Wills to go up the creek as far as the depot and to place a note in the plant there, stating that we were on our road to South

Australia. He also was to bury there the field-books of the journey to the Gulf. Before starting he got three pounds of flour and four pounds of pounded nardoo, and about a pound of meat, as he expected to be absent about eight days. During his absence I gathered nardoo and pounded it, as Mr Burke wished to lay in a supply in case of rain.

A few days after Mr Wills left, some natives came down the creek to fish at some waterholes near our camp. They were very civil to us at first and offered us some fish. On the second day they came again to fish, and Mr Burke took down two bags, which they filled for him. On the third day they gave us one bag of fish, and afterwards all came to our camp. We used to keep our ammunition and other articles in one gunyah, and all three of us lived together in another. One of the natives took an oilcloth out of this gunyah and Mr Burke, seeing him run away with it, followed him with his revolver and fired over his head, and upon this the native dropped the oilcloth. While he was away the other blacks invited me away to a waterhole to eat fish; but I declined to do so, as Mr Burke was absent and a number of natives were about who would have taken all our things. When I refused, one took his boomerang and laid it over my shoulder, and then told me by signs that if I called out for Mr Burke he would strike me. Upon this I got them all in front of the gunyah and fired a revolver over their heads, but they did not seem at all afraid until I got out the gun, when they all ran away. Mr Burke, hearing the report, came back, and we saw no more of them until late that night, when they came with some cooked fish and called out 'white fellow'. Mr Burke then went out with his revolver and found a whole tribe coming down, all painted and with fish in small nets carried by two men. Mr Burke went to meet them, and they wished to surround him, but he knocked as many of the nets of fish out of their hands as he could and shouted out to me to fire. I did so, and they ran off. We collected five small nets of cooked fish. The reason he would not accept the fish from them was that he was afraid of being too friendly lest they should always be in our camp.

We then lived on fish until Mr Wills returned. He told us that he had met

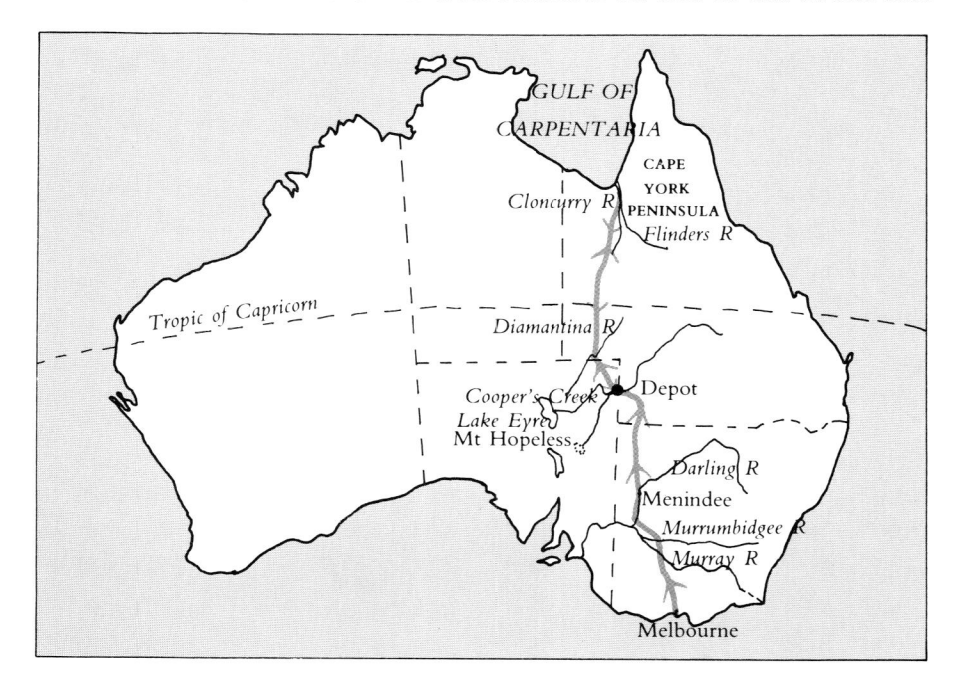

The route taken by the Burke and Wills expedition.

the natives soon after leaving us, and that they were very kind to him and had given him plenty to eat both on going up and returning. He seemed to consider that he should have very little difficulty in living with them, and as their camp was close to ours he returned to them the same day and found them very hospitable and friendly, keeping him with them for two days. Then they made signs to him to be off. He came to us and narrated what had happened but went back to them the following day, when they gave him his breakfast but made signs to him to go away. He pretended not to understand them and would not go, upon which they made signs that they were going up the creek and that he had better go down. They packed up and left the camp, giving Mr Wills a little nardoo to take to us.

During his absence, while Mr Burke was cooking some fish during a strong wind, the flames caught the gunyah and burned so rapidly that we were unable not only to put it out but to save any of our things excepting one revolver and a gun. Mr Wills having returned, it was decided to go up the creek and live with the natives if possible, as Mr Wills thought we should have but little difficulty in obtaining provisions from them if we camped on the opposite side of the creek to them. He said he knew where they were gone, so we packed up and started. Coming to the gunyahs where we expected to have found them, we were disappointed, and seeing a nardoo field close by, halted, intending to make it our camp.

For some time we were employed gathering nardoo and laying up a supply. Mr Wills and I used to collect and carry home a bag each day, and Mr Burke generally pounded sufficient for our dinner during our absence, but Mr Wills found himself getting very weak and was shortly unable to go out and gather nardoo as before, or even strong enough to pound it, so that in a few days he became almost helpless. I still continued gathering, and Mr Burke now also began to feel very weak and said that he could be of very little use in pounding. I now had to gather and pound for all three of us. I continued to do this for a few days, but finding my strength rapidly failing, my legs being very weak and painful, I was unable to go out for several days, and we were compelled to consume six days' stock which we had laid by.

Mr Burke now proposed that I should gather as much as possible in three days, and that with this supply we should go in search of the natives—a plan which had been urged upon us by Mr Wills as the only chance of saving him and ourselves as well, as he clearly saw that I was no longer able to collect sufficient for our wants. Having collected the seed as proposed, and having pounded sufficient to last Mr Wills for eight days and two days for ourselves, we placed water and firewood within his reach and started. Before leaving him, however, Mr Burke asked him whether he still wished it, as under no [other] circumstances would he leave him, and Mr Wills again said that he looked on it as our only chance. He then gave Mr Burke a letter and his watch for his father, and we buried the remainder of the field-books near the gunyah. Mr Wills said that, in case of my surviving Mr Burke, he hoped that I would carry out his last wishes in giving the watch and letter to his father.

In travelling the first day, Mr Burke seemed very weak and complained of great pain in his legs and back. On the second day he seemed to be better, and said that he thought he was getting stronger, but on starting did not go two miles before he said he could go no further. I persisted in his trying to go on and managed to get him along several times, until I saw that he was almost knocked up, when he said he could not carry his swag, and threw all he had away. I also reduced mine, taking nothing but a gun and some powder and shot, and a small pouch and some matches. On starting again, we did not go far before Mr Burke said we should halt for the night; but as the place was close to a large sheet of water, and exposed to the wind, I prevailed on him to go a little further, to the next reach of water, where we camped. We searched about and found a few small patches of nardoo, which I collected and pounded, and with a crow, which I shot, made a good evening's meal. From the time we halted Mr Burke seemed to be getting worse, although he ate his supper; he said he felt convinced he could not last many hours, and gave me his watch, which he said belonged to the committee, and a pocket-book to give to Sir William Stawell, and in which he wrote some notes. He then said to me, 'I hope you will remain with me here till I am quite dead—it is a comfort to know that someone is by; but, when I am dying, it is my wish that you should place the pistol in my right hand, and that you should leave me unburied as I lie.' That night he spoke very little, and the following morning I found him speechless, or nearly so, and about eight o'clock he expired. I remained a few hours there, but as I saw there was no use in remaining longer I went up the creek in search of the natives. I felt

'The following morning I found him speechless, or nearly so, and about eight o'clock he expired'—a pencil and watercolour sketch of Burke's death by William Strutt.

The place where Burke died at Cooper's Creek, by William Strutt.

very lonely, and at night usually slept in deserted wurleys....

Two days after leaving the spot where Mr Burke died, I found some gunyahs where the natives had deposited a bag of nardoo, sufficient to last me a fortnight, and three bundles containing various articles. I also shot a crow that evening but was in great dread that the natives would come and deprive me of the nardoo.

I remained there two days to recover my strength, and then returned to Mr Wills. I took back three crows; but found him lying dead in his gunyah, and the natives had been there and had taken away some of his clothes. I buried the corpse in the sand and remained there some days, but finding that my stock of nardoo was running short, and as I was unable to gather it, I tracked the natives who had been to the camp by their footprints in the sand, and went some distance down the creek shooting crows and hawks on the road. The natives hearing the report of the gun, came to meet me and took me with them to their camp, giving me nardoo and fish.

They took the birds I had shot and cooked them for me, and afterwards showed me a gunyah where I was to sleep with three of the single men. The following morning they commenced talking to me, and putting one finger on the ground and covering it with sand, at the same time pointing up the creek, saying 'white fellow', which I understood them to mean that one white man was dead. From this I knew they were the tribe who had taken Mr Wills's clothes. They then asked me where the third man was, and I also made the sign of putting two fingers on the ground and covering them with sand, at the same time pointing up the creek.

They appeared to feel great compassion for me when they understood that I was alone on the creek, and gave me plenty to eat. After being four days with them, I saw that they were becoming tired of me, and they made signs that they were going up the creek and that I had better go downwards; but I pretended not to understand them. The same day they shifted camp, and I followed them, and on reaching their camp I shot some crows, which pleased them so much they made a breakwind in the centre of their camp, and came and sat round me until such time as the crows were cooked, when they assisted me to eat them. The same day one of the women, to whom I had given part of a crow, came and gave me a ball of nardoo, saying that she would give me more only she had such a sore arm that she was unable to pound. She showed me a sore on her arm, and the thought struck me that I would boil some water in the billy and wash her arm with a sponge. During the operation, the whole tribe sat round and were muttering one to another. Her husband sat down by her side, and she was crying all the time. After I had washed it, I touched it with some nitrate of silver, when she began to yell and ran off crying out 'Mokow! Mokow!' (Fire! Fire!).

From this time she and her husband used to give me a small quantity of nardoo both night and morning, and whenever the tribe was about to go on a fishing excursion he used to give me notice to go with them. They also used to assist me in making a wurley or breakwind whenever they shifted camp. I generally shot a crow, or a hawk, and gave it to them in return for these little services. Every four or five days the tribe would surround me and ask whether I intended going up or down the creek; at last I made them understand that if they went up I should go up the creek, and if they went down I should also go down; and from this time they seemed to look upon me as one of themselves, and supplied me with fish and nardoo regularly.

They were very anxious, however, to know where Mr Burke lay, and one day, when we were fishing in the waterholes close by, I took them to the spot. On seeing his remains, the whole party wept bitterly and covered them with bushes. After this, they were much kinder to me than before, and I always told them that the white men would be here before two moons; and in the evening when they came with nardoo and fish, they used to talk about the 'white fellows' coming, at the same time pointing to the moon.

I also told them they would receive many presents, and they constantly asked me for tomahawks. From this time to when the relief party arrived, a period of about a month, they treated me with uniform kindness, and looked upon me as one of themselves. The day on which I was released, one of the tribe who had been fishing came and told me that the 'white fellows' were coming, and the whole of the tribe who were then in camp sallied out in every direction to meet the party, while the man who had brought the news took me over the creek, where I shortly saw the party coming down.

Cooper's Creek Aborigines covering Burke's remains with bushes.

THE HEROINE OF LIZARD ISLAND

Mary Watson

'Left Lizard Island 2 October 1881 (Sunday afternoon) in tank. Got about three miles or four from the Lizards.'

MARY BEATRICE PHILLIPS *migrated with her parents to Queensland from Cornwall in the late 1870s. For a while she conducted a private school in Maryborough and then worked as a governess in Cooktown. It was there she met Captain R. F. Watson, a bêche-de-mer trader. They were married in May 1880 and went to live on Lizard Island, about thirty kilometres north-east of Cape Flattery between the Great Barrier Reef and the north-eastern coast of Queensland. In September 1881, while Captain Watson was away setting up a fishing station, a party of Aborigines killed one of the Watsons' two Chinese servants and wounded the other. To escape, the 22-year-old Mrs Watson put to sea with the wounded Chinese and her infant son, Ferrier, in part of an iron tank used by her husband for boiling bêche-de-mer. After a perilous and exhausting voyage, they reached No. 5 Island in the Howick Group, about sixty-five kilometres to the north-west, where all three eventually died of thirst. For eleven days Mary Watson kept a diary. The first part was found at the cottage on Lizard Island, the second beside the remains of their bodies on Howick Island No. 5.*

SEPTEMBER 27, 1881. Blowing gale of wind SE. Ah Sam saw smoke in S direction, supposed to be from native camp. Steamer bound for North very close about 6 p.m.; *Corea*, I think.

28 September. Blowing strong SE breeze.

29 September. Blowing strong breeze SE although not so hard as yesterday. No eggs. Ah Leong killed by the blacks over at the farm. Ah Sam found his hat, which is the only proof.

30 September. Natives down on the beach at 7 p.m. Fired off rifle and revolver and they went away.

1 October. Natives (four) speared Ah Sam; four places in the right side, and three on the shoulder. Got three spears from the natives. Saw ten men altogether—

Left Lizard Island 2 October 1881 (Sunday afternoon) in tank. Got about three miles or four from the Lizards.

4 October. Made for the sandbank off the Lizards, but could not reach it. Got on a reef.

5 October. Remained on the reef all day on the lookout for a boat, but saw none.

6 October. Very calm morning. Able to pull the tank up to an island with three small mountains on it. Ah Sam went ashore to try and get water, as

THE HEROINE OF LIZARD ISLAND

ours was done. There were natives camped there, so we were afraid to go far away. We had to wait return of tide. Anchored under the mangroves; got on the reef. Very calm.

7 October. Made for another island four or five miles from the one spoken of yesterday. Ashore, but could not find any water. Cooked some rice and clam-fish. Moderate SE breeze. Stayed here all night. Saw a steamer bound north. Hoisted Ferrier's white and pink wrap but did not answer us.

8 October. Changed anchorage of boat as the wind was freshening. Went down to a kind of little lake on the same island (this done last night). Remained here all day looking out for a boat; did not see any. Very cold night; blowing very hard. No water.

9 October. Brought the tank ashore as far as possible with this morning's tide. Made camp all day under the trees. Blowing very hard. No water. Gave Ferrier a dip in the sea; he is showing symptoms of thirst, and I took a dip myself. Ah Sam and self very parched with thirst. Ferrier is showing symptoms.

10 October. Ferrier very bad with inflammation; very much alarmed. No fresh water, and no more milk, but condensed. Self very weak; really thought I would have died last night (Sunday).

11 October. Still all alive. Ferrier very much better this morning. Self feeling very weak. I think it will rain today; clouds very heavy; wind not quite so hard.

No rain. Morning fine weather. Ah Sam preparing to die. Have not seen him since 9. Ferrier more cheerful. Self not feeling at all well. Have not seen any boat of any description. No water. Nearly dead with thirst.

The first part of the diary was found by police and customs officers who had gone to Lizard Island following a report by a ship's captain that he had seen bushfires on the island and a large group of blacks near the Watsons' hut. For the next two months, mystery surrounded the disappearance of Mrs Watson and her baby and servant. Then

Mary Watson, the heroine of Lizard Island.

The cut-down iron tank (photographed from above) in which Mary Watson made her tragic voyage from Lizard Island to the Howick group with her infant son and wounded Chinese servant. The tank is now in the Queensland Museum.

on 22 January 1882 the bêche-de-mer schooner *Kate Kearney* stopped at Howick Island No. 5 to shelter for the night and a crew member who went ashore to look for firewood found the bodies. Mrs Watson was lying in the tank with the baby resting on her decomposed arm. She had brought a pillow for the baby and an umbrella to shade it from the sun. Beside her were her diary and a loaded and cocked revolver. There was also a chest containing baby clothes, money and jewellery, tins of preserved food and condensed milk, a small bag of rice and some groats. The tank was half filled with rainwater.

The section of north Queensland showing Lizard Island and the Howick group.

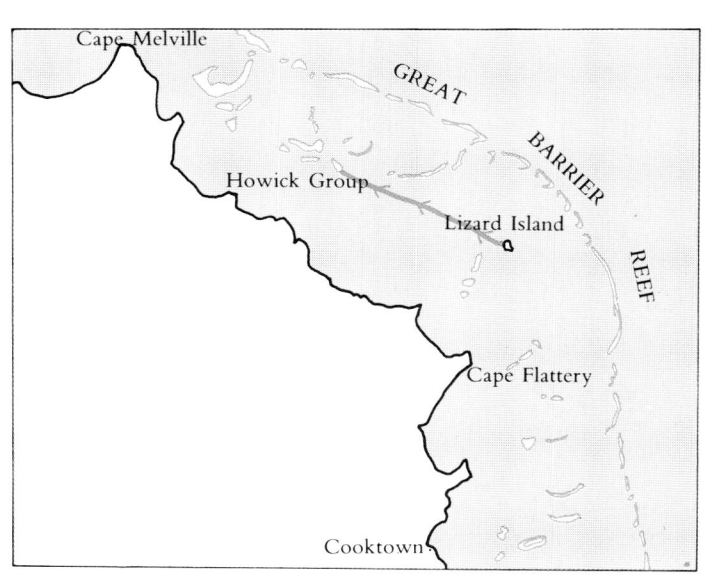

A TRANSCONTINENTAL RAMBLE

G.E. Morrison

GEORGE ERNEST MORRISON—*'Chinese' Morrison, the celebrated* Times *correspondent in Peking and political adviser to the nascent Chinese republic—was an inveterate traveller and an epic walker. In 1880, when he was seventeen, he walked from Geelong to Adelaide, a distance of nearly a thousand kilometres, and years later made a journey, partly by boat but mostly on foot and on horseback, from Shanghai to Rangoon. After attending Geelong College, Morrison had begun medical studies at the University of Melbourne, but failing his second-year examinations he shipped aboard the blackbirder* Lavinia *to observe the evils of the kanaka traffic and subsequently wrote a series of influential articles for the Melbourne* Leader. *He then went to New Guinea on another vessel, transferred to a Chinese junk to work his way back to Australia, and eventually arrived at Normanton, on the Gulf of Carpentaria. He immediately made plans to walk across the continent to Melbourne. It was only twenty-one years since the Burke and Wills expedition, well-equipped and with camels and horses, had come to grief traversing roughly the same route; Morrison, not yet twenty-one years old and equipped with little more than a billy and quart pot, oilcloth and blanket, was about to attempt the journey alone and on foot. He set out from Normanton on 19 December 1882 and arrived in Melbourne 123 days later, having walked more than 3,200 kilometres. His account of the journey appeared in the* Leader *of 19 May 1883.*

*I*T HAD LONG BEEN a wish of mine to cross Australia. Lying in bed in Port Mackay with two crippled knees, I first resolved to do the journey on foot. When I heard on all sides of the long stages between stations and the impossibility of travelling without at least two horses, I decided to go alone, and when everyone croaked to me that the blacks would kill me, if the floods did not drown me, I swore I should go unarmed. Fever I had to fear as well as blacks; quinine would be required to combat the former; a telescope might forewarn me of the latter. My telescope was stolen from me in Cooktown: my quinine, by accident, was thrown away at Thursday Island. Of all things none was more likely to be useful than a compass, yet mine was utterly destroyed in New Guinea. What could I argue from these things but that fever would pass me unharming, blacks would never endanger my life nor would I ever be in a situation from which there was no escape but by the use of the compass. At Normanton, when I gave out my intention of strolling over to Melbourne, people professed to think me mad. The rainy season was impending, and many signs, especially the comet, pointed to its being earlier than usual. 'How reckless,' said one; 'so insane,' put in another; 'it's suicide,' added a third. The elderly landlady of the hotel grew eloquent as to the dangers which awaited me. She was no cur, she assured me, but she wouldn't be game to tackle such a walk. Fearing an attack of nervousness, I hurried out of Normanton to a hotel fifteen miles on the road to Cloncurry. Five teams were camped here. It rained with unpromising severity the better part of two days, and as the next house was seventy-five miles away I had just to wait patiently.

On Friday evening, 22 December, the sky was clear for the first time, and starting at once I was thirty miles on my way before it came on to rain again. The teams hesitated, and have been there ever since, I fancy. This long stage is much dreaded by the carriers. It lies through country lightly timbered with the gutta-percha tree, the stunted bastard box, and the cooliebar, a district said to swarm with blacks, and annually subject to inundation. When I was halfway through there came on a violent tempest of wind and rain. The track became a bog and the knapsack got so soddened with water that I groaned under its weight. It was not safe to rest. The accounts I had heard of the track when flooded made me tremble to sit down, so I wearily struggled on through water and mud up to my knees, forgetting the dangers of this dismal, gloomy country in the fatigue of walking. Suddenly the wind died away, the sun shone out through the clouds, the rain stopped, and in a little while I came to where no rain had fallen at all. It had been merely a local storm. The following morning I came to two huts and a stockyard, the cattle station of Veno Park. Two stages of twenty-five miles each through a country whose monotonous flatness is occasionally relieved by richly wooded sandhills, bring you, the first to a cattle station, the second to a public house. Spear Creek, which has been on your left hand, is now lost sight of. The Sanby is crossed, and you are on that immense plain which stretches to the

George Morrison aged nineteen, a year before he made his journey on foot across Australia.

Flinders River. Between the Cockatoo waterhole, three miles beyond the Sanby, and a low hill called Fort Brown, within three miles of the Flinders, there is a dead waterless flat, almost bare of trees, which is buried some feet under water during the rainy season—carriers tell me thirty feet, and I can well believe it, for the high gums on the banks of the Flinders have drift timber in their very topmost branches.

I had a mate when crossing this plain, an old man who sought my company out of nervousness. He was mounted on a poor wretched moke which had a fistula between its shoulders that was sickening to look at. Yet he was very proud of his horse and was quite disgusted because the only bid he could get for horse, saddle and bridle when he put him up for sale was ten shillings. Locomotion was so painful to the horse that hobbles would have been superfluous. His only fault in the eyes of his owner was that he was not a mare. When buying flour for my mate and myself I asked him how much should we require. 'Six pounds,' he replied. 'Surely,' said I, 'six pounds of flour will not be enough for you and me for three days'—we were eighty-one miles from the next house—but he begged of me to trust him for that. Borrowing the loan of the kitchen he baked a damper of the weight and hardness of a stone. We had no knife strong enough to cut it.

I constantly passed teams now till I got into Cloncurry. Water and grass were abundant, and with the thirty pounds a ton for the two hundred and fifty miles from the Norman to Cloncurry, they had made satisfactory profits. I went some miles off the road to see the first sheep station. The country seems ill adapted for the sheep, though horses and cattle thrive wonderfully; but here, over two hundred miles from the coast, the sheep does splendidly on the open downs with gidya ridges, which stretch away to the north-west of Cloncurry. Between the Norman and Cloncurry I saw neither kangaroos, emus nor wild dogs, though the latter abound. There were native turkeys in scores, and every pool of water swarmed with wildfowl. Kites were more plentiful than crows, and you never stopped for a meal but the trees near became grey with kites waiting for you to leave that they might swoop down upon the scraps.

The wretched blacks are shot without mercy. One night I was at a station, whose owner is said to have shot more blacks than any two men in Queensland, when the mailman came in and reported that he had seen a black prowling about the stockyard. Loading his rifle, Mr ——— at once sallied out after him, but came back in an hour quite disappointed that, though he could pick up the tracks by the stockyard, it was too dark to follow them. Alligators are said to swarm in Spear Creek, as the Norman river is called above Normanton; I hesitate to give the dimensions of the largest that has been seen....

From Cloncurry my route lay to Winton. A publican in town kindly drew me a diagram by which I was to find my way to a hut on the M'Kinlay River, 104 miles distant. That map I keep as a curiosity. A distance of nine miles was made to appear twice as long as one of twenty-two miles, a trifling inaccuracy which caused me unnecessary anxiety and torture. The first night I could not sleep from fear that I had taken a wrong turning. In the morning I started to go thirty-five miles without knowing whether there was water on

> '*Between the Norman and Cloncurry I saw neither kangaroos, emus nor wild dogs, though the latter abound. There were native turkeys in scores, and every pool of water swarmed with wildfowl.*'

the track, or even water where I was making to. My waterbag holds two quarts and a half, but the day was so hot—the thermometer registered 132 deg. in the shade of the hut I refer to—that by midday, although I had hardly wet my mouth, the water was all evaporated. Still I kept moving, but at half past four I just knocked up. It came upon me most suddenly. Without any warning I was seized with an irresistible desire to throw off all my clothes. I had no wish in the world but to lie down. I camped under a tree. The anxiety of mind, for it was but a chance if water was within thirteen miles of me, added to my thirst, and I suffered torments. All through the night I lay naked on my back, my tongue contracted to a point, my body hot and feverish, my brain reeling. Just as day dawned I staggered to my feet, but which way was I to turn, to the right or the left? In a brief intermission of my confusion I recollected that I had turned off to the tree to the right; but during the night I had got my head where my feet should have been, and I actually tried to pick up the track by walking away from it. But Providence watched over me, and set me on my way.

I was so dazed that the track became more blurred and indistinct every minute. A wide plain now stretched before me, and a belt of timber at its further end gave me hope. I reached the creek and threw down my knapsack, and followed up and down the sandy bed for a weary distance, but it was as dry as the Sahara. On again, and another plain, with another belt of timber was to cheer or disappoint me. The creek was drier looking and sandier than the first one. I was throwing myself down in despair, when my eyes lit on a beautiful pool of water under the shade of a weeping teatree. The reaction quite unnerved me. I rested and drank all day. The mailman came up in the evening and gave me information about the country ahead. The contrast struck me forcibly. There were richly grassed instead of arid plains; creeks no longer dry and sandy, but sparkling with water, and plantations of timber, healthy and vigorous, not a parched and stunted forest. The twin parallel channels of the Williams River meander through a country as beautiful as an English park. Then a vast plain extends to the horizon, where, dancing grotesquely in the sun, is the timber marking the course of the Fullarton River.

Two day's walk from here is the M'Kinlay River, which drains an immense area of rolling downs. I was tracing up this river, cutting from one point of timber to another, and wondering whether the hut was above or below me, when I saw a man on horseback driving cattle. I drew nearer and nearer to him, and long before I could see his face I recognised the wild war song which had so often inspired me in my voyage to the islands. This was a young Kanaka, a kindly nice lad, from Motualava, beguiled from his home —one of the most beautiful islands of Polynesia—to tend cattle, to do fencing, to mix with gins, amid all the sultry dreariness and cheerlessness of the most utterly wretched district of the Never Never. The manager of this cattle station was in Cloncurry, and the South Sea Islander was in sole charge. I was taken very unwell when with him, and for three days the Kanaka showed me the greatest kindness and attention.

Leaving now the M'Kinlay River and steering diagonally over to its first sandy billabong, I traced it up till I came to an out-station. In this stage of

'All through the night I lay naked on my back, my tongue contracted to a point, my body hot and feverish, my brain reeling. Just as day dawned I staggered to my feet, but which way was I to turn, to the right or the left?'

thirty miles I was two days without eating anything during which I suffered much from thirst. The next stage was twenty-five miles over the ranges in which the Diamantina takes its source. The heat was something fearful, there was an entire absence of animal life, a faintly marked track which turned and twisted to every point of the compass and continually ran out, and no water, though billabongs and sandy creeks were crossed by the hundred. The only excitement that sustained me in my weakness was the fear of blacks—the wild kalkadoons who are so greatly feared in the hills.

At the headwaters of the Diamantina a sheep station was being formed where the countless billabongs resolve themselves into one of the finest rivers in Australia, a river which shall perpetuate the name of Lady Bowen. The Diamantina from its source trends away to the north-east, and then bends round in the shape of a shepherd's crook. I was on it for 113 miles, having it for 56 miles on my left, then crossing it at Dagworth station, and having it on my right for 57 miles, till its junction with the Western at Elderslie, one of Sir Samuel Wilson's properties. Both here and at Dagworth there was immense activity.... any unskilled man can earn thirty or thirty-five shillings a week; he will be well fed, as a vegetable garden is now an essential part of a large Queensland station. I was out of the country where men are content to exist on salt beef and damper. The money spent by the squatters hereabouts chiefly finds its way into the public houses of Winton, a rising township on the Pelican Waterholes, near the Western River, placed on a high flat, with not a tree near it. The telegraph line is being extended from here to Cloncurry. Vinden station, another magnificent sheep run, is fifteen miles out of Winton. Fifty miles further is Evesham station. Then there is a break in the open downs, and you pass through a lot of gidya scrub country, through Maneroo station to the Thomson River—at this early stage, a trickle of peculiar white water which I stepped across.

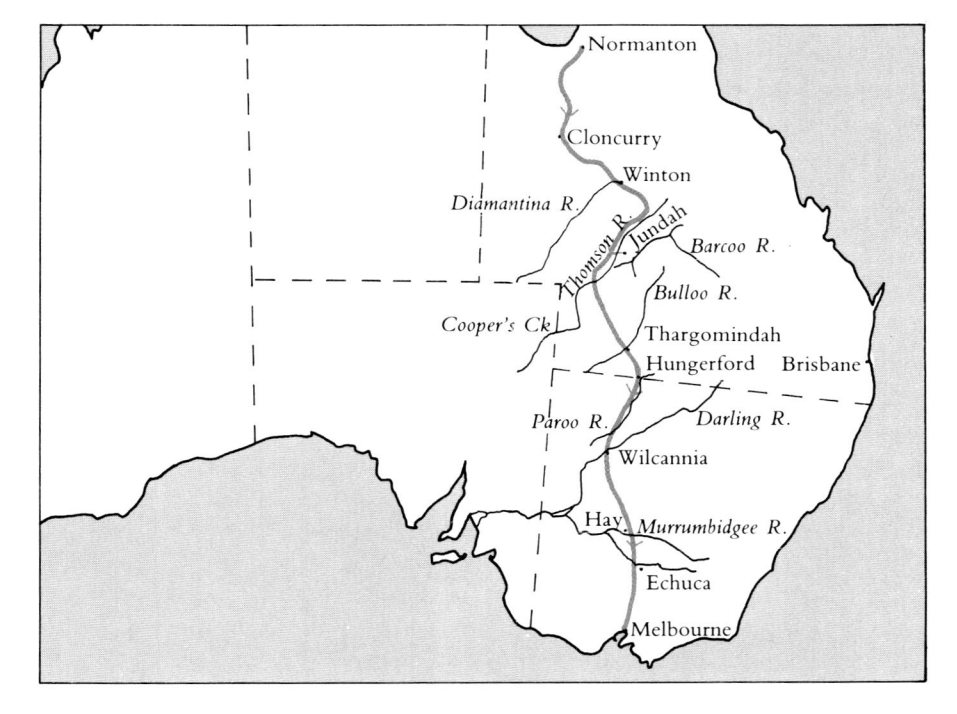

Morrison's track from Normanton to Melbourne. Although he covered much the same route as Burke and Wills twenty-one years before, by 1883 there were settlements along the way where he could obtain provisions.

The day after crossing the Thomson I was overtaken by an old gentleman on horseback whose companionship I found so agreeable that we travelled on together for seventy-five miles. He was a toothless darkie, a native of the Gold Coast of Africa, a cook by profession, and one of the kindest, most considerate men it has been my lot to meet with. He would ride on ahead and open the gates that I might not break my stride. He would stint himself of water if the day were hot that I might have the more. And this is how we fell out. We had to go one day twenty-five miles carrying water. Though parched with thirst he would not take this share. Not to be outdone I also refused any water, and being annoyed I vowed that we must part. I am glad of an opportunity to record my sense of this darkie's kindness. John Smith was his name, and he was the first black man ever seen in Iceland, having been there when a boy on board a Dutch man-of-war which was taking Prince Henry of the Netherlands round the world.

The Thomson River we left some distance on our right, two stations being situated on creeks running into it. On the Bimerah Creek is Bimerah sheep station, which, like all Fairbairn's stations, is being rapidly improved on a princely scale. Twelve miles further there was a sudden change. The water in the Emu Creek was stinking; the fish were rotting in the mud, and the crows were in hundreds. Up to this creek grass had been in abundance. Not till I was overtaken by rain, 250 miles further on, did I again come to any. Now I had to pass through the downs and gidya scrub, which had been the characteristics of the country for the last six hundred miles, till in three days I walked into the township of Jundah. There is a store here, a saddler and public house, and there will be other houses shortly. I shall chiefly remember it because of the splendid dam of water in the Thomson and because of the interesting fact that every man in the township was more or less drunk. All were lost in drunken amazement at my prodigious walk.

I was now an experienced swagman. My swag was carried New Zealand, or knapsack, fashion. The tucker, spare shoes, socks and shirts, some reading matter and a hammock, the matches, baking powder and canvas basil was rolled up in a single blanket, and the whole then enveloped in a strip of oilcloth and borne on my back, being kept by straps passing over the shoulders. In this way only could I secure the untrammelled use of my arms. The swag was seldom less than twenty pounds; above this its weight varied according to the distance I had to carry tucker. I seldom travelled by night; the heat of the day never troubled me. Indeed, it is my favourite boast that I have yet to see the day that is too hot for me. My own dress was cabbage-tree hat, flannel shirt, and tweed trousers, afterwards replaced by moleskins, and a knife belt and sheath. Boots I wore two sizes too large, and as I always cut the stiffening out of the back before using them, I escaped that soreness of heel which has troubled me on my former walks.

Upon arriving at a station I went straight to the store, bought what rations I required, and camped by the most convenient water. The greatest hospitality was always shown me at stations where I was known, but I made it a rule to be as independent of all help as possible. When I had decided to camp I spread the oilcloth and, having lit a fire, put on my salt beef to boil in the billy. By the time it was done, and the quart of tea made, I had a johnnycake or flatjack ready for cooking on the raked-out coals. The former differ only in size and are distinct from a damper in that they are cooked on the hot embers, whereas a damper is baked in the hot ashes with hot embers outside. No wood that I have seen can equal the gidya for giving the very ash and ember most valuable to us. A johnnycake made with baking powder is a most delicious scone—the very best baking powder is Eno's fruit salt. Of course, I did not restrict myself to these two articles of diet. I would vary them with apples and rice, sago or arrowroot, and occasionally with beef tea and potatoes. Preserved potatoes, when prepared in the water in which you have boiled your meat, are most delicious. Soda is an excellent baking powder; the johnnycake becomes a beautiful yellow, so that you can imagine you are eating bread made with milk, butter and eggs. At the stores—every station has its store—flour was ninepence to one shilling per pound, rice a shilling, apples and potatoes one shilling and sixpence, and meat, though most of the stations do not charge for it, was threepence to sixpence a pound for salt beef.

But to return. No one in Jundah could give me any lucid information where water might be in the next sixty-five miles. It is the uncertainty which predisposes to the fever of the palate. With the river in sight on my left, and never more than five or six miles from me, I knew that I could always get water by turning off to it. This, then, was well enough. But the least intoxicated man in Jundah was most positive that there was one stage absolutely without water for eighteen miles. He had offered to fight anyone who contradicted him, yet his statment passed unchallenged. I therefore inferred that he was speaking the truth. If, then, I had been thirsty, had turned off five miles to water and found none this eighteen miles, it would have gone hard with me. As it happened, my anxiety was uncalled for. At several places in the sixty-five miles cattle tracks crossed the path, and by following them I was always brought to water, but so stale and filthy that it gave me severe griping pains in the stomach, which interfered much with my walking. For a greater part of this distance my way lay through a corner of a vast cattle run owned by two men, and in extent larger than Yorkshire and Durham.

On 15 February I came to the most interesting river in Australia. Fifteen miles above this, the Thomson had joined the Barcoo. Wading waist-deep through the combined stream, I paused halfway to admire the glorious reaches of the river opened up above and below me, and the high banks crowned with magnificent timber. Every description of wildfowl floated idly on the unruffled surface of the current, and it was idleness which reigned supreme over the encampment of blacks in the timber on the opposite bank. I was so delighted with seeing Cooper's Creek at last that, despite an empty tuckerbag, I must need camp for the night on its margin.

Seven miles from the crossing I reached a cattle station, and twenty-eight miles further another. The sky now became overcast, the sun was rarely visible, and everything foreboded rain. I rested a day or two and went on. A slight drizzle fell persistently. Not heavy enough to keep me awake, it made all my things sodden. There was no sun to dry them, nor had I sufficient patience to steam them before a fire. Once I lost my box of matches, and

> *'Wading waist-deep through the combined stream, I paused halfway to admire the glorious reaches of the river opened up above and below me, and the high banks crowned with magnificent timber. Every description of wildfowl floated idly on the unruffled surface of the current.'*

Bullock teams at Wilcannia, where Morrison was forced to cool his heels while waiting for money to be telegraphed to him.

calling at a house to replenish them was given as a favour nineteen lucifers. These had to last me two days, sleeping out in the meantime. I cannot imagine any severer trial for one's nerves than when hungry, with no food cooked, nor any house within a day's walk, to have to light a fire in wind or rain with you last match.

On 23 February the Thargomindah and Windorah mailman served me a dirty trick. While I was camped for lunch he and another man came up to me, both well mounted, and driving packhorses. It was a hot, sultry, thirsty day, and I had a larger stock of water than usual, having filled my two-quart billy as well as my waterbag. These men asked me for a drink, and before I could stop them, they had emptied my billy of all but cupful, though they were within two miles of water on horseback, while I was over twenty-eight from it on foot. I made it a rule of my walk never to ask or accept a drink from any traveller, whether on foot or horseback. It gave me satisfaction to be independent even in this.

The same evening of my meeting with the mailman a foot traveller overtook me and we camped together. We made an excellent breakwind, lit a roaring fire, for we were once more in gidya country with abundance of firewood, and calmly settled ourselves for the night. But we were not long asleep before the slight drizzle which had forewarned us was succeeded by a heavy pelting rain that knew no ceasing. One could hardly believe the effect of that rain. In the morning our camp was on the only dry ground within sight. For fifteen miles we did not see land. The track was a clearly defined channel between the bushes. The creeks were running into a very strong current, and we were so often in water up to our armpits that I travelled with nothing on but my shirt. We reached shelter, there to be detained for three days. It rained for seventy-six hours at one stretch. In five days nine inches and thirty points fell. Dams were burst everywhere. The whole country into Thargomindah was become a vast series of swamps and flooded creeks.

Buckling to it, every danger vanished at my approach. Wading through swamps and swimming creeks with long distances to carry food, I yet experienced no fatigue; the dash of excitement kept it away. Where the swamp extended for miles it was but natural that in threading my way among the trees, with no guide but the sun, and water often to my breast, I should wander from the track, but a wide cast on the dry ground would as surely discover it to me. When the water was in motion, centipedes in hundreds and an occasional snake constantly floated across the path in unpleasant proximity.

The snakes I saw in my walk were more varied than numerous. On the red mulga ridges I killed several mulga snakes—a finely marked brown snake nearly six feet in length. When I was at the headwaters of the Diamantina, a black passed me, trailing after him a snake nine feet six inches long and as thick as a cable. It is a kind of rock python, which often attains a length of twelve or fifteen feet. The black would have me to believe that it was not deadly. It is a man's duty to kill every snake he can. I have killed the brown snake, the tiger snake, the poor harmless carpet snake, and a black snake with a blue belly. There were many I had no means of identifying, not the least interesting being an active little fellow which was disturbed by my coming and commenced to wriggle about in a most fantastic way. Just as I turned for a stick it made one spring off the track and vanished down a hole not large enough to introduce your two smallest fingers. Many anecdotes of snakes were told me. People so unkindly take advantage of one's credulous inexperience.

The Bulloo I crossed in a boat; a deep wade then put me on the track to Hungerford. At Thargomindah I had laid in such a large supply of flour and beef that for seventy-five miles I was absolutley independent of everyone. Timber and water were abundant. By this time I had trained myself to do with very little water. I could walk twenty-five miles without wetting my lips. The corellas flock to water at sundown; the thirsty traveller need but be guided by them, and he will infallibly be brought to water. The Paroo was greatly swollen. I had been told to be careful, as the bed of the river is thickly timbered with the Ypunyah. The stream was not less than half a mile wide, and you cannot see the opposite bank till quite close to it. But caution was unnecessary. I walked slap in, and crossed without difficulty. Hungerford is across the river. The boundary between New South Wales and Queensland passes through the centre of the town. The hotel is in Queensland, where the licence is less; the store is in New South Wales, where there is free trade. I had done with Queensland. Drinks were now sixpence, and mutton was to take the place of beef.

In crossing the Paroo, twenty miles below Hungerlord, I waded in a careless way into the stream, with my heavy swag on my back. Gradually it got deeper; it came over my waist; it reached my breast, my chin then was in the water; the next moment I went out of my depth altogether. The current in among the lignum bushes was very strong, and being impeded with my swag and boots I was a long time floundering about before I could get into my depth again. The experience was of use of me. I stripped and found a passage among the trees; then, returning for my things, I swam over with them in comfort.

Not till I was a hundred miles below Hungerford did I overtake the floodwaters of the Paroo and wade through the last of the swamps. There were public houses now every ten or twenty miles into Wilcannia. Away out

'By this time I had trained myself to do with very little water. I could walk twenty-five miles without wetting my lips. The corellas flock to water at sundown, the thirsty traveller need but be guided by them, and he will infallibly be brought to water.'

Countryside in the Darling River area. Morrison found the 'wretched country.... with its uninteresting scrub, its vast flats of saltbush and occasional stretches of barren hills.... the very incarnation of dreary desolation'.

in that wretched country of claypans and sand ridges, with its uninteresting scrub, its vast flats of saltbush and occasional stretches of barren hills, I suddenly came on a beautiful lake which wandered away to the east till its outer margin was hidden. For a little while I felt enthusiastic about the country I was in, but having to toil for some hours through heavy sand my misplaced enthusiasm was turned into ridicule. The scene constantly opening before me seemed the very incarnation of dreary desolation.... Weak and fagged, and badly in need of a spell, I could not rest till I was in Wilcannia.

I got in an hour after the telegraph had closed on Easter Monday; it was Wednesday before I had the means of buying any food. With no money in my pocket, and camped on the flat below the hospital, where those vagrants who have knocked down their cheques in the hells of this town rest till recuperated enough to start away with their swag, my experience of Wilcannia was not a cheerful one. Another young fellow was in a similar predicament to myself, but he knew a Chinese cook at one of the hotels, and twice sponged a supper. On the second evening another of us camped there was put in the lockup and got a fortnight. Another had been living on this flat for months; no one knew how he lived; he hadn't a sixpence.

On the Wednesday I got money and gave a farewell *al fresco* feed to all the tramps and vagabonds, after which I left on the seventy mile track. At the end of the seventy miles is Mount Manaro station, situated in the hollow of the enclosing hills. The way lies through vast clay flats of saltbush and mallee, interspersed with sedges of mulga, boree, leopardwood and sandalwood. The walking is heavy, and there is one stage of twenty-three miles without water. Above Ivanhoe the country is comparatively picturesque. Immediately after leaving it I got into the endless saltbush plains, the few clumps of box and pine on which can be seen such an incredible distance. The large box which gives its name to the One Tree Plain can be seen twenty miles off. There are public houses every ten or twelve miles. The landlady of one of them poses in Melbourne society as a squatter's wife. Up here she is known as the Scrub Turkey.

The hospital of Wilcannia at about the time of Morrison's visit. He camped on a flat near by with a group of fellow vagrants.

I travelled now very rapidly. From Hay I passed through Deniliquin, Echuca, Rochester, Elmore, Heathcote and Kilmore, reaching Melbourne on 21 April. While in my own colony it was a perfect picnic. Instead of immense tracts of country owned by one man, and given up to sheep, there were a succession of beautiful little farms, each with its haystack, its neat little cottage, its substantial fence, and its scene of vigorous activity. Ploughing was in full swing, clearing and grubbing. The beautiful hilly country, seemingly so fertile, and supporting so excellent a class of people, pleased me beyond measure. Certainly, I thought, my colony may be the smallest, but it is the healthiest and most beautiful of them all. This fact I have left to the last. I came seventeen hundred miles through the interior of Australia without seeing a kangaroo. My only objection to writing this account of my walk was a natural one. If it had never been written many people might think that I had done something wonderful. They will read this and see that anyone who cared to take the trouble and give up four months of his time could have done the walk more quickly than I did, more easily, and with less discomfort to himself.

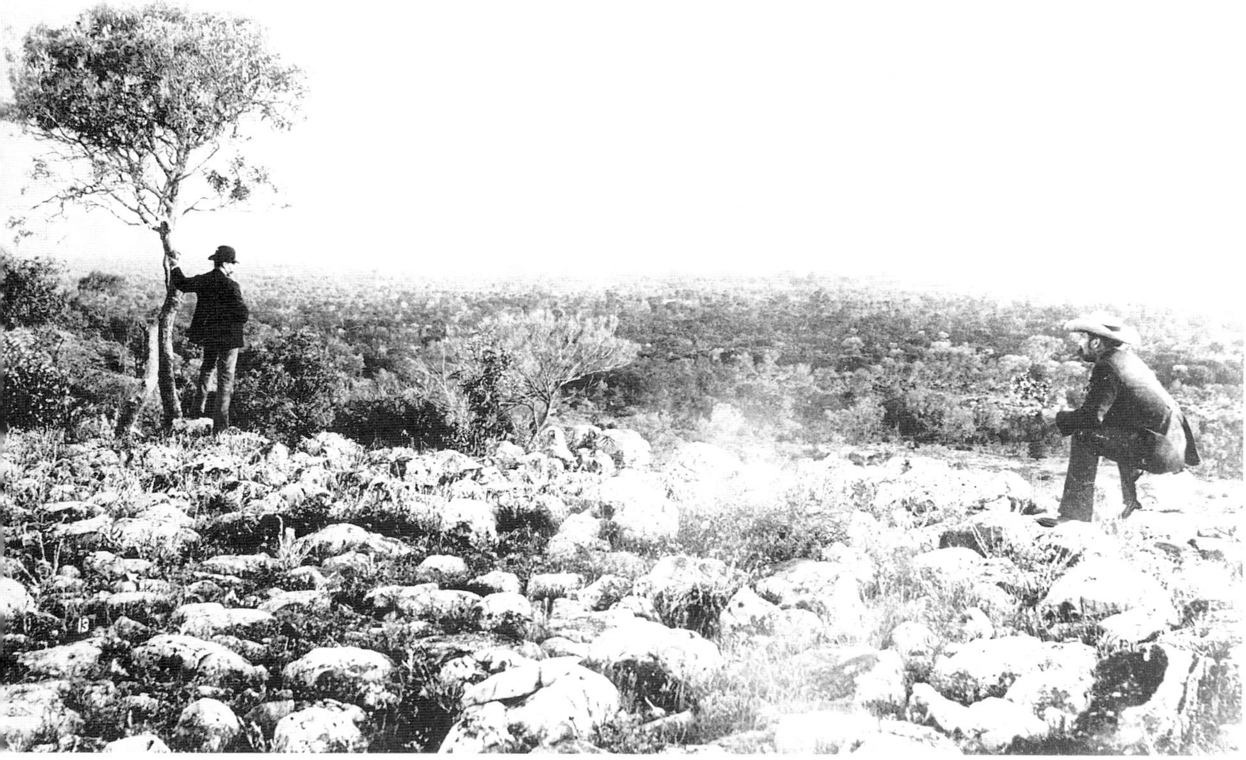

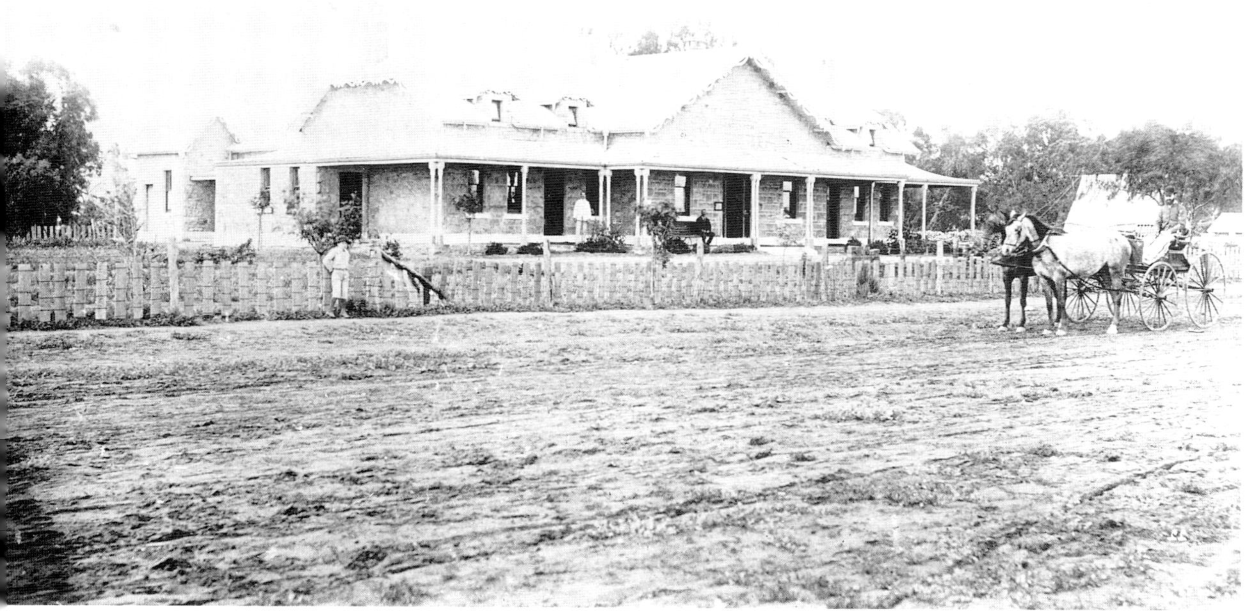

THE GREAT TREK OF THE DURACKS

Mary Durack

'The route from Thylungra stretched north to the Gulf and swung west to no-man's-land. On the map it looked simple enough and measured a fairly neat 2,500 miles.'

ONE OF AUSTRALIA'S great droving exploits was the overlanding of cattle from south-western Queensland to the Kimberley district of Western Australia by members of the Durack family. Brothers Patrick (Patsy) and Michael Durack had founded Thylungra station on Cooper's Creek in the 1860s, and other members of their extended family—with names such as Long Michael, Jerry Brice, Big Johnnie and Black Pat—had taken up properties in the same area. Following the discovery by Alexander Forrest of vast areas of good pastoral land in the Kimberley district, the Duracks decided that this was the land of opportunity for the younger generation of their families. In due course they took up large leaseholds on the Ord River; they now had to stock this land with cattle. In June and July 1883 four parties of drovers with a total of 7,500 head of cattle set out from the Cooper's Creek area to make the trek across nothern Australia to the Kimberleys. They were two years and four months on the track, and during this time they suffered much hardship and misadventure. They were held up for months at a waterhole on the Georgina River waiting for the drought to break, and many cattle died of pleuropneumonia and tick fever along the way. However, they arrived at the Ord in September 1885 with enough cattle to found the herds of Rosewood, Argyle and Lissadel stations. Mary Durack, granddaughter of Patsy Durack, tells the story of the epic trek in her family saga Kings in Grass Castles. Here she describes the beginning of the journey and the way in which they travelled and passed their time.

THE ROUTE from Thylungra stretched north to the Gulf and swung west to no-man's-land. On the map it looked simple enough and measured a fairly neat 2,500 miles. In fact it veered to every compass point from water to water, from grass to grass, and nobody knew how far they must travel in 'drover's miles'.

Halfway up the Thomson River Long Michael's party had caught up with the other mobs and from here they were to travel more or less together, but keeping the four mobs apart as far as possible. Which lot 'went lead' for the day seems to have depended upon which got the earliest start in the morning.

Each party had its wagonette containing supplies, water drums and drovers' swags. This was driven by the cook, who liked to make camp ahead of the drovers and have the billy boiling and the johnnycakes roasting in the ashes when the men rode in off watch. A good camp cook took a tremendous pride in his speed and efficiency. He was traditionally a touchy customer, but the sight of his busy figure, moving briskly among the neat rows of packbags

A mob of bullocks being driven across a river in flood, one of the hazards encountered by long-distance drovers.

and cooking utensils, was a welcome one to a band of hungry men after a long day in the saddle. They judiciously praised the lightness of his dampers and brownies, the succulence of his salt beef and stews.

There were conventions to be observed, small points that marked the experienced stockman from the 'newchum'. Nattiness was one of them, for untidiness meant muddle and delay. It was against all the unwritten laws of the road to waste time looking for one's personal effects. Hat, boots, pannikin and stockwhip must always be to hand, while matches, revolver and pocket-knife were carried in neat leather pouches in their belts. It was 'not done' to linger over meals or get in the cook's way between the packs and the fire, and no one but the cook was ever permitted to meddle with the impedimenta in the wagonette.

Tough customers as many of the old-time stockmen were, some so illiterate that they signed their names with a cross, there was a certain code of etiquette in the cattle camps. Unless he volunteered information, a man was never questioned about his past, and the name he gave himself was good enough. Nothing he said in drink was held against him, and he was not reminded of his indiscretions at a later date. A man could skite as much as he liked, he could leg-pull and lie, but he must on no account be 'flash', though what was considered 'flash' in one district often passed in another.

Letting the cattle spread out over good grass, the drovers 'poked' their mobs quietly north-west up the Darra and over the rugged dividing range to the head of Western River. At Longreach they had taken on as many stores as the packs would carry to avoid bothering station people with their needs. Some settlers resented the passing of big herds through their properties, for in the words of the old ballad: '... They wouldn't steal a copper,/But they

Breakfast in a drover's camp—photographed by the pioneer documentary photographer Charles Kerry.

all steal grass.' Some station owners, however, went out of their way to show hospitality to the overlanders. They never forgot how, on their way down Western River, stockmen from Vindex station had ridden after them with a tribute of fresh vegetables and wished them luck as they moved on.... Already watering-places along the route were dwindling fast, and if rain did not fall soon they could well be trapped in the dreaded western Queensland drought.

No mother fended for her family more diligently than these drovers for their cattle. They battled and thought for their mobs as they nursed them along, aware of the slightest tenderness of hoof and hollowness of flank, grieving for a perishing beast, calling halt for a cow to calve.

Long Michael and his brothers would have considered war well justified against men who cracked their stockwhips at the wrong moment or did anything to excite a mob in hand. They had certain pet theories and prejudices against other methods of working cattle that they would uphold to a point of fanaticism. The fourth brother, Jerry Brice, who lived to the age of ninety-four, gloried to his dying day in having slashed a man's shirt down the back with his whip for having put cattle dogs on to a mob he had nursed down the Birdsville Track to the Burra in '81. Charged with assault and battery and fined ten pounds by the acting magistrate, stock dealer Jenkin Coles, his feelings were bitter indeed, especially since he had previously held Coles's stock knowledge in high regard. Later in the day he met the dealer in the pub and was shaken warmly by the hand:

'Put it here, young fellow,' Coles said (or so the old man's story went), 'I'd have done the same to the so-and-so myself.'

New-born calves were slung into canvas hammocks underneath the wagonettes and when the cattle caught them up were taken into the mob to be claimed by their mothers, but as the weeks passed the new arrivals far exceeded the capacity of the slender hammocks. When as many as thirteen calves would be born in a single dinner camp there was no alternative but to destroy them. It was one of the drovers' saddest reflections that they had been forced to dispose of no less than thirteen hundred new-born calves during the trip. It was a complete waste, for stockmen were oddly squeamish about eating veal or 'staggering Bob' as it was known in the cattle camps.

Keeping the bereft mothers on camp at night was an all-time job. They used every wile of their kind to escape the mob and make back along the route in desperate search of their young. Those that managed to break travelled quickly and sometimes returned three or four day stages before they could be overtaken and brought back. Often they went plodding on, far past the camp where their calves had been born, until the drought closed in on them and they perished on their tracks. This maternal instinct meant extra work for men and horses and the waste of precious time while waters along the route were sinking perilously low....

When the drovers hit a township it was not easy to get them out.

'Give us time to wash the dust down,' they said, but they had collected a lot of dust and there were 'old cobbers' in every outback bar.

At Winton one of the wagon drivers found romance with a full-blown beauty behind the bar of the local pub and became so lovelorn at the Diamantina River that he asked for his cheque and returned to the township as fast as horse and packs would carry him. A bagman camped beside the track was glad enough to take on the job, and the party continued downriver to the Diamantina gates.

The stock route lay over country flat to horizon's end, meandering through a maze of claypan channels edged with teatree, saltbush and wild cotton. Red bare sandhills, beaten by desert winds, broke the skyline as the stock veered

Patrick (Patsy) and Michael (Stumpy Michael) Durack (at back), founders of Thylungra station on Cooper's Creek, with their brother Jeremiah (front right) and cousin 'Long Michael' Durack.

west to Parker Springs, where round wells, warm and bubbing with soda and magnesia, overflowed into a shallow creek. Here, while the drovers enjoyed a plunge in the buoyant, effervescing waters, the cattle were allowed to browse and refresh themselves in preparation for a dreaded fifty miles' dry stage.

At the end of a three days' spell the stockmen filled their waterbags, a small tank and some barrels, gave the cattle a last long drink and headed them into the setting sun. Forcing the pace, they pushed on to daylight, took five minutes for a pannikin of tea and a johnnycake and were off again until noon. They made camp for the hours of intensest heat, to press urgently on at sundown into another waterless night.

Towards dawn the leading cattle were stretching out their heads, eyes and nostrils dilated, until the whole thirsty mob had broken into an urgent trot, bellowing what the drovers knew as 'the water call'. It was still a full day's stage to the Hamilton River, but knowing how thirsty cattle were quick to smell water on the wind the drovers hoped they might be nearing a billabong. When advance riders discovered that the water scent was being wafted from a private tank, all the steadying tactics of the stockman's craft were used to force the cattle in a detour past the tantalising spot to which they continued to turn and strain for miles.

One big, three-year-old bull managed to break from the mob and gallop back. Duncan McCaully turned his mare after it in the moonlight, his long whip flashing out to cut its flank. The beast turned, head down, to charge, but the rider, already off his horse, seized the bewildered animal by the horns, brought it to the ground, and flung sand into its eyes. It was an old trick, cruel but effective, for an angry, half-blinded animal will always charge the nearest moving object—invariably, unless the stockman is extremely unlucky or inexperienced, the travelling herd which quickly envelops the outlaw and carries him along with it.

The mob strung on sullenly bellowing its misery, through another sunrise, another dinner camp, too thirsty now to pull at the tufty, dry remnants of Mitchell grass along the way. A few hours' uneasy spell and off again, the stronger beasts stringing ahead, the weaker lagging painfully.

Towards evening a dull green line of timber marked the winding course of the Hamilton, but advance riders brought news that there was not enough water for the great, dry mob at the nearest hole. The drovers knew too well how the cattle would charge the water in their frenzy of thirst until is was churned to an undrinkable slough in which the weaker animals would hopelessly bog or be smothered in the crush. Grim tragedies of the droving track were known to them all, when perishing herds had stampeded to total destruction in boggy riverbeds.

The stronger cattle were now drafted from the various mobs and taken fifteen miles downstream to a big reach of water while the weaker animals were steadied on to the nearer hole. Only a little water, thick and foul-smelling, floated on slimy mud, but the cattle drained it frantically and then nuzzled and sucked at the evil slime.

Late that night the sturdier mob, breaking at last from the weary drovers, plunged so precipitously into the big hole that when the mighty thirst was

> 'The mob strung on sullenly bellowing its misery, through another sunrise, another dinner camp, too thirsty now to pull at the tufty, dry remnants of Mitchell grass along the way.'

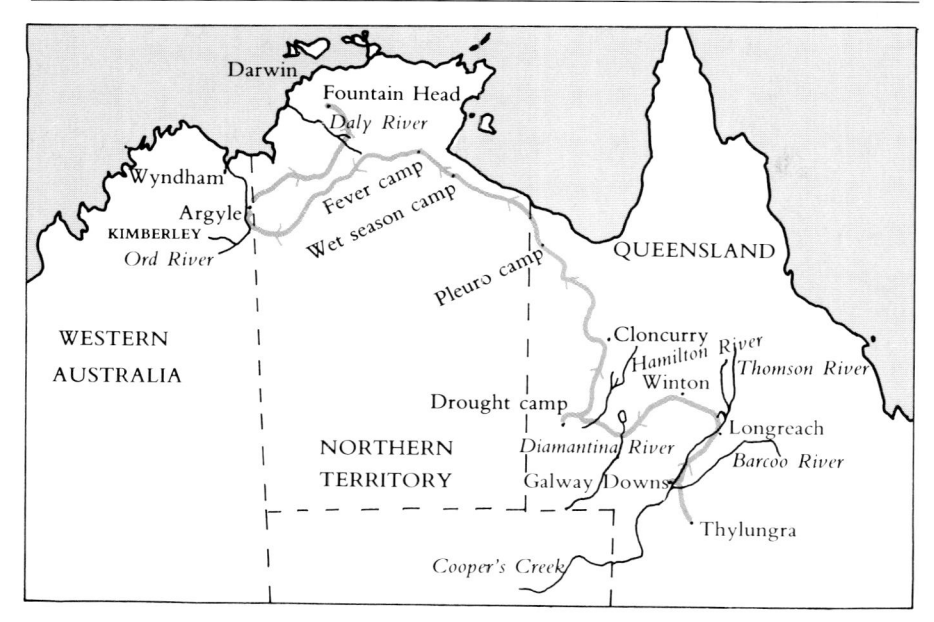

The path of the Durack's cattle drive from south-western Queensland to the Kimberley region of Western Australia in 1883—85.

slaked dozens of smothered fish were found floating in the muddy waters. These provided a rare feast for the tired, hungry men, able at last to relax while the exhausted cattle fed quietly out over the river flat.

By the time they reached the big Parapitcherie waterhole on the Georgina everyone in western Queensland was talking drought and the drovers knew they must camp and wait for rain. Optimists in the party attached hopeful significance to 'the ring around the moon', the 'pinky haze' in the sky at sunset or the antics of insects and birds, but Long Michael at least had no illusions. As the horses had suffered badly over the dry stages and some had died from eating poison weed, he resolved to ride back to Brisbane for a fresh supply. Maybe a 960-mile ride to the capital with an extra mount and pack was no worse than holding cattle on a waterhole and waiting for the drought to break. At all events he seems to have taken it very much as a matter of course....

Back on camp the drovers now had time to kill. Men off watch sat about whittling stockwhip handles from lengths of ironbark that had the pliability of whalebone and was known for some reason as 'dead finish'. They spent hours patiently working bits of greenhide into their favourite types of whip, making rounded 'snake belly' plaits that would cut like knives in a straight thrust. Young Charlie Gaunt started a two-up school, and Jack Sherringham played the concertina and sang the '101 bush melodies' and a few of his own all to the same tune.

Then there was 'mumble-the-peg', so much in vogue among stockmen of the day. Like knuckle bones but played with an open penknife, it kept the players amused for hours on end. Wild applause greeted feats of digital dexterity, with shouts of mirth for the loser who must worry a buried penknife out of the dust with his teeth. So great a grip had the game taken outback that James Tyson when advertising for stockmen added the curt advice: 'No mumble-the-peggers need apply.'

Still, the weeks dragged wearily. The cattle, forced to wander miles to grass, were falling away, and the stockmen began to suffer from a mysterious skin affection like scurvy. Other symptoms followed until, overcome by weakness and lethargy, they lay about in the shade of the scraggy coolibahs, some too weak to ride after the cattle and others too ill even to sit up. The boss drovers, sick themselves, doled out the nostrums of the bush, quinine, Epsom salts and Holloway's mixture, but without avail. The nearest doctor was at Cloncurry, two hundred miles away, but sicknesses such as fever, dysentery and Barcoo rot were regarded as part of a stockman's lot. This seemed like all these common ailments in one, but only when two men died within a day of each other was its seriousness realised.

Two black stockmen whose assistance had been called in to hold the cattle provided a clue to the problem by pointing out that the far end of the Parapitcherie waterhole had always been held taboo as a tribal camping place.

'That belong long time,' they said. 'Must be some reason. Might be poison.'

Acting on tribal custom they dug sand soaks in the dry bed of the Burke and carried water each day in canteens and waterbags to the sick men, who began to recover at once. Realising that the cattle and horses were also being affected by the water, they fenced off the death trap and sank large dry wells, hollowed troughs from tree trunks and filled them with whip and bucket for the perishing stock. Many beasts, however, were already dead or dying, and although attempts were made to burn the carcasses the reek of carrion hung horribly about the waterhole.

Later it was discovered that the Parapitcherie hole was fed by alkaline springs which attained a near lethal concentration as the fresh water level fell.

Light rain fell about the end of April '84, just enough to make a little water and give fresh hope, but it caused the cattle to spread out, feeding over a wide range which made hard work for the weak horses.

About a week later a rider from the nearest station came galloping at dawn.

'Get moving, you fellows. The river's down!'

The drovers knew droughts and they knew floods—those sudden avalanches of water pouring from some distant part of the river into country where perhaps no rain had fallen for many months, filling the long dry channels of creeks and rivers, lifting timber and carcasses to go surging downstream, turning the parched landscape into an inland sea.

'The river's down!'

Expertly the cooks had their equipment into the wagonettes and the stockmen were in their saddles and away. They were always competing over the time they took in catching and saddling a horse, getting a fire alight and a billy boiling, rolling a swag and hitching it to a pack—little things, seemingly unimportant, but on which at certain times might hang the fate of an entire mob and of men and horses too.

The cattle but for the inevitable stragglers were taken at a run to higher ground where, minutes later, drovers watched the waters surging down, swirling into the topmost branches of the river trees under which they had camped for weary months—death-dealing, life-giving water, changing the face of the land.

> 'The drovers knew droughts and they knew floods—those sudden avalanches of water pouring from some distant part of the river into country where perhaps no rain had fallen for many months.'

THREE THOUSAND MILES IN A SIDE-SADDLE

Daisy Bates

IRISH-BORN *Daisy Bates, who was to become famous for her work among the Aborigines, first came to Australia around 1884 seeking a cure for a suspected lung disease. In March 1884, at Charters Towers, Queensland, she married Edwin Henry Murrant (thought by some to be 'Breaker' Morant) but left him soon after. The following February, in Nowra, New South Wales, she went through a form of marriage with cattleman Jack Bates, by whom she had a son, Arnold. In 1894 she returned to England, leaving her husband and son in Australia, and worked for five years in London as a journalist. Commissioned by* The Times *to investigate stories of cruelty to the Aborigines of Western Australia, she arrived at Fremantle in 1901 and began her travels by horse and buggy in the north-west of the state. Her husband and son were already in Western Australia; Jack was working at Roebuck Plains station, east of Broome, and had been looking for suitable country to take up as a cattle run. For some months Daisy lived with Jack and Arnold at Roebuck Plains, where they bought Hereford cattle to stock the run they acquired in the Ophthalmia Range, south-west of Marble Bar. On 23 April 1902 they set out to drive their cattle to their new home. In her book* The Passing of the Aborigines, *Daisy Bates gives a graphic description of the eight-month droving trip. However, she makes no mention of her husband, Jack, apart from a couple of passing references to the 'head drover'. Nor does she indicate that this strenuous journey marked the end of her brief role as a cattleman's wife and her permanent return to journalism and study of the Aborigines.*

THE YEAR'S WORK with the cattle began, and the desire came to stock up my own run of 183,600 acres on Ethel Creek in the Windell area of north central West Australia.

The frightening names of the locality—Ophthalmia Ranges, Dead Man's Hill, Grave Creek, and so on, had hitherto deterred other pastoralists from contemplating settlement there, but they appealed to me, and on my previous journey by buggy, 1899–1900, I had found that far-out area an encouraging proposition. I named the property Glen Carrick, in affectionate remembrance of a dear friend in England, and set about the purchase of the cattle to stock it.

To watch my mob of 770 well-fed Herefords placidly browsing round the fringe of Lake Eda, some forty miles east of Broome, brought back vividly to my mind the inspired lines of Adam Lindsay Gordon, Banjo Paterson and other Australian poets, whose stirring verses lift droving to the realms of high adventure. How little I knew! Today I detest even the picture of a Hereford cow. I loathe their whitewashed faces, for I have ridden behind them with eight of my own drovers, for six months, one thousand miles as the route went but some three thousand as I rode it, zigzagging behind the mob at six or eight or ten miles a day, and every one of the 770 surpassing the Irish pig in contrariness.

This great mob was, perhaps, the largest number that had travelled down from the West Kimberleys in a single herd. Stores and equipment I obtained from Broome, also a cook who was a Maori half-caste, for Broome was mostly 'breed' in those days, with just a few decent whites to leaven the mass. Sundry droving hands were also engaged, whose knowledge of the gentle art about equalled mine. We all armed ourselves with a long stockwhip and, while the head drover and his lieutenant were mustering and branding, tried to flourish them in true stockman style. After much climbing into the trees to disentangle the lash, the stockwhips were quietly rolled up and hidden in the dray, a humble buggy whip or less ambitious instrument of sapling and twine taking their place.

My equipment was a good English pigskin side-saddle with ordinary stirrup; three pairs of laced wallaby-skin shoes; three habits, a felt hat, three pairs of riding gloves, and plenty of fly veiling. A compact hold-all and portmanteau carried all necessaries, and was easily accessible on the dray, which also carried the stores for the trip and the drovers' swags.

I undertook the purchase of the 'plant' myself. Besides the four fine draughthorses, there were some thirty-six riding horses for the use of the drovers, myself, and my son, aged twelve. There were a few good stock-

Daisy Bates at about the time of her droving journey in 1902.

horses in the mob, but not one of the drovers owned a cattle dog, a most necessary adjunct to droving.

On a golden day in the Australian April we lifted the big mob from Lake Eda and started off behind them. The head drover assigned each one his position and duties. Some guarded the flanks, the leader and his second headed the mob; the Maori cook, Davy, took complete charge of the dray, provisions and spare horses, and the others became the 'tailing' hands.

A travelling mob of cows usually shapes itself in the form of a triangle, the strongest beasts forming the apex, while the stragglers make an ever-widening line at the rear in their efforts to find food, as the leaders and flankers consume almost every blade as they go along. All the cattle had been accustomed to surface water, and while the going was over the claypan and well-grassed country south of Broome the big mob travelled easily. My place and that of my boy, which we retained throughout the journey, were the base of the triangle, zigzagging to and fro behind the 'tailers'.

There is no eight-hour day in a droving camp. All hands are roused at peep of dawn. Davy had breakfast ready and steaming, horses were brought in and saddled, and the mob was waked and started. At each night camp, many of the mothers hid their calves, hoping to make back to them later. To watch a cow hide its calf behind a four-inch tussock is a lesson in wild mothercraft. Sunrise generally saw us on the move, the leaders grazing and the stragglers finding their places at the tail. Back and forth along this ever-widening tail of cows and calves we rode, with eyes alert for break-backs. Meanwhile the head man went on to find a night camp. Davy followed the horse-track and only twice failed to turn up in time—but even so, he incurred my extreme displeasure on one occasion. The only greenstuff I had had to eat for weeks, a fresh young lettuce presented as a gift of grace at one of the stations, he took away and boiled!

All went well until the Eighty Mile Beach was reached; here the surface waters ceased and the wells began. Six canvas buckets, each with a twenty-gallon capacity, with pulleys and gear, were brought for emergencies. Most of the wells along the Eighty Mile were in a bad state, owing to the disuse of the stock-route, and there was hefty work for all at the end of each day's droving. The long-disused windlasses, timbering, and platform more than once gave way, burying bucket and gear and effectually closing the wells, so there was nothing for it but to move the thirsty mob onward. The wells were far apart, and cows in calf are slow walkers.

At Whistler's Creek, near Lagrange Bay, the sea became visible and with a 'Hurrah swing' of waving tail, the beasts rushed into the bay. Fortunately the water was shallow at that point, and they were soon on the road again. Nambeet Well, halfway along the Eighty Mile, was the first good well struck, a shallow soak with beautiful and abundant water. Beside the well was a corrugated iron tombstone, telling of the murder of a white man named Hourigan by his native boy, for a few ends of tobacco. The boy was caught and hanged.

Old breakwinds on the slopes surrounding the valley of Nambeet Well showed that the place was once a favourite camping ground, but after the murder no natives would camp there. Some poisonous or stupefying herbage

'There is no eight-hour day in a droving camp. All hands are roused at peep of dawn. Davy had breakfast ready and steaming, horses were brought in and saddled, and the mob was waked and started.'

Daisy Bates's cattle on the move.

laid a score or so of our cattle apparently dead there, but we heard later that they all recovered and returned to their own ground.

The coastline along the beach is only ten to twelve feet above sea-level, and in all the long stretch of plain only two little pinnacles—Barn and Church Hills—raise their heads above the level. These little hills were beacons for the schooners and luggers along the Eighty Mile Beach. A species of bloated rat, with a thick tail, makes shallow burrows on the plain, and these pitfalls added to the difficulty of manoeuvring the thirsty mob. Along the whole length of the beach, we had to carry our firewood in the dray. There was but one tree, an unburnable 'thorny sandpaper', left standing, covered with axe chops, and impregnable still.

The first stampede occurred at Barn Hill, and standing on the little knob I looked down on a sea of horns and tails and dust as the whole mob suddenly started back for home and water. At last the galloping drovers headed them again, the sea of dust subsided, and the runaways were under control.

All along the coast and right out in the bays are fresh springs bubbling up through the mud, and at low tide one can see and taste the beautiful fresh water. Smoke signals of the natives could be seen on the horizon every day, messages carried on for many miles. The signals were all identical—a long spiral drifting away to the south. The inlanders were even in those years coming to the coast from ever-increasing distances to replace the coast groups that had died out, until they, in their turn, succumbed to the new conditions. Practically all the coastal natives are now dead, those frequenting the townships and beaches being far inland 'relatives' of the dead tribes.

The long day's tailing made riding very wearisome, and I frequently changed to the off side. I noticed that many of the drovers rode side-saddle now and then, but generally the quick and arduous work of the wells relieved the weariness of the saddle.

Gradually the Herefords became used to the wells, and our only trouble was the rush to the troughs. We had hoped to reach Glen Carrick before any calves were dropped, so no lorry had been brought along for day-old calves. Many had to be killed, owing to forced marches, and their mothers gave endless trouble and made night hideous with their bellowing. Night-long watches, with great fires at various points, became the rule. More men were needed, and I had to go back to Lagrange Bay to telegraph for extra hands and horses. The way lay over a wide plain, sparsely dotted with high ant hills. I was cantering easily, eyes and thoughts on the scenery, when my mount began to pig-jump and threw me. His trouble was a slipping saddlecloth. I caught the reins, and held them, through all the play that followed, though now and then the flying hoofs came nearer to my head than was pleasant. At last he quietened down. A twisted ankle and no mounting block baffled me for a moment, but the horse had had enough play and came along to an ant hill, from the top of which I mounted and proceeded on the journey.

As we trailed along over the Eighty Mile, prodding a sturdy little calf or clubbing a day-old weakling, those of us who were at the base of the great moving triangle were surprised one morning to see the mob suddenly split in two, leaving a narrow lane along the centre, and along the lane quietly walked a Jew pedlar with his huge pack strapped to his back. Drovers and horses stood like statues as Moses passed through the Red Sea, never once hastening. The drovers were waiting for him—fortunately out of earshot. All he remarked at the close of their tirade was, 'Who iss the lady mit the veil?'

At Wallal we came to the end of the dreadful Eighty Mile, good herbage, good water, and a blessed spell. At the time of our passing, there were six white men and over a hundred natives at this isolated station. Supplies were brought to it quarterly by schooner, and though they were always depleted by travellers long before the schooner was due, the white men bravely carried on in good times and lean. The new country was better for the cattle, but the size of the mob necessitated our reaching water always in good time.

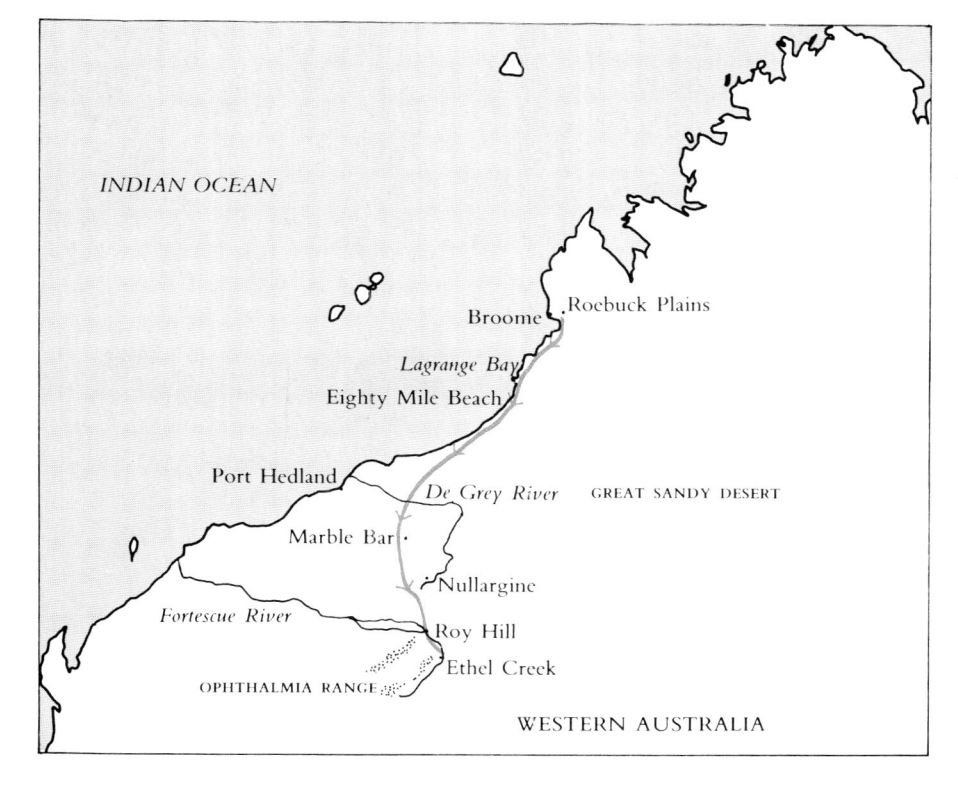

The north-west of Western Australia, showing the route taken by Daisy Bates and her cattle from Roebuck Plains, inland from Broome, to Ethel Creek in the Ophthalmia Range.

The station owners showed us every courtesy in free paddocks and water rights, and we, on our part, paid due attention to time-limit rules.

One night we camped at a beautiful waterhole called Jalliung. Native legend made Jalliung a bottomless pool and the home of a magic snake who devoured any strange blackfellow who drank of it.

At Balla-Balla we replenished our supplies at the little tin store of a barefooted and bearded gentleman who told me that he was a brother of Tiffany, the millionaire jeweller of New York. Such was the adventurous and polyglot population of the north-west at that time that he may have been.

We were accorded a great welcome at the stations. Pardu had suffered a willy-willy a few weeks before our visit, but the roofless house was covered by the hospitality of its owners. At the de Grey the finest four-in-hand of greys that I had seen in West Australia drove out to greet and take me back for a day's spell.

In the saddle for eighteen hours a day, from dawn till the sharing of the night watches, we plodded on. The drovers and cattle stopped for a siesta at midday, in the worst of the blazing heat. Never able to sleep in the daytime, I seized this opportunity for explorations and collections of botanical and geological novelties, which I later forwarded to the museums.

Marble Bar, which received its name from the mottled bar of quartz which crosses the Coongan River, is 130 miles from Port Hedland, and Nullagine, 80 miles south of Marble Bar—all mineral-bearing and good pastoral country. We kept well west of both these townships. It was a dry year, but the feed was splendid. The mob spread itself out on the flats, wading knee-deep in lush herbage, grazing leisurely along the wide swathe of their going. Ashburton pea made a green carpet in the riverbeds, so that the riverbeds sometimes became the stock route. At last we came to the Shaw Hills, denuded masses of granite, silent and sombre. No sound greeted us as we climbed hill after hill; the songs of birds are never heard. Mine was the first dray that ever passed through the Shaw Gorge, where floodmarks showed some sixty feet above the riverbed. Our last night there was a nightmare. The rain came down with the darkness. We were all in a cul-de-sac, cattle, men and horses, our only outlet the riverbed, along which the floodwaters would run. Everyone had had some experience of the quick rise of these rivers. No one slept, and we all watched anxiously from our shelters under the rocks. Happily the rain was light and local, but there had been catastrophic floods many times in this area, and we were deemed fortunate.

In a lonely part of the Shaw, I came upon a native with his two women, three children and some dogs, all very emaciated. I made them follow to the camp, and two young calves about a fortnight old were killed and given to them. Each calf weighed about sixty pounds, but when I rode to the camp at dawn there was not a bone left to tell the tale—only six human stomachs incredibly distended, and six happy faces grinning greeting and farewell.

We crossed the Divide, and so came to the Fortescue River and Roy Hill, with excellent fodder to fatten our herd, now increased to nearly a thousand head. Day after day we travelled a land of plenty, thick mulga scrub, succulent saltbush and Mitchell grass. The pioneer of Roy Hill was Peter

'It was a dry year, but the feed was splendid. The mob spread itself out on the flats, wading knee-deep in lush herbage, grazing leisurely along the wide swathe of their going.'

MacKay. A few miles from the homestead is a knobby rise where, in the early days, he was once assailed by a horde of savages. He had his gun and ammunition, and he was a dead shot, as they well knew. There he remained for two days without sleep, eking out his portion of damper and mutton, and keeping the crowd of cannibals at bay. They hurled their spears and clubs at him, but he had learnt to dodge these weapons. On the third day help came from the station.

Our worst stampede occurred on Roy Hill property, on one of the station wells in a fenced paddock. The cattle had had a long and trying day, the tired calves reluctant to move, and their mothers half maddened with thirst and distracted with mother love. Horses and men were down and out with watching and guiding the troublesome beasts, and it was dark when they had all been safely passed through the fence.

Relying on the security of the mob and the safety of the fence, all hands immediately unsaddled for a drink of tea, when the cattle broke camp and rushed the fence, heading straight for Roy Hill and the pools there. The whole mob, except those too weak to travel, were away in a twinkling. About four hundred tailers, cows and calves, were left to three of us to water—myself, my little son, and one droving hand, with Davy and the dray to look after our inner man. The other drovers headed back to many days of trouble before the stampeders were collected and brought on. Our mob was too tired to move, even when it heard the squeak of the windlass. My son and I shared work with the twenty-gallon buckets from early dawn till late at night, and managed to satisfy our charges by steady lifting and emptying. The paddock was full of feed, and with plenty of water there need be no anxiety.

We all divided the night watch. Nights were still and cloudless. Hercules and Lyra, Aquila and Cygnus were my fellow-watchers in the silence, on their way to the mystical west. No sound was heard save the quiet breathing of the sleeping herd—the little calves snuggled up beside their mothers in full content. I was thankful that their hard times were over.

A chastened mob was brought back to the paddock, and after a few days' spell we moved on the last eighty miles to Glen Carrick. Pools were full and frequent in the many creeks and tributaries which rise in the Ophthalmia Ranges and from the headwaters of the Ashburton and Fortescue. There was no dearth of good feed, and the last part of the journey was without event. In such good grass was my own little run that in three months' time the cattle had put on wonderful condition and it was possible for them to take the six weeks' trip to Peak Hill, there to be disposed of as 'forward stores'.

There was no homestead but a bough shade at Glen Carrick, but I remained there happily for a short period, waiting the opportunity to return to Port Hedland. At last I secured a passage with one 'Black Johnson' a man who had been taking out a buggy-load of dynamite to a far-distant mine. We arrived, without any trouble, at Port Hedland, within nine or ten days. I was in time to embark on the steamer *Sultan* on the downward journey to Perth.

LONG-DISTANCE CYCLIST

Francis Birtles

'Bowling along with a strong breeze on a good track, I enjoyed to the full the glorious weather and "put it all on" as I sent mile after mile under wheel. The track was ideal, for miles level and no ruts to speak of.'

WHEN FRANCIS BIRTLES *arrived back in Australia in December 1905 after spending two years with the Transvaal Constabulary, he disembarked at Fremantle and, on Boxing Day, mounted a bicycle and rode it to Melbourne. It was the beginning of a long-distance cycling career that by 1912 had taken him around Australia twice and across the continent seven times. His first transcontinental ride was completed in August 1907. Soon after arriving in Sydney from Fremantle he set off again, cycling to Brisbane, Normanton, Darwin, Alice Springs and Adelaide before returning to Sydney, having ridden more than thirteen thousand kilometres in thirteen months. During this epic cycling journey he sent back occasional reports to* Australian Country Life, *which noted in its December 1907 issue that he carried 'a one and a half gallon bronze metal tank for holding water (waterbags are useless, as the evaporation is too great, and the salt-dust of the lake country makes the water brackish), a Winchester repeater and two hundred rounds of ammunition, a camera (Harrington and Co.'s), etc., waterproof ration bag, folding double billycan—one cooking and the other for tea—a small outfit of clothes, a compass, and other odds and ends, making a total weight of sixty pounds'. The following excerpts from the* Country Life *articles tell of some of his experiences in North Queensland.*

BOWLING ALONG with a strong breeze on a good track, I enjoyed to the full the glorious weather and 'put it all on' as I sent mile after mile under wheel. The track was ideal, for miles level and no ruts to speak of. At last I got into rocky country, but still good travelling. A tree across the road in front turned me off the track amongst the grass and up a sloping shelf of rock. Every cyclist must take risks—one of mine came along just at that spot. On swerving back to the road I suddenly found my machine leave the rocky shelf and take a flying jump through long grass with a sudden drop of fully three feet. The machine landed squarely upright, but the force of the impact with the ground buckled the front wheel into a figure eight and snapped the steering tube right off above the crown.

I sat on the soft grass and the evening sky smiled down on me. The trail looked more inviting than ever. I wished I had learnt how to smoke. I am told that it is a solace and a stimulant when the mind is troubled. The position was hopeless, and it looked as if my machine was past mending. The track was a lonely one to a distant station which I had hoped to reach that night. To make matters still more trying, I had barely food enough for supper, so I had a bushman's meal, viz., three holes tighter in the belt.

I had strapped the machine together as best I could and was just about to hoist it, kit and all, on my shoulder, and preparing to foot it, when I heard the music of distant horse bells. I dropped my load and awaited events, and in due time there came along the road towards me what looked like a Boer family on the trek. There were two wagon-loads of household effects with a mixture of children, poultry, cats, and caged cockatoos on top. Accompanying these were some half-dozen men and youths on horseback, while three females, who wore the big Queensland sun-bonnet and rode astride, brought up the rear beside a ramshackle buggy containing two old ladies. Now this was a picture I had dreamed about—a true bush picture—and I was not ready with my camera: all the plates in slides were exposed, and before I could have unstrapped my bag and filled up, the picture would be gone.

I waited dejectedly to watch them pass by, but that was not their intention. In their estimation it was camping time, and it did not take them long to unlimber and turn out. It proved to be a selector's family moving 'down south'. They had been three weeks on the road already. As soon as they heard of my trouble they overwhelmed me with kindness. I passed a most pleasant evening with them, and before a roaring fire that night, listening to their happy chatter that hinted of contented lives, I forgot my accident and enjoyed their quaint society.

Next morning, bright and early, I photographed them in a group, which they enjoyed immensely, and we parted with many expressions of friendship and, on my part, of thanks for their timely help and the food supply (nearly a week's), which they had forced on me, and, as I saw them disappear in the distance, I felt that life 'on the land' had much in it that was heart-pulling.

I got under way, changing positions with my bike, which I now carried

Francis Birtles kitted out for his cycling trip through the heart of Australia.

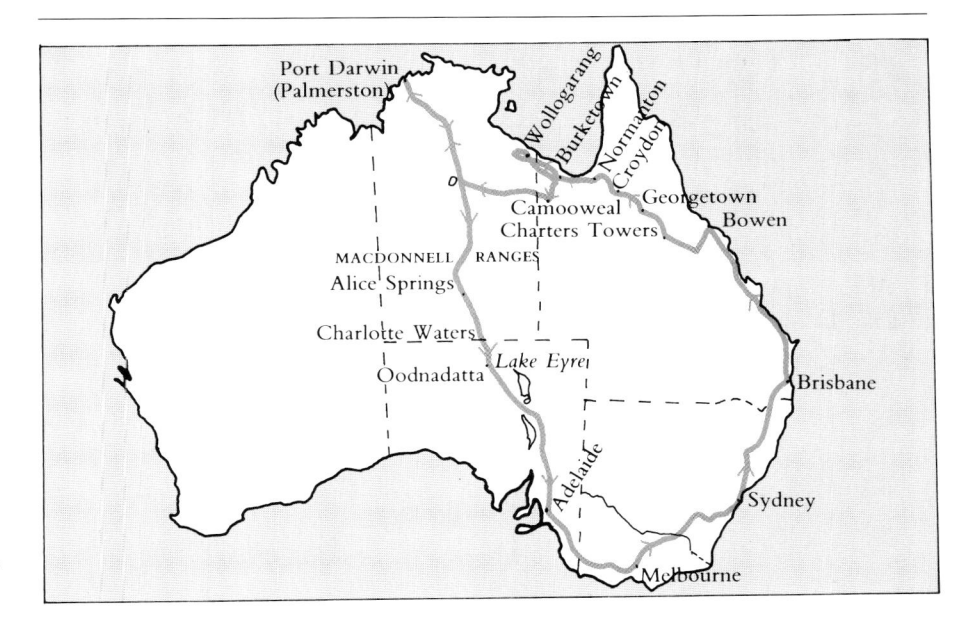

The route of Francis Birtles's bicycle trip in 1907–8. Much of the journey was over unmade roads and through territory that was almost trackless.

on my shoulder, and, by sundown, I reached the station. I can best describe my journey as a day's wrestling match and a fine trial of patience, as many times I got angry with the inanimate 'horse' that found out the tenderest bones of my shoulders and back, and I thought of hanging him to the nearest tree. I spent the next day at the station repairing things, and when I again started I'm sure I must have impressed the good people of the station as a most unlikely looking cyclist to cross the continent. After covering another 120 miles, walking and riding as best I could, I reached Bowen. Here I further repaired the machine and faced the road to Charters Towers, a distance of 300 miles, with much misgiving, and arrived there after fourteen days' battling....

At Charters Towers Birtles had his bike repaired, and after a two-day spell he pushed on towards Georgetown over a dusty, stony track.

Most of the beds of rivers and creeks back in North Queensland show nothing but sand—the waterholes being few and far between; so I have to pass a lot of my time grubbing for water, which is generally to be found about a couple of feet down. I have worn my nails right off. A powerful thirst often adds energy to my quest. The water when procured is always good and beautifully cool....

I am now in the land of insect pests. The flies and mosquitoes are awful. In the daytime I have to wear wire goggles or I would not be able to steer, for one hand would have to be engaged brushing the flies out of my eyes, and it takes both hands on the machine to get along these roads.

The ants are, perhaps, the worst of all pests. The little black ones—the highly flavoured gentlemen—are the worst; they are everywhere in millions. They have regular pads running, often half a mile, to water. The ground on these little roads is worn quite bare for a couple of inches wide, and along this the little beggars stream in countless thousands, one half going for a drink and the other going back, licking their chops after having had one. The best place to sleep or sit or rest is in the middle of a dusty road. Your ant does not like fine dust. Snakes and all other bush animals seem to prefer camping on the roads—I suppose to get away from the ants.

Owing to this, travelling at night is none too safe, as snakes are apt to get mixed up with the wheels and bare legs of the cyclist. Riding along in the early morning I see the tracks and camping places of all manner of snakes, from those of the bulk of a stockwhip to the fellow as big as a ship's hawser. Tracks in the sand would form a volume in themselves.

Here and there I caught sight of old deserted miners' camps, and here and there came to an out-of-the-way cattle station, at one of which I was refused rations. 'None to sell or give, not enough for ourselves,' I was told in a tone of voice which implied that I had no right in that part of the country.

The great drawback to cycling in this part of the country is the thorny bushes which are for ever puncturing the tyres. Dried-up branches of these bushes lie across the track in every direction. One day I mended ten punctures and had to sit down to repair damages in the blazing sun. Three times I attempted to leave one spot, but by the time the back tyre was right the front one was down, and so on.

It was a weary journey through desolate country to Georgetown. But the kindness of the 'sports' there soon made me forget the weary journey I had made. The next morning I was on the road again all well, save for one eye 'bunged up' by the bite of a bulldog ant two days before.

A coach runs betwen Georgetown and Croydon. The distance is seventy miles, which is negotiated in a day and a half, which is good travelling considering the deep sandy road. When I can, I always travel with a coach for company; and I notice they put on the pace when a bicycle is alongside. They don't like being passed....

After leaving Wollogarang I travelled out for a day along cattle tracks. Here I struck the first rain of the season. The wind blew with cyclonic force, and the rain set all the creeks and rivers running a banker. To make matters

Birtles's cycle loaded up for one of his later journeys, carrying 127 kilograms of equipment.

worse, the track petered out. I hunted up and down one river but could not see the faintest resemblance of a track. The country is very rough and scrubby, and then the rains completed all. The track disappeared.

The natives are afraid of the bike. Coming along a 'pad' one evening, I saw two gins walking along with their backs toward me. I got to within a couple of yards before they saw me. They bolted down the deep scrubby valley screaming and running parallel with the track. When they saw that I was gaining on them they nearly went frantic. At last they found an opening in the scrub and disappeared. One of them had a big goanna in her hand.

My provisions would not allow me to lose time like this, and although only two days out I returned to Wollogarang; the track was impossible. I am now glad that I did so, for the country 'down below' is flooded. Returning to just below the Nicholson, and shooting 'squatter' pigeons for meat—the country is swarming with them—I travelled to Egilabria, and thence south, on to the sweet-tasting flowing waters of the Gregory River. Waters full of magnesia and lime; the more one drinks the more is wanted. A little pinch of tea goes a long way with this water. Here I spent an afternoon fishing. This is one of the best rivers for sport that I have come across. Fish of all kinds are plentiful. Down in the clear water one can gaze into a natural aquarium. Big black cod, black bream, garfish, catfish, and brightly coloured fish such as the salmon trout and rifle fish are all to be seen. The rifle fish gets his name from the method in which he gets his food. He is not a very big fellow, might occasionally weigh half a pound. His great speciality is spitting. For precision of aim he would beat the smartest of Sydney larrikins. Any insect flying within a yard of the surface is not safe for a moment. He swims along quietly, suddenly pauses, a little ball of water jumps up, and—the fly is floating on the surface and then gone! I could scarce believe it when I heard about it. I have since caught him on a fine hook dangling over the water....

After following the Gregory for one hundred miles I branched away to the south-west. I had had good travelling, although muddy, and there were occasional rains. Once more I was in open scrub country and had to carry water.

I was now travelling up the slopes of the tableland country. Two days and the open rolling plains could be seen ahead, and no chances of being flooded out, though the creeks and rivers do run a banker, but after a day without rain at their sources they go down. Twenty-four hours later, one has to walk miles up and down stream to get a drink. Three times during a 160-mile ride I had to sit down on the banks and wait for the waters to go down. One evening I camped with a teamster on a hill near a river, which was, like nearly all Queensland rivers, dry. While we were having tea a strange murmuring could be heard; a little later it was a gurgling moan. We went down; the stream was running fast and coming up to its banks. Even while we watched, our retreat was nearly cut off. We got back by wading knee deep. About midnight that night I woke up and looked out from under the mosquito curtain. The water was on both sides of us. I was lying on the ground. No more sleep that night. The water did not rise much more. In the morning the road looked exactly like a river with trees hanging over the sides. For half a mile along I could see this view. That day I had a swim

At the rabbit-proof fence between Queensland, New South Wales and the Northern Territory.

along the road in the still backwaters, the current being a few hundred yards away. I had a two-day wait here, then I had to wade through mud, silt and water and carry the bike and outfit in two separate loads. Going down the steep, slippery banks I slipped, sat down suddenly, and, before I knew where I was, landed into a couple of feet of water. I left an alligator-like trail twenty yards long behind me. The teamster and boy were delighted—I wasn't.

This is a sampling of the 'cycling' I am having. In between rivers there are seas of black mud, sticky as glue. I have had to carry my bike and then go back for the kit. Lack of food and sometimes lack of water made me keep travelling. I have been bogged on the blacksoil plains and, strange as it may seem, have had to go back for water. The country is like a sponge for soaking up moisture. At a place called The Thornton I expected to get provisions but could not get anything. I still had fifty miles to go for my next chance. Fifty miles does not seem much, but here it meant, at this time of the year, about four days' hard travelling. Luckily I overtook a team (also bogged) and got a few supplies. On arriving at the 'fifty miles' (the O'Shanassy River) I found the inhabitants inhospitable. I managed to get a couple of cups of flour for which I paid sixpence a cup. I went straight on with thirty miles of blacksoil mud ahead of me. I got out two miles and then camped, hoping that by daybreak the road would be drier. I had barely made my damper (flour and water baked) when the rain started again. I spent a wretched night—was hungry, tried, bedding and clothes damp, then the small black ants got at me. I moved camp several times during the night, but it was of no use. I got up about three in the morning, had a drink of cold tea and a few tablespoons of sugar, of which I had plenty, and got under way. The road was no better. I could see rising ground ahead, some three miles away. I thought that the country would be drier, but it was not. The rain started again, so I hung the bike on a bush, covered it with a waterproof, and went back to the O'Shanassy. A teamster was camped here with his wife and family. They treated me most kindly. He was going north with an empty wagon. I am afraid that he too was short of provender. He left two days after for the next waterhole, three miles away over some stony ridges.

That night the rain came down in floods. I got under one of the outer sheds of the 'farm'. For three days I camped there. A few hours interval of fine weather and then rain, keeping the roads sticky. The old man was cleaning out his well and wanted help to wind the windlass. He offered to let me have food to help him—which I was glad to do.

Late one afternoon I made another start with only my former bit of damper to carry me through. It was sour and had long sticky threads in it. I intended to bake it again. The old miser did not even offer me a cup of tea or a bite to eat along the road. I would not ask for it after that. I crossed the river, which was waist deep and flowing strong, got out to the bike, loaded her up, and started out to walk all night, it being impossible to ride. I was getting up a mighty big hunger and intended to get to the damper when I saw a mounted man against the skyline some miles away. It was the mail man with packhorses—his buggy was bogged along the road. I told him of my plight and he unearthed half a loaf of bread, some corned meat and a piece of cake. It was all he had, but he said that there was plenty at the O'Shanassy. I made a good meal that night.

All night I travelled. Showers would drift across the road, and over these patches I had to carry the bike. Sometimes sweating with my exertions and then chilling as the cold night winds came along, I reached the Chester Creek just before daybreak. I had travelled eighteen miles and by this time I was dog tired. I lay down and went to sleep for a few hours, but the hot sun woke me up. I made lunch off the sour damper; after cooking it afresh on the coals it was sticky as glue. Then I walked to Camooweal, twelve miles.

The rainy season has started, and I am in for a tough trip. One is likely to be left stranded between stages without food. There is another danger, that of being caught between two flooded rivers—they run too fast to swim. The river here is up and is already a swim. Two months ago cattle were dying by the hundred for want of water—the deaths are estimated at one thousand. If I get to Palmerston by the end of March I will be lucky. There is one consolation: I will have better travelling to Adelaide. I intend to try for the record on leaving Port Darwin.

> 'I crossed the river, which was waist deep and flowing strong, got out to the bike, loaded her up, and started out to walk all night, it being impossible to ride.'

THE FIRST CROSSING OF AUSTRALIA BY MOTOR CAR

Geoffrey Dutton

AUTHOR, EDITOR AND POET *Geoffrey Dutton recounts his father's crossing of Australia from Adelaide to Darwin in a Clement-Talbot car in 1908.*

IN 1908 MY FATHER, Henry Hampden Dutton, and his mechanic, Murray Aunger, set out to drive the first motor car across Australia. In the 2,100 miles south to north, from Adelaide to what was then called Port Darwin, there were probably 200 miles of roads. As for the rest, there were tracks over hard earth and mud, rocks, and sand, across dry riverbeds, huge sandhills, and tropical rivers.

There is a boundary beyond which enterprise crumbles into foolhardiness. Imagination, essential in conceiving any enterprise, has to be tested by truth in the shape of timetable, planning, a boring attention to detail. But the truly enterprising are those who are not daunted by failure. The best plans are subject to chance, to what insurance companies in a secular age still call Acts of God.

So my father, whom I shall call HHD ('Dutton' seems disrespectful, even though he has been dead for more than fifty years), had in 1908 already seen the collapse of all his plans. He and Aunger had set off earlier in 1907, and had completed some fifteen hundred miles of their journey when the transmission failed and could not be repaired without new parts. Also the wet season was upon them, and the monsoonal rains of tropical Northern Australia were turning the country into a swamp. So they had to abandon the car and return to Oodnadatta by horse and thence by rail to Adelaide.

In 1908 HHD and Aunger set off once more for Port Darwin in a 25-horsepower English Clement-Talbot (the first car had been 20/24 h.p.). Cans of petrol were sent ahead by donkey or camel. Unfortunately the Afghan camel drivers, ignorant of such things, often left the four-gallon cans in the fierce sun, where a number of them burst. As there was no town between tiny Oodnadatta and the mining outpost of Pine Creek, a thousand miles further north, supplies had to be sent ahead to the telegraph stations or cattle or sheep stations along the track. In all, petrol supplies were sent to thirteen depots, sometimes including such luxuries as sardines, tinned pineapple, and a bottle of brandy.

HHD was twenty-nine, Aunger a few years younger. The mechanic was a sturdy and highly intelligent man who later founded a successful business

H. H. Dutton and Murray Aunger (at the wheel) leaving Alice Springs telegraph station for Barrow Creek on their first attempt to drive across Australia.

supplying motor accessories. HHD had already had quite an enterprising career. Born of pioneering land-holders who ran sheep in New South Wales and South Australia, he had a degree in geology from Oxford, had rowed in the Oxford Eight, and had hunted in Morocco, Newfoundland, and Wyoming. He had a beautiful wife, Emily, and a son, John, born in 1906.

Extreme variations in terrain called for technological ingenuity. There was an extra set of wheels and tyres, known as Stepney wheels, which bolted on to the existing wheels to give extra traction when crossing sand or mud. There were rolls of coconut matting to be spread in front of the wheels when traversing sand. There were no mudguards, so thick grass or bushes would not jam the tyres, and the body consisted of a seat and a high box full of spares and equipment, with drums of water and the Stepney wheels tied to its top and sides. On the first car, but not on the second, there was a canvas hood to keep off the sun. There were even brass acetylene lamps and a curved brass horn. In the box at the back was a Spanish Windlass by which a car bogged in mud or sand could be attached to a tree by a wire rope and hauled out. (One had to hope for a handy tree.) Strapped across the box behind the heads of driver and passenger was a 12-bore gun in a leather case, hopefully for shooting ducks and other game along the track. There were also eight tyres and tubes, spare tailshaft and back axles, goggles against dust storms, and a pick and shovel.

The second Talbot is still going strong, housed in the Birdwood Mill Motor Museum in South Australia, its brass radiator and lamps glistening, its wooden wheels still free of creaks or cracks. It has some odd features. The four cylinders are cast in two separate blocks. The fan revolves around a shaft bolted right through the immensely strong honeycomb of the radiator. On the dashboard there are glass tubes through which oil can be seen dripping down into the engine, at a pace to be adjusted by brass knobs. There is no speedometer, but the original mechanic who worked on the car at the Talbot agents in Adelaide told me, when he was a very old man, that each Talbot when properly tuned was required to cover a flying mile in one minute.

The Talbot has no self-starter, since it has no electrical gear outside the magneto. It is started by the crank handle; when cold, it requires four pulls with the ignition (which looks like an old-fashioned domestic light switch) turned off, then 'Contact!' and one sharp pull, and the low-revving engine with its huge flywheel chugs into steady life. When moving off from rest, the enterprising driver should beware: the clutch has a very small movement between stop and go. Too lusty a movement of the foot means a kangaroo hop and a stalled engine.

HHD liked giving his cars names. The 1907 20/24-horsepower Talbot was called Angelina; the 1908 25-horsepower model was the Overlander.

For the first journey, after they left Adelaide on 15 November 1907, crowds turned out along the way to wish them luck. On 26 November they left Anlaby, HHD's home, and had the best run, on made roads, of the whole journey: 160 miles to Quorn in just under eight hours.

They drove beside the railway line up to its terminus at Oodnadatta, 688 miles north of Adelaide, a funny little narrow-gauge line. HHD learnt to distrust the Afghans' and other stock drivers' comments on the way ahead. 'Good going' turned out to mean sandy country, which was soft for feet or hooves, but bad news for car tyres. 'Real crook country' meant hard, pebbly plains, across which the Talbot could happily cruise at forty-five miles an hour. Some hazards were particularly bad for cars.

The dry creek beds, for instance. The Alberga River, north of Oodnadatta, was one of the worst obstacles they met with in the entire journey. Dodging the trees, they rushed the quarter-mile-wide expanse of burning sand (that particualr day it was 113 degress in the shade) only to have the heavily laden Angelina sink up to the axles thirty yards from the bank. Then followed hours of sweaty work, jacking up the Talbot on the heavy boards brought for such emergencies, digging out the sand under the wheels and laying strips of coconut matting, fitting the Stepney wheels. When all else failed, the car had to be winched along by the Spanish Windlass.

To vary the torture, there were occasional, totally unexpected heavy rains,

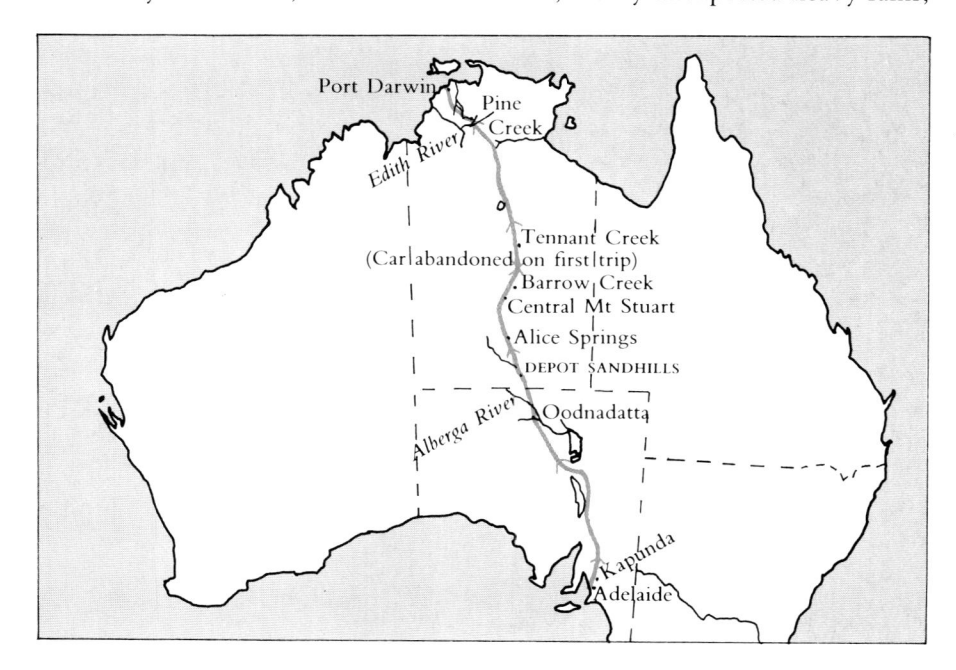

The route through the centre of Australia which Dutton and Aunger followed in the first crossing of Australia by motor car.

and Angelina had to be extricated from deep mud, the engine exhaust blowing bubbles in the water.

Then there would be the blessed relief of gibber country, dead-flat treeless plains covered with glittering ironstone pebbles, hated by the camels, loved by the Talbot.

Most of the way they were following the Overland Telegraph Line, which had been completed, after stupendous difficulties, in 1872. However, the tracks sometimes led away from the line, and once they were given bad directions and drove 130 miles out of their way.

Some of the rocky gorges were almost insuperable. Fortunately the Talbot had an immense ground clearance and could be coaxed along from rock to rock without demolishing the lower parts of engine and chassis. But such slow grinds were a terrible test of the engine in conditions of extreme heat, made much worse by the bare rocks on every side, with the cliffs keeping off any helpful breeze.

It remains a puzzle why HHD, having organised the enterprise so well, should have set off in summer. This meant travelling in conditions of extreme heat (Aunger's diary frequently reports temperatures of well over a hundred degrees) and also, north of the Tropic of Capricorn, facing the hazards of the heavy rains of the wet season.

Angelina coped amazingly well with the low-gear work over boulders and through sand. The worst obstacle of the whole journey came at the Depot Sandhills between Horseshoe Bend and Alice Springs. Splendid to look at, the deep red sand ceaselessly sculpted by the wind, these great drifts are often fifty feet high and cannot be avoided, as they run east and west parallel across the track. These parallel sandhills are a grave hazard even for four-wheel-drive vehicles.

A true enterprise must be infinitely flexible. Imagination must not only be tested by reality but be inventive, capable of modification. It was clear to HHD that the Talbot would never be able to cross the Depot Sandhills, even if coconut matting trails were laid. The angle was so steep and the sand so soft that the scrabbling wheels would pull the matting in and throw it out the back of the vehicle. It was extremely difficult to steer the Talbot in the heavy sand. Aunger's diary (HHD's has, alas, been lost) reads for 11 December: 'Only about 200 yards hard ground in seven miles, first five miles worst, has 13 bad hills all heavy loose sand.'

The problem was solved by donkeys. Together with camels, donkeys were the heroes of early inland transport. Infinitely tough, able to survive in dry country on poor food, donkeys are also renowned for working intelligently together. Despite their small size, a team of twelve or fourteen donkeys can pull almost anything. The Talbot's Stepney wheels were fitted and strips of canvas wrapped around the twin tyres, and as the donkeys heaved, the engine roared and the wheels spun while they searched the sand for a grip. It was odd that despite the steepness of the sandhills the donkeys had also to tow the Talbot *down* the slopes, so soft was the hot sand.

Near the Depot Sandhills they passed His Majesty's Mail being carried by a string of six camels.

The arrival in Alice Springs was sensational. Where a flourishing large town now stands on the plain north of Heavitree Gap in the MacDonnell ranges, in 1907 there was only a tiny township and, three miles away, the telegraph station. The first motor car ever seen in Alice Springs caused consternation. Horses bolted and were not seen for days. Aboriginal women climbed trees, clutching their screaming children. Aboriginal warriors confronted something too big and strange for boomerang or spear. The daughter of the telegraph stationmaster, who was about eight years old at the time, told me that the old descriptive term 'horseless carriage' was absolutely right; there was something utterly strange about this object on wheels which moved all by itself, needing no horse, camel, or donkey.

The next telegraph station to the north, Barrow Creek, had been the scene of a massacre in 1874, when the natives attacked the whites stationed there and speared to death the stationmaster, a linesman, and an Aborigine working for the whites. Whatever the causes of the tragedy, and such attacks were seldom unprovoked, a terrible revenge was taken on the Aborigines. Nevertheless, by 1907 the tribes all along the route were very friendly. HHD was an ardent, talented photographer, and the Barrow Creek Aborigines had no objections to being photographed. The naked men and women were still carrying out their ceremonies and dances, living in wurlies made of boughs and leaves, an accommodation always shared with numerous dogs.

Not long before Barrow Creek they had passed Central Mount Stuart, at the heart of Australia, and now as they travelled toward Tennant Creek they were well past the Tropic of Capricorn. The bare plains of the Centre were giving way to the rank grass of the semitropics which was as high as the shoulders of the men in the Talbot in areas where water was lying. In other areas they found themselves among what they called ant hills (now more correctly known as termite mounds). Often ten or more feet high, these thousands of red monoliths give one the uncanny feeling that one is being watched. One is certainly not alone; the population of the visible ant hills alone runs into hundreds of millions.

The big termite mounds were easy to avoid. Smaller ones, like stumps, were a menace to tyres and undercarriage.

One day, following the steel posts of the telegraph line across a grassy plain, they were amazed to see what looked like a man on a bicycle coming toward them. And indeed it was: the remarkable Francis Birtles riding the first bicycle across Australia, from Port Darwin to Adelaide. A lean brown man in dusty shorts, with the barest minimum of equipment strapped to his machine, Birtles had the great advantage of being able to push his wheels over soft sand and through deep mud. They had a cup of tea together, then went off in opposite directions.

They were now moving from extreme dry heat into the downpour and steamy days of the wet. Aunger's diary reads: 'Heavy going...boggy.... Very coarse sand.' There are ominous references to a failure of transmission bearings, which were replaced, and then to the collapse of the pinion in the differential.

Angelina had to be abandoned. The enterprise was at an end. They had got as far as Edinburgh Flat, south of Tennant Creek. They tapped the overland telegraph line and called up Tennant Creek. Four riding horses and four

'One day, following the steel posts of the telegraph line across a grassy plain, they were amazed to see what looked like a man on a bicycle coming toward them. And indeed it was: the remarkable Francis Birtles riding the first bicycle across Australia, from Port Darwin to Adelaide.'

packhorses were procured, and with a Mr Perry and an Aboriginal boy they set off on the long ride back to the railhead at Oodnadatta, and thence to Adelaide.

Perhaps to be truly enterprising one needs to be disappointed, to be crossed in the full flush of adventure. To overcome consecutive difficulties, however severe, calls for a body and mind working together in harmony, in perfect training. It also calls for belief that the enterprise is possible and worth while. Ease up, and it becomes very difficult to resume. This is especially true when more than one person is involved.

In 1907 it had been a triangle, Angelina, Murray Aunger, and HHD. The two men had to get on with each other under the most trying conditions of heat, discomfort, and even despair. The mud of swamps or rivers after flash floods, the sand of dry rivers or parallel sandhills negated the basic principle of the motor car, the driving wheel. Most modern cars have wheels of fourteen to sixteen inches in diameter; the Talbot's were 24 inches. But even these huge old wheels (often with the Stepneys on) could spin and sink until the frame of the car had bottomed, sunk onto the mud or sand. The donkeys had saved them at the Depot Sandhills, but there were no other saviours available. All that was left was the skill of the men and the strength of the machinery.

After fifteen hundred miles of the most extreme conditions, the two men knew exactly how to use and conserve that strength. A mad revving of power could damage the engine or break an axle. A rock or a piece of ant hill at speed could break a spring. (The Talbot had no shock absorbers.) It was a major effort just to hold those huge wheels straight with the thick-rimmed steering wheel. In sandy country they would pull one way and then the other with a will of their own, rearing to seduce Angelina off the track and threatening to pile the car up.

And then there was always the consciousness of hundreds of moving parts in what was still a primitive piece of machinery. After all, it was only twenty-two years since Carl Benz had run his first automobile, a three-wheeler powered by a two-cycle, one-cylinder engine, and eighteen years since Gottlieb Daimler had first driven his four-wheel car with a chassis, rear engine, and four-speed drive.

It is amazing that in those few years something as strong and reliable as the Talbot was available to cross a continent on unmade tracks without breaking down. Also amazing was the durability of the pneumatic tyres, in the infancy of development. They had very few punctures, which is incredible given the presence along the track of stumps, rocks, ant hills, and pieces of wood or root which in central Australian trees are iron-hard.

Now, as HHD and Aunger returned to Adelaide and Anlaby, HHD's sheep-station home, the whole enterprise sagged. Angelina was out there in the wilderness, an astonishing sight for tribes of wandering Aborigines, a totally inexplicable object in its complete remoteness from their lives and knowledge. Would they ignore it? Attack and attempt to destroy it? Keep away from it in fear? There was no way of telling.

To HHD it was clear that the enterprise could not be abandoned. Despite his commitment to new technology he was in some respects a very conservative man. He set great store by the family motto, *Servabo Fidem*, which may be translated as 'I will keep good faith; I will keep my word.'

The only solution was to set off again in another Talbot (by now any other make of car was unthinkable), collect Angelina, and drive the two vehicles on to Port Darwin.

He went down to Adelaide and bought the latest 25-horsepower model, with a slightly more powerful engine and modifications which gave more strength to the rear suspension. Although ultimately known as the Overlander, this car throughout the trip was called '474', that being her South Australian motor registration number. Angelina's was 319. Of course 474 had to be fitted out with all the same equipment as carried by Angelina, and petrol and supplies had once more to be sent ahead.

On 30 June 1908, HHD and Aunger set off once more on the two-thousand-mile track to Port Darwin. They had to do it all again—the sandy creek crossings, the rocky gorges, the Depot Sandhills, the easy runs across the gibber plains. They were driving in winter, and although the days were sunny there was often an icy wind, and 474, like Angelina, had no windshield. There are violent changes of temperature in central Australia, and the temperatures will go over 110 degrees in the shade by day and drop below freezing at night. On some mornings the water in the canvas water bags was frozen.

They had no trouble with 474, and the knowledge gained from their experiences on the first trip enabled them to make better time. On 16 July they reached Alice Springs, and finally through the long, dry grass and the light scrub they saw the outline of Angelina with its tarpaulin still tied down. After all those months she was untouched. But all around her in a ring was a circle of stamped-down grass and sand. The Aborigines had indeed found her but were so terrified of this strange apparition that they would not approach her, let alone touch her; instead they simply walked round and round her, watching.

Angelina as Dutton and Aunger found her on the second trip.

Descending one of the Depot Sandhills, with four Stepney wheels attached to the ordinary wheels to aid traction.

Aunger stripped down the differential and installed the new pinion, and Angelina started without difficulty. Both automobiles were driven on to Tennant Creek. On the way they passed through an area of huge boulders, some split in two by frost, others perched on top of each other, and one weighing hundreds of tons balanced across a gap between two other boulders as if a giant had rested it there.

The shade of the wide verandas of Tennant Creek telegraph station was welcome, and from here HHD sent a message south to his wife, Emily, that Angelina was safe and they were on their way with both cars....

The Warramunga Aborigines at Tennant Creek, once they had got over their alarm at the sight of the two Talbots, were as friendly as those at Barrow Creek had been. They also were naked, although some of the men dressed up magnificently for the motorists in patterns of feathers and pipeclay with enormous headdresses four feet wide. HHD was allowed to photograph a group of a dozen native women in mourning, daubed all over in white pipeclay, sitting on the ground chanting....

By a strange conjunction of ancient and modern, the Aborigines, however unwittingly, were nearly the cause of the whole trans-Australian enterprise ending in tragedy. In the thick bush and high dry grass of northern Australia the Aborigines have from time immemorial set fires to flush out game and bring on new green growth. In some places the grass was so high that the Talbots were almost invisible. HHD and Aunger were following the telegraph line north of Daly Waters telegraph station when they realised that the black smoke they had been watching on the horizon was coming much closer. Soon they were circled by fires running with the extra wind generated by the flames. With the shade temperature at over ninety-five degrees, it already was unbearably hot before the fires reached them. They wrapped wet cloths around the carburettor, where petrol vapour could rise from the crude needle valve, and hoped that the cans of spare fuel would not explode. At times the vehicles had to stop while the flames went around them. Once they charged right through the flames to get upwind of the fire.

Water had never looked as beautiful as it did when they reached lily-covered lagoons and the great northern rivers—the Roper, the Katherine, the Daly, the Adelaide—flowing by palms and white-trunked paperbarks. But water presented new problems. These were not flash-flood rivers as in the south; these waterways flowed all year round and were full of crocodiles and that most delicious of fish, barramundi. They had to be crossed, and there were no bridges.

The cars crossed the Katherine without much trouble at a ford between the long, tranquil reaches. But the Edith, as the Daly was called where it crossed the track between Elsey and Pine Creek, imposed severe difficulties. The river was four feet deep, over the wheels of the vehicles, and the only way to get across was to tie a tarpaulin across the radiator and back around the engine, and then charge the water 'all out', in HHD's phrase. A huge bow wave rose up in front as 474 roared in between the reeds and the paperbarks, but she made it with comparative ease. Angelina did her best, but the engine died when she was within six feet of the opposite bank. But 474 towed her out and they were both on their way again.

At Pine Creek, a railhead and old mining settlement some two hundred miles south of Port Darwin, HHD decided to give Angelina a rest and put her on the train to Port Darwin.

The country varied now between thick tropical growth near the rivers and open plains with the most majestic ant hills they had seen on the whole journey, some of them ten to twelve feet high, dwarfing 474. With the track, such as it was, quite overgrown, the Talbot had to push its way through thick grass up to six feet high. Only five miles from Port Darwin they had to scramble along a narrow path cut through dense jungle.

They reached Port Darwin on 20 August 1908. The Overlander, as 474 could now be justly called, had taken fifty-one days to cover 2,100 miles across the continent. It had been the best of enterprises, one crowned with success after some difficulties, and a refusal to give in after the first failure.

HHD, Murray Aunger, and the two Talbots went back to Adelaide by sea. Angelina was sold, and the Overlander went to Anlaby station where for many years she did the daily mail run to Kapunda, the local town. After that she was honourably retired and kept in a shed on the property.

There is a postscript to the Overlander's story. In 1941, in World War II, HHD's eldest son, John, was in the 9th Division, besieged in Tobruk in the North African campaign. As soldiers do, he was yarning with an old friend, Jimmy Gosse (grandson of the explorer who discovered Ayers Rock), about what they would do after the war. John thought of old 474 in the shed at Anlaby. He decided on a grand enterprise. He would completely overhaul her and with Jimmy and myself (the youngest brother, then a pilot in the RAAF), fifty years after the original journey the Overlander would once again cross Australia.

And so in 1958 the Talbot completed the journey, much of it over bad, unsealed roads, in the remarkable time of ten days. She is now, still in good running order, in the Birdwood Mill Museum in South Australia, awaiting her centenary journey in 2008.

'The river was four feet deep, over the wheels of the vehicles, and the only way to get across was to tie a tarpaulin across the radiator and back around the engine, and then charge the water "all out", in HHD's phrase.'

A LONE TREK IN ANTARCTICA

Douglas Mawson

'*Our fellow, comrade, chum, in a woeful instant, buried in the bowels of the awful glacier.*'

THE AUSTRALASIAN ANTARCTIC EXPEDITION *of 1911–14, led by Douglas Mawson, left Hobart in the ship* Aurora *in December 1911 and set up their main base camp at Commonwealth Bay, King George V Land, a month later. The following November, after wintering at the base, Mawson and two colleagues, B. E. S. Ninnis and Xavier Mertz, set out with three dog teams to explore eastward from their winter quarters. They had reached a point five hundred kilometres from Commonwealth Bay when Ninnis and a sledge carrying most of their provisions disappeared into a crevasse. The story of the heroic struggle back to winter quarters is told by Mawson in his book* The Home of the Blizzard. *The account is interspersed with entries from a diary which he was miraculously able to write during this appalling journey.*

THE HOMEWARD TRACK! A few days ago—only a few hours ago—our hearts had beat hopefully at the prospect and there was no hint of this, the overwhelming tragedy. Our fellow, comrade, chum, in a woeful instant, buried in the bowels of the awful glacier. We could not think of it; we strove to forget it in the necessity of work, but we knew that the truth would assuredly enter our souls in the lonely days to come. It was to be a fight with Death and the great Providence would decide the issue.

On the outward journey we had left no depots of provisions en route, for it was our bad fortune to meet such impossible country that we had decided to make a circuit on our return to winter quarters sufficiently far inland to avoid the coastal irregularities. As a matter of fact, on the very day of the calamity, preparations had been made to cache most of the food within twenty-four hours, as during the last few days of the journey we were to make a dash to our 'farthest east' point. Such were the plans, and now we were ranged against unexpected odds.

With regard to the dogs, there were six very miserable animals left. The best of them had been drafted into the rear team, as it was expected that if an accident happened through the collapse of a snow-bridge the first sledge would most probably suffer. For the same reason most of the food and other indispensable articles had been carried on the rear sledge....

A silent farewell!—and we started back, aiming to reach our camping ground on 12 December before a snowstorm intervened, as several things had been left there which would be of use to us in our straitened circumstances. The weather still held good and there were no signs of approaching snow or wind. So Mertz went ahead on skis, while we plodded slowly up the hills and dashed recklessly down them. During the descents I sat on the sledge and we slid over long crevassed slopes in a wild fashion, almost with a languid feeling that the next one would probably swallow us up. But we did not much care then, as it was too soon after losing our friend.

At 2.30 a.m. on 15 December the discarded sledge and broken spade came into sight. On reaching them, Mertz cut a runner of the broken sledge into two pieces which were used in conjunction with his skis as a framework on which to pitch the spare tent-cover, our only tent and poles having been lost. Each time the makeshift shelter was erected, these props had to be carefully lashed together at the apex, which stood four feet from the ground. Inside, there was just room for two one-man sleeping-bags on the floor. However, only one man at a time could move about and neither of us could ever rise above a sitting posture. Still, it was a shelter which protected us from the bad weather, and, with plenty of snow blocks piled around it, was wonderfully resistant to the wind.

When we retired to rest, it was not to sleep but to think out the best plan for the return journey.

It was obvious that a descent to the frozen sea would be dangerous on account of the heavily crevassed nature of the falling glacier; delay would undoubtedly be caused and our distance from the hut would be increased. To decide definitely for the sea ice would be to take other risks as well, since, from the altitude at which we were placed, we could not be sure that the floe ice which covered the sea would provide a good travelling surface. In any case it was likely to be on the point of breaking up, for the season was nearing midsummer. On the other hand, there was on the sea ice a chance of obtaining seals for food.

After due consideration we resolved to follow the shorter route, returning

Xavier Mertz and B. E. S. Ninnis, with dog teams and sledges, arriving at Aladdin's Cave on an earlier occasion before their fatal journey.

inland over the plateau, for it was reckoned that if the weather were reasonable we might win through to winter quarters with one and a half weeks' rations and the six dogs which still remained, provided we ate the dogs to eke out our provisions. Fortunately neither the cooker nor the kerosene had been lost.

George, the poorest of the dogs, was killed and partly fed to the others, partly kept for ourselves. The meat was roughly fried on the lid of the aluminium cooker, an operation which resulted in little more than scorching the surface. On the whole it was voted good though it had a strong, musty taste and was so stringy that it could not be properly chewed.

As both mugs and spoons had been lost, I made two pannikins out of tins in which cartridges and matches had been packed, and Mertz carved wooden spoons out of a portion of the broken sledge. At this camp he also spliced the handle of the broken shovel which had been picked up, so as to make it temporarily serviceable.

It was midsummer, and therefore we found it easier to drag the sledge over the snow at night when the surface was frozen hard. Camp was not finally broken until 6 p.m., when the long and painful return journey commenced.

For fourteen miles the way led up rising snow slopes to the north-west until an elevation of 2,500 feet had been reached. After that, variable grades and flat country were met. Though the sledge was light, the dogs required helping and progress was slow. The midnight sun shone low in the south, and we tramped on through the morning hours, anxious to reduce the miles which lay ahead.

Early on 16 December the sky became rapidly overcast. The snowy land and the snowy sky merged to form an enclosed trap, as it seemed to us, while showers of snow fell. There were no shadows to create contrast; it was

Douglas Mawson.

impossible to distinguish even the detail of the ground underfoot. We stumbled over unseen ridges of the hard névé, our gaze straining forward. The air was so still that advantage was taken of the calm to light the primus and melt some snow in the lee of the sledge. The water, to which were added a few drops of primus alcohol, helped to assuage our thirst.

The erection of the makeshift tent was a long and tedious operation, and so, on our return marches, we never again took any refreshment during the day's work excepting on this occasion. At 6 a.m., having done twenty miles and ascended to an elevation of about 2,500 feet, we pitched camp.

There was very little sleep for me that day for I had an unusually bad attack of snow-blindness. During the time that we rested in the bags Mertz treated one of my eyes three times, the other twice, with zinc sulphate and cocaine.

On account of the smallness of the tent a great deal of time was absorbed in preparations for 'turning in' and for getting away from each camp. Thus, although we rose before 6 p.m. on 16 December, the start was not made until 8.30 p.m., notwithstanding the fact that the meal was of the sketchiest character.

On that night ours was a mournful procession; the sky thickly clouded, snow falling, I with one eye bandaged and the dog Johnson broken down and strapped on top of the load on the sledge. There was scarcely a sound; only the rustle of the thick, soft snow as we pushed on, weary but full of hope. The dogs dumbly pressed forward in their harness, forlorn but eager to follow. Their weight now told little upon the sledge, the work mainly falling upon ourselves. Mertz was tempted to try hauling on skis, but came to the conclusion that it did not pay and thenceforth never again used them.

Close to the magnetic pole as we were, the compass was of little use, and to steer a straight course to the west without ever seeing anything of the surroundings was a difficult task. The only check upon the correctness of the bearing was the direction in which trended the old hard winter sastrugi, channelled out along a line running almost north and south. The newly fallen snow obliterated these, and frequent halts had to be called in order to investigate the buried surface.

At 2 a.m. on the 17th we had only covered eleven miles when we stopped to camp. Then Mertz shot and cut up Johnson while I prepared the supper.

Johnson had always been a very faithful, hard-working and willing beast, with rather droll ways of his own, and we were sorry that his end should come so soon. He could never be accused of being a handsome dog; in fact he was generally disreputable and dirty.

All the dogs were miserable and thin when they reached the stage of extreme exhaustion. Their meat was tough, stringy and without a vestige of fat. For a change we sometimes chopped it up finely, mixed it with a little pemmican, and brought all to the boil in a large pot of water. We were exceedingly hungry, but there was nothing to satisfy our appetites. Only a few ounces were used of the stock of ordinary food, to which was added a portion of dog's meat, never large, for each animal yielded so very little, and the major part was fed to the surviving dogs. They crunched the bones and ate the skin, until nothing remained.

A fresh start was made at 7.30 p.m. and a wretched, trying night was spent, when we marched without a break for twelve and a half hours. Overhead there was a dense pall of nimbus from which snow fell at intervals. None of the dogs except Ginger gave any help with the load, and Mary was so worn out that she had to be carried on the sledge. Poor Mary had been a splendid dog, but we had to kill her at the camp in the morning.

After a run of eighteen and a half miles we halted at 8 a.m. on 18 December. At 5.30 p.m. a light south-easter blew and snow fell from an overcast sky. Soon after a start was made, it became apparent that a descent was commencing. In this locality the country had been swept by wind, for none of the recent snow settled on the surface. The sastrugi were high and hard, and over them we bumped, slipping and falling in the uncertain light. We could not endure this kind of travelling for long and resolved to camp shortly after midnight, intending to go on when the day had advanced further and the light was stronger.

'*19 December.* Up at noon and tried a few more miles in the snow-glare. Later in the afternoon the sky began to break and we picked our way with less difficulty. Camped at 5 p.m., having done only twelve miles 1,050 yards since the morning of 18 December.

'Up at 8 p.m. again, almost calm and sun shining. Still continuing a westerly course we dropped several hundred feet, marching over rough, slippery fields of sastrugi.'

In the early morning hours of the 20th the surface changed to ice and occasional crevasses appeared. It was clear that we had arrived at the head of the Ninnis Glacier above the zone of serac we had traversed on the outward journey. It was very satisfactory to know this, to be certain that some landmark had been seen and recognised.

Soon after this discovery we came near losing Haldane, the big grey wolf, in a crevasse. Miserably thin from starvation, the wretched dogs no longer filled their harness. As we pulled up Haldane, after he had broken into a deep, sheer-walled crevasse, his harness slipped off just as he reached the top. It was just possible to seize hold of his hair at that moment and to land him safely; otherwise we should have lost many days' rations.

He took to the harness once more but soon became uncertain in his footsteps, staggered along and then tottered and fell. Poor brutes! that was the way they all gave in—pulling till they dropped.

We camped at 4 a.m., thinking that a rest would revive Haldane. Inside the tent some snow was thawed, and we drank the water with an addition of a little primus spirit. A temperature reading showed minus one degree Fahrenheit.

Outside, the hungry huskies moaned unceasingly until we could bear to hear them no longer. The tent was struck and we set off once more.

Haldane was strapped on the sledge as he could not walk. He had not eaten the food we had given him, because his jaws seemed too weak to bite. He had just nursed it between his paws and licked it.

Before the dogs became as weak as this, great care had to be taken in tethering them at each camp so as to prevent them from gnawing the wood of the sledge, the straps or, in fact, anything at all. Every time we were ready

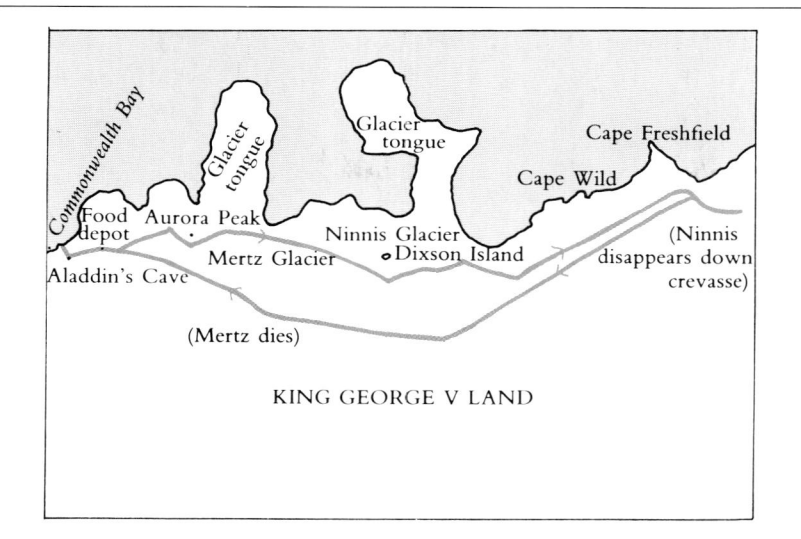

King George V Land, showing the track of Mawson, Mertz and Ninnis from their winter quarters at Commonwealth Bay to the spot where Ninnis disappeared and the appalling journey back to base camp.

for a fresh start they seemed to regain their old strength, for they struggled and fought to seize any scraps, however useless, left on the ground.

The day's march was completed at 10.30 a.m. and fourteen and a half miles lay behind.

'We were up again at 11.20 p.m. Sky clear; fifteen-mile breeze from the south-south-east and the temperature 3° F. By midnight there was a thirty-mile wind and low, flying drift.

'*21 December.* The night march was a miserable one. The only thing which helped to relieve it was that for a moment Dixson Island was miraged up in the north, and we felt that we had met an old friend, which means a lot in this icy desolation. The surface was furrowed by hard, sharp sastrugi.

'We camped at 9 a.m. after only eleven miles. Haldane was finished off before we retired. We were up again at 9 p.m., and when a start was made at 11 p.m. there was a strong south-south-east wind blowing, with low drift; temperature, zero Fahr.

'*22 December.* The surface of hard, polished sastrugi caused many falls. The track was undulating, rising in one case several hundred feet and finally falling in a long slope.

'Pavlova gave in late in the march and was taken on the sledge.

'Camped at 6.40 a.m. in a forty-mile wind with low drift. Distance marched was twelve miles 1,400 yards.'

Before turning in, we effected sundry repairs. Mertz re-spliced the handle of the shovel which had broken apart and I riveted the broken spindle of the sledge-meter. The mechanism of the latter had frozen during the previous day's halt, and, on being started, its spindle had broken off short. It was a long and tedious job tapping at the steel with a toy hammer, but the rivet held miraculously for the rest of the journey.

'Up at 11.30 p.m., a moderate breeze blowing, overcast sky, light snow falling.'

On 23 December an uphill march commenced which was rendered very heavy by the depth of the soft snow. Pavlova had to be carried on the sledge.

Suddenly, gaping crevasses appeared dimly through the falling snow which surrounded us like a blanket. There was nothing to do but camp, though it was only 4.30 a.m., and we had covered but five miles 1,230 yards.

Pavlova was killed and we made a very acceptable soup from her bones. In view of the dark outlook, our ration of food had to be still further cut down. We had no proper sleep, hunger gnawing at us all the time, and the question of food was for ever in our thoughts. Dozing in the fur bags, we dreamed of gorgeous spreads and dinner parties at home. Tramping along through the snow, we racked our brains thinking of how to make the most of the meagre quantity of dogs' meat at hand.

The supply of kerosene for the primus stove promised to be ample, for none of it had been lost in the accident. We found that it was worth while spending some time in boiling the dogs' meat thoroughly. Thus a tasty soup was prepared as well as a supply of edible meat in which the muscular tissue and the gristle were reduced to the consistency of a jelly. The paws took longest of all to cook, but, treated to lengthy stewing, they became quite digestible.

On 24 December we were up at 8 a.m. just as the sun commenced to gleam through clouds. The light was rather bad, and snow fell as the track zigzagged about among many crevasses; but suddenly the sun broke forth. The sledge was crossing a surface of deep snow which soon became so sticky that the load would scarcely move. At last a halt was made after four miles, and we waited for the evening, when the surface was expected to harden.

A small prion visited us but went off in a moment. It is very remarkable how far some Antarctic seabirds may wander inland, apparently at such a great distance from anything which should interest them. We were then more than one hundred miles south of the open sea. As the bird flew away, we watched it until it disappeared in the north, wishing that we too had wings to cross the interminable plateau ahead.

Lying in the sleeping-bag that day I dreamt that I visited a confectioner's shop. All the wares that were displayed measured feet in diameter. I purchased an enormous delicacy just as one would buy a bun under ordinary circumstances. I remember paying the money over the counter, but something happened before I received what I had chosen. When I realised the omission I was out in the street, and, being greatly disappointed, went back to the shop, but found the door shut and 'early closing' written on it.

Though a good daily average had been maintained on the march whenever conditions were at all favourable, the continuance of bad weather and the undoubtedly weaker state in which we found ourselves made it imperative to dispense with all but the barest necessities. Thus the theodolite was the only instrument retained, and the camera, photographic films (exposed and unexposed), hypsometer, thermometers, rifle, ammunition and other sundries were all thrown away. The frame of the tent was made lighter by constructing two poles, each four feet high, from the telescopic theodolite legs, the heavier pieces of sledge-runner being discarded.

We were up at 11 p.m. on 24 December, but so much time was absorbed in making dog stew for Christmas that it was not till 2.30 a.m. that we got under way. We wished each other happier Christmases in the future, and divided two scraps of biscuit which I found in my spare kitbag....

The surface was a moderately good one of undulating, hard sastrugi, and, as the course had been altered to north-west, the southerly wind helped us along. The sun shone brightly, and only for the wind and the low drift we might have felt tolerably comfortable. On our right, down within the shallow depression of the Ninnis Glacier, the low outline of Dixson Island, forty miles to the north, could be seen miraged up on the horizon.

The tent was raised at 9.30 a.m. after a run of eleven miles 176 yards. An ounce each of butter was served out from our small stock to give a festive touch to the dog stew. At noon I took an observation for latitude, and, after taking a bearing on to Dixson Island, computed that the distance in an airline to winter quarters was 160 miles.

'26 December. Got away at 2 a.m.; the surface undulating and hummocky with occasional beds of soft snow. Sun shining, wind ranged between thirty and forty miles per hour with much low drift; cold; camped about noon having done ten miles 528 yards.

'We have reached the western side of the Ninnis Glacier. Ahead are rising slopes, but we look forward to assistance from the wind in the ascent.

'I was again troubled with a touch of snow-blindness, but it responded to the usual treatment.

'At 11 p.m. we were at it again, but what with preparing dog stew, packing up within the limited area of the tent and experimenting with a sail, it was five hours before the march commenced.

'The sail was the tent-cover, attached to the top of one ski lashed vertically as a mast and secured below to the other ski, lashed across the sledge as a boom.'

A start was made at 4 a.m. on the 27th in a thirty-mile wind accompanied by low drift. The surface was smooth but grew unexpectedly soft at intervals, while the ascent soon began to tell on us. Though the work was laborious, notwithstanding some aid from the sail, the bright sunlight kept up our spirits, and, whenever a halt was called for a few minutes' spell, the conversation invariably turned upon the subject of food and what we should do on arrival on board the *Aurora*.

At noon the sledge-meter showed nine miles 1,400 yards, and we agreed to halt and pitch camp.

The wind had fallen off considerably, and in the brilliant sunshine it was comparatively warm in the tent. The addition of the heat from the primus stove, kept burning for an unusually long time during the preparation of the meat, caused a thaw of drift-snow which became lodged on the lee side of the tent. Thus we had frequently to put up with an unwelcome drip. Moisture came from the floor also, as there was no floor-cloth, and the sleeping-bags were soon very wet and soggy. As soon as the cooking was finished, the tent cooled off and the wet walls froze and became stiff with icy cakes.

At this time we were eating largely of the dogs' meat, to which was added one or two ounces of chocolate or raisins, three or four ounces of pemmican and biscuit mixed together, and, as a beverage, very dilute cocoa. The total weight of solid food consumed by each man per day was approximately fourteen ounces. Our small supply of butter and Glaxo was saved for

'At this time we were eating largely of the dogs' meat, to which was added one or two ounces of chocolate or raisins, three or four ounces of pemmican and biscuit mixed together, and, as a beverage, very dilute cocoa.'

emergency, while a few tea-bags which remained were boiled over and over again.

The march commenced on 28 December at 3 a.m. in a thirty-mile wind accompanied by light drift. Overhead there was a wild sky which augured badly for the next few days. It was cold work raising the sail, and we were glad to be marching.

Our faithful retainer Ginger could walk no longer and was strapped on the sledge. She was the last of the dogs and had been some sort of a help until a few days before. We were sad when it came to finishing her off.

On account of the steep upgrade and the weight of Ginger on the sledge, we camped at 7.15 a.m. after only four miles 1,230 yards.

We had breakfast off Ginger's skull and brain. I can never forget the occasion. As there was nothing available to divide it, the skull was boiled whole. Then the right and left halves were drawn for by the old and well-established sledging practice of 'shut-eye', after which we took it in turns eating to the middle line, passing the skull from one to the other. The brain was afterwads scooped out with a wooden spoon.

On sledging journeys it is usual to apportion all foodstuffs in as nearly even halves as possible. Then one man turns away and another, pointing to a heap, asks 'Whose?' The reply from the one not looking is 'Yours' or 'Mine' as the case may be. Thus an impartial and satisfactory division of the rations is made.

After the meal I went on cooking more meat so as to have a supply in readiness for eating. It was not till 2 p.m. that the second lot was finished. The task was very trying, for I had to sit up on the floor of the tent for hours in a cramped position, continually attending to the cooker, while Mertz in his sleeping-bag was just accommodated within the limited space which remained. The tent was too small either to lie down during the operation or to sit up comfortably on a sleeping-bag.

At 9.30 p.m. Mertz rose to take a turn at the cooking, and at 11 p.m. I joined him at 'breakfast'. At this time a kind of daily cycle was noted in the weather. It was always calmest between 4 p.m. and 6 p.m. During the evening hours the wind increased until it reached a maximum between four and six o'clock next morning, after which it fell off gradually.

We were away at 2.30 a.m. on the 29th in a thirty-mile wind which raised a light drift. The sail was found to be of great assistance over a surface which rose in terraces of fifty to one hundred feet in height, occurring every one to one and a half miles. This march lasted for six hours, during which we covered seven miles 528 yards.

On 30 December the ascent continued and the wind was still in the thirties. After several hours we overtopped the last terrace and stood on flat ground—the crest of a ridge.

Tramping over the plateau, where reigns the desolation of the outer worlds, in solitude at once ominous and weird, one is free to roam in imagination through the wide realm of human experience to the bounds of the great Beyond. One is in the midst of infinities—the infinity of the dazzling white plateau, the infinity of the dome above, the infinity of the time past since these things had birth, and the infinity of the time to come before they shall

> *'One is in the midst of infinities—the dazzling white plateau, the infinity of the dome above, the infinity of the time past since these things had birth, and the infinity of the time to come before they shall have fulfilled the Purpose for which they were created.'*

have fulfilled the Purpose for which they were created. We, in the midst of the illimitable, could feel with Marcus Aurelius that 'Of life, the time is a point.'

By 9 a.m. we had accomplished a splendid march of fifteen miles 350 yards, but the satisfaction we should have felt at making such an inroad on the huge task before us was damped by the fact that I suddenly became aware that Mertz was not as cheerful as usual. I was at a loss to know the reason, for he was always such a bright and companionable fellow.

At 10.15 p.m. the sky had become overcast, snow was falling and a strong wind was blowing. We decided to wait for better conditions.

On New Year's Eve at 5.30 a.m. the wind was not so strong, so we got up and prepared for the start. Mertz said that he felt the dogs' meat was not doing him much good and suggested that we should give it up for a time and eat a small ration of the ordinary sledging food, of which we had still some days' supply carefully husbanded. I agreed to do this and we made our first experiment on that day. The ration tasted very sweet compared with dog's meat and was so scanty in amount that it left one painfully empty.

The light was so atrocious for marching that, after stumbling along for two and a half miles, we were obliged to give up the attempt and camp, spending the day in sleeping-bags.

In the evening at 9.30 p.m. the sun appeared for a brief moment and the wind subsided. Another stage was therefore attempted but at considerable cost, for we staggered along in the bewildering light, continually falling over unseen sastrugi. The surface was undulating with a tendency to down grades. Two sets of sastrugi were found crossing one another, and, in the absence of the sun, we could not be sure of the course, so the camp was pitched after five miles.

'*1 January* 1913. Outside, an overcast sky and falling snow. Mertz was not up to his usual form and we decided not to attempt blundering along in the bad light, believing that the rest would be advantageous to him.

'He did not complain at all except of the dampness of his sleeping-bag, though when I questioned him particularly he admitted that he had pains in the abdomen. As I had a continuous gnawing sensation in the stomach, I took it that he had the same, possibly more acute.

'After New Year's Day he expressed a dislike to biscuit, which seemed rather strange. Then he suddenly had a desire for Glaxo and our small store was made over to him, I taking a considerable ration of the dogs' meat in exchange.

'It was no use, however, for when we tried to cover a few more miles the exertion told very heavily on him, and it was plain that he was in a more serious condition than myself.

'*2 January*. The same abominable weather. We eat only a few ounces of chocolate each day.

'*3 January*. In the evening the sky broke and the sun looked through the clouds. We were not long in packing up and getting on the way. The night was chilly and Mertz got frostbitten fingers, so camp was pitched after four miles 1,230 yards.

'*4 January*. The sun was shining and we had intended rising at 10 a.m., but

Mertz was not well and thought that the rest would be good for him. I spent the time improving some of the gear, mending Mertz's clothing and cooking a quantity of the meat.

'5 January. The sky was overcast, snow was falling, and there was a strong wind. Mertz suggested that as the conditions were so bad we should delay another day.

'Lying in the damp bags was wretched and was not doing either of us any good, but what was to be done? Outside, the conditions were abominable. My companion was evidently weaker than I, and it was apparently quite true that he was not making much of the dogs' meat.

'6 January. A better day but the sky remained overcast. Mertz agreed to try another stage.'

The grade was slightly downhill and the wind well behind. Unfortunately the surface was slippery and irregular and falls were frequent. These told very much upon my companion until, after consistently demurring, he at last consented to ride on the sledge. With the wind blowing behind us, it required no great exertion to bring the load along, though it would often pull up suddenly against sastrugi. After we had covered two and a half miles, Mertz became so cold through inaction in the wind that there was nothing to do but pitch the tent.

Mertz appeared to be depressed and, after the short meal, sank back into his bag without saying much. Occasionally, during the day, I would ask him how he felt, or we would return to the old subject of food. It was agreed that on our arrival on board the *Aurora* Mertz was to make penguin omelettes, for we had never forgotten the excellence of those we had eaten just before leaving the hut.

Reviewing the situation, I found that we were one hundred miles south-east of winter quarters, where food in plenty awaited us. At the time we had still ordinary rations for several days. How short a distance it would seem to the vigorous, but what a lengthy journey for the weak and famished!

The skin was peeling off our bodies and a very poor substitute remained which burst readily and rubbed raw in many places. One day, I remember, Mertz ejaculated, 'Just a moment,' and, reaching over, lifted from my ear a perfect skin-cast. I was able to do the same for him. As we never took off our clothes, the peelings of hair and skin from our bodies worked down into our under-trousers and socks, and regular clearances were made.

During the evening of the 6th I made the following note in my diary:

'A long and wearisome night. If only I could get on; but I must stop with Xavier. He does not appear to be improving and both our chances are going now.'

'7 January. Up at 8 a.m., it having been arranged last night that we would go on today at all costs, sledge-sailing, with Xavier in his bag on the sledge.' It was a sad blow to me to find that Mertz was in a weak state and required helping in and out of his bag. He needed rest for a few hours at least before he could think of travelling. 'I have to turn in again to kill time and also to keep warm, for I feel the cold very much now.'

'At 10 a.m. I get up to dress Xavier and prepare food, but find him in a kind of fit.' Coming round a few minutes later, he exchanged a few words and did not seem to realise that anything had happened. '... Obviously we can't go on today. It is a good day though the light is bad, the sun just gleaming through the clouds. This is terrible; I don't mind for myself but for others.... I pray to God to help us.'

'I cook some thick cocoa for Xavier and give him beef tea; he is better after noon, but very low—I have to lift him up to drink.'

During the afternoon he had several more fits, then became delirious and talked incoherently until midnight, when he appeared to fall off into a peaceful slumber. So I toggled up the sleeping-bag and retired worn out into my own. After a couple of hours, having felt no movement from my companion, I stretched out an arm and found that he was stiff.

My comrade had been accepted into 'the peace that passeth all understanding'. It was my fervent hope that he had been received where sterling qualities and a high mind reap their due reward. In his life we loved him; he was a man of character, generous and of noble parts.

For hours I lay in the bag, rolling over in my mind all that lay behind and the chance of the future. I seemed to stand alone on the wide shores of the world—and what a short step to enter the unknown future!

My physical condition was such that I felt I might collapse in a moment. The gnawing in the stomach had developed there a permanent weakness, so that it was not possible to hold myself up in certain positions. Several of my toes commenced to blacken and fester near the tips and the nails worked loose.

Outside, the bowl of chaos was brimming with drift snow and I wondered how I would manage to break and pitch camp single-handed. There appeared to be little hope of reaching the hut. It was easy to sleep on in the bag, and the weather was cruel outside. But inaction is hard to brook, and I thought of Service's lines:

> Buck up, do your damnedest and fight,
> It's the plugging away that will win you the day.

If I failed to reach the hut it would be something done to reach some prominent point likely to catch the eye of a search party, where a cairn might be erected and our diaries cached. And so I commenced to modify the sledge and camping gear to meet fresh requirements.

The sky remained clouded, but the wind fell off to a calm which lasted for several hours. I took the opportunity to set to work on the sledge, sawing it in halves with a pocket tool. A mast was made out of one of the rails of the discarded half of the sledge and a spar was cut from the other rail. The sledge-meter, very much battered, was still serviceable. Lastly, the load was cut down to a minimum by the elimination of all but the barest necessities.

Late on the evening of the 8th I took the body of Mertz, wrapped up in his sleeping-bag, outside the tent, piled snow blocks around it and raised a rough cross made of the two half-runners of the sledge.

On 9 January the weather was overcast and fairly thick drift was flying in a wind reaching about fifty miles an hour. As certain matters still required attention and my chances of re-erecting the tent were rather doubtful if I had decided to move on, the start was delayed.

> 'My comrade had been accepted into "the peace that passeth all understanding". It was my fervent hope that he had been received where sterling qualities and a high mind reap their due reward.'

The half sledge that Mawson improvised for the last stage of his journey.

'I read the burial service over Xavier this afternoon. As there is little chance of my reaching human aid alive, I greatly regret inability at the moment to set out the detail of coastline met with for three hundred miles travelled and observations of glacier and ice-formations, etc.; the most of which latter are, of course, committed to my head.

'The approximate location of the camp is latitude 68°2'S, longitude 145°9'E. This is dead reckoning, as the theodolite legs have been out of action for some time, splinted together to form tent-props. I believe the truth lies nearer latitude 67°57'S, longitude 145°20'E, as the wind must have drifted us to the north.'

During the afternoon I cut up Mertz's burberry jacket and roughly sewed it to a large canvas clothes bag, making a sail which could be readily set or furled, so as to save delay in starting out or in camping.

The 10th of January was an impossible day for travelling on account of thick drift and high wind. I spent part of the time in reckoning up the amount of food remaining and in cooking the rest of the dogs' meat; the last device enabling me to leave behind some of the kerosene, of which there was still a good supply. Late in the afternoon the wind fell and the sun peered amongst the clouds just as I was in the middle of a long job riveting and lashing the broken shovel.

It was on 11 January—a beautiful, calm day of sunshine—that I set out over a good surface with a slight downgrade. From the start my feet felt lumpy and sore. They had become so painful after a mile of walking that I decided to make an examination of them on the spot, sitting in the sun on the sledge. The sight of my feet gave me quite a shock, for the thickened skin of the soles had separated in each case as a complete layer, and abundant watery fluid had escaped into the socks. The new skin underneath was very much abraded and raw. I did what appeared to be the best thing under the circumstances: smeared the new skin with lanoline, of which there was a good store, and with bandages bound the skin soles back in place, as they were comfortable and soft in contact with the raw surfaces. Outside the bandages I wore six pairs of thick woollen socks, fur boots and a crampon over-shoe of soft leather. Then I removed most of my clothing and bathed in the glorious heat of the sun. A tingling sensation seemed to spread throughout my whole body, and I felt stronger and better.

When the day commenced with ideal weather I thought I would cover a long distance, but at 5.30 p.m., after six and a quarter miles, I felt nerve-worn and had to camp, 'so worn that had it not been a delightful evening, I should not have found strength to erect the tent.'

Though the medical outfit was limited, there were a fair number of bandages and on camping I devoted much time to tending raw patches all over the body, festering fingers and inflamed nostrils.

High wind and much drift put travelling out of the question on 12 January, and in any case my feet needed a rest.

'*13 January*. The wind subsided and the snow cleared off at noon. The afternoon was beautifully fine. Descended hard ice-slopes over many crevasses —almost all descent—but surface cut my feet up; at 8 p.m. camped, having done five and three-quarter miles—painful feet—on camping find feet worse than ever; things look bad but shall persevere. It is now 11 p.m. and the glacier is firing off like artillery—appears to send up great jets of imprisoned air.' During the march Aurora Peak showed up to the west, about twenty miles away, across the Mertz Glacier. I felt happy at thus fixing my position, and at the sight of the far plateau which led onwards to winter quarters.

The glacier was the next obstacle to advance. To the south-west it descended from the plateau in immense broken folds. Pressing northward it was torn into the jumbled crush of serac-ice, sparkling beneath an unclouded sun. The idea of diverging to the west and rounding the icefalls occurred to me, but the detours involved other difficulties, so I strove to pick out the best track across the valley.

A high wind which blew on the morning of the 14th diminished in strength by noon and allowed me to get away. The sun was so warm that the puckered ice underfoot was covered with a film of water and in some places small trickles ran away to disappear into crevasses.

Though the course was downhill to the Mertz Glacier, the sledge required a good deal of pulling owing to the wet runners. At 9 p.m., after travelling five miles, I pitched camp in the bed of the glacier.

Between 9.30 p.m. and 11 p.m. the 'cannonading' heard on the previous night recommenced. The sounds, resembling the explosions of heavy guns, usually started higher up the glacier and ended down towards the sea. When I first heard them, I put my head outside the tent to see what was going on. The reports came at random from every direction, but there was no visible evidence as to how they were produced. Without a doubt they had something to do with the re-freezing and splitting of the ice owing to the evening chill; but the sounds seemed far too loud to be explained by this cause alone.

The 15th of January—the date on which all the summer sledging parties were due at the hut! It was overcast and snowing early in the day, and in a few hours the sun broke out and shone warmly. The travelling was so heavy over a soft snowy surface, partly melting, that I gave up, after one mile, and camped.

At 7 p.m. the surface had not improved, the sky was thickly obscured and snow fell. At 10 p.m. the snow was coming down heavily, and, since there were many crevasses in the vicinity, I resolved to wait.

On the 16th at 2 a.m. the snow was as thick as ever, but at 5 a.m. the atmosphere lightened and the sun appeared.

Without delay I broke camp. A favourable breeze sprang up, and with sail set I managed to proceed through the snowy deluge in short stages. The snow clung in lumps to the runners, which had to be scraped frequently. I passed some broken ridges and sank into several holes leading down to crevasses out of which it was possible to scramble easily.

After laboriously toiling up one long slope, I was just catching my breath at the top and the sledge was running easily when I noticed that the surface beneath my feet fell away steeply in front. I suddenly realised that I was on the brink of a great blue hole like a quarry. The sledge was following of its own accord and was rapidly gaining speed, so I turned and, exerting every effort, was just able to hold it back by means of the hauling-line from the edge of the abyss. I should think that there must have been an interval of quite a minute during which I held my ground without being able to make it budge. Then it slowly came my way, and the imminent danger was past.

The day's march was an extremely hard five miles. Before turning in I had an extra supper of jelly soup, made by boiling down some of the dogs' sinews, strengthened with a little pemmican. The acute enjoyment of eating under these circumstances compensates in a slight measure for the suffering of starvation.

The 17th of January was another day of overcast weather and falling snow. Delay meant a reduction in the ration which was low enough already, so there was nothing to do but go on.

When I got away at 8 a.m. I found that the pulling was easier than it had been on the previous day. Nevertheless I covered only two miles and had to consider myself fortunate in not winding up the whole story then and there. This is what happened, following the account in my diary:

'Going up a long, fairly steep slope, deeply covered with soft snow, broke through lid of crevasse but caught myself at thighs, got out, turned fifty yards to the north, then attempted to cross trend of crevasse, there being no indication of it; a few moments later found myself dangling fourteen feet below on end of rope in crevasse—sledge creeping to mouth—had time to say to myself, "so this is the end", expecting the sledge every moment to crash on my head and all to go to the unseen bottom—then thought of the food uneaten on the sledge; but as the sledge pulled up without letting me down, thought of Providence giving me another chance.' The chance was very small considering my weak condition. The width of the crevasse was about six feet, so I hung freely in space, turning slowly round.

A great effort brought a knot in the rope within my grasp, and, after a moment's rest, I was able to draw myself up and reach another, and, at length, hauled myself on to the overhanging snow-lid into which the rope had cut. Then, when I was carefully climbing out on to the surface, a further section of the lid gave way, precipitating me once more to the full length of the rope.

Exhausted, weak and chilled (for my hands were bare and pounds of snow had got inside my clothing) I hung with the firm conviction that all was over except the passing. Below was a black chasm; it would be but the work of a moment to slip from the harness, then all the pain and toil would be over. It was a rare situation, a rare temptation—a chance to quit small things for great—to pass from the petty exploration of a planet to the contemplation of vaster worlds beyond. But there was all eternity for the last and, at its longest, the present would be but short. I felt better for the thought.

My strength was fast ebbing; in a few minutes it would be too late. It was the occasion for a supreme attempt. New power seemed to come as I addressed myself to one last tremendous effort. The struggle occupied some time, but by a miracle I rose slowly to the surface. This time I emerged feet first, still holding on the rope, and pushed myself out, extended at full length, on the snow—on solid ground. Then came the reaction, and I could do nothing for quite an hour.

The tent was erected in slow stages and I then had a little food. Later on I lay in the sleeping-bag, thinking things over. It was a time when the mood of the Persian philosopher appealed to me:

> Unborn To-morrow and dead Yesterday,
> Why fret about them if To-day be sweet?

I was confronted with this problem: whether it was better to enjoy life for a few days, sleeping and eating my fill until the provisions gave out, or to plug on again in hunger with the prospect of plunging at any moment into eternity without the great luxury and pleasure of the food. And then an idea presented itself which greatly improved my prospects. It was to construct a ladder from alpine rope, one end of which was to be secured to the bow of the sledge and the other carried over my left shoulder and loosely attached to the sledge harness. Thus, if I fell into a crevasse again, it would be easy for me, even though weakened by starvation, to scramble out again by the ladder, provided the sledge was not also engulfed.

Notwithstanding the possibilities of the rope ladder, I could not sleep properly at all; my nerves had been so overtaxed. All night considerable wind and drift continued. On the 19th it was overcast and light snow was falling. I resolved 'to go ahead and leave the rest to Providence'.

As they wallowed through the deep snow my feet and legs kept breaking through into space. Then I went right under, but the sledge was held back and the ladder 'proved trumps'. A few minutes later I was down again, but I emerged again without much exertion, half-smothered with snow. Faintness overcame me and I stopped to camp, though only a short distance had been covered. All around was a leaden glare, the snow-clouds corralling me in. The sun had not shown up for some days and I was eager to see it once more, not only that it might show up the landscape but for its cheerful influence and life-giving energy. A few days previously my condition had been improving, but now it was going back.

During the night of the 18th loud booming noises, sharp cracks and muffled growls issued from the neighbouring crevasses and kept waking me up. At times one could feel a vibration accompanying the growling sounds, and I concluded that the ice was in rapid motion.

The sun at last appeared on the 19th, and I was off by 8.30 a.m. The whole surface was a network of crevasses, some very wide. Along one after another of these I dragged the sledge until a spot was reached where the snow-bridge looked to be firm. Here I plunged across, risking the consequences.

After three hours' marching nothing serious had happened and I found myself on safer ground with a 'pimply' surface visible ahead, close under the slopes of the highlands. Once on this I became over-reliant, and in consequence sank several times into narrow fissures.

At 1 p.m. the Mertz Glacier was at last crossed and I had reached the rising hills on its western side. Overlooking the camp, five hundred feet above the glacier, were beetling, crevassed crags, but I could trace out a good road, free from pitfalls, leading to the plateau, at an elevation of three thousand feet.

To lighten my load for the climb I threw away alpine rope, finnesko crampons, sundry pairs of worn crampons and socks, while I rubbed a composition on the sledge runners which prevented them from sticking to wet snow.

The 20th of January was a wretched day; overcast, with wind and light drift. In desperation I got away at 2 p.m. in a wind which proved to be of considerable assistance. I could see nothing of my surroundings; one thing was certain, and that was that the ascent had commenced and every foot took me upward. The day's work amounted to about two and a half miles.

On the 21st the sun shone brightly and there was a good following wind. Through deep snow I zigzagged up for three miles before deciding to camp.

Wind and drift prevailed early on the 22nd but fell away towards noon, and I was then favoured with a glorious sunny day. Away to the north was a splendid view of the open sea; it looked so beautiful and friendly that I longed to be down near it. Six miles had been covered during the day, but I felt very weak towards the end on account of the heavy pulling.

During the early hours of the 23rd the sun was visible, but about 8 a.m. the clouds sagged low, the wind rose and everything became blotted out in a swirl of driving snow. I wandered on through it for several hours, the sledge capsizing at times owing to the strength of the wind. It was not possible to keep an accurate course, for even the wind changed direction as the day wore on. Underfoot there was soft snow which I found comfortable for my sore feet but which made the sledge drag heavily at times.

When camp was pitched at 4 p.m. I reckoned that the distance covered in a straight line had been three and a half miles.

Erecting the tent single-handed in the high wind was a task which required much patience and some skill. The poles were erected first and then the tent was gathered up in the proper form and taken to the windward side of the legs where it was weighted down. The flounce on the windward side was got into position and piled up with snow blocks. Other blocks of snow had previously been placed in a ring round the legs in readiness to be tumbled on to the rest of the flounce when the tent was quickly slipped over the apex of the poles. In very windy weather it was often as much as two hours after halting before I would be cosy within the shelter of the tent.

High wind and dense driving snow persisted throughout the 24th and I made five and a half miles, sitting on the sledge most of the time with the sail up. The blizzard continued on the 25th, but after the trying experience of the previous two days, I did not feel well enough to go on. Outside, the snow fell in torrents, piled up round the tent and pressed in until it was no bigger than a coffin, of which it reminded me.

I passed most of the day doctoring myself, attending to raw and inflamed places. Tufts of my beard and hair came out, and the snowy floor of the tent was strewn with it at every camp.

'*26 January*. I went on again in dense, driving snow. There was no need of the sail. The wind, which was behind, caught the sledge and bundled it along so that, though over a soft surface of snow, the travelling was rapid. The snow was in large, rounded grains, and beat on the tent like hail. Altogether nine miles were covered.

'*27 January*. Blizzard-bound again. The previous day's exertions were too much for me to undertake the same again without a long rest.

'*28 January*. In the morning the wind had moderated very much but the sky remained overcast and snow continued to fall. It was a long job digging the tent out. Soon after the start the sun gleamed and the weather improved. The three-thousand-foot crest of the plateau had been crossed and I was bearing down rapidly on Commonwealth Bay, the vicinity of which showed up as a darker patch on the clouds of the north-west horizon.

'The evening was fine and I really began to feel that winter quarters were approaching. To increase my excitement Madigan Nunatak came into view for a time in the clear, evening light. Distance covered, over eight miles.'

The calm of the previous evening was broken again, and I started on the morning of 29 January in considerable drift and fairly strong wind. After going five miles I had miraculous good fortune.

Mawson emerging from his makeshift tent.

I was travelling along on an even down grade and was wondering how long the two pounds of food which remained would last, when something dark loomed through the drift a short distance away to the right. All sorts of possibilities fled through my mind as I headed the sledge for it. The unexpected happened—it was a cairn of snow erected by McLean, Hodgeman and Hurley, who had been out searching for us. On the top of the mound was a bag of food, left on the chance that it might be picked up, while in a tin was a note stating the bearing and distance of the mound from Aladdin's Cave (E 30° S, distance twenty-three miles); that the ship had arrived at the hut and was waiting; that Amundsen had reached the Pole; and that Scott was remaining another year in Antarctica.

It was rather a singular fact that the search party only left this mound at eight o'clock on the morning of that very day (29 January). It was about 2 p.m. when I found it. Thus, during the night of the 28th, our camps had been only about five miles apart.

With plenty of food, I speedily felt stimulated and revived, and anticipated reaching the hut in a day or two, for there was then not more than twenty-three miles to cover. Alas, however, there was to be another delay. I was without crampons—they had been thrown away on the western side of Mertz Glacier—and in the strong wind was not able to stand up on the slippery ice of the coastal slopes. The result was that I sat on the sledge and ran along with the wind, nibbling at the food as I went. The sledge made so much leeway that near the end of the day, after fourteen miles, I reckoned that I had been carried to the east of Aladdin's Cave. The course was therefore changed to the west, but the wind came down almost broad-side-on to the sledge, and it was swept away. The only thing to do was to camp.

On the 30th I cut up the box of the theodolite and into two pieces of wood stuck as many screws and tacks as I could procure from the sledge-meter. In the repair bag there were still a few ice-nails which at this time were of great use. Late in the day the wind fell off, and I started westward over the ice-slopes with the pieces of nail-studded wood lashed to my feet.

After six miles these improvised crampons broke up, and the increasing wind got me into difficulties. Finally, the sledge slipped sideways into a narrow crevasse and was caught by the boom (which crossed from side to side at the lower part of the mast). I was not strong enough for the job of extricating it straight away, and by the time I had got it safely on the ice, the wind had increased still more. So I pitched camp.

The blizzard was in full career on 31 January and I spent all day and until late at night trying to make the crampons serviceable, but without success.

On 1 February the wind and drift subsided late in the afternoon, and I clearly saw to the west the beacon which marked Aladdin's Cave.

At 7 p.m. I reached this haven within the ice, and never again was I to have the ordeal of pitching the tent. Inside the cave were three oranges and a pineapple which had been brought from the ship. It was wonderful once more to be in the land of such things!

I waited to mend one of the crampons and then started off for the hut; but a blizzard had commenced. To descend the five miles of steep icy slopes with my miserable crampons, in the weak state in which I found myself, would

'At 7 p.m. I reached this haven within the ice, and never again was I to have the ordeal of pitching the tent. Inside the cave were three oranges and a pineapple which had been brought from the ship. It was wonderful once more to be in the land of such things!'

only have been as a last resort. So I camped in the comfortable cave and hoped for better weather next day.

The high wind, rising to a hurricane at times, continued for a whole week with dense drift until the 8th. I spent the long hours making crampons of a new pattern, eating and sleeping. Eventually I became so anxious that I used to sit outside the cave for long spells, watching for a lull in the wind.

At length I resolved to go down in the blizzard, sitting on the sledge as long as possible, blown along by the wind. I was making preparations for a start when the wind suddenly decreased and my opportunity had come.

In a couple of hours I was within one mile and a half of the hut. There was no sign of the ship lying in the offing but I comforted myself with the thought that she might be still at the anchorage and have swung inshore so as to be hidden by the ice-cliffs, or on the other hand that Captain Davis might have been along the coast to the east searching there.

But even as I gazed about seeking for a clue, a speck on the north-west horizon caught my eye and my hopes went down. It looked like a distant ship; it might well have been the *Aurora*. Well, what matter! the long journey was at an end—a terrible chapter of my life was finished!

The Aurora, *framed by a striking ice formation produced by the freezing of spray, lies in Commonwealth Bay. The ice slopes of the mainland in the distance rise to a height of six hundred metres.*

Mawson reached the hut, where full preparations had been made for wintering a second year. Only that morning the Aurora *had left. A wireless message was sent recalling the ship, but the weather was too bad for a landing to be made, and after steaming up and down Commonwealth Bay for a day, the ship left to relieve the men at the western base on the Shackleton Ice Shelf. Mawson was eventually picked up by the* Aurora *when it returned in December 1913.*

Trapped by the pack-ice in the Weddell Sea, the Endurance *leans perilously after one of the convulsions of the ice that eventually crushed the ship.*

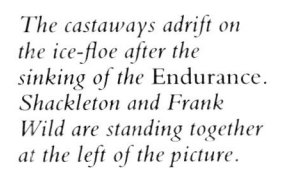

The castaways adrift on the ice-floe after the sinking of the Endurance. *Shackleton and Frank Wild are standing together at the left of the picture.*

SHACKLETON'S ARGONAUTS

Frank Hurley

PHOTOGRAPHER-ADVENTURER *Frank Hurley, who accompanied Douglas Mawson on his expedition to the Antarctic in 1911–12, was invited to join the British Trans-Antarctic Expedition led by Sir Ernest Shackleton in 1914. Travelling in the beautiful barquentine-rigged auxiliary* Endurance, *of 350 tons, the expedition planned to land at the head of the Weddell Sea and cross the Antarctic continent by way of the South Pole to the Ross Sea, where another ship would pick them up. It was not to be. Before reaching land, the* Endurance *was trapped in pack ice, and for the next eight months the ship slowly drifted northwards through the Weddell Sea while held fast in the grip of the ice. On 27 October 1915 the* Endurance *was crushed by the force of the ice and the party of twenty-eight men were forced to abandon ship and make camp on an ice-floe. Before the ship sank, they were able to salvage food and equipment, including Hurley's films and camera, and the ship's three boats, the* James Caird, *the* Stancomb Wills *and the* Dudley Docker. *For another five months they drifted northwards on the ice-floe, hoping that before their gigantic raft disintegrated they would reach the open sea and be able to launch the boats and make their way to the nearest land. Frank Hurley tells the remarkable story of their ordeal in the boats in his book* Shackleton's Argonauts.

IT WAS NOW 8 April 1916. The Antarctic winter had already set in and the nights were rapidly lengthening. Shortly after 6 p.m. the watchman raised the alarm that the floe was splitting. We hurried from the tents in the gloom and observed a dark, jagged line gradually broadening through the centre of the camp. It passed directly under the *James Caird*, separating the other two boats from us. In a few minutes we rushed the boats across to the section where the tents stood. Our camp was reduced to an overcrowded, rocking triangle, and it was evident that we must take the first opportunity to escape, no matter how desperate the chances might be. During the night a strong breeze sprang up from the south, and under its influence the pack began to scatter.

On 9 April we found that the previous night's wind had loosened the ice, but it was impossible to launch the boats, for the leads were opening and closing so rapidly that if we had attempted to navigate them we would have been crushed like eggshells. Changes took place so rapidly that a clearing which appeared to offer an excellent opening at one moment was a grinding ice-mill a few minutes later. In our awful dilemma we all turned our eyes to the leader, who was standing surveying this baffling maze. Action was imperative at the first opportunity. After a hurried breakfast, tents were struck and all made ready to launch the boats. Crews were allotted. The leader, Frank Wild, and eleven men, of whom I was one, manned the *James Caird*, the largest but frailest boat. Captain Worsley with nine others formed the crew of the *Dudley Docker,* and Tom Crean had charge of the *Stancomb Wills* with the remainder of the men. These preparations proved to be opportune, for, as we stood by, the ice parted beneath our feet. Hastily we hauled the boats and gear to temporary safety on the larger piece, which was barely big enough to accommodate everything. The ice had cracked in an uncanny fashion through the old camping site, which the leader and myself had vacated but an hour previously. We stood on the brink of the widening fissure and watched the raft on which we had slept for four months drift away amidst the churning ice. How insecure it had been! The warmth of our bodies had thawed the ice, until we were sleeping, happily unconscious of the fact, barely a foot above the surface of the sea.

The first desperate chance came just after lunch. At one o'clock a lead opened up through the heaving ice. Sir Ernest gave the order to launch the boats. We slid them over the jagged edge of the floe into the inky waters. The gear and supplies were hurriedly stowed and we rowed for dear life through the winding channel and entered a vast lake of gently heaving deep blue water in which floated a solitary mammoth berg. At last we were free. No longer idle captives with capricious winds and tides for gaolers, but free to shape our own destinies. Our adventures during those 159 days on the floe had come to an end. How thoroughly the happenings of the next six days were to eclipse them...!

The *James Caird* took the lead, and as we bent to our oars we sang joyfully—we were bound for Elephant Island at last. But we sang too soon.

We had covered only a few miles when we observed the eastern horizon of pack-ice in violent agitation and rapidly bearing towards us. The noise of the oncoming water and ice sounded like the rush of a tidal bore up a river. We stopped rowing for a brief moment and observed that the whole surface of the sea was covered by a mass of churning ice and foam, which was driving towards us in a broad crescent in the grip of a furious tide rip. The horns were converging, and it seemed as though we would be trapped in a rapidly closing pool. Sir Ernest shouted to the boats to make for the lee of the mammoth berg. Tossing, plunging and grinding, the ice-laden surge swept after us, and though we pulled with all our might we could not draw away. It was only one hundred yards behind, and tongues of ice were flicking out ahead of it. One of these reached to within a few yards of the *Stancomb Wills,* which was bringing up the rear; disaster was averted only by the greatest exertion of her crew and by Crean's skilful piloting.

After a fifteen minutes' race for life, the phenomenon ceased as quickly as it had begun. All became quiet, save for the groaning and creaking of the floes as they fretted in the swell. The waters were littered with ice, and, night falling swiftly, the leader decided to rest his weary men on an old floe. The cook with his small stove and his assistant were put ashore first, and, by the time the boats were discharged and hauled up, and the tents pitched, hoosh

'We stood on the brink of the widening fissure and watched the raft on which we had slept for four months drift away amidst the churning ice. How insecure it had been!'

Frank Hurley, one of the world's great adventurer photographers. He accompanied both Mawson and Shackleton to Antarctica, and after being rescued from Elephant Island in 1916 became an official war photographer on the Western Front and in Palestine.

was ready. The hot meal set our cold bodies aglow and, with the cheerful prospect of a night's rest, laughter and song came from the tents.

We had lived so long in this perilous vortex that we had become almost indifferent to hazards and dangers. We cared little that our camp was pitched on a brittle ice-raft, scarcely more than fifty paces across.... Nor did we heed the schools of killer-whales patrolling the neighbouring waters in search of prey. Guards being set—each man taking an hour's watch—we snuggled down into our sleeping-bags and were soon rocked to sleep by the swaying floe. But the hope of a night's rest was shattered. Shortly after 11 p.m. a loud cracking caused us to hasten from our sleeping-bags and to investigate. A minute examination of the floe by the light of hurricane lamps displayed nothing more than a subsidence of the surface snow. Once more we turned in and had just dozed off when another report aroused us.

It was no false alarm this time—the watchman was yelling that the floe was splitting. The crack passed beneath the tent occupied by the sailors, and so quickly did it draw apart that before the men could escape one fell through into the sea. By marvellous good fortune Sir Ernest was near, and rushing to the breach flung himself down by the brink and hauled seaman Holness, who was floating in his sleeping bag, from the water. An alarm was raised that a second man was missing, but, before a search could be made, the fractured floes came together again with a terrific impact. The *James Caird*, which had been separated from the body of the camp, was hurried across the rift, which was opening again. So rapidly did it widen that Sir Ernest, who was waiting on the far side till the boat reached safety, was unable to leap across. A few minutes later he drifted away and was swallowed up in the darkness and falling snow. We heard a voice calling for one of the boats, but Wild had already anticipated the order and had manned the *Stancomb Wills*.

Owing to the darkness and the congestion of the ice, we had great difficulty in rescuing our leader. Then the roll was called, and with deep relief all hands were accounted for. A roaring blubber-fire was kindled, and, since the floe was rocking badly in the increasing swell and might fracture again, the tents were struck. We huddled close to the fire and spent the rest of the night longing for the dawn and praying that our camp would remain intact. Dawn came at 6 a.m. and the sight it revealed was frightening, for the sea was closely packed with ice. A good hot hoosh and a cup of hot milk banished our fatigue to some extent, and we stood by, waiting for an opportunity to get under way. At 8 a.m. a lead opened and the boats were launched and loaded. The previous day's experience had shown that the boats were too deep in the water, so we left behind some cases of dried vegetables, a number of picks and shovels, and sundry oddments which we considered could be dispensed with. A strong east wind was blowing, which gradually increased to a moderate gale. At noon we won through to what appeared to be the open sea. Heavy rollers were running outside and breaking on the margin of the pack-ice, and the deeply laden boats began to labour badly. Sprays continually broke over them, freezing as they fell. Everything became sheathed in ice, and our soaked garments froze as still as mail and cracked as we moved.

It was too hazardous to face the dangerous sea, and we were reluctantly compelled to run back to the shelter of the pack, where the sea was broken down by the weight of ice. We continued sailing westward until late afternoon, when we entered an extensive, calm pool in which drifted a massive friendly floe—an excellent camping place. Soaked to the skin, weary through lack of sleep, and utterly worn out, we were thankful for any place on which we might lie down and snatch a few hours' rest. Guards were set to watch over the safety of the camp, and we managed to get more sleep then we had had for a fortnight.

The dawn broke, foggy, cheerless and sinister. A piercing wind was

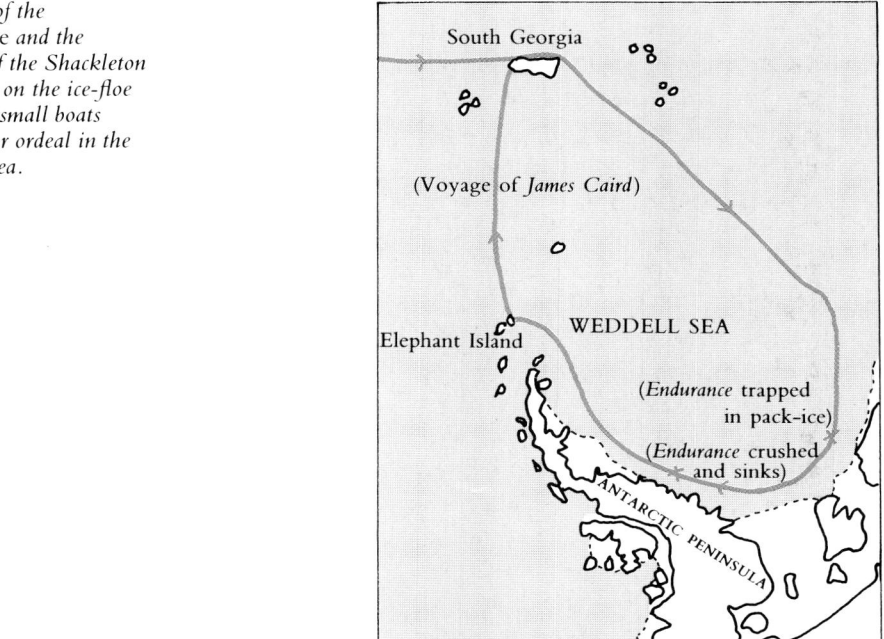

The path of the Endurance *and the members of the Shackleton expedition on the ice-floe and in the small boats during their ordeal in the Weddell Sea.*

blowing from the north-west, bringing sleet which froze in a glassy veneer. While we were making ready to get under way, fields of pack-ice came rapidly driving down from the north. But our floe appeared capable of withstanding a buffeting, so Sir Ernest decided to remain and await events.

Driven on by the swift tides and heavy swell, the ice swirled round our floe, bearing it along, rolling and rocking alarmingly. In less than an hour the bosom of the sea was obscured by a seething expanse of crushing pack-ice. Climbing to the top of a reeling knoll, we gazed spellbound on a terrifying spectacle. Furious warfare was raging on one of nature's age-old battlefields. We had reached the northern limit of the ice-pack, where the endless streams of ice cast adrift from the polar continent were being lashed back remorselessly by temperate seas. Here the conclusion of a cycle in nature's equilibrium was taking place. The ice-packs, pounded up and eroded by the action of the waves, were returning to their primal element. Around us churned the mill of the world. Gnarled old ice-floes, weather-worn bergs, fragmentary stumps, and decayed ice masses were crowded together in one heaving, rolling grind. To the girdling horizon stretched this tempest-ridden, battling confusion. It was sublime, irresistible, terrible. Our rocking floe was suffering the fate of its neighbours. We experienced a series of sickening impacts as its ramparts were torn asunder. What helpless atoms we felt—mere human flotsam, caught in a maelstrom of unlimited power and separated from eternity by only a thin partition of crumbling ice.

We stood by the boats, ready to launch them should our frail raft shatter. A large section of it sheared from its margin, and a broad ice foot formed, over which the surf swirled and on which masses of ice were stranded. It would be difficult to launch the boats over this lunging ice reef. Sir Ernest and Wild stood on the peak of our foundering berg, patiently watching and waiting for a chance. There was a cry of 'She's splitting.' We manned the boats, waited, but nothing happened it was only the surface snow subsiding. But our floe was wallowing like a sinking ship before the last plunge, and the end seemed near.

Sir Ernest called out that a lead was approaching, and that we were to stand by to launch the boats. On the horizon we noticed a dark line cleaving through the tortured ice—a narrow, open lead. Would it never reach us? A flock of seabirds circled over us like messengers of freedom, a few seals drifted past, sleeping peacefully and safely on rocking floes; but we, in spite of our superior intelligence, were in peril, powerless to help ourselves; how anomalous it seemed! Slowly, stealthily, with exasperating deliberation, the lead crept closer. At last it reached our floe. Sir Ernest stood by the rising and falling ice foot, directing the launching, which was extremely hazardous. When the floe rolled favourably, the order was given, 'Launch boats.' The *James Caird* had barely swung free when the uprising ice caught her bow and she was nearly swamped. We flung stores and gear aboard, leapt in and rowed desperately. The three boats in procession headed along the lead to the west and soon entered large stretches of water, sufficiently open to allow the sails to be hoisted. Light snow and biting winds numbed us to the bone, but our spirits were cheered by the excellent progress.

Wild was at our helm, and Sir Ernest stood up in the stern keeping a

'We had reached the northern limit of the ice pack, where the endless streams of ice cast adrift from the polar continent were being lashed back remorselessly by temperate seas. Here the conclusion of a cycle in nature's equilibrium was taking place.'

watchful eye on the two boats following in our wake, and occasionally shouting words of direction. As night drew on, we ranged up alongside a floe that promised shelter, and made fast. The cook was put ashore just long enough to prepare some hoosh. We had had enough of the floes, and prefered to remain in the boats until daylight. We were compelled to cast off in the dark, for streams of ice threatened to hole the boats. It was a stern night: snow and sleet fell; killer whales skirmished round, and we dreaded that they might rise to 'blow' beneath the boats, or capsize them with their massive dorsal fins. We had seen the killers charge and upset heavy masses of ice on which luckless seals basked....

Dawn rose on a pitiful scene. Haggard, drawn faces, with beards encrusted with ice, peered out from garments shrouded with snow. The boats were drifting idly on a stagnant, mushy sea. Before getting under way we set about looking for a suitable floe on which the cook might land to prepare breakfast. Such a floe was difficult to find without running into the body of the pack, and it was interesting to note the keenness that was displayed in searching for a friendly ice island. At last we drew up alongside one. The cook—excellent fellow—though stiff with cold, soon had a hot hoosh ready, which heartened us for what the immediate future might bring.

The day proved to be clear and radiant with sunshine. Sails were set and the purl of a silver bow wave sang merrily in our ears as we moved over the deep blue. For the first time for months we admired the callous beauty of the pack-ice, eroded by the waves into countless fanciful forms. Penguins rode on crystal gondolas, and countless seals basked on marble-white slabs, which swayed gently in the swell. Beyond the margin of the pack rolled the seas, deep furrowed and white crested.

Ever since we embarked on 9 April, thick weather had obscured all view of land, and there had been no opportunity of determining our position by sun observations. We knew we had been sailing west, but, since we knew little about the set of the currents, our precise location was a matter of conjecture. We imagined, however, that it must be highly favourable as far as Elephant Island was concerned. With keen speculation we awaited noon, when Captain Worsley would check up our dead reckoning by a sun shot. As the time approached we watched Worsley stand up in the *Dudley Docker*, put his arm around the mast to steady himself, for the boat was rolling badly, and manipulate his sextant. We then rowed the *James Caird* alongside the *Dudley Docker* and the leader jumped into it. After the observations were worked out, he returned to the *James Caird* and held a whispered discussion with Wild. The outcome was that our destination was changed from Elephant Island to Hope Bay—roughly eighty miles to the south-west—on the Antarctic mainland. Fearing the reaction it might have had on the party at the time, we were not made aware of Worsley's calculations, though Sir Ernest informed us that our progress was not as favourable as we had anticipated. In fact, we were actually thirty miles east of the position where the boats had been launched three days previously. Though sailing west during the day, the currents had carried the ice-floes on which we had rested during the night swiftly to the east. Not only had we lost all the distance sailed, but the drift had actually carried us thirty miles off our course. This was heartbreaking.

'For the first time for months we admired the callous beauty of the pack ice, eroded by the waves into countless fanciful forms. Penguins rode on crystal gondolas, and countless seals basked on marble-white slabs, which swayed gently in the swell.'

Throughout the day we continued, until dusk made navigation dangerous, and we then set about finding a suitable floe behind which to shelter for the night. The ice was so broken and tossed by the surge that it was unapproachable. At last, in the darkness, we succeeded in making the boats fast to a large floe, tethering one behind the other. The swell prevented the cook from being put ashore, so hoosh had to be prepared with the aid of primus stoves. This was a lengthy business, for the boats were rolling violently, and sprays occasionally broke over them, extinguishing the stoves.

It seemed as if evil forces were arrayed to torment us. No sooner was one peril overcome than another arose in its place. Streams of ice fragments, borne along by surface currents or driven by the winds, were attracted to the lee side of our floe, and this became a new annoyance. For several hours we staved off the ice with boat-hooks and paddles, and then, shortly after midnight, the wind suddenly changed and began to drive the boats back broadside on to the ice spurs of the floe. There was no time to cast off, so reluctantly we cut our valuable mooring line and backed away, to save the boats from being holed.

So that we might not drift apart, we kept the boats tethered to one another, and all night long they lay hove to in the freezing sea. We huddled together, clasped in each other's arms, so that we might glean a little warmth from each other's bodies and consolation from whispered hopes. Where our bodies touched, the warmth thawed our frozen garments and, when we moved, the icy wind stabbed through us. Night seemed an eternity. Where our wet clothes chafed, boils swelled up, throbbing intolerably in the piercing cold. It seemed that the limit of human endurance must soon be reached.

Dawn came at last. We were denied the cheer of a hot breakfast, for everything was iced and the sea was running high. But there were compensations. No restraint was placed on the amount of cold rations we might eat, the sun was rising, and the wind had changed fair for Elephant Island....

The pack-ice had closed up to the south in the direction of Hope Bay, so the boats were again headed for Elephant Island, which now lay a hundred miles to the north. Sails were hoisted, and with a strong, fair breeze our three small vessels sped forward to the land of hope. The pack was rapidly thinning out, and it appeared as if we were nearing its northernmost limit. Shortly after noon we passed through a narrow belt of ice and unexpectedly emerged into the open ocean.

Had we not been driven by desperation, we would not have dared to venture into the heavy seas in three such frail boats. It was amazing that our spent and weather-beaten bodies reponded so heroically to the occasion, and I doubt if any creature but man could have survived the excesses of exposure, fatigue, hunger, and lack of rest to which we had been subjected. It was our wills that made it possible—the wills that enabled us to rise above suffering and to dominate and drive our jaded bodies.

Again, I cannot speak too highly of our leader. The piloting of the party through perilous adventures, from the time the ship was beset up to our escape from the ice without loss of life, was a far greater achievement than the realisation of the original plans of the expedition would have been. If ever an environment was likely to breed pessimism, ill feeling and revolt,

'No restraint was placed on the amount of cold rations we might eat, the sun was rising, and the wind had changed fair for Elephant Island.'

it was that which surrounded us during the monotonous months on the floe. Scientists and sailors of widely diverse natures, training and outlook, cooped together in tiny tents, hungry, cold, with tempers exasperated by nature's despotism, betrayed neither enmity nor discontent. All this I attribute to Sir Ernest, whose magnetic personality inspired cheerfulness, hope and encouragement.

The three small boats and their weather-beaten refugees had proved themselves in the conflict with the ice—now they were to measure their worth against the sea. The ocean seemed an old friend and, though our vessels were mere cockleshells, their pilots were skilled mariners, and He who had directed the floe through its tortuous wanderings was surely still with us. In an indefinable way we felt that our escape was no matter of mere chance. Always, when on the brink of doom, an outlet of escape had saved us in some miraculous way. So our hearts swelled with exultation as our crazy boats bounded over the glinting seas. . . .

During the afternoon an icy wind lashed the water, and sails were reefed. Spray, dashing on board, froze and caked boats and men with ice; the salt water saturated our garments and provoked our split skin and boils to fresh miseries. Some of the men had seasickness added to their afflictions. Even under these conditions we were still capable of seeing the humorous side of things. One of the party, who had consistently skimped and saved titbits from his frugal rations, keeping them reserved in a bag against the day of starvation of which he lived in constant dread, became violently seasick and was unable to eat even a crumb of the liberal rations that were issued and on which the more fortunate gorged themselves. This brought smiles to cracked lips, for we felt our doubting companion was doing just penance for his lack of faith.

Most of us were badly frostbitten, and it was notable that the old campaigners, Shackleton, Wild, Crean, and myself, though not seriously affected by most conditions, were not immune from frostbite. My hands became badly frozen through the continual wearing of wet mitts. Sir Ernest, noticing my endeavours to restore circulation, took off his warm gloves and handed them to me. 'Take these until your hands are right,' he said. Since he was suffering himself, I refused. But he was determined that I should have them. 'All right,' he replied, 'if you don't take them I'll throw them into the sea.' It was a brave action characteristic of the man.

We had burst so unexpectedly into the open sea that we had not taken any ice aboard for drinking purposes, nor had we any drinking water. To alleviate our burning thirsts, we had eaten raw seal meat, cut into squares, but this had unfortunately been drenched with salt spray, and only aggravated our condition. One wondered what additional anguish and suffering the body was capable of feeling and the mind of withstanding.

Night fell, and, though we wished to continue and to take advantage of the fair wind, our leader decided to heave to. This was a wise policy, for it would have been impossible to keep the boats together in the darkness. Sails were lowered, a sea-anchor was hastily made by lashing the oars together, and the boats were tethered to it one behind the other. Owing to the cross currents, the boats would not keep head on to the seas and kept continually

> *'The three small boats and their weather-beaten refugees had proved themselves in the conflict with the ice—now they were to measure their worth against the sea.'*

bumping together. The temperature fell below zero, and as our vessels tossed and plunged the sprays broke over them and quickly froze. The added weight of the accumulating ice caused the boats to wallow, and we spent the night chipping the ice away, staving off the boats and trying to keep ourselves from freezing. They were hideous hours, and the flame of hope all but died in many a heart. Indeed, many of the party were unhinged by their agonies. It was a night of terror, horror and despair.

Sharp indeed are the contrasts in these latitudes. With the dawn came an abatement of the sea and a glimpse of land. It was a sublime revelation. I am convinced that nothing less could have brought the party from its state of death-like apathy back to life again. A grey fog hung over the sea, screening all distant prospect. Then the sun burst through pink vapours. Like an enchanted curtain the mists rolled skyward, revealing a sun-gilt mountain, like a colossal pyramid of gold rising from the purple seas. It was Clarence Island. Magical had been its appearance, and magical the reaction on us. Our moribund party flickered into life again. A little later we observed on our port bow, some thirty miles away, seven domed peaks, the ice-clad summits of Elephant Island.

The tethering lines were cast off, and our sea anchor of bundled oars, which had grown to the thickness of tree trunks through accumulated ice, was chipped clean and taken on board. Sails were hoisted with difficulty, for the ropes and pulleys were fouled with ice, and the sheets were frozen stiff like metal plates. With a fair breeze, the three boats headed for Elephant Island. Breakfast rations were served, but we could only nibble at them, for our cracked lips bled painfully and our parched throats and swollen tongues would not permit us to swallow. The sun mounted in the sky and beat down on thirst-maddened men, but somehow we seemed indestructible in spirit and body. At last the land lay within our grasp—the land that we had been patiently longing to reach for sixteen long months. We could stand a few hours' more suffering. A few hours and we would be walking on good solid rock.

At noon the breeze died down and we took to the oars. How we laboured! How anxiously we watched the land gradually draw closer and the snowy peaks grow clearer. 'I can see rock!' cried one. And 'Look! the crevasses are now showing up!' cried another. We strained our eyes towards the goal, measuring the distance by details gradually revealed as we drew closer.

At 3 p.m. we were within eight miles of the island. Wild picked out a little bay, sheltered by white peaks, with rocks standing out boldly from the ice-clad shores. It was to us a sunlit, homely prospect. We rowed with joyful eagerness—tonight we would be camped on solid rock. Oh heavenly prospect!

The minutes grew into hours. The sea was calm, the water was rippling from our bows, but somehow, in spite of our efforts, we were drawing no closer. Then the terrible truth burst upon us—we were caught in an adverse current. It was only just possible to hold our own against it. Curdling despair crept into us, and all the agonies that hope had dulled throbbed with fresh acuteness. We could not row much longer. The reserve energy which the near realisation of freedom had called up was almost spent. It was cruel, uncharitable, relentless. There was not a man whose soul did not cry out in

'Then the sun burst through pink vapours. Like an enchanted curtain the mists rolled skyward, revealing a sun-gilt mountain, like a colossal pyramid of gold rising from the purple seas.'

anguish to the controller of the winds and tides not to forsake us. Throughout the dreary, suffering months we had quelled our heartaches with the consoling thought that the future would one day reward our hopes; that time, the panacea for all tribulations, would solve the problem of our destinies as our hearts desired. Barrier after barrier had raised itself and had been surmounted, but now, on the very threshold of salvation, it seemed we must fail. Only a miracle could save us—the wind! A favourable wind, which would swell our sails and tear us from the merciless suck of the tide. Our plight had never been so desperate as now. Most of the party were at the last gasp, crazed and dazed, and could row no more.

Night shut down, black and pitiless. The open ocean lay to the right, and the tide was hurrying us into its greedy spaces. Down fluttered the snow, coming from the south-east in whirling flurries. It fell in a soft shroud over forms huddled down in the boats, listless and careless of death. An occasional moan came from the men. We were helpless. Then a great, black cloud filled the sky and the wind came. It came from the south, at first gently—it seemed a sigh. Then the waters rippled under its caress. More strongly it came, till the sea swept up in rolling waves—waves rolling to the shore. The miracle had happened. It was not chance: our prayers had been heard.

Shackleton called to the men in the boats to hoist sails. Those aboard the *Stancomb Wills* were too far spent, so we took them in tow. On through the dark, towards our goal, now swallowed up in the blackness, plunging through a void of waters swelling up in the gale. Those who were able trimmed the boat as she heeled to the wind's press—the others lay corpse-like. The noise of tumbling crests was all around, and the spume flung forward by the wind raked the boats.

Wild had not left the helm for forty-eight hours and was now so frozen that his arms and hands would not function. He was relieved by Chips, the carpenter, but he, too, overcome by exhaustion, swooned at his post. Instantly the boat turned broadside to the seas and a huge wave leapt aboard, drenching everything and nearly swamping us. Wild carried on again. In the darkness and agonising cold the worn-out party fought the storm, chipping away the accumulations of frozen spray, and frantically baling the boats to keep them afloat. Every billow brought a spasm of misery. Each black gulf, viewed

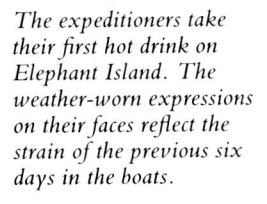

The expeditioners take their first hot drink on Elephant Island. The weather-worn expressions on their faces reflect the strain of the previous six days in the boats.

from the crest of a spuming comber, yawned to swallow us. Scoured by the winds, mocked by the storm, we wondered if the night would ever end.

With the *Stancomb Wills* in tow, we were making heavy weather. It seemed from moment to moment that we would have to part the line and leave her to her fate. Sir Ernest, in the stern, strained his eyes into the darkness, watching that black object tossing in the dark torment, and shouting at intervals words of cheer and inquiry. 'She's gone!' one would say, as a hoary billow reared its crest between us. Then, against the white spume, a dark shape would appear, and through the tumult would come, faint but cheering, Tom Crean's reassuring hail, 'All well, sir!' So we lived through each wave and through the night. In the darkness we lost sight of our third boat, the *Dudley Docker*.

Anxiously we peered through the mists and snow-whirls towards the land. As we drew closer, the watery moon broke fitfully through the storm-racked sky and shone on nebulous contours of peaks and phantom-like glaciers. The land seemed like a spectral fantasy conceived by our distressed minds. Our overwrought nerves were steadied when we heard the growl of surf on the reefs. It must be real! We stood off till the dawn, which came at last to reveal leaden clouds, great grey seas, and the land.

After a great deal of difficulty, they were able to make a landing on Elephant Island, and for the first time in sixteen months they were on solid ground. But it was an inhospitable place, devoid of vegetation and swept by the ice-laden surges of the South Atlantic. Their refuge on the island was a spit of rock thrusting out into the sea with a sheer ice cliff behind. Within days the fierce winds had ripped their tents to pieces. On 24 April Shackleton and five others set off in the James Caird *to try to get to South Georgia and bring relief. After sixteen days at sea and a heroic march across the previously uncrossed South Georgia Island, Shackleton reached the whaling station of Grytviken. But it was another four months before a relief vessel could reach Elephant Island. Meanwhile, the twenty-two marooned men, by this time suffering badly from deprivation and exposure, made their home under the two upturned boats on their frozen strip of land. At last, on 30 August 1916, the Chilean trawler* Yelcho, *the fourth vessel to attempt the rescue, reached Elephant Island, and Hurley and his comrades were taken to safety.*

The James Caird *being launched on its relief voyage to South Georgia. Its improvised deck was made from fragments of canvas and packing-case lids.*

THE FIRST FLIGHT FROM ENGLAND TO AUSTRALIA

Ross Smith

IN MARCH 1919 *the Commonwealth government offered a prize of ten thousand pounds to the first Australian crew to fly a British-made aircraft from Great Britain to Australia within thirty consecutive days before the end of the year. There were five official entries, four of which crashed on the way, causing the deaths of four of the fourteen airmen involved. A French crew in a French plane also took part, although they were ineligible on both counts. The prize was won by a crew led by Captain Ross Smith, a 26-year-old South Australian who had distinguished himself as a pilot with the Australian Flying Corps in the Middle East during the 1914–18 war. His brother Keith was assistant pilot and navigator, and two AFC sergeants, James Bennett and Walter Shiers, were the mechanics. The aircraft was a Vickers Vimy, a fabric-covered biplane powered by two Rolls-Royce engines with a cruising speed of 130 kilometres an hour and carrying enough fuel for thirteen hours flying. The crew occupied two open cockpits exposed to the elements. Here is Ross Smith's account of the flight: the first extract is from a brief account he wrote soon after the race; the second is from his book* 14,000 Miles through the Air.

THE MACHINE was at Hounslow, but winter had set in and the weather was quite unsuited for flying. For a fortnight we had only had variations in snow, sleet and fog.

We were called at 4.30 a.m. on 12 November 1919, and I was delighted to find clear frosty weather. Two hours later a ground haze drifted up, and the Air Ministry Weather Bureau forecasted bad weather, totally unfit for flying. But we had made up our minds, and we decided to start. The machine was wheeled from the hangar and Commander Perrin, of the Royal Aero Club, marked and sealed five parts of the machine in accordance with the rules of the competition. At 8.30 a.m. we started the engines, climbed into our seats, and took off from the snow-covered aerodrome. The flight to Australia had begun!

We were, of course, not alone in the race. The gallant Frenchman Poulet had twenty-eight days' start. His handicap was a machine totally unsuited for such an enterprise. It was not till we reached Karachi in India on 24 November that we had news of him; thence in a series of day stages, Delhi, Allahabad, Calcutta, we had the excitement of learning of his progress, and the satisfaction of finding that we were catching up. On approaching Akyab, in Burma, we noticed another machine at an aerodrome. It turned out to be Poulet's. In the flight from Akyab to Rangoon, Poulet was also in the air and reached the city shortly after we did. We greatly admired his pluck in tackling the huge job in a small machine, accompanied only by a single mechanic. The gallant Frenchman received with us the hospitality of His Excellency Sir Reginald Craddock, the Lieutenant-Governor of Burma, and Lady Craddock, at Rangoon. Monsieur Poulet had made a daring and glorious endeavour. Great honour and credit are due to him, but after leaving Rangoon we, in our modern Vickers Vimy, left him behind. Matthews had also begun a flight to Australia about ten days before us. Thus in the early part of our flight we had the incentive of the chase besides the zest and excitement of our adventure.

The perils of our fight soon began. Shortly after reaching the French coast at Boulogne we ran into a big bank of snow-clouds. We could not get underneath it, for it practically reached the ground. We therefore climbed above it, to a height of eight thousand feet. The cold was bitter, twenty-five degrees of frost, and for three hours our breath froze on our face-masks, and our sandwiches were frozen solid. It took us five days to cross Europe to Taranto in Italy. The circumstances were most trying, for the weather was execrable. The flight was made almost all the way through dense clouds, snow and blinding rain. Only an occasional burst of sunshine cheered us on our way. The cloud belts were too thick to fly above them, and we were obliged to keep for the most part at dangerously low altitudes.

We had intended to fly from Rome to Athens, but at Rome we received certain information which made us doubtful as to whether it would be wise to adhere to our first route. So we went to Crete and stayed a night at Suda Bay. We had a deal of rain, and clouds were troublesome, as we had to clear a high mountain range in the centre of the island and feared we might crash. However, we escaped this peril and made a non-stop flight of seven and a half hours from Crete to Cairo, arriving at the Heliopolis Aerodrome on 18

Ross Smith (right) and his brother Keith (left) with one of their mechanics, Walter Shiers, camped beside their aeroplane in the Northern Territory towards the end of their pioneering flight.

November. We met many old friends of the Royal Air Force, and they treated us well and did all in their power to help us.

On the 19th we left Cairo for Damascus. We were told it was raining hard in Palestine, but we determined to go ahead, as I knew the country. Our route lay over the old battlefields, Romani, El Arish, Gaza and Nazareth. It revived many memories for me, for this land over which we were passing was the arena of my war service. At Damascus we were welcomed by a squadron of the Royal Air Force, who looked after our comfort.

Next day, the 20th, we got off in a break of the bad weather at about ten o'clock and headed for Baghdad across the Syrian desert, via Abu Kemal to Ramadi, making our landing on the old Turkish battlefield. Here we were taken care of by the Tenth (Indian) Lancers, and invaluable to us was their help. For that night a simoom swept down and nearly put an end to our efforts. We lashed the machine to the ground and, assisted by a great crowd of the Indian Lancers, hung on to it through that wild night of storm. By morning the wind died down, and after six hours spent in adjustments and clearing away the sand we made another start. This was 21 November, and our objective was Basra, which is the modern spelling of Bussorah, that famous seaport of the *Arabian Nights*. Our route was famous in both recent and ancient history. For we flew over Kut-el-Amarah, the scene of General Townshend's surrender, and over the legendary site of the Garden of Eden. This was the first good flying day we had had since we left England.

Next day, the 22nd, we were all feeling very tired, and as the machine needed a certain amount of attention we decided to put in the day at Basra and give her a thorough overhaul. This was done with the assistance of the Royal Air Force, but we chafed at the delay. On the 23rd we left Basra for Bandar Abbas, on the Persian Gulf, and landed there after a flight of eight hours over desert and mountainous country.

On 24 November we reached India at Karachi, and Delhi on the 25th. From Basra to Delhi we had travelled sixteen hundred miles and spent $25\frac{1}{2}$ hours out of 54 in the air. Everything had gone remarkably well, both with

The route of the Vickers Vimy from London to Adelaide on the first flight from England to Australia in November 1919.

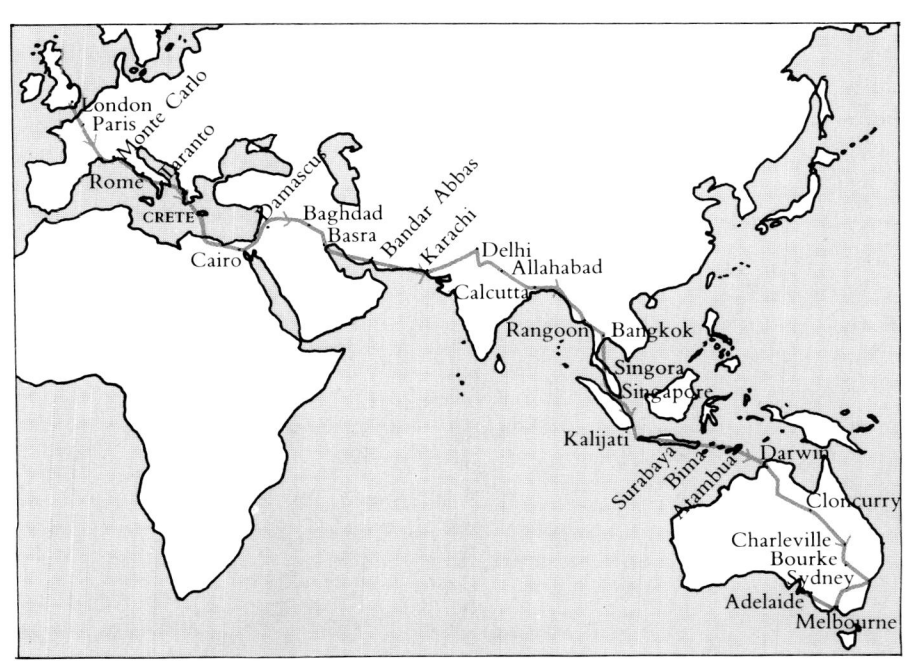

the machine and the engines. The health of the crew had been excellent and the weather had improved. We intended as usual starting again next day, though we were well up to time; but when next day came we were all so tired from the three preceding long flights that we decided to rest, and so we spent the day in Delhi working on the machine. On the 27th we reached Allahabad, and on the 28th Calcutta. We had expected to rest a day in Calcutta, but as the machine was going so well and all were feeling so fit we decided to go on, making Rangoon in two days, staying the first night at Akyab. We had a most hospitable and popular welcome in Rangoon, which we left on December, for Bangkok in Siam. Here we had every assistance from the civil and military authorities.

We had intended to fly direct from Bangkok to Singapore, but as we were informed that there was a good aerodrome at Singora, about halfway, we decided to halt there. The Siamese notion of a good aerodrome nearly brought us all to an untimely end. A square patch had been hewn from the jungle, the trunks and upper portions of the trees had been removed, but the stumps were allowed to remain. We made a safe and miraculous landing, missing the stumps by inches. On 3 December the heaviest rain I had ever experienced kept us tied up at Singora, and Sergeant Bennett was busy repairing the tail skid which had found one of the obstacles on the Singora aerodrome.

On 4 December, my birthday, we arrived at Singapore. The racecourse had been prepared for us to land on, and proved very suitable, though, if anything, too small. That night we were entertained by the Australian and New Zealand Association of Malaya. Next day, the 5th, we left Singapore for Kalijati, near Batavia in Java. This was a distance of nearly seven hundred miles and the worst stage of the journey as regards landing grounds. We travelled two hundred miles down the eastern coast of Sumatra, which was so densely wooded that it would have been impossible to have made a forced landing. Then we turned seawards to Batavia.

We arrived at Kalijati, where we were received by the Governor-General of the Dutch East Indies. We had expected that the last stage of the journey, from Singapore to Darwin, would be the most difficult. But the Governor-General, on learning that aeroplanes were flying from England to Australia, ordered aerodromes to be constructed at different points in the Dutch Islands. These greatly facilitated our flight....

Nearing Surabaya, flying became very bumpy, and it was no small relief when the town, like a magic carpet of multicoloured fabric, spread beneath us. Heading the Vimy down, we made a low circle above the town, to the infinite amazement of the teeming native population that swarmed out into the streets, petrified, evidently, by the visitation.

From above, the surface of the aerodrome on which we were to land appeared to be ideal, but the whole ground was somewhat small. I landed along the south side intending to open up one engine and swing the machine round on the ground if there appeared any danger of over-shooting and running into a bank of earth at the end. This manoeuvre, however, I discovered to be unnecessary. We made a good landing and were easing off to

'The Siamese notion of a good aerodrome nearly brought us all to an untimely end. A square patch had been hewn from the jungle, the trunks and upper portions of the trees had been removed, but the stumps were allowed to remain.'

rest when the machine seemed to drag, and from past experience I knew at once the Vimy was becoming bogged.

Opening up the starboard engine, we began to swing slowly, but the port wheels immediately sank into the mud and we tilted onto our fore-skid. At once I shut off both engines and the Vimy gradually eased back to her normal position. I then discovered that our aerodrome was a stretch of land that had been reclaimed from the sea; the top crust had set quite hard, but underneath was a layer of liquid mud.

The natives and people, who had been kept back by the Dutch soldiers, rushed the ground, and their weight on the sun-dried crust soon broke it up, and mud began to ooze through. In a very short while the Vimy subsided to her axles and was surrounded by a pond of semi-liquid mud.

The proposition literally was a decidedly sticky one. It was midday, broiling hot, and the tenacity of the mud reminded me forcibly of that clinging tendency familiar to our black-soil plains. Moreover, only four days of our prescribed time remained, in which we must make Port Darwin.

The engineer of the Harbour Board arrived, and together we discussed the situation. He collected a horde of coolies and a large quantity of bamboo matting, and so we set to work to dig out the wheels.

After some hard work we got the matting almost under the wheels, started up the engines and, aided by the coolies and Dutch soldiers, the Vimy was hauled from the bog. I then stopped the engines, tied ropes to the undercarriage, and the machine was pulled on to a pathway of mats.

After a couple of hours the machine was safe out of the morass, and the ground on which we stood felt quite solid; so I thought we had landed on the only soft spot on the aerodrome and decided to taxi to the opposite end under our own engine power. I was soon disillusioned, for, after moving but ten yards, down went the wheels again. More digging, tugging, and pushing, and we, apprehensive all the while as to whether the coolies would drag off the undercarriage, finally had to lay down a pathway of bamboo mats and have the machine hauled by two hundred coolie power.

We had landed at 12 noon, and after six hours of hard work under a boiling tropical sun we had the Vimy on a platform of bamboo mats at the end of the aerodrome. Some of the matting had large nails sticking out of it, and two of our tyres were punctured. Bennett and Shiers as usual attended the engines first, while Keith and I replenished our tanks with petrol and oil. Fortunately we did not have to put in so much petrol as usual, and we then attacked the two punctured tyres. By this time it was dark, but we worked on by the light from the lamps of a motor car.

The Vimy, fully loaded, weighs about six tons, and just as we had got one wheel jacked up the ground beneath sank under the weigh and the jack broke. We borrowed another jack from our friend with the motor car, but this also suffered a similar fate. We had had no food since early morning, so tired and disconsolate we decided to leave the machine for the night and resume our efforts in the morning. I don't think I have ever felt so tired or so miserable in my life as I did then. Here we were only twelve hundred miles from Australia; we still had four of our thirty days left in which to do it, and yet to all intents and purposes we were hopelessly stuck in this quagmire

> *'In a very short while the Vimy subsided to her axles and was surrounded by a pond of semi-liquid mud. The proposition literally was a decidedly sticky one.'*

without a chance of getting out of it. Furthermore, I knew that this was the only flat stretch of land within four hundred miles from which it was possible to get the Vimy into the air. It seemed as if victory were to be snatched from us at the last moment.

But just when things were looking blackest a bright idea occurred to my brother. We knew that it would be impossible to get off this aerodrome in the usual way, but why not construct a roadway of mats to prevent our wheels sinking into the mud, then run along it and so get into the air!

Straightway we sought out the Harbour Board engineer, but he said it would be impossible to get so many mats together in so short a time. However, after much persuasion he agreed to have as many mats as possible at the aerodrome next morning. This cheering news considerably revived our sinking spirits and we went off to our hotel in a much happier frame of mind.

The British Consul had invited us to a 'quiet little dinner' that evening, but when we arrived at the restaurant, an hour late, we found that all the British residents in Surabaya had gathered there to welcome us. It was a very happy party and a most enjoyable diversion from our efforts of the past few hours.

Next morning saw us at the aerodrome by daylight, and a gladsome sight met our eyes. Natives were steaming in from every direction bearing sheets of bamboo matting—they were literally carrying their houses on their backs—and already a great pile of it lay by the Vimy.

At first a pathway of mats was merely laid down, but in our keen anxiety to set off we had overlooked the slipstream from the propellers. The engines were opened up and we were just gathering speed nicely when some of the sheets were whisked up and blown into the tailplane. This threw the machine out of control, and to our dismay the Vimy ran off the matting and bogged again. Once more we had to dig deep down and place great planks under the

The runway of bamboo mats laid over the boggy airfield at Surabaya from which the Vimy took off during the final stages of its flight to Australia.

wheels and haul the Vimy back into the matting. I have never been able to understand how the machine stood the rough handling she received; it speaks volumes for the material and thoroughness of her construction. Of course the coolies had no idea which parts were safe to pull and which were not, and to try and watch two hundred of them and get anything like teamwork out of them was somewhat of a problem. More matting arrived on a motor lorry, so we made the road about three hundred yards long and forty feet wide and this time pegged it all down and interlaced the mats so that they could not blow up. At last all was ready, and just twenty-four hours after our arrival at Surabaya we started up the engines, ran along the roadway, and with feelings of intense relief felt the Vimy take off and get into the air.

We circled low over the town and anchorage, so as to give the engines time to settle down to normal running, and then headed on a direct compass course for Bima.

From the point of view of a prospective forced landing, the four-hundred-mile flight to Bima was impossible. Not a single flat occurred on which we might have landed. Scenically, this lap was glorious. We skirted the coast of Bali and Lombok, keeping three thousand feet above the sea. Not a ripple disturbed its surface, and looking over the side from time to time I could see a lot of small splashes in the water in the form of a circle. For a time these splashes puzzled me, and then I caught a glint of silvery wings and knew that they were made by flying fish. My brother also had seen them, and we were both rather surprised to be able to see flying fish from a height of three thousand feet. It made me think that perhaps after all the hawks and other birds that we see flying about have not such wonderful eyesight as we imagine, because it is undoubtedly easier to see an object from the air than on the ground.

Bima aerodrome in the island of Sumbawa was in excellent condition and clearly marked with a huge white cross in the centre, which we saw several miles away. The natives scampered in all directions and would not venture near until they saw us walking about the machine.

The local Sultan and the Dutch Commissioner met us and proffered the hospitality of a native bungalow a couple of miles from the machine. Here we aroused intense interest; eyes taking little furtive glimpses at us peered through every crack and gap.

During the night we were awakened to hear some fellow prowling about outside. I waited until he was opposite the doorway, then a shot from my Very light pistol put him to a screaming and, I have no doubt, a terror-stricken flight.

The natives had recovered from their shyness by next morning and on our arrival were swarming around the machine with presents of coconuts sufficient to start a plantation; evidently they thought the Vimy a very thirsty sort of bird.

We took a cargo of nuts on board, as the water was unsuited for drinking, and, setting off in dazzling sunshine, once more pursued our course above scenes of tropical enchantment and alluring charm.

After following the north coast of Flores to Reo, we crossed over to the south side of the island and ran into isolated rainstorms. Once we saw a small

'Scenically, this lap was glorious. We skirted the coast of Bali and Lombok, keeping three thousand feet above the sea. Not a ripple disturbed its surface'

active volcano in the distance and were tempted to go off and gaze down into its smoking crater, but as the weather indicated a change for the worse we could not afford to make a deviation. We flew on as far as Pandar, and then swung off direct for Timor.

We had by this time acquired such confidence in our engines that it mattered little what lay below us—sea or land.

A thick haze soon obscured the land and all distant vision, but we eventually picked up the Timor coast a few hundred yards from our calculated position. Ten miles inland we came down on the aerodrome at Atambua, our last landing ground before Port Darwin.

The Dutch officials had thoughtfully arranged our petrol and oil supply close at hand, saving us a good deal of valuable time, which we were able to devote to a thorough overhaul. Tomorrow would be the great day whereupon reposed the destiny of hopes, labours, and ideals.

This was one of the aerodromes specially made by the Governor-General of the Netherlands Indies for the Australian flight and had been completed only the day before our arrival. A guard of Dutch soldiers kept watch over the machine while we proceeded with their officers to camp, some six miles away.

It is hardly necessary to say that none of us overslept. We were too excited at the prospect of the morrow. We felt sure that if it dawned fine and hot, our homing was assured; but as we stepped out, before sunrise, into the still, sluggish air, we realized that our hopes of an early start were small. A heavy haze lay over the sea and the coast, obscuring everything; so we decided to await its clearing.

We were at the aerodrome before sun-up to discover that a great swarm of natives were even earlier risers than ourselves. Most had come afoot, but many had ridden their ponies, and they clustered on and around the fence, behind and beside the Vimy, like swarming bees. We had hauled the machine well back with the tail against the fence in order to take advantage of every foot of the short run.

Our start-off was brightened by one of those incidents that usually make material for comic papers. The propellers were just kicking over, like two great fans, and those natives sitting on the fence in the line of the slipstream were enjoying the cool breeze and looking pleased with themselves. When I opened the engines and both propellers swung into action, the sudden blast of air sent these particular spectators toppling back into the crowd, where ponies and natives made a glorious mix-up, at which we all laughed heartily.

If an aeroplane is forced to land in the sea it usually floats for a time, then the forward part sinks and only the tail remains above water. Remembering this, just before leaving Timor we tied a parcel of food, a bottle of water, the Very pistol and some cartridges on to the tail so that we would have something to fall back upon in case of emergency.

Soon after 8 a.m. the fog began to thin, and at 8.35, to be exact, I opened up the engines and just managed to scrape out of the 'drome. Scrape is exactly the word, for the branch-tops of the gum tree rasped along the bottom of the machine as we rose. It was indeed one of the closest shaves of the trip.

'I opened up the engines and just managed to scrape out of the 'drome. Scrape is exactly the word, for the branch-tops of the gum tree rasped along the bottom of the machine as we rose. It was indeed one of the closest shaves of the trip.'

In front of us rose a chain of high hills, and, as the atmosphere was hot and we climbed very slowly, we made a detour to avoid them. Still flying low, we approached the coast and pulled ourselves together for the final lap—the jump across the Arafura Sea that lay between us and Port Darwin.

Keith took all possible bearings, noted wind direction, and made numerous calculations of ground speeds. Then we set compass course for Darwin, and with a 'Here goes!' we were out over the sea. All our hearts were beating a little quicker; even our fine old engines seemed to throb a trifle faster.

This was to be our longest stretch over open sea, and I did not relish the prospect of being out of sight of land for five hours. However, as the coastline of Timor receded and disappeared behind us, my thoughts turned back to the great transatlantic fight made by the late Sir John Alcock in a Vimy similar to our own. What had we to fear with only a few hundred miles of open sea to cross, while he had nearly two thousand?

The Australian government had arranged that a warship should patrol the sea between Timor and Port Darwin in case we should need help, and anxiously we scanned the distant horizon for the first glimpse of her.

Our watches registered 11.48 when Keith nodded ahead, and dead on the line of flight we made out a faint smoke that soon resolved itself into the smoke plume of a fighting ship. It was HMAS *Sydney*, and we knew now that, whatever might befall, we had a friend at hand.

We swooped low, and exactly at twelve minutes past noon passed over the vessel, seeing plainly the upturned faces of the sailors and their waving hands. It was a cheer of welcome quite different from anything that we had experienced on the long journey. Perhaps it is not to be wondered at that the result of our snapshot was blurred through the shaking of the camera.

We took the opportunity of snatching a speed test and found that we were averaging seventy-five miles an hour.

Two hours later both of us saw ahead and to port what appeared to be haze, but which we hoped was land, though neither dared express his hopes. They were justified, however, ten minutes later, and hailing Bennett and Shiers, we pointed joyfully to Bathurst Island lighthouse.

It was just 2.06 p.m. when, as our diary prosaically notes, we 'observed Australia'. At three o'clock we not only observed it, but rested firmly upon it, for, having circled over Darwin and come low enough to observe the crowds and the landing place, we landed on Terra Australis on 10 December, twenty-seven days, twenty hours after taking off from Hounslow.

We had won the race against time and the ten-thousand-pound prize with just fifty-two hours to spare!

Ross and Keith Smith were both knighted for their achievement, and Bennett and Shiers were promoted lieutenants and awarded the Air Force Medal. In April 1922 Ross Smith and Bennett were killed in an air crash while test-flying a Vickers Viking amphibian in which the four men had planned to fly round the world.

FRANCIS BIRTLES DRIVES FROM LONDON TO MELBOURNE
T. R. Nicholson

FRANCIS BIRTLES, *whose cycling exploits are mentioned earlier in this book, switched from long-distance cycling to overlanding by motor car in 1912 when he accompanied S. R. Ferguson in a single-cylinder Brush on the first west-east crossing of Australia by car. In 1927 he made two heroic attempts to drive from London to Melbourne in a massive 25-horsepower Bean. On his first attempt, accompanied by the journalist and author Malcolm Ellis and Billy Knowles, he got as far as Delhi, where sickness, a crippled car and the onset of the monsoon prevented him from going any further. On his second try, which he undertook alone, he made it, arriving in Melbourne on 25 July 1928 after driving twenty-five thousand kilometres in just over nine months. This account of his second attempt is from T. R. Nicholson's book* Five Roads to Danger.

H E HAD NO COMPANION, and his car was an old trusted friend—Sundowner, the special Bean which in two years had seen him through some of the world's worst motoring country. This car was a very rakish, narrow two-seater with stark coachwork, a drilled chassis, stiffer-than-normal springs and an extra fuel tank. Its petrol was supplied by Shell and its tyres by Dunlop; Bean's themselves gave comparatively little assistance. Birtles planned to camp out all the way and carry his own food supplies. Leaving in October, he anticipated no difficulty reaching Burma before the 1928 monsoon began, and reckoned that the trip to Melbourne, his ultimate destination, would take only five or six months. As before, it was to include an absolute minimum of sea travel.

Most of those who took it upon themselves to advise him had other ideas. 'Responsible people along the route had been writing to equally responsible people in England with a view to deterring me, but I set off in spite of their efforts.' Birtles took his leave of England by giving the motor industry a very thorough slating in the columns of the *Autocar*, attacking it for its apathy towards the Australian market, which was so promising. The motor vehicle was vital to inland communications in Australia, so that there was a ready-made market crying out for more cars, so long as they were suited to Australian conditions. Mainly they needed strong sumps, cleanly designed undersides, strong radiator mountings and waterproof brake and clutch linings. None of these features would call for radical alterations in the design of any British car, but without them the American car would continue to

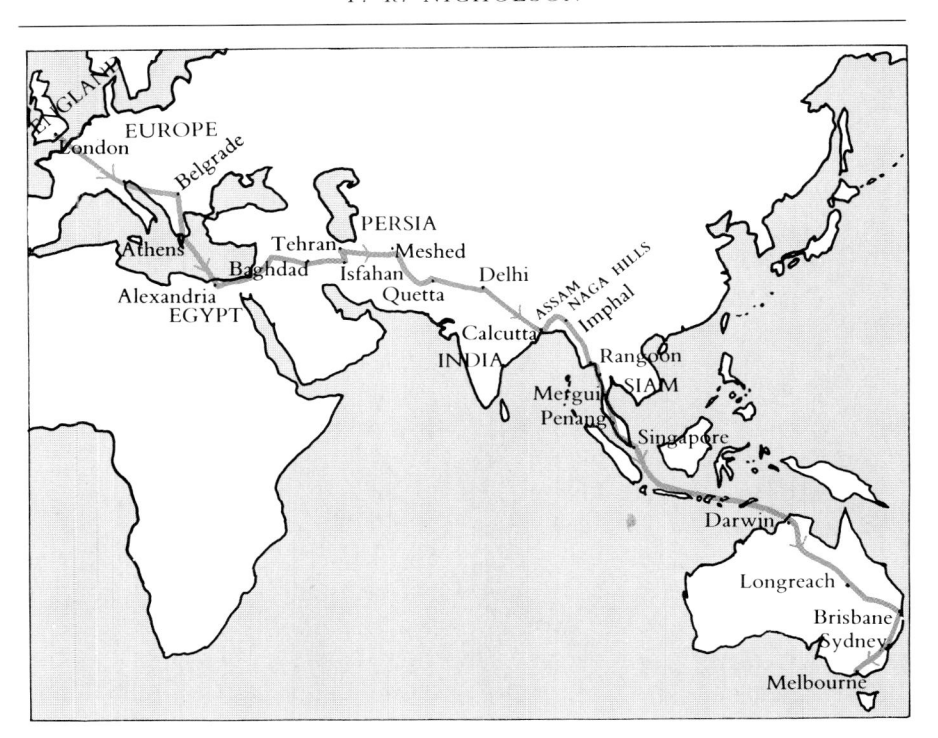

The route taken by Francis Birtles in his second attempt to drive from England to Australia.

dominate the roads. Birtles was better qualified than any man alive to make such comments.

Instead of making for Constantinople, Birtles headed south for Athens. In Greece he encountered a bridge which had been smashed by a landslide, on a mountain road so narrow that it was impossible to turn the car round. He reversed five miles to find a detour. Customs formalities held the Bean up for nine days in Athens, where it had arrived on about 8 November, but the British consul telegraphed to the Foreign Office, which solved Birtles's problems for him. Up to his arrival in Athens, he had averaged two hundred miles a day across Europe. On 17 November he sailed for Alexandria. In spite of his expressed aim to keep sea travel to a minimum, Birtles preferred to add to this rather than risk once more the appalling delays he and Ellis had experienced in Turkey. From Alexandria the Bean struggled through the soft sand of the Sinai Desert to Palestine. It had no difficulty on the Syrian Desert crossing. On his first night out, Birtles camped well off the frequented route, concealed in a ravine. On the next night, when he arrived at dusk at a fort twenty-five miles from Baghdad, the police prevented him from driving on through the darkness, for his own safety. On 28 November he was in Baghdad, and out of it on the same day. So far his time and his luck had both been excellent. The car had suffered no more than a fractured petrol pipe.

But now Birtles's troubles began—he ran straight into the Persian winter. The main road to Tehran was deep in snow, so he determined to cut across country to Isfahan, keeping below the snowline, then turning north to Tehran and east to Meshed. That, at least, was the idea. It did not work out in practice. Having abandoned the good road for cart-tracks, the car was soon pushing through snowdrifts. Every landmark was blotted out by a dense, swirling white curtain. Drifts bogged the Bean down in the hollows between hills, calling for prolonged shovelling and the fitting of chains. Although much of the route lay downhill, the radiator boiled from continual low-gear work in the thin air of the mountains. Birtles always aimed to get under way early in the day, before the sun could thaw the snow. In a snowstorm near Tehran, he ran across a party of seven Persians sitting in their car, which was stationary by the roadside. They had been frozen to death. The blizzard was so fierce that progress had become impossible, so Birtles pitched camp, using the stranded car with its grisly load as a windbreak. He stretched a waterproof sheet between the two vehicles, his camera tripod doing duty as a tent-pole. Even where a caravanserai was at hand, he preferred to sleep out in the car, protected only by a tarpaulin against the snow and wind, for these establishments were infested with thieves and insect life, both of which would prevent him from sleeping. Without the experience of his bush training, Birtles could hardly have survived this spartan regimen.

One evening the car stuck in a drift of sand, and while Birtles was scouting ahead to find the best way out, all his blankets and weatherproof clothing were stolen. This was a first-class disaster, for now he could not camp out at all. There was no firewood near by to supply the missing warmth. Sick and freezing, he turned back to Isfahan, where the British mission hospital filled him up with hot coffee and gave him a bed. There Birtles stayed for two days recuperating.

For a while the snow was left behind, and the Bean began to cross frozen desert. It was buried to the axles in a sandstorm, so that its driver had to dismount, let tyres down and spread his blankets in front of the rear wheels to give them something to grip. When the car reversed out, the wind blew the blankets away and buried them. Near Sultanabad in north-eastern Persia, the snow began to fall again, but Birtles went on thrashing himself and his car unmercifully. As it ground along in bottom gear through the drifts, the radiator boiling and the exhaust-pipe red hot, icicles would form all over the body and chassis.

The road, or rather track, south through the mountains from Meshed was a hard one at the best of times, but in winter it was murder. The boulder-strewn goat path was steep, narrow, slippery with ice and shrouded in thick mist. Soon a great wind arose which swept away the fog and replaced it with driving snow and sleet. The drifts became deeper and deeper and the car's sojourns in them more frequent and prolonged. One evening, Birtles was in such despair that he was actually trying to reach the shelter of a caravanserai, but failed. He spent a fantastic night in a village goat-pen, guarded by a ferocious but easily deceived hound which thought he was one of its charges. He was kept awake by a goat licking his face, and by the howling of hyenas outside. To cross one rapid, shallow river the Bean was forced to follow its bed for some distance. Halfway over, a front wheel jammed between two boulders, and the car began to slew round in the fierce current. Birtles left the engine running, so that the water and oil would not freeze, then jacked the machine out of its crevice, only to find that it would not move. The brake drums had become iced-up while immersed in the water.

Birtles experienced no particular difficulties in Baluchistan, reaching Sibi

'He spent a fantastic night in a village goat-pen, guarded by a ferocious but easily deceived hound which thought he was one of its charges. He was kept awake by a goat licking his face, and by the howling of hyenas outside.'

beyond Quetta on Christmas Eve, but he had taken all the punishment he could absorb. Struck down by dysentery, he went into hospital at Quetta for several days. As for the car, it had suffered a broken crown wheel and pinion, but nothing else very serious had happened to it, yet. On 5 January 1928 Birtles's Bean passed through Delhi on the way to Calcutta. There had been no news of Birtles since he left Baghdad five weeks earlier, and it was widely feared that the Australian had perished in the snows of the Persian winter. In Calcutta Birtles picked up a companion: Percy Stollery, a footloose young Canadian. They were going to need each other, for the next stage of the journey was to be far and away the most difficult. Indeed, if the resident experts of Calcutta were to be believed, no car could possibly be taken over it, and only madmen would attempt to do so.

The two madmen duly set out on 15 January, with blood-curdling stories of trackless, jungle-clad mountains, headhunters, elephants, tigers and malaria ringing in their ears. It was a sober fact that they were faced by two thousand miles of country never traversed by car before, for which omission there were good and sufficient reasons. Once again Birtles disappeared completely from human ken. Swamps made it impossible to drive south-east down the coast of Burma, so the Bean headed north for the Brahmaputra valley and Assam. There were innumerable small rivers to be crossed by various means, including rickety local ferries or rafts improvised from canoes and bamboos. Crossing the Brahmaputra, Birtles turned eastward through Assam, running along narrow jungle paths, and then south towards Imphal. Over the last stretch into Imphal there was an excellent road. After a week's rest the two men were off again, their car laden with a live goat, an assortment of vegetables and cake, a hundred yards of rope, a crowbar, an axe and other implements. Their difficulties were about to begin in earnest, for now the Naga Hills, the barrier to Burma, had to be climbed.

The road became a cart-track, and the cart-track a one-man coolie path for which the car was much too wide. On 12 February the party passed Manipur Road railhead. Suddenly the path vanished skywards, corkscrewing at impossible angles up a mountainside—or rather, up a series of sixty mountainsides. Birtles and Stollery sat down at the bottom for a week, planning their assault. They reconnoitred and plotted the first three miles of the ascent, deciding where corners had to be opened out by cutting away the cliff on the inside, where the track had to be widened, and where boulders would have to be dug out of it with the crowbar. Then they set to with picks and shovels, and built their road. They spent a whole day widening the path at a hairpin bend so that the car could be skidded round it without losing momentum on the one-in-two gradient at that point. In a mile and a quarter the track rose fourteen hundred feet, an average incline of one in four. Next, the car itself had to be made ready. It was stripped of everything detachable, and the engine brought to the finest possible pitch or tune. The crown wheel was reversed on the pinion, so that the Bean now had one forward gear (its lowest ratio, which had been reverse), and three reverse gears. At maximum engine revolutions its top speed forwards was eight miles an hour, while its theoretical maximum in reverse was eighty, which would have been quite exciting.

> 'On 12 February the party passed Manipur Road railhead. Suddenly the path vanished skywards, corkscrewing at impossible angles up a mountainside—or rather, up a series of sixty mountainsides. Birtles and Stollery sat down at the bottom for a week, planning their assault.'

Negotiating a cart-track in the Naga Hills, on the border of India and Burma. At times the side of the cliff had to be cut away to allow the Bean to negotiate a corner, and sometimes this was only possible with the help of a block and tackle.

Backing a hundred yards to give himself plenty of room to gather momentum, Birtles waited for the sun to dry out the path, then flung his car screaming at the first slope. He slid at full throttle round the lower bends, but was soon brought to a halt. The next two corners were too sharp to be turned by normal means. Instead, out came the jacks and block and tackle, so that the Bean could be lifted and its front pulled sideways in the direction of travel without any forward motion, for which there was no room. In some places the path, even when widened, was so narrow that part of the width of the tyres on the outside might actually be over empty air—and this on cliff-edges that were likely to crumble away at any moment. Before tackling the next hill, half a mile ahead, Birtles and Stollery built a ramp four feet high, up which they reversed the car so that it could obtain a flying start. While halted on this slope, sump oil ran out past the rear of the crankshaft and over the clutch, but luckily this was castor oil and did not cause clutch-slip.

On some of the descents a combination of brakes fully applied and deflated tyres fitted with chains refused to hold the car. It would begin to slide if stopped. As a precaution, a rope would be attached to the dumb-irons. As the Bean moved off, Stollery would stay behind paying out the slack. If the car showed signs of running away, he at once lashed his free end round a tree. Sometimes the rope would break, in which case Birtles would stop the car as best he could and begin praying, while his companion hunted frantically for a substitute. If, as might happen, the path sloped outwards as well as downwards, a short length of rope attached to the dumb-irons would be tied to the nearest tree. When the brakes were released, the nose of the car would be pulled sharply inwards as the rope became taut.

As the path climbed higher and higher into the hills, so it became colder and colder. Most of each day was taken up in reconnoitring the road on foot, rebuilding it, stripping the car and carrying baggage up mountains. 'For a few desperate minutes daily', as Birtles put it, the motorists motored. When they camped, there was almost no dry wood with which to build a fire, so cans of petrol were made ready to ward off any elephant which came too close for comfort. The petrol would be scattered in a circle round the camp, and then set alight. Once, a tiger sniffed about so close to the recumbent Birtles that he could smell the beast. Generally the hillmen were friendly and respectful, plying the travellers with rice whisky and roast stuffed puppy, for they endowed the car with magic properties. Only at one point did they become menacing. One evening the Bean had been stopped by a gradient, but had been hauled halfway up by nightfall with block and tackle. Birtles moored it with ropes to nearby trees and camped on the spot. During the night a herd of some hundreds of buffalo, driven by armed hillmen, descended the path. There was just room for each beast to pass the stationary vehicle in single file, but they stubbornly refused to do so, fearing the strange object. Their herdsmen wanted to cut the ropes and send the car over the edge to perdition, but changed their minds when Birtles picked up his elephant gun. He covered the car in bushes, effectively disguising it, whereupon the buffalo consented to be led past it one by one; a performance which took many hours but which was preferable to having one's head and various other component parts adorning a Naga house.

In this fashion the Naga Hills were surmounted, at the rate of a mile a day. In twenty-eight days thirty-six miles were covered, and the two men were next heard of at Tammu, where they arrived on 19 March. Ten days before, there had been talk of asking the Australian government to organise a search party, for no news of the Bean had been received, and it was taken for granted that Birtles was lost in the jungle. Leaving the mountains behind them for a while, the motorists hacked their way through dense forest to the Irrawaddy, which they tried—and failed—to cross. To reach an alternative crossing-place, another range of hills had to be attacked, but fortunately this was traversed by a cart-track. The Bean ran down to Pakokku on the Irrawaddy along a road through teak forests, where a thick carpet of leaves concealed holes and stones. Although they were ragged, unshaven and unwashed, the crew were received with increasing adulation by the Burmese. However, their appearance did little to recommend them to their fellows. When he saw that he was about to be accosted by a pair of motorised tramps, a British resident of Pakokku, the first white man the travellers had seen for many days, hastily ordered his chauffeur to accelerate. Near Rangoon they received their proper deserts, being welcomed by a crowd of cheering motorists and over-optimistic journalists, who acclaimed them as the pioneers of 'a new motor trade route'.

Birtles and Stollery in the Bean after their eventual arrival at Rangoon.

The Bean reached Rangoon on 10 April, two months and twenty-six days out of Calcutta. It left again six days later, though its crew were exhausted, penniless and in tatters. Birtles was also suffering from a poisoned hand, but once he had replenished his supplies and equipment with the help of his sponsors, he pushed on for Singapore, for the monsoon was now only three weeks away. He fought his way east and south over paddy fields and through jungle occasionally relieved by a stretch of good road. By the 23rd, Birtles had reached the frontier of Siam eighty miles east of Moulmein, but was forced to turn back for reasons not specified; his report had said, 'all well'. Next he tried to get through to Singapore by running due south through lower Burma, but was foiled by the breaking of the monsoon. There were innumerable river crossings on this coast, all in flood. The car fell right through one rotten ferry, and where there was no ferry the fords were so deep that the floorboards were awash, the exhaust pipe was submerged, and a combination of oil and river water was sloshing about in the sump. Stollery would be wading along behind, waist-deep. Once, the Bean was stuck in a tidal creek when the tide was rising. The rain descended in a solid, relentless stream. The motorists' clothes rotted off their backs, their biscuits went green, and mushrooms grew on their blankets. At Mergui in the south of lower Burma, Birtles acknowledged defeat. He put himself, his companion and his car on a boat for a relatively short hop of three hundred miles to Penang. Once again early delays had put paid to his chances. He had been beaten, but only just.

From Penang Birtles motored down through Malaya to Singapore, and on 29 May sailed on an oil tanker bound for Darwin. He arrived there on 10 June, penniless once more. His official welcome to Australia was provided by the customs, who seized his car and demanded duty on it. It was released only after a direct appeal to the Prime Minister of Australia. On 13 June began the last stage of the long journey, one very well known to Birtles, who was now on his home ground. His route took him from Darwin to Katherine, then across north-western Queensland to Camooweal, Longreach, Toowoomba and Brisbane, which was reached on 4 July. The car lost a day *en route* when Stollery fell ill with malaria. By the 15th they were in Sydney, and ten days later Sundowner and its crew drove into Melbourne. Their sixteen-thousand-mile expedition had lasted nine months and five days. Still running perfectly, Sundowner made its last journey to the Australian National Museum at Canberra, but Birtles himself, beyond being presented with a new vehicle by the Bean company, received precious little recognition for what he had done. . . .

Francis Birtles had failed to complete the land link between England and Australia by only the smallest margin. It is almost certain that this was not finally accomplished until the Land Rovers of the 1955–56 Oxford and Cambridge Far Eastern Expedition, travelling in the dry season and taking advantage of the ruinous but usable Ledo and Stilwell Roads built across northern Burma in the Second World War, motored from Calcutta to Singapore via Bangkok. A generation of technical progress and another war were necessary before the trail Birtles had begun to blaze was driven through.

> 'There were innumerable river crossings on this coast, all in flood. The car fell right through one rotten ferry, and where there was no ferry the fords were so deep that the floorboards were awash.'

TO CAPE YORK BY BABY AUSTIN

Hector MacQuarrie

WHILE FRANCIS BIRTLES *was driving from London to Melbourne in his massive 25-horsepower Bean, a lantern-jawed New Zealander named Hector MacQuarrie was motoring from Sydney to the tip of Cape York in a Baby Austin. MacQuarrie and his companion, Richard Matthews, drove, pushed, and hauled the Baby through quicksand, over sandhills, and across rivers, sometimes with the aid of donkeys, horses, and some helpful young Aborigines. MacQuarrie wrote a light-hearted account of the journey called* We and the Baby. *Here is how he describes the final leg of the trip, to the northernmost tip of Australia.*

TOWARDS THE END of the day we began making a very gradual descent; the pad became very sandy and the telegraph pole numbers assured us that we were approaching the great river, against which many people believed we could not prevail. Actually we were in its wet-weather bed, for the Jardine is several miles wide during the wet. We must have disturbed an amorous brown snake somewhere about here, for he began chasing us. We did not see him, but Joe, hurrying behind us, saw him following our wheel tracks, and killed him.

At five o'clock we reached the Jardine River.

I recall looking across the great expanse of running water to the far bank, and saying to myself, 'Ah—when once we are there!'

The Jardine is a good hundred and fifty yards wide, and during the dry season it runs over and between snowy white sandbanks. We had our plans made for the crossing, but an attempt could not be thought of that night. When the boys rejoined us, Mickie led me down the river to the cattle ford. He said, 'You and me go across and look him.' I shuddered, but agreed. Unquestionably the Jardine is crocodile-infested, and if the reptiles had any courage no one would dare to ford the river. I could not allow myself to appear frightened before Mickie, and so we both waded in.

Stockmen say that the Jardine is always a swim; but for once in its history it was unusually and agreeably low. The sand was very soft and unpleasant, but we were never in water above our armpits. Our progress was distressingly slow, and it occurred to me halfway across that a shy crocodile might become bold at any minute. The current was swift, but not actually swift enough to knock a man down. I discovered that the river shoaled very badly near the far bank and that the sand in this shallow water was quicksand.

Hector Macquarrie (left) and Richard Matthews lunching beside the Baby in a dry creekbed on the main northern highway of Queensland in 1928.

One sank up to one's knees and the withdrawal of feet was difficult. I saw that a raft would not float in this shallow water; and after consultation with Dick that night we decided to enter at the cattle ford and to make our way up the river against the current to a firmer landing.

After a few minutes' examination of the far bank, Mickie and I began the return crossing. I was chatting gaily with him, but my nerves were on edge. I recalled how people had said that crocodiles need not bother one at the Jardine because the water is so clear that they could be seen coming. I estimated the speed of a crocodile at thirty miles an hour in the water; Mickie's and my own utmost speed was perhaps one mile an hour. It seemed to me that a croc would have it all his own way if he made a rush at us when we were anything more than three feet from the bank. I must admit that I was seriously scared, and that I hurried! Dick, I may say, was at the telegraph clearing two hundred yards higher up the river.

It was most unfortunate that he should decide to practise with his revolver by shooting at a black stump floating down with the current at the moment when Mickie and I were in midstream. I heard the shots in rapid succession, and I decided at once that a crocodile was his target, and that the reptile was tearing downstream. Obviously it would pick me up *en route*.

At the first bang I jumped from the water. 'My hat, a crocodile!' I yelled; and jumped higher at the next shot. Mickie nearly collapsed in the stream with merriment. I was not altogether reassured, but I thought it best to laugh too, and to make many more little bounds from the rushing water to show Mickie that I was doing it merely for fun!

That night, before turning in, we made our plans for the crossing. I would leave the camp two hours before dawn and go with the boys two miles back along the clearing to a spot where cyprus pine grew. All the timber near the Jardine is hardwood and will not float. We would return with as much timber as possible. Dick would drive to the cattle ford and there dismantle the car, removing the battery, the magneto, the carburettor, and what cushions could be removed. (We still thought of the prospect of Thursday Island!)

This worked out well to the point when the raft was completed. But then we discovered that, while the raft would hold Mickie if he stood very still, it would not hold Mickie plus Charlie. The cyprus pine would float, but it seemed to have as much as it could do to keep itself afloat without bothering about any further burden. It certainly could not hold the Baby. Then Dick saw that I had placed the main logs across the raft instead of lengthways, and, deciding that it might be a case of occasionlly pushing the raft along the bottom, he thought it best to make an alteration which meant pulling my craft to pieces. This was not difficult; she was held together by telegraph wire!

Finally we hit upon an ingenious idea. The McDonnell folks keep a small dinghy at the river for ferrying stores across. This was chained and locked to a tree, and in a very leaky condition. It was much too small to take the car. But the buoyancy of even this small boat was infinitely greater than any raft we could make; and so we decided to borrow the dinghy by chopping down the branch to which it was chained. Then we made shafts—long, stout poles bound along the length of the raft and projecting the length of the dinghy.

We backed the dinghy in between the shafts and lashed her firmly, under and over. Then we placed two long stout poles across the stern of the raft for the boys to hold, to keep the stern buoyant.

The raft had her stern aground at the edge of the bank and her bow was held up well by the dinghy, which incidentally had to be kept baled. The Baby ran very obligingly on to the raft and was securely lashed to it. The dinghy took the weight easily.

But when once we had pushed into deep water and the stern had left the bank, our situation seemed most precarious. For while the dinghy held up

The Baby's route from Cairns to Cape York. At the time of the journey, the road connecting the major towns of the eastern Australian coast ended at Cairns; from there on it was a matter of following the occasional wagon road, bridle track or cattle pad.

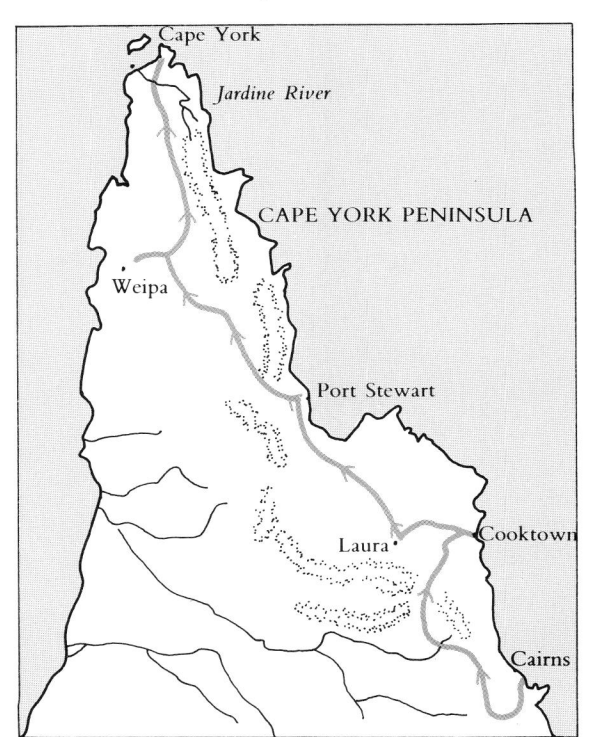

well, the boys and I could not keep the stern far from the bottom of the river. I would have suggested a pause for more thought; but Dick took up a position at the dinghy and said, 'Come on, now—let's get across!'

If Mickie, Joe, Charlie, and Peter had been capable of concerted action, all might have been well; but it happened that Mickie and Joe on the port side tired at a moment when Charlie and Peter were lifting. Thus Charlie's and Peter's side would often rise dangerously when Mickie's and Joe's sank, and often the car threatened to topple. Then Charlie and Joe would lose courage, and down would go the stern of the raft to the sand, the Baby's bonnet emerging in an attitude of supplication from the rushing water.

The only thing to do was to shout and shriek, even to make bad jokes—anything, to keep the boys going. I sang songs and yelled for some dozen yards with great success, until I made a shocking *faux pas*. I shouted, 'Come on Mickie and Joe—give her ten—whoop!'

Mickie and Joe responded magnificently; but Charlie and Peter did not. Up rose the Baby's port side dripping with water; down went her starboard side! The car trembled, threatening to topple over, but righted herself in time. It was a trying moment!

'What's the joke?' Dick shouted icily. 'You want to capsize the car, do you?—very funny!' I believe he was seriously annoyed; but I could think of nothing sufficiently rude to fling back at that moment.

Besides, my thoughts were occupied with crocodiles. The current was rushing against us—especially when, eventually, we were forced to turn into its teeth to avoid a shoal in front of us! After a time the boys seemed to give up trying to keep their end up, and it became a matter of pushing the stern of the raft along the sand, which was dangerously soft. Altogether it was an exceedingly difficult and dangerous operation, which succeeded more by good fortune than by anything else.

Dick, who, from the moment he took hold of the dinghy at the near bank never ceased to pull with all his strength until the far bank was reached, tells me that his greatest trouble was thirst, which seems absurd in view of the fact that he was in water often up to his shoulders; he dared not release an ounce of strength to bend to drink!...

After a fight of two full hours against soft sand and the current, we ran against the far bank, and thanked God. During those hours there was not a minute which did not contain serious risk. The boys were as pleased as we were to get across, and immediately danced a dance of joy.

Rafting the Baby across the Jardine.

We paid off our men when again we were on the telegraph clearing. Mickie called it 'the best pay-off in the whole world'. It was certainly the most interesting—old pipes, three safety razors which had reached the expensive stage of cutting more strops than they should, bachelor's buttons, pencils, tobacco, old coats, much flour, tea, sugar, and tobacco—and a few shillings each to clinch the business with. When at last we bade them goodbye and they cried, we both felt a tightening in the region of the throat; we had all become great friends....

On then with less than forty miles before us. There were two hours of daylight left in that fair day; and we hoped to cover ten miles. But, alas, turkey-brush gave us six punctures in rapid succession and we were forced to camp hardly more than two miles north of the Jardine.

Turkey-brush is a very pretty sage-like scrub which seldom grows higher than four or five feet. Its twigs and small branches have the capacity of steel to pierce rubber, and even leather, we were told. Few horses will face turkey-brush willingly. We discovered, too, that if we carried on for more than a yard after a puncture, the twig, piercing the outer cover, tore great rents in the inner tube. It looked very bad for that prospect on Thursday Island! We reached close to the necessity of stuffing the tyres with grass or sand, which would have been a great pity, because the little car was still in perfect condition.

We hardly ate that night; and we hardly slept. Thirty-eight miles separated us from Cape York. Should we get there? Could we? Until that night we had never doubted our ability to reach the end of Australia. Now it seemed almost impossible.

But hope came at dawn, when we were ready to start. We had all the tyres tight, and three or four good hours of coolness before us. Alas, we had only travelled three hundred yards when flat went a tyre. Having mended this, we proceeded—but, to make a sad story short, I had better say at once that at the ninth puncture, with only four miles covered, we were seriously discouraged. Discouragement was a new sensation to us; we had not known it before. Hot day with its offering of small flies was upon us. Dick looked very depressed and miserable; he looks like that only once in five years.

But fortunately, after the ninth puncture, the turkey-brush ceased, and we began making excellent progress.

Benzine was now becoming scarce. Only good luck, we were amazed to find, would get us through.

We reached the neighbourhood of Red Island, where the Fresh Food and Ice Company of Thursday Island slaughter beasts. It was the first sign of our renewed connection with the outer world. We found a Japanese charcoal burner called Tokita, who gave us tea and pineapples. We ran the mile down Tokita's road to the sea, but that glory of blueness meant little to us that day.

Going a little farther north and branching off from the pad, we called in at the Red Island slaughter yard, and told that very good soul, Mrs Gibson—I must mention her—that we were short of benzine.

'I've got plenty,' she said, and instantly produced six bottles of the precious fluid. She used it for her iron. It was natural enough for Mrs Gibson to have benzine for her iron, and lucky that she had but newly accumulated a fresh store; but it seemed a miracle to us.

On then for Cape York!

Cape York was less than twenty miles ahead of us, and we had every chance of getting there before dark. But a very bad creek called Takanau, less than nine miles south of our journey's end, held us up for some hours, and when we were free of Takanau it was getting dark.

We should have camped; we could not! Indeed we had hardly eaten that day. Flinging caution to the wind, we struggled on in the dark. I can hear at this moment that brave little British engine singing away as sweetly as she had sung in Sydney. Sometimes she had to struggle very seriously over the pad, which was becoming more sandy as time passed, but she never failed us. I was walking twenty yards ahead with an electric torch, giving Dick warning of stumps, ant heaps, and watercourses. The sand here is the home of many small death-adders effectively camouflaged white and grey, but no death adder crossed my path. I can still see the Baby's brilliant headlights swinging this way and that across the great avenue which forms the telegraph clearing, and I can easily recall the joy I felt when at last they lit up some sliprails ahead of us.

'Sliprails, Dick,' I called, 'we shall soon be there!'

I heard no reply; the little engine was still singing sweetly; the Baby was bobbing and creeping her confident way like a clever insect along the pad. She seemed quite unconcerned. I might have been amazed had she suddenly given tongue and said, 'What's all this fuss about? I can get there all right!' But if she had said, 'Well—what's the big idea anyway? What did you lead me here for?' I should have been puzzled to find an answer.

We reached the sliprails and entered the home paddock of Cape York telegraph station. We crept over very soft sand for some time, and then that avenue of hundreds of miles ended abruptly.

We saw lights in a house; we honked our horn; soon a little pool of brilliant light came dancing over the ground towards us. It was Mr Gunn, the postmaster, watching his steps with an electric torch; Mr Gunn knows his local death adders!

Finally we reached a sand mound, the most northerly end of Australia, and stopped. Dick got out of the car and took my hand.

'Thank God!' he said.

'Thank God!' I said.

Macquarrie and Matthews look out over Torres Strait from the tiny Baby Austin which had taken them to the end of Australia.

PACIFIC FLIGHT OF THE SOUTHERN CROSS

Charles Kingsford Smith and C.T.P. Ulm

CHARLES KINGSFORD SMITH, *Australia's most famous airman, nurtured an ambition from early in his career to be the first to fly an aeroplane across the Pacific Ocean. So did Charles Ulm. They met in 1927 and, after much difficulty in obtaining sponsorship, raised enough finance to get them to America, where they bought the Fokker monoplane that the Arctic explorer Hubert Wilkins had used on his latest Arctic expedition. The plane was renamed the* Southern Cross. *On 31 May 1928 Kingsford Smith, Ulm, and two Americans—radio operator James Warner and navigator Harry Lyon—took off from Oakland, California, in the* Southern Cross *for the east-to-west flight across the Pacific, stopping at Hawaii and Fiji before landing at Brisbane on 8 June. The flight was exhausting and uncomfortable (the noise of the three Wright Whirlwind engines allowed no spoken conversation in the plane and so deafened the flyers temporarily that they were unable to hear reporters' questions when they landed), and it was not without hazards. Here, in an extract from their account of the flight, Kingsford Smith and Ulm tell of some blind flying in bad weather on the long leg from Kauai, Hawaii, to Suva.*

WE HAD much more drinking water on this hop. That was a necessary precaution, because in the last six hours flying before we landed at Wheeler Field, there was a parching drought aboard the *Southern Cross*. We had drunk all the water during the night and early hours and did a rigorous thirst after sunrise.

On this occasion we determined that if possible we would not again suffer the pangs of drought. Our food was practically all in the form of sandwiches. Nothing else was so easily handled in the confined space in which we lived. We have never eaten so many sandwiches in our lives, and when we left Kauai we brought with us whole regiments of them, thanks to the kindness of Mr and Mrs Faye, our hosts at Kauai. So far as was possible, we planned to defeat thirst and hunger on the long hop.

From 7 a.m. to 8 a.m. we bowled along at a ground speed of 81 knots. Our altitude was still only 500 feet. We were figuratively hugging the sea as long as we could to save that vital gasoline. But it was apparent that our best-laid plans in this respect would very shortly 'gang agley'.

Visibility was still good, our oil pressures and temperatures were perfect, but far ahead the horizon was blotted out by low drifting clouds. It was

People in Sydney flocked to Mascot aerodrome to welcome the Southern Cross *after the record trans-Pacific flight.*

Harry Lyon, Charles Ulm, Charles Kingsford Smith and James Warner beside the Southern Cross *after their pioneer flight across the Pacific.*

growing duller. The sun was obscured by murk. There seemed to be water in the air. Rain apparently was blowing up many miles ahead.

Again we had just breakfasted on sandwiches and coffee, and were feeling in excellent humour, when we were suddenly jolted out of our comfortable frame of mind once more. Warner sent through a note. We had lost the radio beacon. Its signals had faded away at 8.15, and we were only three hours out. We had expected that its friendly buzz would have accompanied us for seven hours.

This, however, was not the worst news.

We had just completed a little more than an hour's flying without the radio beacon when Warner reported that our radio equipment was completely out of action. We were then flying towards what looked like a barrier of rain in the far distance. Our altitude was only 550 feet, and our airspeed was 77 knots.

Between eight and ten o'clock the rosy promise that seemed to have been held out at sunrise had changed for the worse. A stern tussle with rainstorms looked inevitable in an hour or so, and we found ourselves again cut off from the world. The radio beacon had failed us, our own instrument had decided to declare a strike, and for the second time in five hours' flying we found ourselves in that isolated world whose limits were set by the front windshields and the exhaust pipes. And this time it was a more dismal world than on the first occasion when we had been isolated from the radio voice of the world. There was no sun awakening a flash and sparkle from the sea. The innocuous cumulus packs had given place to wicked-looking rain clouds that seemed to be charged with all the evaporated waters of the globe.

We missed the chats with the world. With every mile the loss of the radio words became greater. Our sense of loneliness increased. We felt in the miserable position that a man must feel who suddenly has lost the use of his voice. Our radio voice was silent, the radio voices of the two continents were also silent, and there we were plunging into gloom actual and temperamental. The actual gloom came down on us like a damp blanket. The ship was slipping along splendidly at a ground speed of 90 knots, when the wind began to freshen. Its sudden puffs turned to tugs and slaps and punches. Ahead, great dark clouds tumbled in a headlong rush. The wind whipped up from ten to twenty miles an hour. The sun was blotted out. At 11.40 a.m. we plunged into the squall, still voiceless.

Right ahead the nimbus clouds dissolved in a curtain of rain. The fringe of it splashed us before we flew round the main deluge. From that moment began a wild aerial jazzing out of the way of rain. The storms that had been lurking ahead for the previous three hours flung themselves across our path. Like ominous grey curtains that trailed their fringes across the surface of the sea, rainstorms charged at us from every direction, driven before a fresh wind. Ulm swung the ship out of the way of one storm, and Smith steered her clear of a second. But the dark curtains closed in—beset us from every side, and merged into a great belt of swishing water.

It was a cheerless hour. Visibility shrank from seven or eight miles to one, then to half or less. Just when a dim and dismal path seemed to be opening out before us through these walls of water, the wind chopped round and closed the murky corridor. Kingsford Smith set the nose of the *Southern*

The path taken by the Southern Cross from Oakland, on San Francisco Bay, to Brisbane via Hawaii and Fiji between 31 May and 9 June 1928.

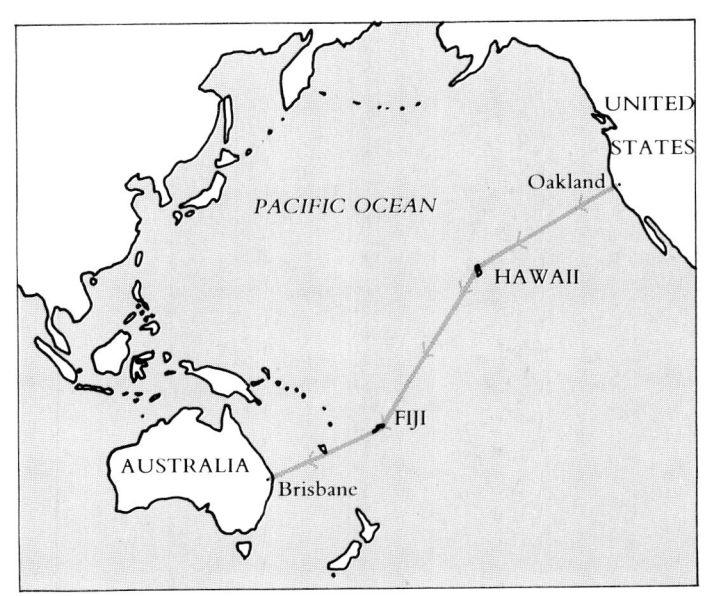

Cross down one of these watery corridors in a dash between the merging squalls. He got through, and we earned a slight respite from the battering by the wind. But it was only a passing lull.

The rainstorms surged in round us again. We were 600 feet up, and as we had been flying for only six and a half hours our petrol load was still tremendous. To fly low in such atrocious conditions, heavily overloaded, was an experience that did not at all add any to the peace of mind.

To dodge around the fringes of the storm and to climb through the murk were the kind of manoeuvres that were going to mop up our gasoline at a disconcerting rate. To fly low overloaded in the face of the savage chopping gusts with visibility shrinking to a few hundred feet was to flirt a little too dangerously with risk. We were indeed on the horns of a dilemma. We were forced to decide on a policy, as we had not the faintest idea how long this battering by the storms might continue. That policy was to climb, to risk a heavier petrol consumption, and to hope for the best. So we opened up the motors to 1,775 revolutions, and ploughed up through rain and storm and a jolting nasty wind which blew in sudden gusts.

Visibility shrank at an incredible rate; the rain became thicker, and at 11.50 a.m. we were flying blind and climbing to get out of the deluge. The plane bumped heavily in the tearing gusts, and we got out of it at 1,000 feet, only to be faced with another menacing black curtain of water. Our spell of blind flying through slashing rain was not a long one, but the ship bucked and lurched heavily as the wind seemed to chop in three directions at the same moment. Visibility opened up to about 200 feet again just before noon, when we began to glide down to 600 feet to get under a rainstorm that was massing up ready to burst on us in full fury. Just as suddenly as we had to fight these squalls, we tore through into moderately clear air once more. We were, of course, plugging along at 76 knots all the time.

Noon (12.30 Honolulu time) saw us just through the barrier of squalls. Lyon took a sight with the sextant to get our latitudinal position. We were then seven hours from Kauai. Kingsford Smith had flown 4½ hours, and Ulm 2½ hours. There had been a long silence from Jim Warner in the navigating cabin, and it was clear that we were still without our radio voice or ears. Yet we had the utmost faith in the ability of Jim. If the radio equipment could be readjusted, Jim was the man to fix it.

In the thrill of sidestepping, or rather side-sliding, out of the path of storms, we had forgotten the atmospheric conditions. It dawned on us as we emerged from the tumult of rain that it was oppressively hot in the cockpit. The heavy water-laden air, the passage into a definite tropical zone, and the waves of heat from the motors caused us to perspire. As we took our coats off, we swept past a cloudbank abeam that was just dissolving into a rainstorm that looked more wicked than those through which we had passed.

At 12.45 (Honolulu time) we had flown 630 miles in just seven hours, at an average ground speed of 90 miles an hour. Lyon, after his observations, then passed through our position as being 'latitude by observation, 12 deg. 47 min.; by dead reckoning, 12 deg. 58 min.; longitude 163 deg. 13 min.'

Rainstorms came sweeping up at us endlessly, lashing the plane, beating a lively tattoo on the windshield, and making us fly through a murky soaked

'Rainstorms came sweeping up at us endlessly, lashing the plane, beating a lively tattoo on the windshield, and making us fly through a murky soaked world that seemed to have no boundaries.'

world that seemed to have no boundaries. Conrad's skipper preferred to plough through a China Sea typhoon rather than run up his coal bill. Like him, we became misers of petrol. We resolved to keep flying at 600 feet, because if we went higher, we would burn more fuel. When we plunged into a heavy rainstorm at 12.50 there was only one bright spot in a most cheerless aspect. The motors were fighting the storms with such stubbornness that our ground speed was maintained in a most satisfactory way. Kingsford Smith flew seven minutes blind through the new storm. The rain poured in rivulets from our windshield, and though it was high noon, and a tropic noon at that, we tore through a wall of water where visibility ceased to exist.

Already in seven hours we had experienced more blind flying on this stage of our flight than on the $27\frac{1}{2}$ hours between Oakland and Honolulu.

What is blind flying? Most long-distance airmen know, but to the average man in the street the term may be rather vague.

If you have ever tried to drive a motor car along a bush road on a pitch black night without a headlight or a rear light, or even a match, you will gain some slight idea of the meaning of blind flying. But even then, with that nightmare experience, you would not have lived through all the thrilling uncertainty of flying a plane in a dim opaque world of nothingness. That is because in a car you could only go forwards or backwards.

In a plane there are any number of movements that have to be regulated. It not only goes forward, but may climb or drop or bank or sidestep, or drift.

How do you know when a plane in banking, when all round you is inky blackness? How can you tell its drift sideways? You can do none of these things without the proper instruments, and without the blindest, the most implicit faith in them. In blind flying when a plane charges through lashing rain in a black void, there is a contest between your senses and your instruments. Your senses may lead you to believe that the ship is climbing or descending. They may tell you that the plane is banking steeply. And it is possible for the senses to be quite inaccurate.

It seems revolutionary to oppose the dictum of the senses in such a matter as this. Yet in blind flying, if the instruments show that the plane is banking when your senses indicate that it is thrashing its way forward on an even horizontal wing, the instruments are correct, and not your senses. It is not easy to allow the mind to become as elastic as this. The process is in the same category as that which a dentist demands of a patient when he asks him not to sit rigid against the forceps but to relax. To relax the mind in such a way as to doubt your own senses is no joke. Yet that is what blind flying demands during every minute when visibility is definitely cut out.

Your whole world is reduced to an instrument board illuminated by an electric torch. Over the edge of the windshields of the cockpit there is nothing but blank greyness. At the sides there is nothing but blank greyness. Behind you there is nothing but blank greyness. Unlike the darkened car on the darkened road, however, there is nothing to hit if the altitude is correct.

If the altitude was not carefully adjusted and watched, however, with us there was the ghastly posibility of hitting the surface of the ocean. That was where our altimeter played its important part. It told us constantly how far from the sea we were when we were plunging through that soupy greyness.

> *'If you have ever tried to drive a motor car along a bush road on a pitch black night without a headlight or a rear light, or even a match, you will gain some slight idea of the meaning of blind flying.'*

Without those instruments it would have been impossible to fly blind for an hour without disaster.

At 1.22 p.m., when we came out of our third spell of blind flying, on the new stage of the flight, Warner had good news for us to relieve the gloom that is apt to settle on one in those patches of blank greyness. Both radio transmitters were working normally again. Once more we had our link with the world, and, to speak, figuratively, we had 'come back to life'.

A little later we again dashed into heavy cloud banks. We climbed, and once more had to sidestep two savage bursts of rain that came tearing at us. The cloud curtains thickened; the rain lashed us with greater fury, and again we were in that dim opague world flying blind. The windshields began to leak, and water started to trickle in on us. Then our real personal discomfort commenced. Water splashed into the cockpit and soaked our feet and legs. In less than half an hour we were very damp and a little disgruntled. For an hour we flew low against oblique sheets of stinging rain.

There was one vast difference between this hop of the flight and the trip to Honolulu. That crushing monotony of calm sea and cloud beauty did not linger with us. We were about ten hours out, and there had not been a consecutive half hour of monotony. Things seemed to happen in a steady sequence. There was the losing of the radio beacon, the capriciousness of our own radio instrument, the supposed gas leak, the opening lively rounds with the rain-squalls, and the sudden transitions from murk to blind flying. We had plunged on through the driving rain for about another hour, and we were beginning to believe that the rush of incident was about to ease when there was another scare and a few moments of anxiety. We were just changing over at the controls, working them on an hourly duty roster.

Kingsford Smith had taken over the controls, when there was a sudden tremulous cough in the starboard engine. It was not a bad spluttering cough, but just sufficient to break that wonderful harmonious chorus that the motors had played for us now over three thousand miles of ocean.

We thought hard for a few seconds. Then came a note from Lyon to ask about the motor. Our ears were so attuned to the steady thunder of the three motors that in the navigating cabin Lyon and Warner had also instantly detected the unusual highpitched bark of the starboard engine.

What was wrong? We were nearly a thousand miles out over a stretch of ocean that could not possibly have looked more inhospitable or forbidding.

Were the motors going to let us down after the wonderful comradeship they had shown us since we left the Golden Gate? We were secure in the fact that at least all three motors would not—to use the boxing term—'sky the towel' at the same moment, or even in the same hour.

It would have been extremely bad luck for one of them to have refused duty, but it would not have been altogether desperate.

Yet that cough sounded menacing. For three thousand miles across the great sweep of ocean that we had covered, our ears had become sensitised to the slightest irregularity in the beat of those motors. We were constantly on the alert, listening, so to speak, like an Indian with his ear to the ground, with the essential difference that our ears were very far from ground of any kind. Mile after mile one could not dull this tense ear strain for the possible cough or splutter of one of the engines. It was only a natural inclination, as the motors were to be either our salvation or our destruction.

Yet, though only one of the motors had coughed suddenly in the midst of that cheerless rain-soaked afternoon, and we looked at the bright side even of possible trouble with the starboard engine, in so far as the outcome was concerned, the prospect of tinkering with a misbehaving motor out there over strange sea, and in the midst of savage gusts, was not the least reassuring.

The cough ceased as quickly as it began. We were all ears.

Was it only a passing irregularity? But no. It came again, definite and unmistakable. There was a splutter and a sort of kick. Nothing could be left to chance. We could not charge on through the rain disregarding that motor, and possibly laying the foundation of disaster. We started out to investigate. We did not for a moment believe that the cough was caused by a fault in the motor itself. The first theory that ran through our minds was that a defect had developed in the gasoline feed line. An inspection by Ulm discovered no visible trouble in the gas lines. It was possible, however, that rain had percolated into the carburettor stoves, and that this had led the starboard motor to dance a little.

At any rate, the revolutions of the starboard motor were normal at 1,600, and the oil pressure and temperature were right. Intermittently, for about eight minutes, came this discordant note in the roar of that engine. Then the coughs stopped abruptly. The roar, steady and rhythmic, swelled out as before. Ulm entered in the log probably one of the most historic jottings that the book contained. It read: 'Starboard engine has quit shimmying.'

At the moment, that entry was as pleasing to us as if he had to put down on paper that Fiji was in sight. Our altitude was 550 feet, and our speed 77 knots. All was well with the world. Yet the temporary irregularity of the engine had caused us to train our ears with greater concentration for a possible renewal of the shimmying. That, too, was but a natural result of the scare. The rain seemed to get a little lighter, and at 4.22 p.m. we had been eleven hours in the air for the day. Our estimate was that we had averaged a hundred or more statute miles hourly. Lyon worked up the longitudinal position, and in a note that he passed through he told us that at 4 p.m. (*Southern Cross* time) and 4.25 (Honolulu time) we were in latitude 7° 27' N and 167° 30' W longitude. We had covered 1,026 nautical miles at an average hourly speed of 106.55 miles.

We had now broken free from the wet cloudbanks, the rain had stopped, and although a thick haze lay along the horizon ahead, it looked as if we would have a clear night with good flying conditions. We felt that we certainly deserved such a night, as from before noon the rain had made our lives miserable.

We plotted our probable progress, based on the favourable outlook that the checking of our longitudinal position had given us. Given favourable conditions, we believed that we would pass over the Islands of the Phoenix Group that night. It was then 6.10 p.m., and dry, all except our feet and legs, where the water had cascaded on us from the windshields.

Again our forecast of a fine night went astray. When you are bowling along at a ground speed of 85 knots, you sometimes overlook the fact that great sweeps of sea are being left behind rapidly, and that while the weather indications may look promising at one point, two hours' flying further on may bring you into the foulest of weather.

It was so with us. As the daylight began to wane fast, we started to climb for our night flying. This was our settled policy, as it was safe at a good altitude, and, in addition, it was the means of prolonging the day. High up there we had the advantage of the rays of the sun as it slid under the horizon, even though darkness may have fallen completely at the ground or sea level.

The clearness that had appeared ahead was now no more. New mountain peaks of cloud heaped up on the south-western horizon. They were thick and dark. We climbed steadily at 69 knots. We expected that we would get above the menacing peaks at 5,000 feet, but we had not pulled up to more than 1,200 feet when rain burst on us once again from the foothills in this vast range of cloud. We opened up the motors to 1,700 revolutions, so that we could climb more rapidly, and at the moment had to swing right off our course to fly round a wall of rain of tropical violence that charged right at us.

We began to fly in circles always steadily upwards. This was the sort of thing that always reawakened those qualms about the terrific drain on our gasoline. We probably in our mental state on this occasion exaggerated the thirst of those motors when they began to haul the heavy load aloft, because it was one of the longest and most strenuous climbs of the whole flight.

There was always, too, the feeling that while we were seeking to soar over these cloud pinnacles we were getting nowhere. Progress was cut down to a few miles. It was a breathless race between the *Southern Cross* and the clouds. First we gained, then they puffed up beneath the plane. Rain battered at the windshields, and the wind seemed to stand off like a boxer and punch us. We had been battling upwards in this way for about ten minutes when the flexible lead of the exhaust pipe carried away off the centre motor. No damage was done, and we did not worry unduly over the incident. As long as nothing more vital fell off we were quite at ease in mind. As we climbed, the rain grew worse. It slashed and tore against the windshields. The clouds seemed to get blacker and thicker the further we struggled aloft, and for the fourth time since we left Barking Sands we were flying blind.

In the midst of that cloud bank it was as black as the blackest night, yet the altimeter told us that we were climbing at the rate of 250 feet a minute, and at 6.20 p.m. we had mounted to nearly 2,000 feet. We burst out of the first prison house of clouds and found ourselves above the lower ranges of them. We could see about us again, and the dying sun lit up the tumbling cloud masses in a picture as striking as that which we had seen just before we reached Honolulu. But there was a difference. It lay in the fact that there was nothing kindly in these great cloud valleys down which we looked from the sides of the cockpit. They were the colour of heavy coal smoke, and inspired a certain amount of awe. And the rain was dogging us for every mile. It often blotted out everything, and our damp feet and legs grew more damp as it tumbled in rivulets over the windshield.

We were forcibly reminded of the 2,500 miles of rain through which we had battled on our 7,500 miles flight round the Australian continent. The rivulets coming over the windshields turned to rushing cascades, and we

'And the rain was dogging us for every mile. It often blotted out everything, and our damp feet and legs grew more damp as it tumbled in rivulets over the windshield.'

The Southern Cross *in a demonstration flight over New Zealand. On 10–11 September 1928, three months after their trans-Pacific crossing, Kingsford Smith and Ulm set another aviation record in the* Southern Cross—*the first flight across the Tasman.*

got sodden from the knees down. At 5,000 feet, and after a sudden swing almost at right angles to our course, we shook off the clinging rain clouds, but there were still higher mountains of cloud before us, and the haulage was heavy on the three roaring motors.

From this point, a little after seven o'clock in the evening, it became a tense race between the *Southern Cross* and the clouds to reach 10,000 feet. Only such an altitude, we felt, would carry us into clearer flying conditions. At 7.15 p.m. we had reached 7,500 feet, but there was none of the sunset glory that had enlivened our lot a little on the previous hop. Inky blackness, rain, and capricious winds made up the cheerless outlook for the night. So it was with the greatest fervour with which anything was ever penned that Ulm included in the log the sentence 'We see a rotten night ahead.' Clouds completely surrounded us, and we passed through another of those frequent periods when we were unable to take our bearings. It rained hard in bursts, and we kept flying in circles.

But after a long and grim fight we won that race. At 8,000 feet we had beaten the uprush of the cloud banks. We looked down into a world of tumbled vapour, ranging away in ragged fringes on every side. Yet the struggle up there through the cloud masses was well worth the reward that awaited us when we scaled them.

Above us, as we emerged from the murk, glittered the Southern Cross, the constellation whose name we were proud to bear on our ship. It winked out a genial welcome to us after the stress of the battle far below. It glimmered on the port bow like a shower of diamonds in a vault of the deepest blue. There were other stars there too, of course, but we hardly saw them. The Southern Cross was to us the symbol of success. It seemed to hang there beckoning its namesake with the three droning motors. It looked good. We were still far from our goal, the sea swept by, the tangled cloud wreaths far below looked just as relentless, yet the sight of the Southern Cross seemed to give us the impression that the worst was over, that we would win our way through to Suva.

DEPRESSION TRACKMEN

Mick Healy

DURING THE GREAT DEPRESSION of the early 1930s, thousands of unemployed went on the track as swagmen. They made long journeys in the outback and up and down the coast in search of work, travelling on foot or jumping the rattler. Many stories of the Depression were gathered by the oral historian Wendy Lowenstein for her book Weevils in the Flour. *Here is how Mick Healy, swagman, told her his story of life on the track.*

I LEFT IRELAND for New Zealand in 1925. I'd no trade. Just a general knockabout sort of a fellow. When the depression set in there, we had enough money to keep going for a few months. We decided to leave New Zealand for Australia, knowing full well that everyone was out of work here. We went straight on to the dole in Sydney. We went down to this place near Circular Quay. There were thousands of people. We enrolled and got ration tickets, about six shillings worth of food. The Lang government was in office. It was late in 1931.

We started off on the track. You should have seen us. We must have been

Unemployed pass through the dole lines.

the best-dressed swagmen that ever hit Australia! When we got out at Hornsby I had a lovely brown nap overcoat, Bostock shoes and a Borsalino hat. My mate, the Canadian, had a lovely eiderdown quilt. He wouldn't part with it under any circumstances. And we had ports! We camped there overnight and in the morning I went to get some water in my nice new billy. There was an old fellow camped in the bandstand. He'd a big long beard. He said, 'Oh, you're new, eh? A new chum!' I asked him, 'How long have you been carrying your swag?' He said, 'Let me see now. It was 1905 when I picked up my swag first!' 'My God!' I said. 'This is a terrible country. This fellow has been on the track since the year I was born!'

We didn't find the police hostile. In fact they were quite sympathetic. Tobacco was a problem, so we used to buy half a pound of tea and take it to the Greek cafe and he'd give you a couple of ounces of cheap tobacco. Make a fat profit for himself, but what could you do? We learnt to bandicoot spuds. We'd feel the drill where the potatoes were and take a good sized one. We'd fill the earth back so it wouldn't interfere with the rest of his crop. We were quite thoughtful really!

We went up the coast, and at Newcastle we started to meet young fellows going south on their way home for Christmas. They'd been to Cairns. It was amazing really. They'd have presents for their mothers. Perhaps a little tin of Arnott's biscuits. We had no idea where Cairns was, of course. We had a railway timetable with a map of Australia on it, and we'd look to see where all these places were. We'd say, 'Cairns! My goodness! That's a long way.' And we'd look at the scale to see how many miles it was.

We had a Danish mate: the most lovable liar I've ever met. He'd kidded us that there was gold on the Laura River up near Cooktown, and he wanted us to go there. We were enjoying ourselves. We were young, and in a new country. Life was interesting and the climate was excellent, and we still looked quite respectable. I still had that coat. I never parted with that until I got right up north to Townsville, but we'd given away our ports and had rolled a swag. We had a tuckerbag, too. We were becoming real Australian bagmen.

Someone said there was work sewing wheat bags at Walgett, and we're getting ready to jump this train when another train came in and a lot of bagmen got off. 'Where have you come from?' 'Oh!' he said. 'We were out at Walgett looking for work, but there's more bloody bagmen out there than bags of wheat!' So needless to say we turned back. Spent several weeks in Newcastle. There was a camp there of unemployed. This is where I started to get interested in the Unemployed Movement. There was Lang Planners, there was Douglas Creditites, there was all kinds of ideas. The whole country seemed in a kind of fervour. The unemployed were trying to find some kind of a solution. I hadn't thought much about politics at all before the depression. I was an easygoing young fellow.

We decided to jump our first train. I think the police were glad to see you move on and they didn't interfere. And if there were two or three hundred people trying to get on a train, it was quite impossible anyway. The unemployed actually held up a train once to get on it. It was between Townsville and Mount Isa. Someone told us there was work at Aberdeen, so we got off

'We were enjoying ourselves. We were young, and in a new country. Life was interesting and the climate was excellent, and we still looked quite respectable. I still had the coat.'

Jumping the rattler during the Depression.

there, but of course there was no work. We camped at the Showgrounds and went to the pictures. After all the paying customers had gone in, the unemployed could go in free.

At Scone, it became necessary to do a bit of begging for food. I went to the Convent and I was very Irish! The Mother Superior was very sympathetic. I told her I had two mates with me and one was a Canadian. 'Would he be a good axeman?' she said. 'Oh!' I said. 'He'd be a topnotcher. He comes from British Columbia where the real axemen are!' 'Well, he's the man we want,' she said, 'to have a look at this big tree in the schoolyard. I can't get anyone to chop it down. If it falls, it could fall on the school. Do you think he could do it?' 'He'd be the very one,' I said. I went and told Percy. His father was a wheat farmer and he knew nothing about felling trees, but he said, 'Well, we've got nothing to lose!' They'd got an axe and a crosscut saw, and wire and ropes. We had a nice cup of tea with home-made biscuits. All the kids were out there to see the great work. And then we started. You wouldn't believe what happened. Luck was our way, and the tree fell in just the right direction. We were really the heroes, and old Mother Superior would have done anything for us. She wrote little notes out. We had to go to the local hairdresser, and he cut our hair. The local publican gave us a meal at night, and we went to the pictures!

We moved up though Tamworth and Armidale and camped at Guyra. We were getting into the mountains and, even though it was Christmas, it was cool at night. I was always worried about snakes and got on to some kind of a veranda at a railway station or a goods shed if I could. There was always plenty of company at these places. Some of the greatest liars and story-tellers I've heard in my life. It was very interesting!

At Guyra we somehow all got separated. One chap got sick of jumping goods trains so he got on to the mail train. There were a few shearers playing cards and he told them the problem. They had a rug over their knees and he got in under the rug and travelled quite a long way. Jumping trains wasn't de luxe travel by any means. Sometimes it was hot and horrible, and sometimes the opposite, particularly at night. Some wagons would have quite big openings between the boards and, oh my goodness, the wind would be blowing up and you would have a crook back! Our longest trip was from a place near Maryborough right through for twenty-four hours to Rockhampton. You had food and water with you, of course. As for the needs of nature, it was over the side! At Rockhampton the unemployed camped at the Giggle House, a disused mental hospital.

We finished up right out at Moree this first trip. They were building a railway to Boggabilla. We didn't get work there, and were depending more and more on handouts. But you'd only get really hungry away from civilisation, out in the back country. You might walk two miles to a homestead and there'd be no one home. But they would usually give you a bit of flour and salt and a little corned beef. In the towns you got a few knock-backs but not a great number. As I got more experience I was inclined to go to working-class homes. They were better. You'd pick out a house and walk up a couple of steps to the door. By the time they came you'd see what kind of pictures they had. If they were good Roman Catholics, if they were very religious, you would word your story accordingly. You adjusted yourself.

Storekeepers were often good, too. In Mackay, for instance, you could go to Michelmore's, a big wholesale store. They had a certain day. They'd give you two or three potatoes and onions. And there was a local butcher, he had a day too when he'd give you a little bit of meat. This information was passed on. We were in Mackay for a long while at a place called the shelter shed. This was built by the City Council. It was properly built and had a kitchen outside. It was the result of a campaign by Jim Healy and other

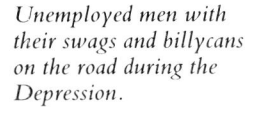

Unemployed men with their swags and billycans on the road during the Depression.

Waterside Workers, by the Railway Union, and by local church people and unemployed. It was an excellent campaign. The rumour was that they were going to build the Mackay Harbour and all the unemployed were pushing up there. Hundreds were camping there, waiting on this project.

We did a lot of reading. We'd go to the School of Arts Library and just sit there. They didn't worry. They were very kind. We'd read the papers and the old *Bulletin*. I liked the Red Page. And I read Henry Lawson and Banjo Paterson and Jack London. I read all about Australia. Picture shows were the great entertainment at this time. They'd have special family nights when you got in cheap, and they'd have a lucky number on the ticket. If you were successful you got a basket of groceries. They had popular artist nights. We had a little Irish fellow with a beautiful voice and we nominated him for this concert. At this stage we were getting a day's work a fortnight so we had a little money and we went along to give Paddy the hooray. He sang 'Mother Machree' and the 'Mountains of Mourne', and we cheered the bloody hall down! As the prize was given on acclamation he won. A five-pound prize! He bought a keg of beer and we had a lovely time!

The Unemployed Movement was very good in Mackay, and by this time I was getting active in it. They used to have lectures on a Sunday night and talk about socialism. To me it seemed, 'Why should people be out of work? Why shouldn't they have homes to live in?' At last we got to Townsville and set off to go to Mount Isa. We finally got to a place called Chorregon. My mate got on to a train and I got left. I was in a terrible predicament. I didn't want to leave the railhead because of the water supply, and I was worried to billy-o about snakes. All those panics. I think I'd be the greatest sap new chum that ever came to this country!

The blokes had me believing that death adders were as big as cobras. That they'd get up on their tails and wait on you. Instant death! One night we had a big fire with all the bagmen camped round it. And they told the old story that if you drew a ring in the dirt with a stick the snake won't come across it. I was so silly about snakes that I didn't know they were pulling my leg. So as soon as they'd gone to sleep or pretended to, I drew a ring. I throught, 'If one line drawn around is good enough for a snake I'll draw quite a few!'

I was on my own at Goondiwindi early in 1932. It was a bad time and it was very hot. An old fellow picked me up, and said, 'I could give you a job ringbarking.' I said, 'Could you? I'd like that!' 'Have you ever done it?' I said, 'I could try.' So he took me to this camp. The fellows there were from Inglewood and Texas. Bloody rural idiots they were! It was dreadful. They only had damper and corned beef to eat and they'd be up before dawn. Though at least they went home at the weekend. I had to stay there in the camp. It was the first time I'd come across prickly pear. I fell head over heels into it. It gets into your skin. It was awful. I was that weak with hunger that I was ringbarking and I stumbled. I put the axe into my foot; you can see the mark there. It bled and bled and they didn't want to take me to hospital. 'Oh!' I said. 'You've got to take me to hospital!' So they took me. I was there nine or ten days and, being Irish, the Mother Superior from the Convent and the priest came to see me.

Then I was back on the track again on my own. I was in a store one time

'The Unemployed Movement... used to have lectures on a Sunday night and talk about socialism. To me it seemed, "Why should people be out of work? Why shouldn't they have homes to live in?"'

and there were half a dozen bagmen all there with their coupons. One smartie asked for something that was up on the shelf, and the fellow had to get the ladder. By the time he had the ladder they were chaining stuff out. Tins of biscuits and everything. A fellow was outside the door with a sugar bag. But on the whole the swagmen were very honest. They never took food from the farmer's mailbox, or touched anything in the trains.

News used to be passed along the grapevine. You had to watch out for Wingy Conellan, a famous one-armed railway detective at Maryborough, but they reckoned that Proserpine was a good place to get caught. One of the best places. Another fellow and I decided to get caught there. So coming in on the train we got our heads well up, and the copper come and caught us. We were lagged, got seven days in the lock-up. It was all worked out. It seems that the progressive people in the town were building tennis courts and croquet for the women. If you looked young and healthy, as if you could do a bit of work, you'd get seven days. If you were old and worn out they'd send you on your way! You didn't mind working because it was worthwhile. You had morning tea with the Country Women's Association. You had dinner at the pub and tea at the pub. You went to the pictures at night, and then you went back to the lock-up. And they never shut the door.

On the track, the worst thing was to be on your own. I was on my own one time and I was getting very dispirited. A squatter came along and picked me up. His name was McGovern. He said, 'I could give you a job!' I said, 'My goodness, that would be very good. A job! That would be wonderful!' I didn't know such a thing as a job existed. The wages were a pound a week! There was a very severe drought on, and my job was to chop down the leaves of the gidgee tree. The sheep would follow you around and eat the leaves. I worked like the dickens, because the sheep were so hungry. The water had receded and the little lambs would get stuck. You'd pull them out. I had nothing to read but a Holy Bible. I'm sure I must have read the Bible more times than anyone else. I knew everything in it. To keep myself from getting silly—I was camped on my own in a tent—I'd see how many words I could make out of 'raspberry jam'. Dingoes were howling. It started to rain. It must have been about four inches of rain. And afterwards there was hot sunshine. I never endured anything like it in my life. There were big grey-backed March flies. If they'd bite you they'd draw blood. There were little black flies that'd get in your eyes, and I finished up getting sandy blight and what was known in the west as Barcoo rot. This was the result of a lack of vegetables. I tried to take the billy off, and I couldn't see because of the sandy blight and I burnt my hand in the fire. The dingoes were still howling. I heard a motor horn. It was the boss. He said, 'I've brought you some fresh meat.' 'Look!' I said. 'You take me in. I'm finished! Quick as hell. Get me on a train to Brisbane, and if they ever get me out of the cities again, out of the lights of Brisbane, they can do what they like to me. Never again!'

After I got to Brisbane I was so sick with sandy blight and the Barcoo rot that I went to hospital. The little sores, they wouldn't heal up. I had to go back to the hospital for weeks and weeks, and that's when I got active in the Unemployed. I was about eighteen months on the track altogether I suppose. From that time on I never moved from Brisbane.

IAN FAIRWEATHER'S RAFT VOYAGE

Nourma Abbott-Smith

WHEN IAN FAIRWEATHER *achieved fame and success as an artist, he was in his late sixties and living in a thatched hut he had built from bush materials on Bribie Island in Moreton Bay. He had set up house on Bribie in 1953, and, except for a brief visit to London, he lived there—alone, painting, sometimes translating Chinese legends from Mandarin into English—until he died in 1974. Never before had he remained long in one place. His restless nature had taken him from his native England to Europe, Canada, China, Bali, the Philippines, Malaya, Singapore, and India, as well as to Australia.*

In 1950 he had fetched up in Darwin, where he made his home for two years in the after end of a beached and abandoned American supply ship of the Second World War. The Darwin residents, who are used to eccentrics, accordingly dubbed him the Rear Admiral. But in due course Fairweather's restlessness overtook him again. This time he decided to attempt to navigate a raft from Darwin to Timor, some six hundred kilometres to the north-west across the Timor Sea. Thor Heyerdahl's account of the Kon Tiki *expedition had recently been published, and Fairweather thought he would have a* Kon Tiki *expedition of his own.*

He made his raft out of aircraft belly tanks which had been discarded in the sea, decked with driftwood and dunnage he picked up on the beach. He added a mast, a centre-board and a rudder; even so, the raft was built to sail downwind only. Having studied the tides and currents of the north and spent some time in the library reading all he could find on seamanship, he was ready to go. Author and journalist Nourma Abbott-Smith recorded Fairweather's recollections of the trip in her book, Ian Fairweather: Profile of a Painter.

HIS PREPARATIONS for food were simple. He had cut bread into strips and dried it on the roof and had also provided himself with a tin of dried milk, a box of Quaker Oats, and sixteen cans of tinned meat. For water he had two four-gallon kerosene tins. He was counting on not more than ten days' crossing and in any case he could not carry more, for the raft was already loaded down to the gunwales. He had managed to buy a small wrist compass.

When the wind did at last set in it came at night with a blast that tore the raft from its moorings, carried it across the harbour, and piled it up on the rocks. Fairweather went round the next morning and found it jammed in some wreckage, its tail in the air. But the high tide floated it off, seemingly

The derelict wartime supply ship in which Ian Fairweather lived at Darwin before making his raft trip.

not much worse for the experience. This time he took it to a corner of the harbour where it was hidden behind some mangroves and fish traps. The tanks had been badly scraped and dented but not holed.

His concern now was to leave the harbour without coming under the scrutiny of the port authorities. They were known to be sticklers for the book and would produce all sorts of reasons why a ship could not sail. They were also very chary of giving papers to unconventional craft.

> I would have liked to test the tanks for leaks, but now I was impatient to be away. The water cans were filled from a tap in the navy yard and, when it was dark, I began to carry the rest of my stuff to the raft. I had to make several trips passing a lighted warehouse in the goods yard. The tide had reached full and started to ebb when all was stowed. I thought I would have time for a last look at Darwin and a beer at the pub.

Within an hour Fairweather had pushed out the boat but miscalculated the position of the fish traps and found himself caught and unable to estimate the position of those further out. He was forced to go back around the beach end. The tide was now running out fast, and when he neared the shore he ran onto a mud bank and stuck fast. By jumping overboard, sharks and crocodiles notwithstanding, he was able to push the raft into deeper water, though still dangerously near the lighted jetty.

When he set out there was no wind, a dead clear night, and the ebb of the tide helped to carry him round the point to where he would have a clear run down the harbour.

> I had an idea that I might call in at Bill Harney's place and overhaul the raft before going any further, but a slight breeze sprang up. This grew steadily stronger and I was soon racing towards the harbour entrance, too late to turn aside.
>
> I tried various ways of fixing the ropes from the rudder to hold her straight but none seemed to work and there was nothing for it but to lie down and hold the ropes in my hands.
>
> The square sail cut out all view ahead so I lay with my feet aft, watching the stars over the stern and steering by them. The light on Charles Point at the harbour mouth was now past and I was at sea.

He now made good going, but the wind was still rising and he began to be alarmed for the sail and mast, both of which were flimsy. The waves were now high, with hissing white tops, and he did not like to experiment with sail shortening as that would mean leaving the tiller.

> At first light there was a big sea running, huge rollers that threatened to roll over the stern, and as they lifted the raft it seemed to me that I was standing on my head.

From that moment on through the voyage he was never to be dry, for the raft settled just below the waterline and the deck was always awash to a depth of about six inches.

> The wind slackened towards evening and the sea calmed down, but not sufficiently to allow me to fix things. It freshened after dark and it was another night of bright starlight and racing whitecaps on a black sea.

Fairweather now began to suffer the pangs of thirst, but to get a drink was a complicated matter. The water cans were stowed out on the two side tanks and each cupful had to be pumped out. He dozed fitfully until dawn.

At first light Bathurst Island showed up. This meant that he had made good progress and was on the right course: perhaps a shade north, but that was all to the good for he should then run up amongst the islands and avoid the danger of entering the Indian Ocean.

By midday it was calm and he was able to lay to and rest. The sail was beginning to tear badly between the ribs, and he lowered it a little and fixed a

Ian Fairweather in the 1950s. Born in 1891, Fairweather was sixty when he made his madcap raft voyage.

guy rope to steady the mast which had worked loose, a simple job ordinarily but difficult and painful working with hands sore and skinned from holding the tiller lines for so long.

Towards evening a pearling lugger circled the raft and hove to. In broken English the Malay crew, thinking Fairweather to be in difficulties, offered him a lift back to Darwin. This he refused, saying, 'I'm going to Portuguese Timor. Is this the right way?'

Though he did not know it, he and his raft had already been missed from Darwin. An Australian air force plane had made a three-day search of the area in which it was thought he might be found. At the end of this time the search was abandoned and Fairweather's obituary appeared in the Australian newspapers.

> I kept the raft headed north-east, but I could sense that she was drifting west. I tried to check this by the wake but could not be sure, and even when I threw things overboard and watched them fall astern I was still undecided.

All he could be certain of was that he was making little headway. The sail was now badly torn and he thought it best to leave it alone save for fixing a blanket to it, which helped to fill some of the holes.

Unable to put the centre-board to any good use, for it was attached to the frame that also supported the mast, and very shakily at that, he threw it into the sea, which at least lightened the raft.

The sack of rusks he had so carefully dried and tied to the mast were now soaked by the waves and had become quite mouldy. Always willing to experiment, he ate some of them and said they tasted not bad though rather gamey. He used the remainder as a cushion to sit on, to cover a hole that had sprung up in the floorboards which sent up a spout of water every few minutes like a geyser.

Before long there were only water and tins of meat left, and the water was going down rather quickly. For three days the wind blew hard and the sea ran high, but things calmed down on the fourth day and the lone voyager

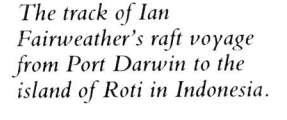

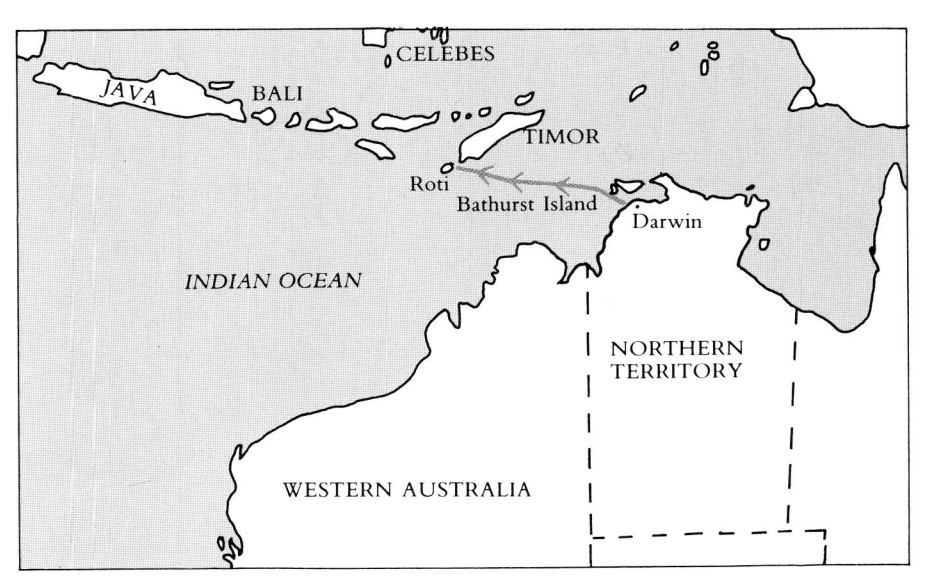

The track of Ian Fairweather's raft voyage from Port Darwin to the island of Roti in Indonesia.

was able to get a little sleep and managed to dry out his shirt and pullover.

Below his waist it was impossible to be dry, for he was lying and sitting in salt water day and night; sores had now begun to develop on his back and shoulders, and the ends of his fingers had swelled to the size and shape of mushrooms.

> Every movement was painful and my eyes were beginning to suffer from the constant strain of watching either bright clouds or the stars by which I steered. On the fifth day I began to see things which most certainly were not there.
>
> The starlight was intensely bright and a luminous haze seemed to fill the sky, glowing brighter towards the horizon. The sea was quite black and the haze took on the appearance of a mosquito net hanging down all over the raft through which the stars would move and jump about as the boat rocked, but always the net remained stationary. I could not understand this. On the net I could see lines, drawings of figures behind which danced other figures. I lay and contemplated these, for they were better than any drawings I had made on land. I could even see colours faintly amongst the lines. The net coming down around the raft was bright where it touched the horizon. It appeared so close that I felt I could reach out my hand and touch it.
>
> The same illusion was repeated on many nights to follow. Towards one dawn I had the impression that I was running between fog banks and fancied I could see the outlines of trees above me. I was so sure this was so that I stood up and with the oar tried so steer away from the fog banks, for the sea was running high and I did not want to be wrecked on possible rocks. I even saw what I took to be fish traps and, through the fog, lights in houses and people moving about. As I tried to fend the raft off the poles of the fish traps which I could plainly see were touching the forward end, I found I was reaching for the horizon. In my dazed state it did not occur to me until later that fish traps could not have survived in that sea.
>
> Worn out by my efforts, I lay down and spent the rest of the night, it seemed to me, being hurled down a lane of fog, and I was sure I had lost all sense of direction.
>
> The next day, or perhaps the one after, for I was beginning to lose count of the days, there was a row of thunderheads along the horizon. As night drew on they came nearer, rising like white towers with flashes of lightning striking from their bases in the sea.
>
> I had left Darwin about the time of the new moon and now it was bright moonlight, and as the towers of cloud came nearer, they rose before me like gleaming white cliffs. Beneath them all was blackness.
>
> The wind would freshen and I could feel the raft racing beside those cliffs. I tried to steer away from them but they would follow. I was steering by the moon and would find suddenly that it was in the wrong direction. The wind had veered without my noticing it and the raft with it. Most of the night passed thus and by dawn I was utterly confused.
>
> Towards morning I lay to and let the raft drift. I felt I could no longer cope with the elements. In the daytime the wind would usually die down and the raft would make little progress. The wind was always in the east or north-east, and it was a temptation to turn downwind and go with it.
>
> I told myself that I had made a good northing and could now afford to run west, but things thrown out gave this the lie. I was actually making very little northing, mostly drifting west and even a little to the south of west.

'On the net I could see lines, drawings of figures behind which danced other figures. I lay and contemplated these, for they were better than any drawings I had made on land. I could even see colours faintly amongst the lines.'

The rolling was a strain on the mast. One of the stays had snapped and I feared that the mast would not be able to take it much longer, but the dread of the Indian Ocean kept me trying, heading the raft north-east.

The thunderheads piled up every night, and every morning found Fairweather completely fuddled by the night-long game of blindman's buff. So far, they had come near, menacing and black, but never quite over him. One night, however, two of them came together, forming an arch, a black hole in the wall of dazzling whiteness. It was like a cave, and as it came nearer, the raft was drawn into it, sucked in as though by a whirlpool.

> As we entered the mouth of it some birds that had come to spend the night on the raft gave cries of alarm and flew into the air. The raft went in out of the bright moonlight to pitch darkness, the roof of the 'cave' so low that it seemed to be touching the top of the mast. Then, in the blackness, the rain and wind struck.
> In the morning I was soaked and very cold. My fingers were still swollen. I had still not learnt how to fix the rudder and sail so that the raft would steer itself; and I could, by now, scarcely hold the ropes. It was not until the eleventh day that I hit on the combination and so got some much-needed rest.
> There were aeroplanes flying about overhead nearly every day. I could hear them but never saw one. It was not until much later that I learnt that one of these had been lost and that the others were looking for it. The missing plane was that of a young Australian airman and his wife who had married in England and were flying home in the small plane. They had disappeared somewhere between Timor and north Australia.

'In the morning I was soaked and very cold. My fingers were still swollen. I had still not learnt how to fix the rudder and sail so that the raft would steer itself; and I could, by now, scarcely hold the ropes.'

Somewhere about this time the rudder rope frayed through and Fairweather had to climb out on the tail to fix a new one. 'Nothing much of a job but most painful, the saltwater sores making every movement an agony.' The yardarm too, originally fixed with wire to the mast, broke loose and had to be bound with rope. This became an almost daily chore as the constant movement soon frayed the rope through.

> Fortunately it did not entail as many acrobatics as fixing the rudder, but at times it came near to pitching me off the raft.
> I think I suffered most from my eyes. They were so painful that, in the end, I could not look at anything in the sunlight or even the stars at night. I had to steer by lying face down and watching the needle of the compass which I shaded with my hand.

He had still no idea whether he was north or south of Timor. At morning and evening there were cloudbanks on the horizon which he hoped might be covering land, but he was always disappointed.

> I had counted on, at most, ten days at sea, for I had read that the *Kon Tiki* had made an average of fifty miles a day and I thought my small craft with its streamlined belly tanks and even with its inadequate sail should be able to make at least that. Downwind it certainly would have, but as I had to bear north all the time, I was making little progress.

On the tenth day, having sighted no land, Fairweather cut rations down to half. He knew he must be either to the north of Timor, and might strike

Celebes, or to the south, in which case he should now be in the Indian Ocean. This was something he had to push into the back of his mind.

> The birds that left me when the raft entered the 'cave' in the thunderheads picked me up the next night and came in every following evening to roost. I think they were a kind of tern, swallow-like in shape and a dark brownish colour. I was later joined by a cormorant who sat on the raft day and night and watched other birds when they began to fish and then went out and joined them. Sometimes he would fly off for an hour or so but he always returned. I would see him bearing down on me and he would land with a great flapping of his wings and his large webbed feet.

The birds were always welcome, for they were splendid company, much to be preferred to the fish which followed the raft and which were, for the most part, sharks.

> I had the company of sharks from the time I left Darwin, sometimes one or two, at other times what seemed to be a whole school of them. Whether they were the same ones or even the same species I could not tell, but certainly they all had the same multiple rows of teeth and, when they turned to bite at the timbers of the raft, their pearly underbellies were as sinister as those of any grey nurse. When there were a lot of them they would swim beneath the raft and bump it about. I made myself very secure and guarded against allowing a limb to protrude over the side; indeed, I kept one leg constantly hooked around the mast in case I should doze off and slide into the waiting jaws.

On the fifteenth day Fairweather sighted land, but it was not the landfall he had expected. This could not be Portuguese Timor, for there were no mountains. It lay to the north-west, and all day he struggled towards it, but the wind was in the north-east and he seemed to be drifting west along the coast. On the morning of the sixteenth day he could see a bit of the island curving down towards the south. Hoping to make a landing, he took up the oars, but rowing for an hour or so made little difference.

About noon he could make out a small speck on the horizon but could not be sure that this was not a cloud. Before long, however, the island stood out unmistakably.

> I turned the raft to run with the wind and joyfully listened to the cheerful gurgle it made as it picked up way.
>
> As I drew nearer, the centre of the island rose like a hump and I could make out two arms stretching to the north and south. The target was getting wider and my hopes rose.
>
> I had expected there must be a reef and kept a good lookout for surf, but it was getting near dusk and I was still some way out. I could just make out what might be surf to the north so had to bear a little south, but I was afraid that, with the north-east wind, I might be blown past the island.
>
> As darkness began to set in I thought it better to take a chance on the reef and I headed straight for the centre of the island. I could discern some brown islands along the coast which I took for mangroves, and I made for the space between them.
>
> It was too dark to see any more, only the dark outline of the hump against the sky. It must have been around ten o'clock at night when a

big wave came aboard and then another. The raft bumped harshly on what seemed to be a small coral atoll. I could hear the bottom of my trusty craft being ground with every succeeding wave. Suddenly a huge wave appeared, seemingly out of the blue, to lift the raft over the reef. I breathed a sigh of pure relief as I felt it slide into calm water.

I was out of danger and in the lagoon. In the failing light I could make out a line of posts and brushwood, and this time I knew they were really there and that I was caught in them.

The voyage had ended, as it had begun, caught in a fish trap. The sixty-year-old voyager had made his landfall.

Fairweather had landed on the island of Roti, south of Timor, in the newly independent Republic of Indonesia. He was interrogated and held under house arrest for three months, on suspicion, apparently, that he was a spy of the Dutch rebel 'Turk' Westerling. He was then taken to Bali, where he was held for a further period of some weeks under house arrest as an 'immoralee'. Eventually, through the intercession of Maie Casey, who prevailed upon her husband, R. G. Casey, Minister for External Affairs at the time, to take up Fairweather's case at diplomatic level, he was allowed to leave and so made his way to Singapore and ultimately to London. He returned to Australia in 1953.

SAILING ALONE TO ANTARCTICA

David Lewis

AT THE AGE OF FIFTY-FOUR, *seagoing adventurer David Lewis decided to sail a yacht single-handed to Antarctica. Not only had no one done it before, but no relatively small craft, even with a crew, had made the passage. Lewis had already sailed round the world in a catamaran and crossed the Pacific without instruments, following a legendary Maori course and using only the sun and stars to steer by. On 19 October 1972 he sailed out of Sydney in his 9.75-metre steel yacht* Ice Bird; *fourteen weeks later, after experiencing mountainous seas, constant gales, snowstorms, freezing temperatures—and two capsizes and a dismasting—he arrived at the US Palmer Antarctic Station on the Antarctic Peninsula. The following extract from his book* Ice Bird *describes the first capsize, six weeks out from Sydney and about as far from land as it is possible to be.*

ICE BIRD continued to make steady, if unspectacular, progress eastward, keeping generally about 61°S. A progression of gales—north-west with heavy snow and falling glass, as the warm front of the depression rolled over us—would be succeeded abruptly after eight to twelve hours by the cold front, with its falling temperatures, clearing sky and rising glass—and intensified south-west gale. The resulting jumble of cross seas kept the ocean's face in a state of furious confusion even without the rogue seas which, every now and then, reared up and dashed right across the line of the prevailing swells. I kept the yacht running with the wind on one or other quarter, nearly downwind. Usually she carried only the storm jib, sometimes the storm tri-sail as well. The mainsail had been put to bed somewhere in the mid-fifties and had remained furled ever since.

One of the most awkward operations that had to be carried out in the brief intervals between gales was filling the petrol tank. Balancing a four-gallon plastic can on a deck rolling at a thirty-degree angle was not easy, but at least it had the advantage that the considerable spillage was soon washed overboard. This was more than could be said when I performed the chore of topping up lamps and stove with kerosene. Inevitably a good deal of kerosene spilled over as the yacht lurched and wallowed, and this made of the cabin floor a skating rink on which I slithered helplessly.

The fresh water in the tank let into the keel froze. Fortunately I had a supply of plastic cans to fall back upon. The drop in sea temperature was because we were now south of the Antarctic Convergence. Fogs, due to relatively warm north-west winds blowing over a colder sea, became more frequent and persistent than ever. Heavy snow showers became the norm.

Navigation was far from easy. A quick sight of the sun emerging from cloud cover; a dubious horizon as the sloop, rolling her gunwales under, lifted on a crest; numb fingers feverishly manipulating the sextant. To balance things a little, radio time signals were being received very clearly. Not so radio transmissions. An attempt to keep a schedule with Sydney on the 22nd, not unexpectedly, failed.

Evening, 26 November, the worst gale so far, a raging fifty-knot, force-ten north-wester that drove long lines of foam scudding down the faces of enormous waves and literally whipped away their crests. Each time a breaker burst against *Ice Bird* everything loose in the cabin went flying and I was for ever thankful for the steel plates protecting her windows. The bilge water appeared to defy gravity by distributing itself everywhere. It surged violently uphill and whizzed round the hull.

I kept *Ice Bird*, under snow-plastered storm jib, running off before the seas at about twenty degrees from a dead downwind run, so that she moved diagonally across the faces of those huge waves at a slight angle. During the night the gale backed to the south-west and the glass began to rise. It must eventually blow itself out, but when? I was shocked with the scene that full daylight revealed; scared, then gradually fascinated; though still terrified on looking out through the dome. It seemed as if the yacht's stern could never lift to each wave that reared up behind us. But rise it did; each time with a sensation like being whisked up in a lift. The yacht was being steered by the wind vane, assisted from inside the cabin by occasional tugs at the tiller lines.

Ice Bird *leaving Sydney on 19 October 1972.*

A weatherbeaten and drawn David Lewis shortly after his arrival at the United States' Palmer Base on 29 January 1973.

'She's bloody near airborne,' I wrote, and added that she was running incredibly smoothly. But was this in spite of, or because of, my tactics? Were they the right ones?

This last is a perennial query in storms. Vito Dumas, the heroic Argentine farmer who in 1944 circumnavigated alone through the roaring forties in a yacht the same size as *Ice Bird*, never took in his jib. He did the same as I was doing now. Bernard Moitessier, after his memorable non-stop voyage from Tahiti to Spain, had also suggested the tactics I was adopting—running before gales at an angle under headsail, the sail being necessary to give control and manoeuvrability.

Dumas and Moitessier had been two of the successful ones, but so many had come to grief in the Southern Ocean. I recalled reading in Captain W. H. S. Jones's book, *The Cape Horn Breed*, that out of 130 commercial sailing vessels leaving European ports for the Pacific coast of America in May, June and July 1905, four were known to have been wrecked and *fifty-three* were still missing in Cape Horn waters in November—four to six months later.

The 37-foot Australian ketch *Pandora*, the very first yacht ever to round Cape Horn—this was in 1911—was capsized and dismasted off the Falkland Islands. She was towed into port by a whaler. The Smeetons' big British *Tzu Hang* was pitchpoled and dismasted on her first attempt to round the formidable cape; on her second gallant try she was rolled and lost both masts. She succeeded the third time. Only the previous year the 34-foot *Damien*, crewed by two young Frenchmen, was thrice capsized off South Georgia, the first time righting herself only after a considerable interval. Again the mast was a casualty.

Yet here I was, traversing even stormier waters than they. No wonder I was scared. The gale seemed to be bearing out what I had somewhat wryly termed Lewis's law—for every point the wind increases your boat shrinks and becomes one foot shorter. This great truth has been my own discovery. I was brought back from my musings about other voyagers by bilge water surging up over the 'permafrost' that coated the inside of the hull these days, as an exploding crest threw the yacht over on her beam ends. She righted herself, water streaming off her decks. So far there had been no damage. But there was very little respite. This 26–27 November gale was barely over before, on the night of the 27th, the barometer started dropping again.

These repeated gales were at last seriously beginning to get me down. Gradually my morale was being sapped and increasing physical exhaustion was taking its toll. My whole body was battered and bruised and I was suffering from lack of sleep. Increasingly I dwelt on my in many ways disastrous personal life; what a mess I had made of things. I could hardly remember when my storm clothes had last been removed; standing in squelching boots had become habitual but was hardly comfortable. To make matters worse, my left hip, damaged in a skiing accident the previous winter, ached intolerably. I no longer daydreamed about the voyage and its outcome—I had already dreamed and was now living it.

Instead, present reality became illusory. In my exhausted state the wild irregular seas that were tossing us around like a cork were only half apprehended. I jotted down in the log that everything was an effort; there were constant mistakes of every kind in my sight workings; I could no longer grasp simple concepts. Twice, I recorded with scientific detachment that I heard ill-defined imaginary shouts. I drifted out of reality altogether....

A girl companion and I are ploughing through the long fragrant grass of autumn towards the Ginandera Falls. Green scarlet lorikeets flash by in streaks of vivid colour. We push our way through some heavy scrub, then go stumbling thigh-deep over slippery stones across the icy Murrumbidgee. A tangle of deadfall, tall gums and casuarinas, then a grassy glade under lichen-covered rock walls and ahead the leaping cascade. Imperceptibly the scene changes to the coast. A water-lily covered secret lake behind the sandhills. The same girl, and Susie and Vicky, naked and laughing in the hot sunshine, splashing up into the shallows.

Such are my memories, false and nostalgic though they be, of 27 November, the last day of my great adventure; such was my mental condition on the eve of disaster.

On the 28th the bottom fell out of the glass. How true, even if unintended, were the words of the poet MacNeice.

> The glass is falling hour by hour, the glass will fall for ever,
> But if you break the bloody glass you won't hold up the weather.

Nothing I or any other man might do could control the barometer. The pointer moved right off the scale and continued downwards to about twenty-eight inches or 950 millibars during the night. This time it was for real. Long before the barometer had reached this point it was apparent that something altogether new had burst upon us—a storm of hurricane intensity. This was the home of the unthinkable 105-foot waves the Russians had recorded, I recalled with dread. A breaker half as tall, falling upon *Ice Bird*, would pound her flat and burst her asunder.

The waves increased in height with unbelievable rapidity. Nothing in my previous experience had prepared me for this. Yet I had known the full fury of North Atlantic autumn gales when homeward bound in 25-foot *Cardinal Vertue* from Newfoundland to the Shetlands in 1960 (coincidentally, the Shetlands straddle the 60th *north* parallel).

Barry and I had weathered Coral Sea cyclone 'Becky' in *Isbjorn*, only partially sheltered by an inadequate island. Severe gales off Iceland, Magellan Strait and the Cape of Good Hope had been ridden out by *Rehu Moana*—the most seaworthy catamaran built so far—in the course of her Iceland voyage and her circumnavigation.

But this storm was something altogether new. By evening the estimated wind speed was over sixty knots; the seas were conservatively forty feet high and growing taller—great hollow rollers, whose wind-torn crests thundered over and broke with awful violence. The air was thick with driving spray.

Ice Bird was running downwind on the starboard gybe (the wind on the starboard quarter), with storm jib sheeted flat as before. Once again I adjusted the wind-vane to hold the yacht steering at a small angle to a dead run, and laid out the tiller lines where they could be grasped instantaneously to assist the vane. This strategy had served me well in the gale just past, as it had Dumas and Moitessier. But would it be effective against this fearful storm? Had any other precautions been neglected? The Beaufort inflatable life raft's retaining strops had been reinforced by a criss-cross of extra lashing across the cockpit. Everything movable, I thought, was securely battened down; the washboards were snugly in place in the companionway; the hatches were all secured. No, I could not think of anything else that could usefully be done.

Came a roar, as of an approaching express train. Higher yet tilted the stern; *Ice Bird* picked up speed and hurtled forward surfing on her nose, then slewed violently to starboard, totally unresponsive to my hauling at the tiller lines with all my strength. A moment later the tottering breaker exploded right over us, smashing the yacht down on to her port side. The galley shelves tore loose from their fastenings and crashed down in a cascade of jars, mugs, frying pan and splintered wood. I have no recollection of where I myself was flung—presumably backwards on to the port bunk. I only recall clawing my way up the companionway and staring aft through the dome.

The invaluable self-steering vane had disappeared, and I found, when I

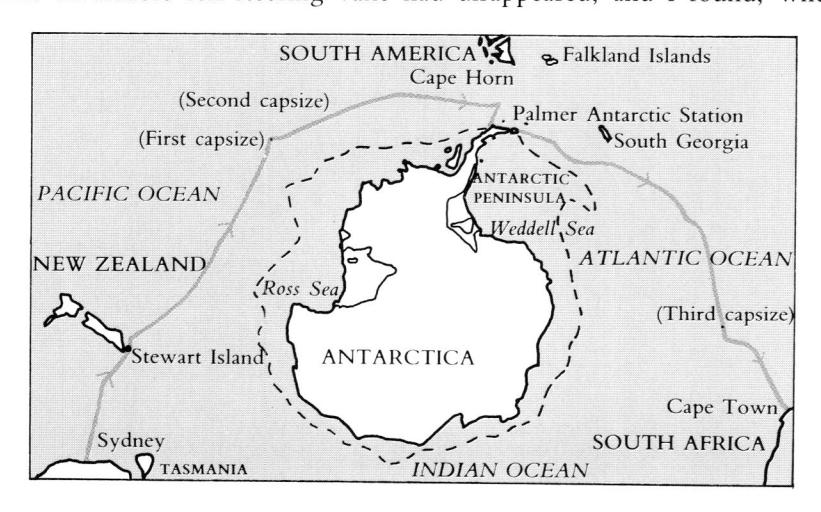

The route of the Ice Bird *from Sydney to Stewart Island, New Zealand, and thence by way of a track about 61 degrees south to the Antarctic Peninsula. Lewis later continued his voyage to Cape Town.*

scrambled out on deck, that its vital gearing was shattered beyond repair—stainless steel shafts twisted and cog wheels and worm gear gone altogether. The stout canvas dodger round the cockpit was hanging in tatters. The jib was torn, though I am not sure whether it had split right across from luff to clew then or later. My recollections are too confused and most of that day's log entries were subsequently destroyed.

I do know that I lowered the sail, slackening the halyard, hauling down the jib and securing it, repeatedly unseated from the jerking foredeck, half blinded by stinging spray and sleet, having to turn away my head to gulp for the air being sucked past me by the screaming wind. Then lying on my stomach and grasping handholds like a rock climber, I inched my way back to the companionway and thankfully pulled the hatch to after me.

I crouched forward on the edge of the starboard bunk doing my best to persuade *Ice Bird* to run off before the wind under bare poles. She answered the helm, at best erratically, possibly because she was virtually becalmed in the deep canyons between the waves; so that more often than not the little yacht wallowed broadside on, port beam to the sea, while I struggled with the tiller lines, trying vainly to achieve steerage way and control.

And still the wind kept on increasing. It rose until, for the first time in all my years of seagoing, I heard the awful high scream of force thirteen hurricane winds rising beyond seventy knots.

The remains of the already-shredded canvas dodger streamed out horizontally, flogging with so intense a vibration that the outlines blurred. Then the two stainless steel wires supporting the dodger parted and in a flash it was gone. The whole sea was white now. Sheets of foam, acres in extent, were continually being churned anew by fresh cataracts. These are not seas, I thought; they are the Snowy Mountains of Australia—and they are rolling right over me. I was very much afraid.

> *'These are not seas, I thought; they are the Snowy Mountains of Australia—and they are rolling right over me. I was very much afraid.'*

Some time later—I had no idea how long—my terror receded into some remote corner of my mind. I must have shrunk from a reality I could no longer face into a world of happier memories, for I began living in the past again, just as I had in my exhaustion in the gale two days earlier. It is hard to explain the sensation. I did not move over from a present world into an illusory one but temporarily inhabited both at once and was fully aware of doing so, without feeling this to be in any way strange or alarming. My handling of the tiller was quite automatic.

Mounts Kosciusko, Townsend, the broken crest of Jagungal; sculptured summits, sweeping snow slopes streaked with naked rock; all this mighty snow panorama rolled past like a cinema film. It was moving because those snow mountains were simultaneously the too-fearful-to-contemplate watery mountains of paralysing reality.

I am watching, as from afar, four of us gliding down off the snow-plumed divide, four dots in a vast whiteness. Then I am striving for balance under the weight of my pack, skis rattling a bone-shaking tattoo over a serration of ice ridges. We ski to a rest under a snow cornice overlooking the headwaters of the Snowy River, where we tunnel a snow cave to shelter us for the night—a survival exercise in preparation for my present venture.

But why are those snow mountains rolling onward? Where are they going? I have drifted away even further from the present and my tired brain baulks at the effort of solving the conundrum.

The picture blurs. I am leading a party up this same Kosciusko during the winter lately past, something like three months ago, amid the same rounded shoulders and rolling summits—literally rolling. My little Susie, refusing help with her pack, plods gamely up the endless snow slope, eyes suffused with tears of tiredness. We halt to rest. Almost at once with the resilience of childhood, Susie is away—laughing, her tears forgotten, the swish of her skis answering the song of the keen mountain wind.

The intolerable present became too intrusive to be ignored; the past faded into the background. Veritable cascades of white water were now thundering past on either side, more like breakers monstrously enlarged to perhaps forty-five feet, crashing down on a surf beach. Sooner or later one must burst fairly over us. What then?

I wedged myself more securely on the lee bunk, clutching the tiller lines, my stomach hollow with fear. The short sub-Antarctic night was over; it was now about 2 a.m.

My heart stopped. My whole world reared up, plucked by an irresistible force, to spin through giddy darkness, then to smash down into daylight again. Daylight, I saw with horror, as I pushed aside the cabin table that had come down on my head (the ceiling insulation was scored deeply where it had struck the deck head)...daylight was streaming through the now gaping opening where the forehatch had been! Water slopped about my knees. The remains of the Tilley lamp hung askew above my head. The stove remained upside down, wedged in its twisted gimbals.

Ice Bird had been rolled completely over to starboard through a full 360 degrees and had righted herself thanks to her heavy lead keel—all in about a second. In that one second the snug cabin had become a shambles. What of the really vital structures? Above all, what of the mast?

I splashed forward, the first thought in my mind to close that yawning fore hatchway. My second—oh, God—the mast. I stumbled over rolling cans, felt the parallel rules crunch underfoot and pushed aside the flotsam of clothes, mattresses, sleeping-bag, splintered wood fragments and charts (British charts floated better than Chilean, I noted—one up to the Admiralty). Sure enough the lower seven feet of the mast, broken free of the mast step, leaned drunkenly over the starboard bow and the top twenty-nine feet tilted steeply across the ruptured guard wires and far down into the water, pounding and screeching as the hulk wallowed.

The forehatch had been wrenched open by a shroud as the mast fell. Its hinges had sprung, though they were not broken off, and its wooden securing batten had snapped. I forced it as nearly closed as I could with the bent hinges and bowsed it down with the block and tackle from the bosun's chair.

Then I stumbled back aft to observe, incredulously, for the first time that eight feet of the starboard side of the raised cabin trunk had been dented in, longitudinally, as if by a steam hammer. A six-inch vertical split between the windows spurted water at every roll (it was noteworthy, and in keeping with the experience of others, that it had been the lee or downwind side, the side

'My heart stopped. My whole world reared up, plucked by an irresistible force, to spin through giddy darkness, then to smash down into daylight again.'

underneath as the boat capsized, that had sustained damage, not the weather side where the wave had struck).

What unimaginable force could have done that to eighth-inch steel? The answer was plain. Water. The breaking crest, which had picked up the seven-ton yacht like a matchbox, would have been hurtling forward at something like fifty miles an hour. When it slammed her over, the impact would have been equivalent to dumping her on to concrete. The underside had given way.

Everything had changed in that moment of capsize on 29 November at 60° 04′S, 135° 35′W, six weeks and 3,600 miles out from Sydney, 2,500 miles from the Antarctic Peninsula. Not only were things changed; everything was probably coming to an end. The proud yacht of a moment before had become a wreck: high adventure had given place to an apparently foredoomed struggle to survive.

For the next three days Lewis struggled to bale out the yacht, retrieve some of his damaged and sodden equipment, cut away the fallen mast and shrouds, and, when the wind eased, rig a jury mast and set a kind of sail. With his hands frostbitten and in constant pain, and with little hope of reaching his destination 2,500 miles away, he nevertheless continued his struggle to survive. Despite another capsize two weeks later and periods of contrary winds and, ironically, of calms, Lewis gradually came to realise that it was at least possible to make landfall. After negotiating a difficult passage through icebergs, he tied up at Palmer Antarctic Station on 29 January 1973. There the shattered boat was repaired, and in the following December Lewis set sail again, only to capsize for a third time before eventually reaching Cape Town.

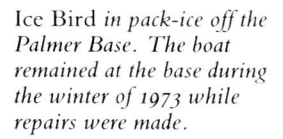

Ice Bird *in pack-ice off the Palmer Base. The boat remained at the base during the winter of 1973 while repairs were made.*

CAMEL TRACKS THROUGH THE CENTRE

Robyn Davidson

IN APRIL 1977, *27-year-old Robyn Davidson set off from Alice Springs to cross 2,700 kilometres of desert and bush with four camels, named Dookie, Zeleika, Bub and Goliath, and a dog called Diggity. Eight months later she arrived at Hamelin Pool on the West Australian coast south of Carnarvon. For most of the journey she walked, leading the camels, which carried drums of water, bags of food, camping equipment and other necessities. (At first it took her two hours or more to load them each day.) Only when she became footsore did she ride, and then not without some misgivings—the one camel with a saddle designed for riding was the temperamental Bub, and the thought of being thrown and breaking a leg far from human contact acted as a restraint. Before she left, she spent two years in Alice Springs learning how to train, ride and doctor camels and how to maintain her equipment and survive in the bush and cope with whatever problem arose. An ever-present danger in the desert was an attack by wild bull camels, as she describes in the following extract from her book* Tracks. *At this point she had just left the Docker River settlement, heading towards Pipalyatjara through land dotted with Aboriginal sacred sites where women were not allowed to go; she was unhappy that she had been unable to find an old Aboriginal man willing to come with her and show her the way.*

'My ears thumped, cold sweat stuck to the hollow of my back. My vision was distorted by fear.'

As I LEFT the settlement, alone, I was aware only of a flatness, a lack of substance in everything. My steps felt achingly slow, small and leaden. They led me nowhere. Step after step after step, the interminable walking dragged out, pulling my thoughts downward into spirals. The country seemed alien, faded, muted, the silence hostile, overwhelming.

I was twenty miles out, tired and thirsty. I drank some beer. I was about to turn off and make camp when through the beer-hazed afternoon heat came striding three large strong male camels in full season.

Panic and shake. Panic and shake. They attack and kill, remember. Remember now one—tie up Bub securely, two—whoosh him down, three—take rifle from scabbard, four—load rifle, five—cock, aim and fire rifle. They were just thirty yards away and one was spurting a cylindrical arch of red blood. He didn't seem to notice it. They all came forward again.

I was scared deep in my bones. First, I could not believe it was happening, then I believed it was never going to stop. My ears thumped, cold sweat stuck to the hollow of my back. My vision was distorted by fear. Then I was past it, not thinking any more, just doing it.

Zzzzt. This time just behind his head and he turned and ambled away. Zzzt. Near the heart again, he slumped down but just sat there. Zzzt. In the head, dead. The other two trundled off into the scrub. Shake and sweat, shake and sweat. You've won for now.

I unsaddled the camels and hobbled them close, glancing around constantly. It was getting dark. They came back. Braver now, I shot one, but only wounded it. Night came too quickly.

The fire flickered on white moonstruck sand, the sky was black onyx. The rumbling sound of bulls circled the camp very close until I fell asleep. In the moonlight, I woke up and maybe twenty yards away was a beast standing in full profile. I loved it and didn't want to harm it. It was beautiful, proud. Not interested in me at all. I slept again, drifting off to the sound of bells on camels, peacefully chewing their cud.

Came dawn, I was already stalking, gun loaded and ready. They were both still there. I had to kill the wounded one. I tried to. Another cylinder of blood and he ran away nipping at his wound. I could not follow. I knew he would die slowly but I could not follow, I had my own survival to think of. There he was, the last young bull, a beautiful thing, a moonlight camel. I made a decision. This one of the three would be allowed to live until he did something direct to jeopardise my safety. Happy decision. 'Yes, maybe he'll tag along right to Carnarvon. And I'll call him Aldebaran and isn't he magnificent, Diggity, what a match for Dookie. I don't have to kill him at all.' I snuck around to catch the camels. He watched me. Now, last camel to catch, Bub. Off he galloped in his hobbles, the new bull pacing lazily beside him. I couldn't catch him with the other bull so close. I tried for an hour, I was exhausted, I wanted to kill Bubby, to dismember him, rip his balls out, but they'd already gone. I took the rifle and I walked to within thirty feet of the now excited young bull. I put a slug right where I knew it would kill him. It did not, and he bit and roared at his wound. He didn't understand this pain. I was crying. I fired again into his head and he sat down, gurgling through his own blood. I walked up to his head, we stared at one another—he knew then. He looked at me, I shot him in the brain, point blank.

Bubby was puzzled. He walked up to the carcass and drank some blood. It was all over his nose, like clown's lipstick, and he threw his lips around. He allowed himself to be caught, I didn't hit him. I walked on.

Robyn Davidson's camel trip took her from the Glen Helen tourist Camp near Alice Springs, in the Northern Territory, to Hamelin Pool on the coast of Western Australia. The journey lasted from April to December 1977.

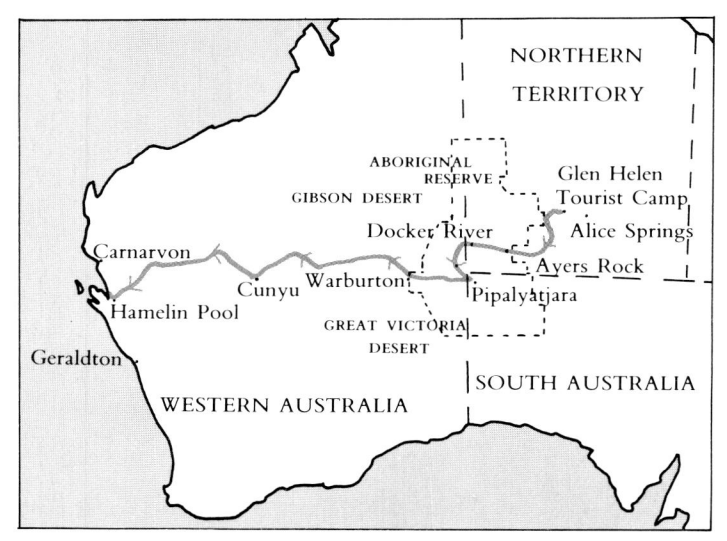

Robyn Davidson and her camels coming into Cunyu station in central Western Australia. By this time the press had discovered the mysterious 'camel lady', and for a while the camels were hidden at the station from the eyes of inquiring newsmen.

I entered a new time, space, dimension. A thousand years fitted into a day and aeons into each step. The desert oaks sighed and bent down to me, as if trying to grab at me. Sandhills came and sandhills went. Hills rose up and hills slipped away. Clouds rolled in and clouds rolled out and always the road, always the road, always the road, always the road.

So tired, I slept in the creek and thought of nothing but failure. I could not even light a fire. I wanted to hide in the dark. I thought it was surely longer than two days, I had walked so far. But time was different here, it was stretched by step after step and in each step a century of circular thought. I didn't want to think like this, was ashamed of my thoughts but I could not stop them. The moon, cold marble and cruel, pushed down on me, sucked at me. I could not hide from it, even in dream.

And the next day and the next day too, the road and the sandhills and the cold wind sucked at my thoughts and nothing happened but walking.

The country was dry. How could the camels be so thirsty and thin. At night, they came into camp and tried to knock over the water drums. I hadn't enough to spare. I rationed them. The map said 'rockhole'. Thank god. I turned off the track somewhere in that haze of elastic time and walked in. More sandhills, then a stretch of gibber flat, wide and dry and desolate with one dead bird and two empty holes. Some string somewhere inside me was starting to unravel. An important string, the one that held down panic. I walked on. That night I camped in those sandhills.

The sky was leaden and thick. All day it had been grey, smooth, translucent, like the belly of a frog. Spots of rain pattered on me but not enough to lay the dust. The sky was washing me out, emptying me. I was cold as I hunched over my meagre fire. And somewhere, between frozen sandhills, in a haunted and forgotten desert, where time is always measured by the interminable roll of constellations, or the chill call of a crow waking, I lay down on my dirty bundle of blankets. The frost clung like brittle cobwebs to the black bushes around me, while the sky turned thick with glitter. It was very still. I slept. The hour before the sun spills thin blood colour on the sand, I woke suddenly, and tried to gather myself from a dream I could not remember. I was split. I woke into limbo and could not find myself. There were no reference points, nothing to keep the world controlled and bound together. There was nothing but chaos and the voices.

The strong one, the hating one, the powerful one was mocking me, laughing at me.

'You've gone too far this time. I've got you now and I hate you. You're disgusting, aren't you? You're nothing. And I have you now, I knew it would come, sooner or later. There's no use fighting me, you know, there's no one to help you. I've got you. I've got you.'

Another voice was calm and warm. She commanded me to lie down and be calm. She instructed me to not let go, not give in. She reassured me that I would find myself again if I could just hold on, be quiet and lie down.

The third voice was screaming.

Diggity woke me at dawn. I was some distance from camp, cramped, and cold to my bones. The sky was cold, pale blue and pitiless, like an Austrian psychopath's eyes. I walked out into the time warp again. I was only half there, like an automaton. I knew what I had to do. 'You must do this, this will keep you alive. Remember.' I walked out into that evil whispering sea. Like an animal, I sensed a menace, everything was quite still, but threatening, icy, beneath the sun's heat. I felt it watching me, following me, waiting for me.

I tried to conquer the presence with my own voice. It croaked out into the silence and was swallowed by it. 'All we have to do,' it said, 'is reach Mount Fanny, and there is certain to be water there. Just one step and another, that's all I have to do, I must not panic.' I could see what had to be Mount Fanny in the hot blue distance, and I wanted to be there, protected by those rocks, more than anything I'd ever wanted. I knew I was being unreasonable. There was more than enough water to get by on to Wingelinna. But the camels, I'd been so sure they'd do a week comfortably. I hadn't planned on the sudden dryness—the lack of green feed. 'But there'll be water there, of course there will. Haven't they told me so? What if there's not? What if the mill's run dry? What if I miss it? What if this thin little piece of string that keeps me tied to my camels breaks? What then?' Walk walk walk, sandhills for ever, they all looked the same. I walked as if on a treadmill—no progress, no change. The hill came closer so slowly. 'How long is it now? A day? This is the longest day. Careful. Remember, it's just a day. Hold on, mustn't let go. Maybe a car will come. No cars. What if there's no water, what will I do? Must stop this. Must stop. Just keep walking. Just one step at a time, that's all it takes.' And on and on and on went that dialogue in my head. Over and over and round and round.

Late in the afternoon—long creeping shadows. The hill was close. 'Please please let me be there before night. Please don't let me be here in the dark. It will engulf me.'

It must be over the next sandhill surely. No, then the next one. OK, all right, the next, no the next, no the next. Please god, am I mad? The hill is there, I can almost touch it. I started to yell. I started to shout stupidly at the dunes. Diggity licked my hand and whined but I could not stop. I had been doing this for ever. I walked in slow motion. Everything was slowing down.

And then, over the last sandhill, I was out of the dunes. I crouched on the rocks, weeping, feeling their substance with my hands. I climbed steadily, up the rocky escarpment, away from that terrible ocean of sand. The rocks were heavy and dark and strong. They rose up like an island. I crawled over this giant spine, where it emerged from the waves, in a fuzz of green. I looked back to the immensity of where I had been. Already the memory was receding—the time, the aching time of it. Already, I had forgotten most of the days. They had sunk away from memory, leaving only a few peaks that I could recall. I was safe.

'The mill will be easy to find. Or the rockhole, it doesn't matter. There will be water here somewhere. Everything will be OK.' Panic melted and I laughed at myself for being so absurd, an effect of emotional and physical exhaustion, that was all it was. I was all right. I was going to be all right. The threads bound together and I touched Diggity. 'Diggity's here, it's OK. It's too dark to find the mill tonight, Dig, but there's a green patch of roly-poly here, that will make them happy, eh, little one? We'll find the mill tomorrow, the birds and tracks will lead us to it. And I'll give the camels a big drink, but right now I'll make a roaring fire and have some tea and feed you, my little friend.'

I slept deeply and dreamlessly, woke early and rose as easily and cleanly as an eagle leaving its nest. There was no trace of the previous day's fatigue, or the previous night's enemy. My mind was rinsed clean and sparkling and light. Everything around me was bursting with life and vibrancy. The colours danced and glistened in the crisp dawn light. Early morning birds, hundreds of them. My spirits high, I packed up quickly, expertly even, like a precision machine. I felt bigger somehow, expanded. I walked a hundred yards around the corner, and there was the mill. The camels drank, Diggity drank and I had a freezing invigorating bath.

About half a mile from the mill, I walked slap bang into a herd of forty camels. The gun came out smoothly and quietly. I had watched them descend like quiet ghosts, from their drinking spot high up in the hills. I looked at them, and they looked at me, sharing the same path. I knew I wouldn't have to shoot this time, but play it safe, that's the rules of this particular game. I smiled at them. They were more beautiful than I could describe. The big boss bull kept them slightly ahead, and glanced back constantly, to size up the situation. They stopped, I stopped—impasse. I shouted, hooted and laughed at them. They looked faintly quizzical. I waved my arms in the direction of the big bull and said, 'Shoo...' in a loud and authoritative shout. He looked infinitely bored. I fired some shot-gun pellets into the air and he recognised that sound. He rounded up his family, nipping as their heels, and they gathered momentum, until forty beautiful wild free camels were bucking and galloping down the valley into an echo and a vortex of dust, and then they were gone. I was remembering exactly who I was now.

That night, I was about to turn in when I heard cars purr in the distance. Such a foreign, incongruous sound. I didn't need them any more, didn't want them. They would be an intrusion. I was even slightly afraid of them, because I knew I was still half crazy. 'Yea or nay for human company tonight, Dig? Well let's let the fire do the talking. But will I make sense to them? What if they ask me questions? What will I say? Best thing is just to smile a lot and keep the trap shut, eh, little dog, what you reckon?' I fossicked around in my head, trying to find the pleasantries of conversation that had been blasted into fragments by the previous week's experience. I muttered them to Diggity. 'Oh god, they've seen the fire, here they come.' I checked myself nervously for signs of dementia.

Aborigines. Warm, friendly, laughing, excited, tired Pitjantjara Aborigines, returning to Wingelinna and Pipalyatjara after a land rights meeting in Warburton. No fear there, they were comfortable with silence. No need to pretend anything. Billies of tea all round. Some sat by the fire and chatted, others drove on home.

The last car, a clapped-out ancient Holden, chug-a-chugged in. One young driver, and three old men. They decided to stay for the night. I shared my tea and blankets. Two of the old men were quiet and smiling. I sat by them in silence, letting their strength seep in. One I especially liked. A dwarfish man with dancing hands, straight back, and on his feet one huge Adidas and one tiny woman's shoe. He handed me the best bit of his part-cooked rabbit, dripping grease and blood, fur singed and stinking. I ate it gratefully. I remembered that I had not eaten properly for the past few days.

The one I didn't like so well was the voluble one who could speak a little English and knew all about camels and probably everything else in the world as well. He was loud, egotistical, not composed like the others.

Early in the morning, I boiled the billy and started to pack up. I talked to my companions a little. They decided that one of them should accompany me to Pipalyatjara, two days' walk away, to look after me. I was so sure it was going to be the talkative one, the one who spoke English, and my heart sank.

But as I was about to walk off with the camels, who should join me but—the little man. 'Mr Eddie,' he said, and pointed to himself. I pointed to myself and said 'Robyn', which I suppose he thought meant 'rabbit', since that is the Pitjantjara word for it. It seemed appropriate enough. And then we began to laugh.

> *'Aborigines. Warm, friendly, laughing, excited, tired Pitjantjara Aborigines returning to Wingelinna and Pipalyatjara after a land rights meeting in Warburton. No fear there, they were comfortable with silence.'*

ROUND THE WORLD IN A HELICOPTER

Dick Smith

SYDNEY BUSINESSMAN, *publisher and adventurer Dick Smith was the first to fly a helicopter solo round the world. His original intention was to take delivery of the helicopter, a Bell JetRanger identified as* Delta India Kilo, *from the manufacturer's works at Fort Worth, Texas, and fly it back to Sydney; later he decided to complete the circumnavigation of the globe. As helicopters are essentially short-distance aircraft, Smith installed an extra fuel tank which gave him enough fuel for seven hours and twenty minutes in the air, a range of about seven hundred nautical miles. Even so, a route had to be plotted mostly over land so that the helicopter could be refuelled regularly and the pilot could find somewhere to sleep each night.*

Smith set off from Fort Worth on 5 August 1982 and flew up the east coast of America, crossed the North Atlantic to Britain by way of Greenland, Iceland and the Faeroes, then came down through Europe, the Middle East, East Asia and Indonesia to Australia, arriving in Sydney on 3 October. He completed his journey the following year, arriving at Fort Worth on 22 July 1983. On his flight from the Second World War fighter base at Biggin Hill in England to Bundaberg in Queensland, Smith followed the path taken by Bert Hinkler fifty-four years earlier when Hinkler made the first solo flight from Britain to Australia. In the following excerpt from The Earth Beneath Me, *Smith tells the story of his terrifying flight from the Burmese capital, Rangoon, to Phuket in Thailand.*

THE REGULAR ROUTES were of no use to me as I wanted to fly down the coast to the island of Aye, about a hundred miles south of Rangoon, where it is believed Charles Kingsford Smith and Tommy Pethybridge crashed in the *Lady Southern Cross* in 1935. Luckily, the flight briefing officer agreed to my proposed flight track down the Burmese coast to the Thai holiday resort town of Phuket, on the Isthmus of Kra. I was very pleased. Kingsford Smith has always been a hero of mine, and by flying over the area in which he disappeared I would be paying tribute to one of the world's greatest aviators. Often during the lonely hours on my flight I had looked at his photograph and speculated about how he had felt and had handled all the problems a solo pilot faces. And of course I had that piece of fabric from his earlier aircraft, the Fokker tri-motor *Southern Cross*, tacked to the instrument panel just near my left knee....

By 6.15 a.m. I was ready to go, feeling on top of the world. The weather forecast looked good right through to Phuket, about 586 miles to the south.

Dick Smith bedding down beside his helicopter on Baffin Island after being forced down by poor visibility. On a number of occasions he was obliged to set down the aircraft on some isolated spot as an emergency measure.

Out of Rangoon I weaved in and out of scattered rain squalls at five hundred feet without any trouble and picked up the coast of Burma as it turned south. After an hour's flying I came across Kalegauk Island, and near it I could recognise the outline of Aye Island.

It was strange and extremely moving to think that I might have been flying over the remains of the *Lady Southern Cross*, somewhere down there, in those dark muddy waters. One day I would like to launch an expedition to search for that historic wreck.

I made a low run over Aye on the course Kingsford Smith would have been flying. The island is rocky and covered with jungle, with cliffs on one side. It would certainly be a dangerous place to fly too close to at night in bad weather and poor visibility. One of the theories about Kingsford Smith's death is that engine trouble forced him down and he clipped the top of the unmarked island while searching in the darkness for a place to make a forced landing.

It was an uncanny feeling to circle the little island, photographing it from every angle. I located and photographed the small beach where the only remains of the *Lady Southern Cross* were found—an undercarriage leg and tyre.

I spent fifteen minutes looking at Aye, and then swung south again, to get back on course for Phuket. Unfortunately, the weather along my track had deteriorated dramatically. I ran into a torrential tropical downpour—a solid sheet of water which drummed on the canopy and lashed the smooth sea beneath me. Visibility had dropped to the absolute minimum. I hastily changed course, moving from my planned track which would have kept me out over the sea, and flew in to pick up the coast. I certainly did not want to get lost somewhere out in the Gulf of Martaban with zero visibility, heavy rain and dwindling fuel.

Once I had picked up the coast I dropped down and skimmed southwards over beaches and headlands and little fishing villages with boats pulled up on the sand. People ran out and waved at the helicopter.

I kept this up for another half an hour, and then the weather, which had been appalling, degenerated even further and became thoroughly dangerous. The rain became so heavy and thick that I could see virtually nothing ahead of me. I had never seen rain like it. My visibility was limited to a small patch immediately below the helicopter. The noise was horrendous and deafening.

I've got to get out of this and very quickly, I thought. I reduced speed to forty knots and headed through the rain at one hundred feet. Luckily there was no wind. Below me I could see waves crashing on a sandy beach, so I dropped the helicopter, moved in sideways and put it down on the beach as quickly as I could, breathing a sigh of relief.

Crikey, I thought, I'm alive! I had been given a terrible fright. When the rain lifted slightly and I looked along the beach ahead of the helicopter, I got a bigger one. There, looming dimly through the murk was a huge dark headland. If I had not landed I could have flown straight into it. Even at forty knots, that would have been the end of me and the JetRanger.

I sat in the helicopter for a few minutes after landing, stunned by the narrowness of my escape, and rather expecting to be surrounded by gaping villagers from a nearby fishing village. I got out, getting drenched in the process, and dragged my wet weather gear out of the luggage compartment.

Back in the cockpit, sopping wet and tired, I was just about to sit back and take it easy until the rain stopped when I noticed something extremely alarming. The helicopter was slowly tilting to one side! The right-hand skid was being forced down by the huge weight of fuel still in the tanks, driven deep into the wet sand at the water's edge.

Dick Smith's journey on the first two stages—Fort Worth to London; London to Sydney—of his solo helicopter flight round the world. He later flew the helicopter north through east Asia, crossed from Japan to Alaska (landing on the deck of a freighter in mid-ocean to refuel), then down through Canada and the United States to Fort Worth, arriving on 22 July 1983.

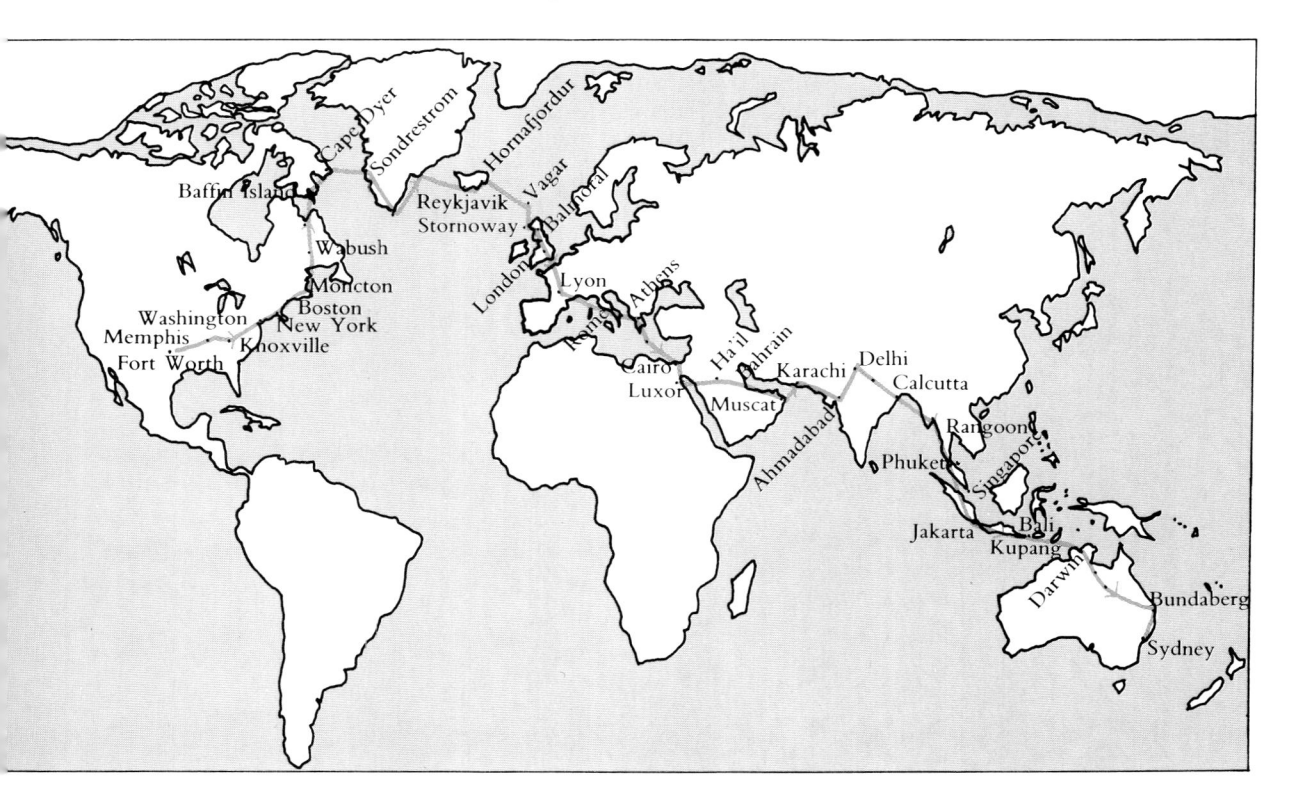

I got out of that helicopter as though it was on fire. Already the JetRanger had a dangerous list. It was several degrees out of the vertical and still sinking. *Delta India Kilo* cannot lift off with a list of more than ten degrees. I dug frantically at the sand for a few minutes to bring the JetRanger back on an even keel, and I realised I was not getting anywhere. The skid was just sinking deeper and deeper.

I jumped in the helicopter and started the Allison. By now the helicopter had developed a fore-and-after list as well as a sideways list and the tail rotor was only a few centimetres above the sand. At 100 per cent power the JetRanger would still not move, so I increased power to 110 per cent for the maximum five seconds allowed and it finally hauled itself clear of the clinging sand. Another few seconds and either the tail rotor would have touched the beach or the list would have increased beyond the maximum take-off angle. Either way, I would have been stuck on that lonely Burmese beach.

Once clear of the sand, I hovered the helicopter up the beach until I could see the dark gloom of the jungle. I dropped down and hoped the sand would stay firm for a while.

I sat and wondered what on earth I should do. There were not many options. It was raining so hard that flying was out of the question. Visibility was for all practical purposes absolute zero. The rain was so heavy that I doubted if a small helicopter could have stayed airborne in it.

I checked my co-ordinates on the VLF Omega, 13°48.0'N, 098°05.0'E, and related them to my chart which was by now decidedly soggy, thanks to the rain. The chart showed that I was about thirty kilometres south-west of the town of Tavoy and about seven kilometres from a road. Unfortunately, between me and the road lay thick jungle and a high mountain range. So walking to the road and hitching a ride back to civilisation was out of the question.

At last the rain began to ease off. I walked up and down the beach, thinking. I also noticed the tide was coming in and the waves were dashing higher and higher up the beach with each surge. The jungle ran down to the beach, and I could hear monkeys chattering and the screech of parrots. It was an incredible situation. Here I was, trapped on a jungle beach and my mind went back to Kingsford Smith's story of his solo Australia-to-England flight in the *Southern Cross Minor*. To the south of where I was now he had very similar problems. His autobiography says:

> The rain was coming down in sheets.... I could see nothing except the lighter colour of the sandy beach below me, and, if I went on blind flying like this at such a low altitude, I might crash into a hill at 70 miles an hour. There was only one thing to do—to come down on that beach and wait until the weather cleared.
>
> Fortunately for me that beach was all right! I taxied the plane up near high water mark, right up almost against the jungle which came right down to the beach....
>
> The rain was coming down in sheets, making a horrible drumming noise on the wing above me; in front of me was the black gloom of the jungle; behind me was the raging sea and the tide was coming in!
>
> I sat there in the cockpit after having stuffed up the exhausts to keep the rain out. Nothing happened except more and more rain. I was tired, hungry, wet, cold and depressed.

Luckily for me the rain continued to ease. After one hour and eighteen minutes on the ground I lifted off in what for those parts was a light shower, but it was still heavy enough. I could at least see for a few hundred metres.

I tracked out to sea for a few miles—I did not want any more scares with headlands—and switched on the autopilot so I could concentrate on navigating. Instantly, the helicopter began swinging violently from right to left. Now what was happening? I had had just about all the frights I could take in one day. I grabbed the controls and flew manually a few hundred feet above the sea in the driving rain, forcing myself to think calmly. I had been taught to always believe my instruments, but now, when I looked at my gyro attitude indicator, it told me that the helicopter was in a tight right-hand turn. I thought, that cannot be right. I could see the water below me between my feet, whereas if I had been in a tight right-hand turn it would have been below my right shoulder.

I glanced desperately around the bucking cabin, trying to get a clue to the helicopter's potentially lethal behaviour. Immediately, I saw what the trouble was. The on-off flags for the attitude and horizontal situation indicators were in the off position. I hastily looked up to the switches in the roof panel and saw that I had forgotten to turn on the switch which operates both of these instruments.

The autopilot had been wildly chasing heading information from a switched-off instrument. With all the flying I had done in helicopters, this was the first time I had failed to do the proper start checks. I can only surmise that the fatigue I was suffering was responsible.

I turned on the switch, took control of the helicopter again and turned south. I shall never forget my flight down the Burmese coast.

Flying through steadily increasing rain, I looked at my soggy chart and decided to keep out to sea and head straight across the water to an island called Malikyun. I chose Malikyun because the chart showed clear water to it from my present position. There were no other islands to fly into if the visibility got worse, as it seemed very likely to do. The rain was now unbelievable with solid water glancing off the windscreen.

Back on autopilot, I bored south through the deluge, feeling increasingly unhappy because, although I could see the sea between my feet, I had virtually no visibility ahead. Despite the weight of rain smashing into it, *Delta India Kilo* was making good speed. The chart showed Malikyun to have some high mountains and I wanted to keep it well to the east by heading out into the gulf.

By now I was feeling sick with worry. It was a most unpleasant experience, flying a few hundred feet over the sea, cocooned in a tiny cabin and unable to see anything at all except the monotonous pouring, thundering rain.

As I came abeam of Malikyun Island the rain must have eased slightly, because I could see its high rugged green shape loom out of the falling torrents like a passing liner. So at least I was on course. The next minute my hair almost stood on end because off to the right, and almost on my track, was a cluster of islands which were not on the map at all! They stuck up out of the sea, five or six hundred feet high—hazards which had obviously not made the charts yet.

'The next minute my hair almost stood on end because off to the right, and almost on my track, was a cluster of islands which were not on the map at all!'

If the rain had not eased off just then, or if I had made a slight westerly changed of course, I would have flown slap bang into one of them and become a statistic in the book of aviation mysteries, joining Kingsford Smith and Pethybridge on the bottom of the Gulf of Matarban. It was a terrifying thought. For the lone aviator in a small aircraft, death is sometimes not far away. One slip, a little miscalculation, one factor taken for granted....

Happily for my morale, which by now was at an extremely low ebb indeed, the weather began to improve, and I turned in towards the coast again. I approached the coast near the village of Mergui, which I was told had an airstrip and a radio. I called Mergui repeatedly on the frequency I had been given in Rangoon, but there was dead silence.

There was nothing for it but to press on, fighting my feelings of mounting depression. The weather was worsening again and I could not get a response from any navigation directional beacon on the entire Burmese coast, although I had been assured in Rangoon that they would all be turned on for me. Fortunately the VLF Omega appeared to be working perfectly.

In fact, I was beginning to feel a little bitter about my friends at Mingaladon Airport. After all, the weather forecast I had been given there had promised me a clear run all the way to Phuket, instead of which I had been flying through a watery hell since shortly after leaving Rangoon.

As I could not raise anyone on the radio, there was nothing for it but to keep heading south. I hugged the coastline at a very low altitude. Most of the land below me seemed pretty swampy—not a good type of terrain to set down in.

The weather began to change from bad to really dreadful again at one of my last Burmese reference points, Sir Robert Campbell Island, on Forest Strait. Tracking almost due south to my next waypoint, Victoria Point, I began to get extremely worried again. The weather had now deteriorated to absolutely marginal conditions. If it got any worse I would have no choice, I would have to land. Desperately I scanned the jungle-covered hills, interspersed with swampy inlets, which passed beneath me.

Victoria Point's NDB, like all the others on that long coast, was not working, so I tracked into Victoria Point with the VLF Omega, with the discomforting knowledge that as I had not started this flight leg with an accurate fix on the beach even the usually accurate Omega could be a few miles out.

I was now flying down the west coast of the Isthmus of Kra, the narrow strip of land on the Malay Peninsula where Burma runs into Thailand. The coast was greatly indented, with scores of bays and headlands, and the green of mangrove swamps right at the sea's edge.

The rain had increased and before long I had no forward visibility. I knew that there must be a landing strip at Victoria Point because I had read about the early aviators landing there on flights to Australia. Even 'Hustling' Hinkler had landed there on his twelfth day out of England in 1928.

The books I had read about Hinkler said he landed 'on an airfield in the jungle'. Well, I could see signs of habitation through the rain. There were many houses and two very old-fashioned looking radio masts which confirmed I was over Victoria Point—but not a trace of an airstrip.

I came in very low on a landing approach over the town, but there was nowhere to land. At one stage I began my descent to what I thought was a clearing, but realised just in time that it was a rice paddy.

By now I was very tired and frightened. It was still raining heavily, and the unpleasant events of the day had shaken my nerves pretty badly. And here I was, going round and round Victoria Point in a tropical downpour. I spotted another clearing which looked like a sports field, but it was surrounded by buildings and palm trees and would have been impossible to approach safely in the present conditions of almost zero visibility. Ahead of me through the rain-smeared windscreen I could see nothing but more rain. It was only directly below my feet that I could see anything at all.

I began to seriously consider ditching the helicopter in the shallow water in front of the town. Then I thought I saw a glimmer of light through the murk, and what seemed to be a boat. Perhaps the visibility was better in that direction, I thought, and flew towards it. No such luck. The shape I had taken for a boat turned out to be a small low coral atoll. But there was a lighter patch in the gloom to the south. It looked as though the rain might be lifting. Gritting my teeth, I flew on down the coast.

The day, which had started so happily in Rangoon, had turned into a nightmare. The rain still fell in solid grey curtains. I kept low and flew very slowly. My eyes ached with the effort of trying to penetrate the almost solid wall of water ahead. The thunder of rain on the JetRanger's metal skin added immensely to my fatigue and nervous strain.

I hung on grimly, alternating from manual to autopilot. Flying was terribly

Although flying alone and navigating through unfamiliar parts of the world, Dick Smith managed to film and narrate a television documentary and take still photographs while piloting his helicopter. Here he has photographed some Western-style houses set among the palms of a Malaysian coconut plantation.

dangerous. Every few minutes a great dark blur would loom up out of the rain and I would have to take evasive action to avoid colliding with an island or a headland. I began to feel quite sick with tension and I thought I would never get out of this weather.

When I was just about at the end of my tether the fates or furies who order the weather must have decided that I had been tested enough, because about twenty miles south of Victoria Point the rain became patchy and at last I could see the sunshine, glorious sunshine, on the sea beneath me. At Ban Khao Ba, a little Thai village, I flew out into clear skies and visibility of twenty miles.

The rest of the flight, down to the Thai village and holiday resort of Phuket, was like a lovely dream after a bad nightmare. The change in the weather had come none too soon. I was sopping wet, thanks to my excursion on the beach near Aye Island, and dead tired and hungry, as I had eaten nothing since attending the ambassador's dinner in Rangoon the night before.

I began calling Phuket Airport when I was about twenty miles out. No reply. Oh my God, I thought, don't tell me there is no airfield at Phuket. I was prepared to believe it at this stage because everything else I had been told to expect on my trip down the Burmese coast had been wrong.

I called again. And again silence. And then, suddenly, unbelievably, the Phuket tower answered and told me to fly right in. It was Gerry Nolan's voice! I learnt later that he had been in the tower for some time, getting increasingly worried about me. He had my time of departure from Rangoon, and simple arithmetic told him that I must have either run out of fuel or landed somewhere. I could hear the relief in his voice.

I landed at Phuket at 1.45 p.m. local time, five hours and forty-eight minutes flying time after leaving Rangoon. I do not know how Hinkler felt after his seven hours and thirty minutes in the Avian to Victoria Point, but I felt absolutely done in.

'The rest of the flight, down to the Thai village and holiday resort of Phuket, was like a lovely dream after a bad nightmare. The change in the weather had come none too soon.'

ACKNOWLEDGMENT OF SOURCES

Thanks are due to the publishers and copyright owners concerned for permission to include copyright material. For future editions, we should be grateful to receive any corrections of sources wrongly credited.

Nourma Abbott-Smith
Ian Fairweather: Profile of a Painter. St Lucia, Qld: University of Queensland Press, 1978.

James Allen
Journal of an Experimental Trip by the 'Lady Augusta' on the River Murray. Adelaide: C. G. E. Platts, 1853. Reprinted in facsimile by the Libraries Board of South Australia, Adelaide, 1976.

Asiatic Mirror, Calcutta
'Voyage of the Sydney Cove's Longboat from Preservation Island to Port Jackson', *Asiatic Mirror*, 27 December 1797 and January 1798. Reprinted in *Historical Records of New South Wales* 3: 757–68.

Daisy Bates
The Passing of the Aborigines. London: John Murray, 1938.

Francis Birtles
'All over Australia with Bike and Camera'. *Australian Country Life*, 2 December 1907; 1 February, 1 April and 1 May 1908.

Gregory Blaxland
Journal of a Tour of Discovery across the Blue Mountains in New South Wales. London: B. J. Holdsworth, 1823. Reprinted in *Blaxland-Lawson-Wentworth 1813*, ed. Joanna Armour Richards. Hobart: Blubber Head Press, 1979.

William Bligh
Narrative of the Mutiny on Board His Majesty's Ship 'Bounty'. London: G. Nicol, 1790. Republished by Australiana Facsimiles,

James Cook
The Journals of Captain James Cook, ed. J. C. Beaglehole. London: Cambridge: Hakluyt Society, Cambridge University Press, 1955–74.

Robyn Davidson
Tracks. London: Jonathan Cape, 1980.

Mary Durack
Kings in Grass Castles. London: Constable, 1959.

Geoffrey Dutton
'The First Crossing of Australia by Motor Car'. *Pegasus*, no. 28. Mobil Services Co. Ltd, 1985.

Edward John Eyre
Journals of Expeditions of Discovery into Central Australia and Overland from Adelaide to King George's Sound. 2 vols. London: T. & W. Boone, 1845. Reprinted in facsimile by the Libraries Board of South Australia, Adelaide, 1964.

Mick Healy
From 'The Trackmen'. In *Weevils in the Flour*, by Wendy Lowenstein. Melbourne: Hyland House, 1978.

Annie Henning
The Sea Journals of Annie and Amy Henning, ed. Joan Thomas. Sydney: John Ferguson, 1984.

Frank Hurley
Shackleton's Argonauts. Sydney: Angus & Robertson, 1948.

John King
'John King's narrative, as delivered to the Royal Commission'. In *A Successful Exploration through the Interior of Australia, from Melbourne to the Gulf of Carpentaria*, by William Wills. London: Richard Bentley, 1863.

C. E. Kingsford Smith and C. T. P. Ulm
Story of 'Southern Cross' Trans-Pacific Flight 1928. Sydney: Penlington & Somerville, 1928.

Ludwig Leichhardt
Journal of an Overland Expedition in Australia from Moreton Bay to Port Essington. London: T. & W. Boone, 1847. Reprinted in facsimile by the Libraries Board of South Australia, Adelaide, 1964.

David Lewis
Ice Bird. London: Collins 1975.

Hector MacQuarrie
We and the Baby. Sydney: Angus & Robertson, 1929.

James Martin
Memorandoms of James Martin, ed. Charles Blount. Cambridge: Rampant Lions Press, 1937.

Sir Douglas Mawson
The Home of the Blizzard, Being the Story of the Australian Antarctic Expedition, 1911–1914. London: Heinemann, 1915.

Alan Moorehead
The Fatal Impact. London: Hamish Hamilton, 1966.

George Ernest Morrison
'Across the Australian Continent on Foot'. *Leader* (Melbourne), 19 May 1883.

Ian Mudie
Riverboats. Adelaide: Rigby, 1961.

T. R. Nicholson
'Heroic Failure'. In *Five Roads to Danger*. London: Cassell, 1960.

Dick Smith
The Earth Beneath Me, ed. Jack Bennett. Sydney: Angus & Robertson, 1983.

Sir Ross Smith
The First Aeroplane Voyage from England to Australia. Sydney: Angus &

Robertson, n.d. [1920].

14,000 Miles through the Air. London: Macmillan, 1922.

Charles Sturt

Two Expeditions into the Interior of Southern Australia. 2 vols. London: Smith Elder, 1833. Reprinted in facsimile by the Public Library of South Australia, Adelaide, 1963.

Mary Watson

The Heroine of Lizard Island. Cooktown: Cook Shire Council, 1956. Original diaries in the Oxley Memorial Library, Brisbane.

John White

Journal of a Voyage to New South Wales. London: J. Debrett, 1790. Republished by Angus & Robertson in association with the Royal Australian Historical Society, Sydney, 1962.

SOURCES OF ILLUSTRATIONS

ABBREVIATIONS
BL British Library; BM British Museum; DG Dixson Gallery; DL Dixson Library; ML Mitchell Library; NLA National Library of Australia; RNK NLA Rex Nan Kivell Collection, National Library of Australia; SLSA State Library of South Australia.
T = top; B = bottom.

P.1 F. Garling, *Steamship*, 1859–68, DG D3 f.8; p. 2 John Gilbert, *South Sandwich Islands*, 1775, Public Record Office, London; p. 7 G. Hamilton, *Bushman's Halt*, ML ZV★ Bush L.1(b); p. 8 Augustus Earle, *Cabbage Tree Forest, Ilawarra* (sic), *New South Wales*, RNK NLA, NK 12/37; p. 11 George Foster, *Ice Islands*, ML PXD 11 f.30; p. 13 William Hodges, *Captain James Cook*, DG ZDG 214; p. 14 Sydney Parkinson, 'Two of the Natives of New Holland Advancing to Combat', in *Journal of a Voyage to the South Seas....* (1773), plate XXXVIII f.p. 134, ML Q980/P; p.19T Sydney Parkinson, 'A View of New Holland', *op. cit.*, ML; p. 19B Sydney Parkinson, 'Kangaroo', *op. cit.*, ML; p. 26 artist unknown, 'Surgeon John White and Others Talking with Aboriginals', c. 1792, BM (Natural History); p. 31 William Bradley, 'City of St Sebastians, Rio Janeiro, Sirius and Convoy at Anchor, 1787, journal, opp. f.37, ML Safe 1/14; p. 32 'A Sea Surgeon's Instruments', in Ernest Gray, *Surgeon's Mate 1756–1762*, opp. p. 26, ML 926.1/K74/2A1; p. 35 William Bradley, 'Cape Town, Table Mountain, Sirius and Convoy in Table Bay, November 1787', journal, opp. f.46, ML Safe 1/14; p. 38 William Bradley, 'Botany Bay. Sirius and Convoy going in. Supply and Agent Division in the Bay, 21 January 1788, journal, opp. f.58, ML Safe 1/14; p. 40 'A Copy of the Draught from which the Bounty's Launch was built', from William Bligh, *A Narrative of the Mutiny on board H. M. Ship Bounty* (1790), RNK NLA NK 785; p. 41 Robert Dodd, *The Mutineers turning Lt. Bligh and part of his crew adrift from His Majesty's Ship the Bounty*, RNK NLA NK 267; p. 44 'The Launch at Sea', from Bligh, *A Narrative of the Mutiny of the Bounty* Dutch edition, f'piece, ML 988/55B1; p. 47 'A page from Bligh's Notebook', NLA Manuscripts—Bligh Notebook, p. 30; p. 50 Juan Ravenet, *Convicts of New Holland*, DG D2 f.5; p. 51 William Bradley, 'Governors House at Sydney Port Jackson 1791', journal, opp. f.225, ML Safe 1/14; p. 53 William Bradley, 'First Interview with the Native Women at Port Jackson, New South Wales', journal, opp. f.70, ML Safe 1/14; p. 55 ML; p. 58 George

SOURCES OF ILLUSTRATIONS

Raper, *H. M. S. Sirius Weathering Tasmans-head*, DG SSV★SHIPS/3; p. 63 The Artist of the Chief Mourner, *Australian Aborigines in bark canoes [April 1770]* BL Add MS 15508, f.10(a) (no. 10); p. 64 Joseph Lycett, *Aborigines Spearing Fish*, NLA R5686; p. 69 Gregory Blaxland, ML ZML 143; p. 73 Augustus Earle, *Waterfall in Australia*, RNK NLA NK9; p. 74 'Blaxland, Lawson and Wentworth, 1813', from William Joy, *The Explorers*, ML; p. 76 SLSA; p. 80 'Junction of the Supposed Darling with the Murray', from Charles Sturt, *Two Expeditions into the Interior of Southern Australia 1828–31* (1833), opp. p. 106, ML 980.1/11902; p. 83 *View of the Morumbidge* (sic) *River, op. cit.*, ML; p. 88T 'Wylie', from J. E. Eyre, *Journal of Expeditions in Central and Southern Australia in 1840*, vol. 1, p. 205, ML 983.7/20A2; p. 88B Edward Eyre, SLSA; pp. 100–101 Lieut. Robert Dale, *Panoramic View of King George's Sound*, 1834, NLA; p. 102 'Arrival at King George's Sound', from Eyre, *Journal*, vol. 2, p. 109, ML 983.7/20A2; p. 104 'Leichhardt in Camp', from J. F. Mann, *Eight Months with Dr Leichhardt* (1888), f'piece, ML 984/24A2; p. 105 Charles Rodius, *Charley and Harry Brown*, from Ludwig Leichhardt, *Journal of an Overland Expedition in Australia from Moreton Bay to Port Essington* (1847), ML 984/32A1; p. 107 'Notes and Drawings', from Leichhardt's diary, 24 Feb 1844, ML MSS 683/1 Item 3/CYREEL 1082 (frame 0227); p. 109 'Peak Range from the N.W.', from Leichhardt, *Journal*, opp. p. 124, ML 984/32A1; p. 110 'Paddy a Badda Man on Durandur Station 18 Jan 1844', ML ON 4606/MSS 683/1 (frame 223); p. 113 The S.S. Great Britain, ML 81; p. 115 Handbill of the Steamer Great Britain, ML MSS 342/1-4x (frame 781) CY 1098—Rachel Henning Letters 1853–90; p. 119 Tucker Family, ML SPF; p. 120 'Sketches on board an emigrant ship', in *Illustrated Australian News*, 24 Mar 1875, p. 40, NLA; p. 123 J. H. Adamson, *The Lady Augusta with the barge Eureka just showing* 1853, SLAS; p. 124T Captain Francis Cadell, SLSA; p. 124B Captain William R. Randell, SLSA; p. 125 'Lady Augusta and Mary Ann, Swan Hill', from James Allen, *Journal of an Experimental Trip by the Lady Augusta on the River Murray* (1853), ML 981/101; p. 130 DG 436; p. 132 Burke Wills and King, DG 276: p. 133 Helena Forde, *Pammamaroo Creek, Menindie*, 1865–66, ML PXA 551 f.10; p. 137 William Strutt, *The Death of Burke*, DL PXX3 129; p. 138 William Strutt, *Grave of Burke the Explorer, Cooper's Creek*, DL PXX4 f.5; p. 139 William Strutt, *With Cooper's Creek blacks who are covering Burke's remains*, DL PXX3 f.15(b); pp. 141, 142 Oxley Memorial Library; p. 144 ML MSS 312 PX★D153–2 70; p. 150 ML PX★D255 20 CY:37:20; p. 153T ML PX★D255 14 CY:37:14; p. 153B ML PX★D255 23 CY:37:23; p. 155 ML PX★D255 22 CY:37:22; p. 156 ML SPF Bush Life; p. 157 from Mary Durack, *Kings in Grass Castles*, opp. p. 192, ML 990.1/21A1; pp. 162, 164 NLA; p. 169 *Weekly Times*, 26 Sept. 1908; p. 171, 173 *Lone Hand*, 1 Mar. 1911; pp. 176, 181, 182 courtesy of Geoffrey Dutton; p. 185 Frank Hurley in Sir Douglas Mawson, *The Home of the Blizzard*, vol. 1, opp. p. 215, ML Q989.8/M; p. 186 ibid., f'piece; pp. 196, 201 Frank Hurley, ibid., p. 266; p. 203 Frank Hurley, ibid., vol. 2 opp. p. 161; pp. 204T&B, 207, 214, 215 Frank Hurley, *Argonauts of the South*, ML 989.8/76N; p. 217 Ross Smith, *1400 Miles Through the Air*, opp. p. 134, ML 910/S; p. 221 ibid., opp. p. 118; pp. 229, 230 Francis Birtles, *Album of Newspaper and Magazine Cuttings*, ML Q910.4/74; p. 233 Hector

SOURCES OF ILLUSTRATIONS

McQuarrie, *We and the Baby*, opp. p. 7; p. 235 ibid., opp. p. 214; p. 237 ibid., opp. p. 271; p. 239T Qantas; p. 239B NLA; p. 246 NLA; pp. 247, 249, 250 John Fairfax & Sons P/L; p. 254 Mirror Australian Telegraph Publications; p. 255 Norma Abbott-Smith, *Ian Fairweather: Profile of a Painter*, opp. p. 138, ML Q759.9901/F172/1; p. 262 David Lewis, *Ice Bird*, opp. p. 48, ML 989.8/228; p. 263 ibid., opp. p. 96; p. 268 ibid., opp. p. 153; p. 271 Mirror Australian Telegraph Publications; p. 276 Dick Smith, *The Earth Beneath Me*, p. 52, courtesy of Dick Smith; p. 282 ibid., p. 200, courtesy of Dick Smith.

BOUNTY